BOOK ONE

WRITTEN, ILLUSTRATED, AND LETTERED BY

TESSA STONE

COLLECTION EDITED BY
ROBIN HERRERA &
BESS PALLARES

DESIGNED BY
FAWN LAU

PUBLISHED BY ONI PRESS, INC.

JOE NOZEMACK, publisher
JAMES LUCAS JONES, editor in chief
ANDREW MCINTIRE, v.p. of marketing & sales
DAVID DISSANAYAKE, sales manager
RACHEL REED, publicity coordinator
TROY LOOK, director of design & production
HILARY THOMPSON, graphic designer
ANGIE DOBSON, digital prepress technician
ARI YARWOOD, managing editor
CHARLIE CHU, senior editor
ROBIN HERRERA, editor
ALISSA SALLAH, administrative assistant
BRAD ROOKS, director of logistics
JUNG LEE, logistics associate

Hiveworks Comics LLC
A creator owned publisher and studio
WWW.THEHIVEWORKS.COM

1305 SE Martin Luther King, Jr. Blvd.
Suite A
Portland, OR 97214

ONIPRESS.COM
facebook.com/onipress | twitter.com/onipress
onipress.tumblr.com | instagram.com/onipress

NOTDRUNKENOUGH.COM

First Edition: July 2017
Retail Edition ISBN 978-1-62010-414-9
eISBN 978-1-62010-415-6
Artist Edition ISBN 978-0-9986886-0-2
Artist Limited Edition ISBN 978-0-9986886-1-9

1 3 5 7 9 10 8 6 4 2

Library of Congress Control Number: 2016960958

Printed in China.

Not Drunk Enough, Book 1. July 2017. Published by Oni Press, Inc. 1305 SE Martin Luther King, Jr. Blvd., Suite A, Portland, OR 97214.

NOT DRUNK ENOUGH

AN ONI PRESS PRODUCTION

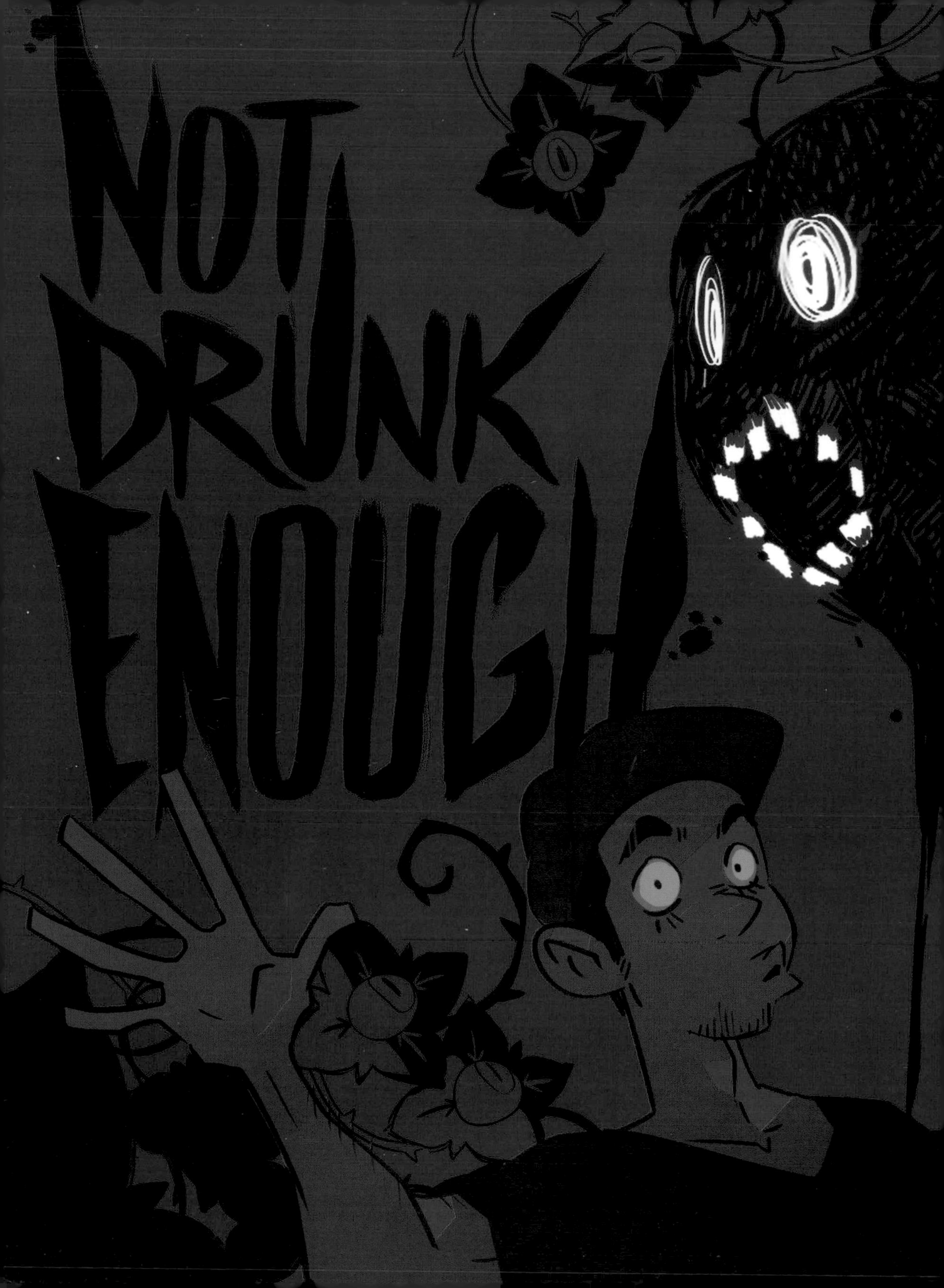
NOT
DRUNK
ENOUGH

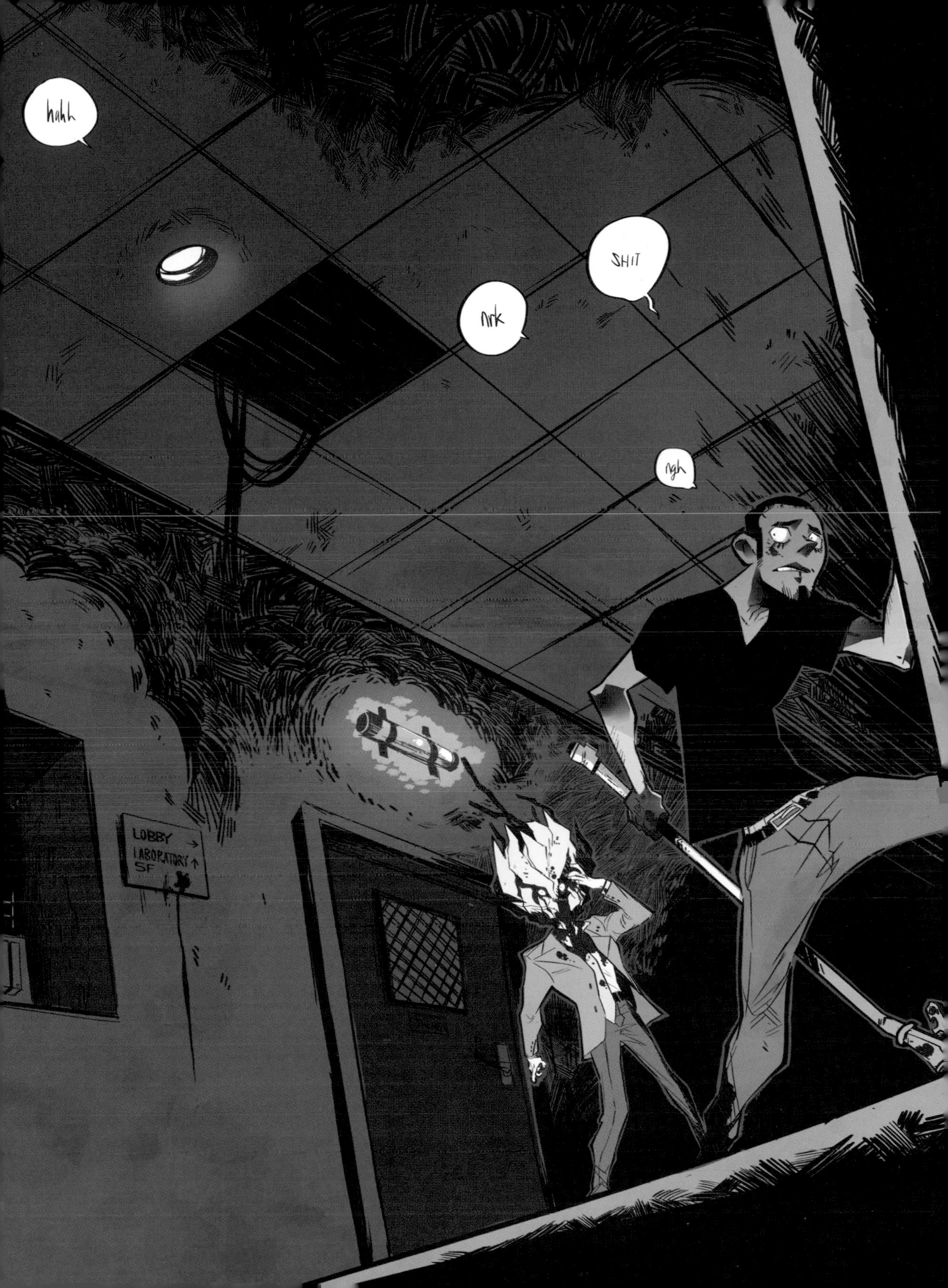
huhh
SHIT
nrk
ngh
LOBBY →
LABORATORY ↑
5F

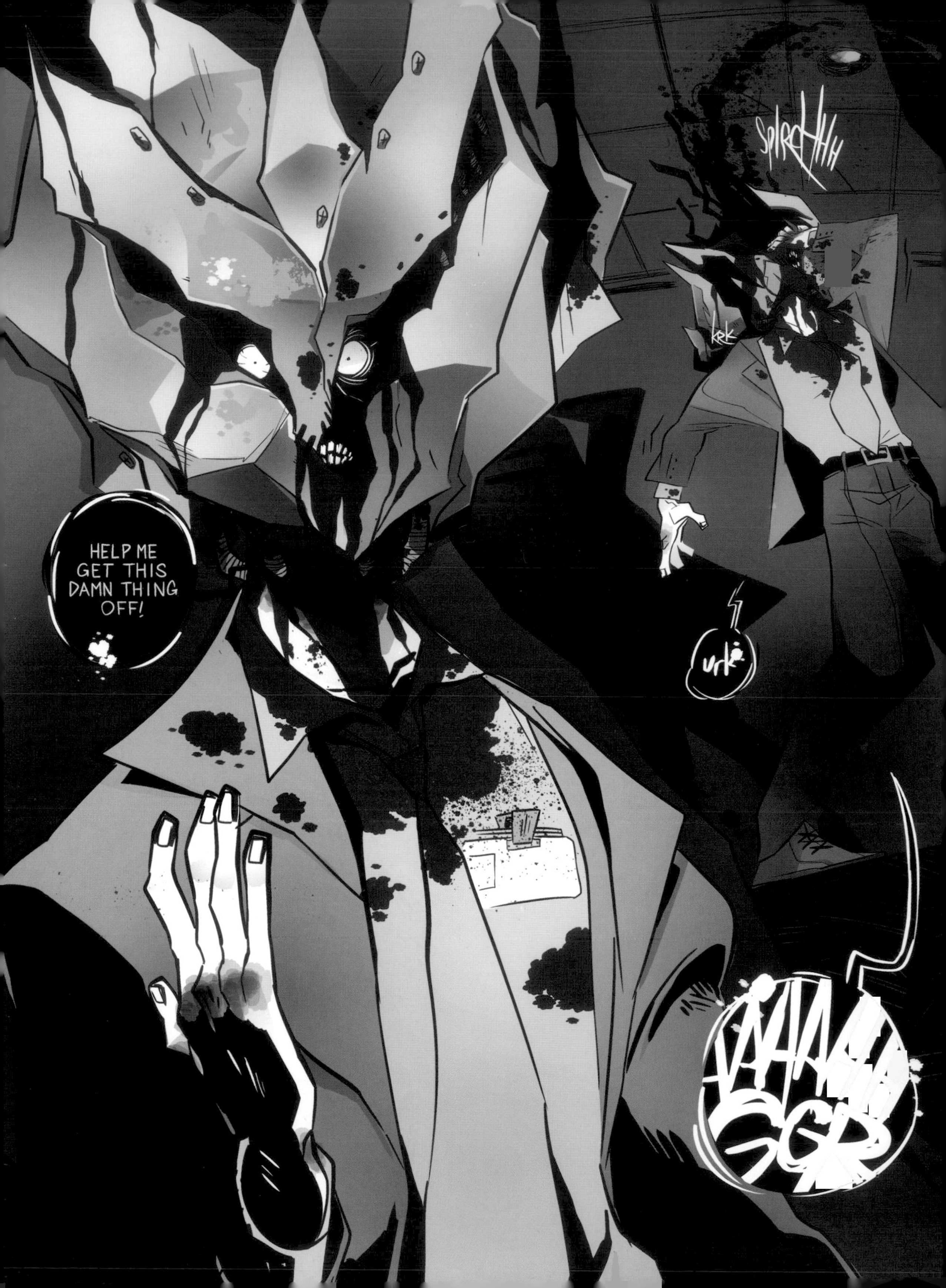
HELP ME GET THIS DAMN THING OFF!
krk
urk

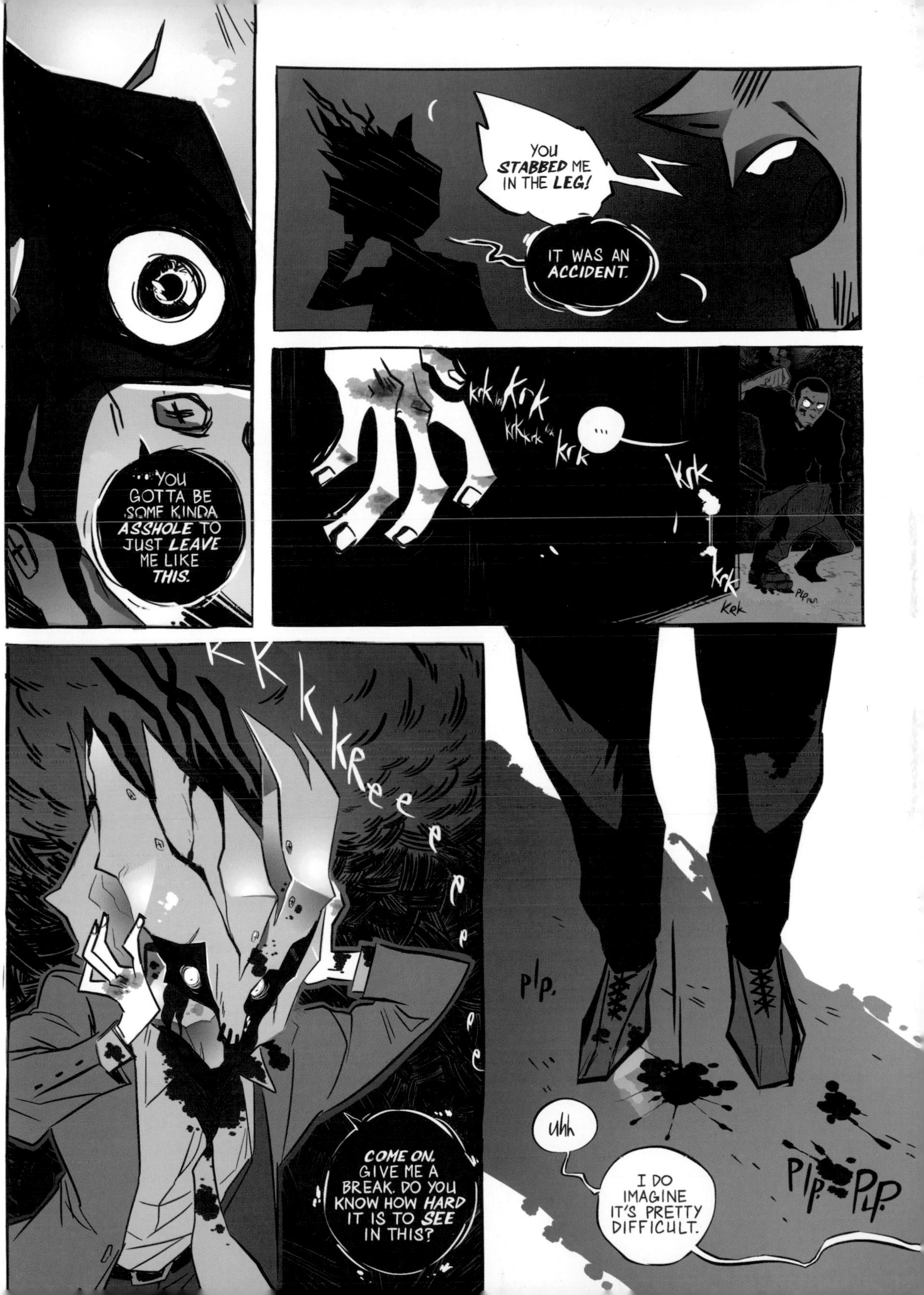
YOU STABBED ME IN THE LEG!
IT WAS AN ACCIDENT.
...YOU GOTTA BE SOME KINDA ASSHOLE TO JUST LEAVE ME LIKE THIS.
krk krk Krk
krkkrk krk krk
...
krk
krk
krk
PLP PLP
KKKKReeeeeeee
COME ON. GIVE ME A BREAK. DO YOU KNOW HOW HARD IT IS TO SEE IN THIS?
PLP.
uhh
I DO IMAGINE IT'S PRETTY DIFFICULT.
PLP PLP.

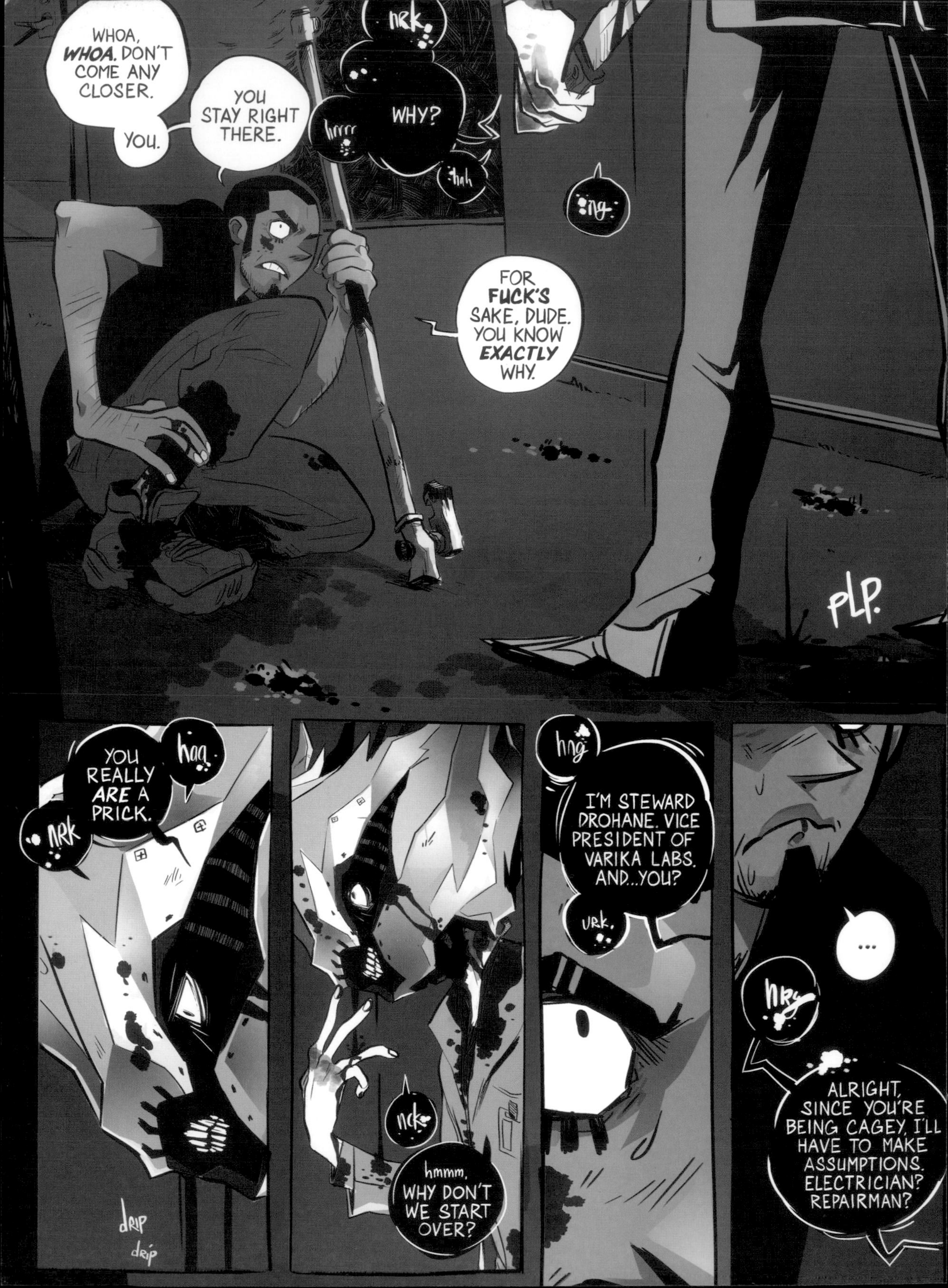
WHOA, **WHOA.** DON'T COME ANY CLOSER.
YOU.
YOU STAY RIGHT THERE.
nrk.
hrrrr
WHY?
hah
ng.
FOR **FUCK'S** SAKE, DUDE. YOU KNOW **EXACTLY** WHY.
PLP.
YOU REALLY **ARE** A PRICK.
hag.
nrk
drip
drip
nrk
hmmm, WHY DON'T WE START OVER?
hng
I'M STEWARD DROHANE. VICE PRESIDENT OF VARIKA LABS. AND...YOU?
urk.
...
ALRIGHT, SINCE YOU'RE BEING CAGEY, I'LL HAVE TO MAKE ASSUMPTIONS. ELECTRICIAN? REPAIRMAN?

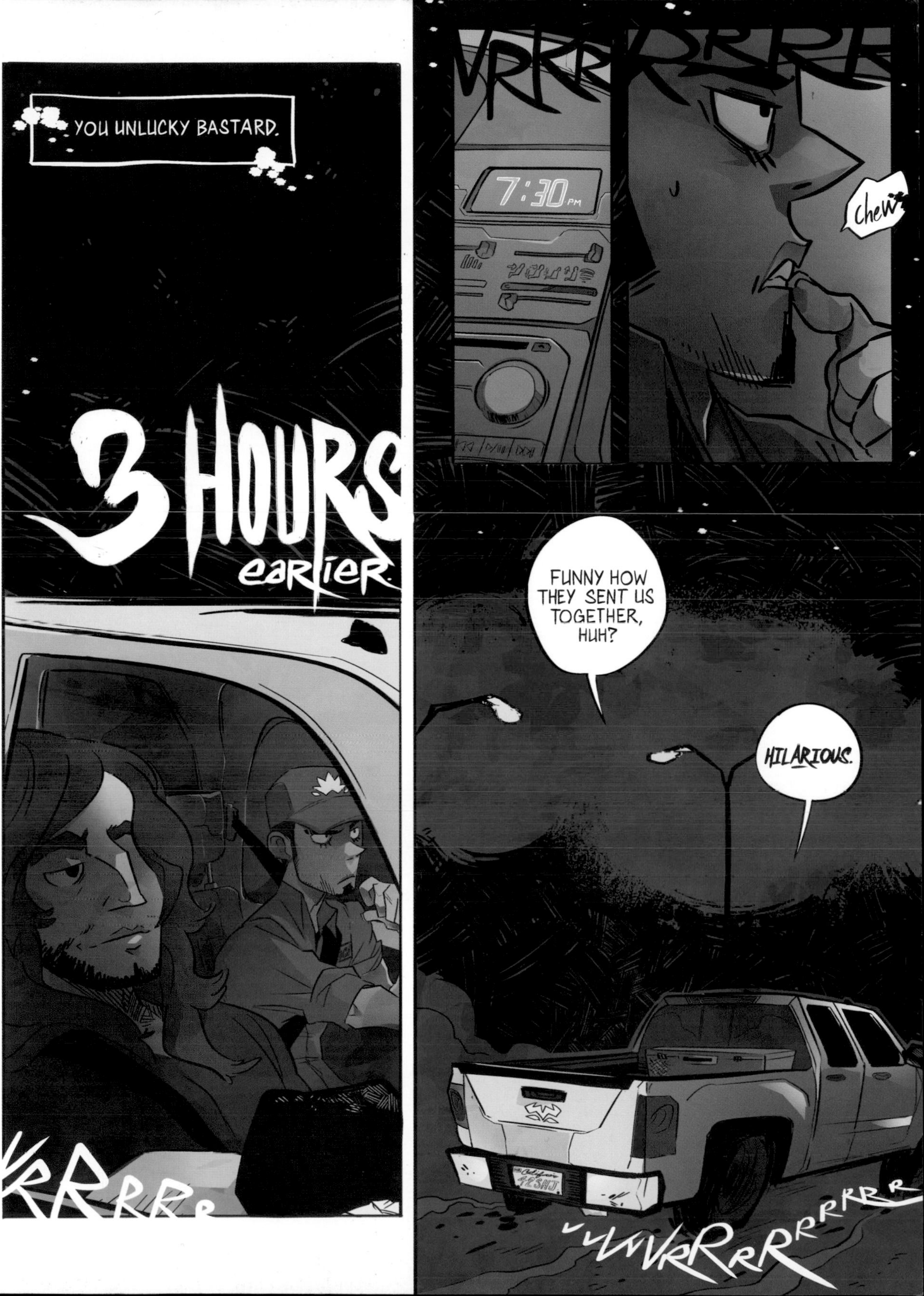
YOU UNLUCKY BASTARD.
3 HOURS earlier
VRRRRR
VRRRRRRRRR
7:30 PM
chew
FUNNY HOW THEY SENT US TOGETHER, HUH?
HILARIOUS.
VVVVRRRRRRRRRR

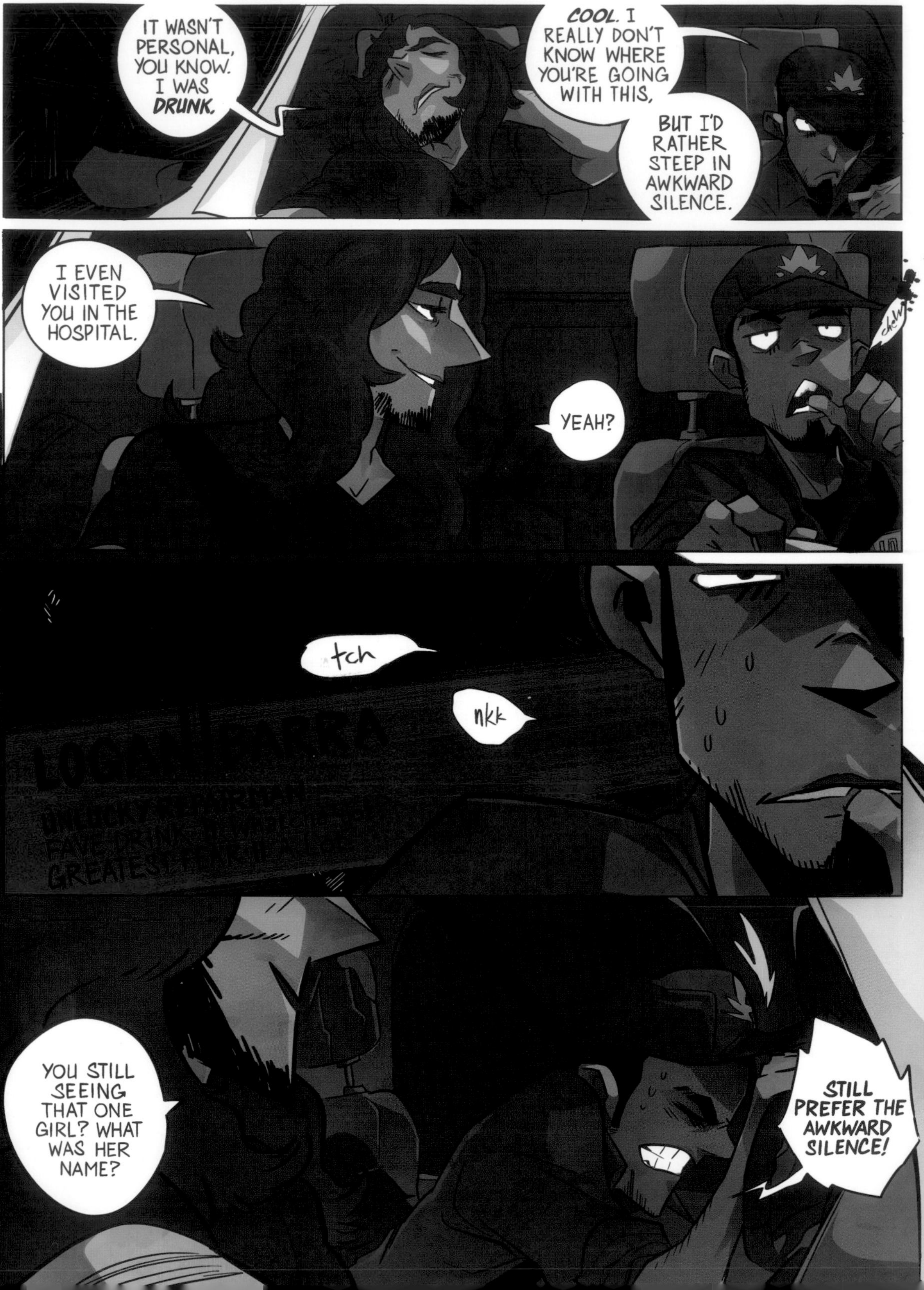
IT WASN'T PERSONAL, YOU KNOW. I WAS DRUNK.
COOL. I REALLY DON'T KNOW WHERE YOU'RE GOING WITH THIS,
BUT I'D RATHER STEEP IN AWKWARD SILENCE.
I EVEN VISITED YOU IN THE HOSPITAL.
YEAH?
tch
nkk
YOU STILL SEEING THAT ONE GIRL? WHAT WAS HER NAME?
STILL PREFER THE AWKWARD SILENCE!

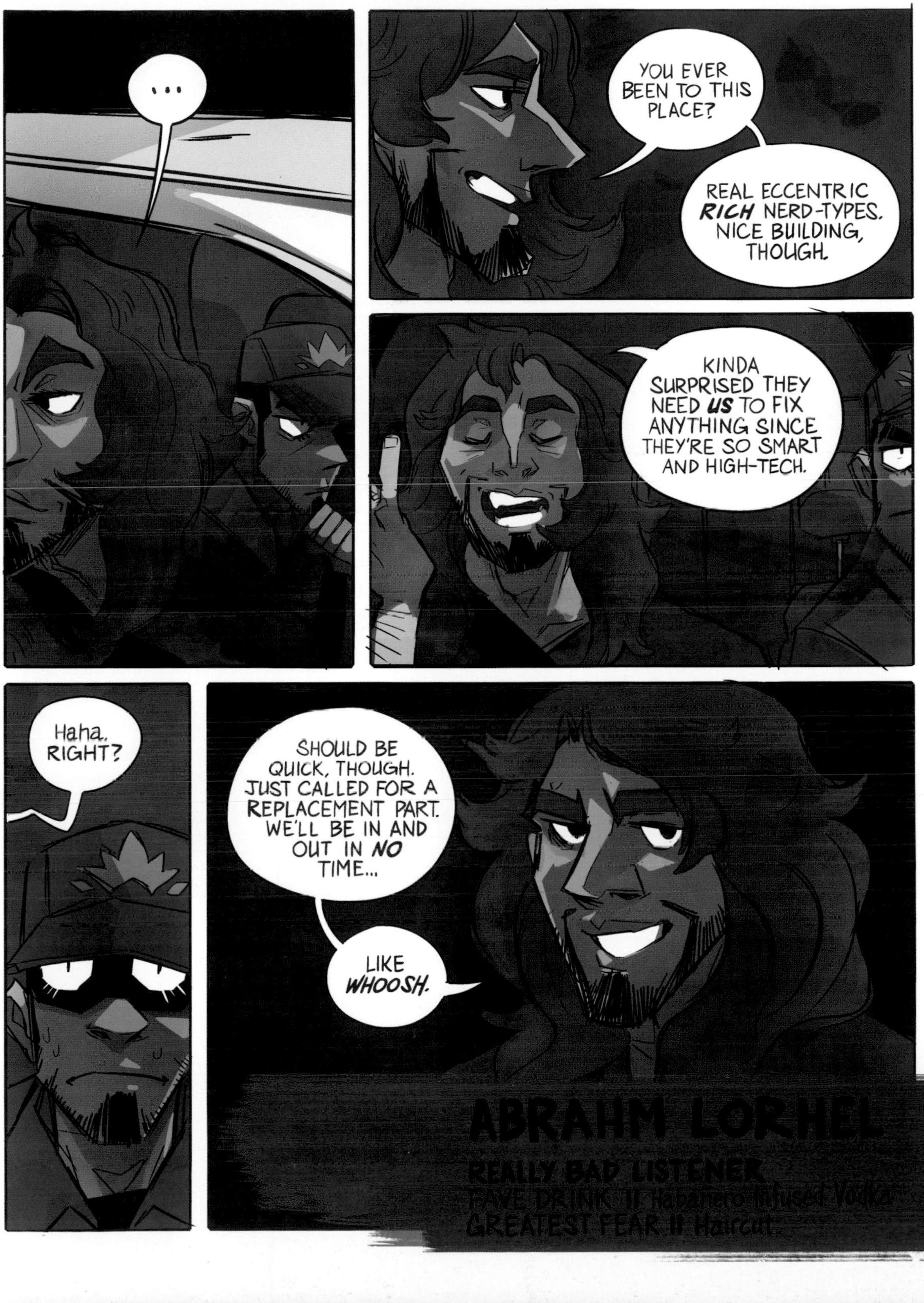
...
YOU EVER BEEN TO THIS PLACE?
REAL ECCENTRIC RICH NERD-TYPES. NICE BUILDING, THOUGH.
KINDA SURPRISED THEY NEED US TO FIX ANYTHING SINCE THEY'RE SO SMART AND HIGH-TECH.
Haha, RIGHT?
SHOULD BE QUICK, THOUGH. JUST CALLED FOR A REPLACEMENT PART. WE'LL BE IN AND OUT IN NO TIME...
LIKE WHOOSH.
ABRAHM LORHEL
REALLY BAD LISTENER
FAVE DRINK // Habanero Infused Vodka
GREATEST FEAR // Haircut.

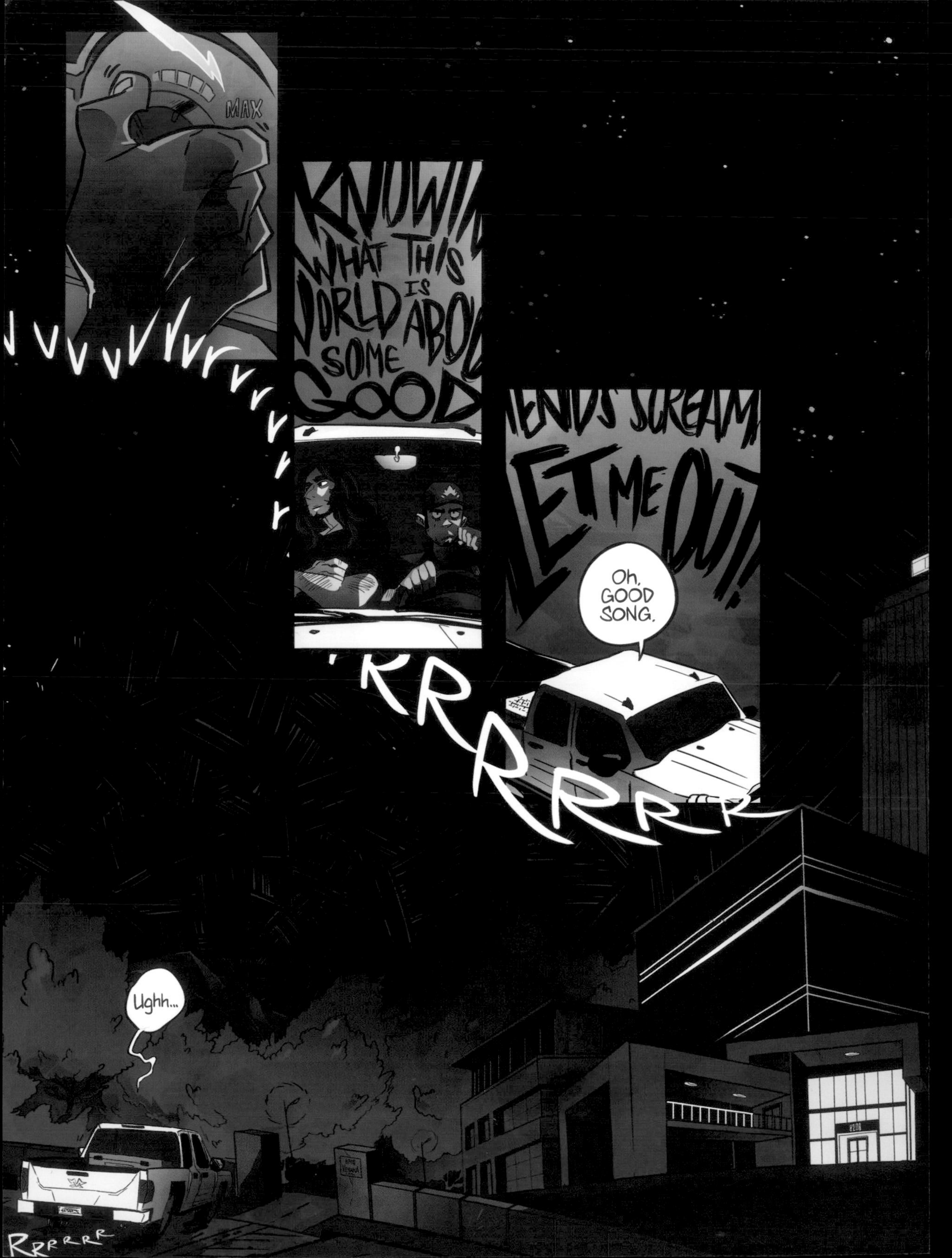
MAX
KNOWIN
WHAT THIS WORLD IS ABOU
SOME GOOD
IENDS SCREAM
LET ME OUT!
Oh, GOOD SONG.
VVVVVVVVrrrrrrrRRRRRRR
Ughh...
RRRRRR

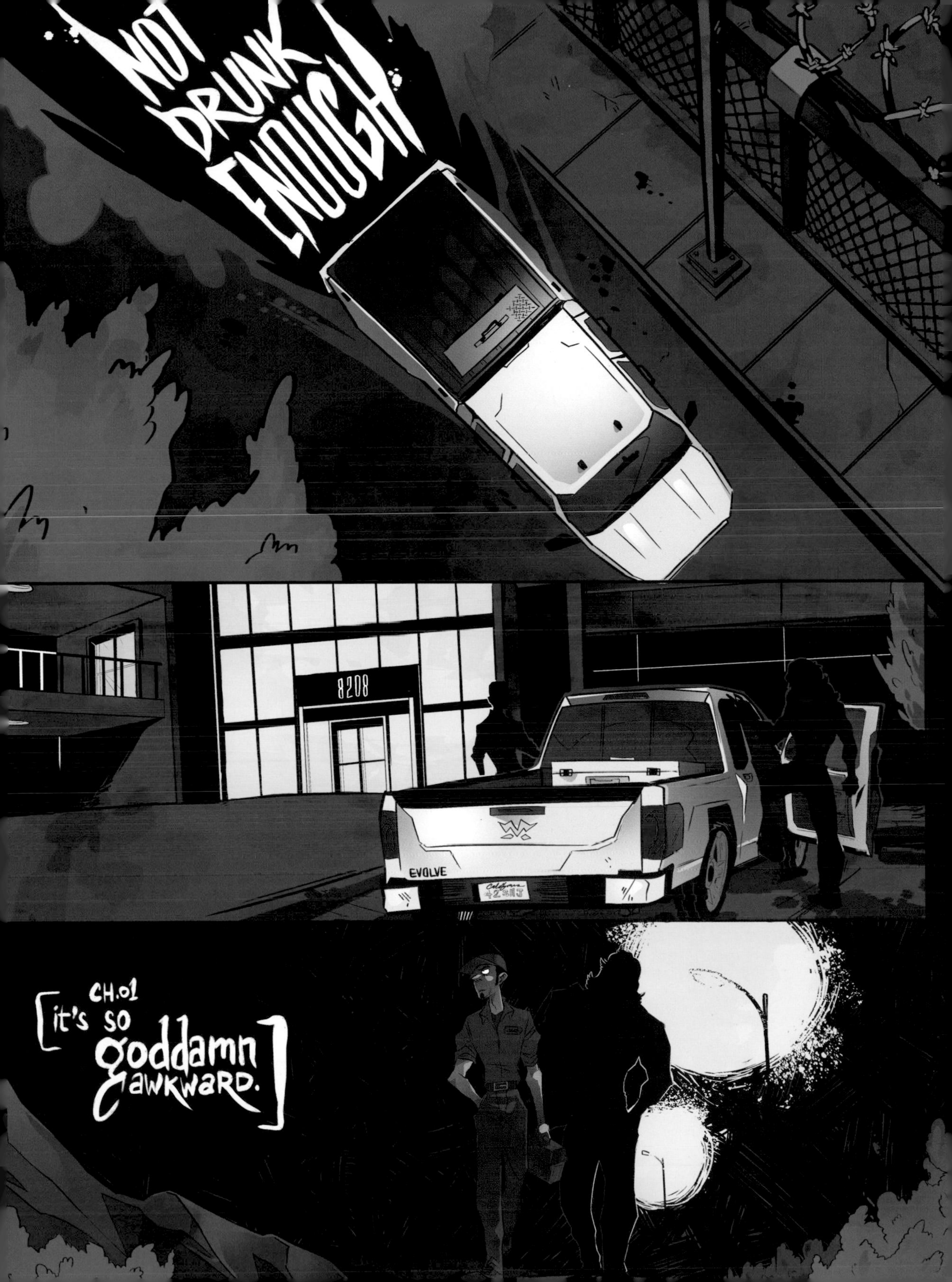
NOT DRUNK ENOUGH
8208
EVOLVE
CH.01
[it's so goddamn awkward.]

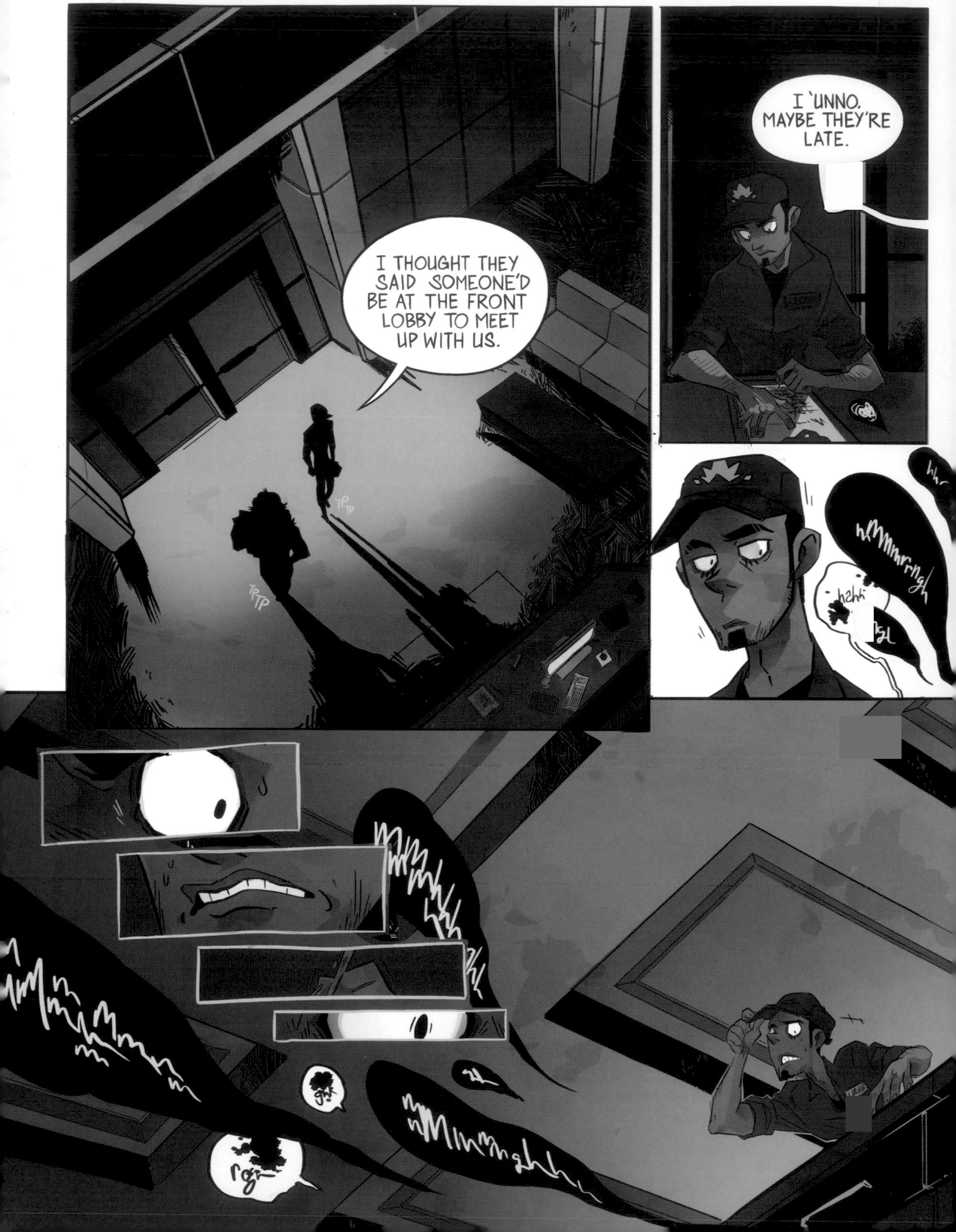
I THOUGHT THEY SAID SOMEONE'D BE AT THE FRONT LOBBY TO MEET UP WITH US.
I 'UNNO. MAYBE THEY'RE LATE.

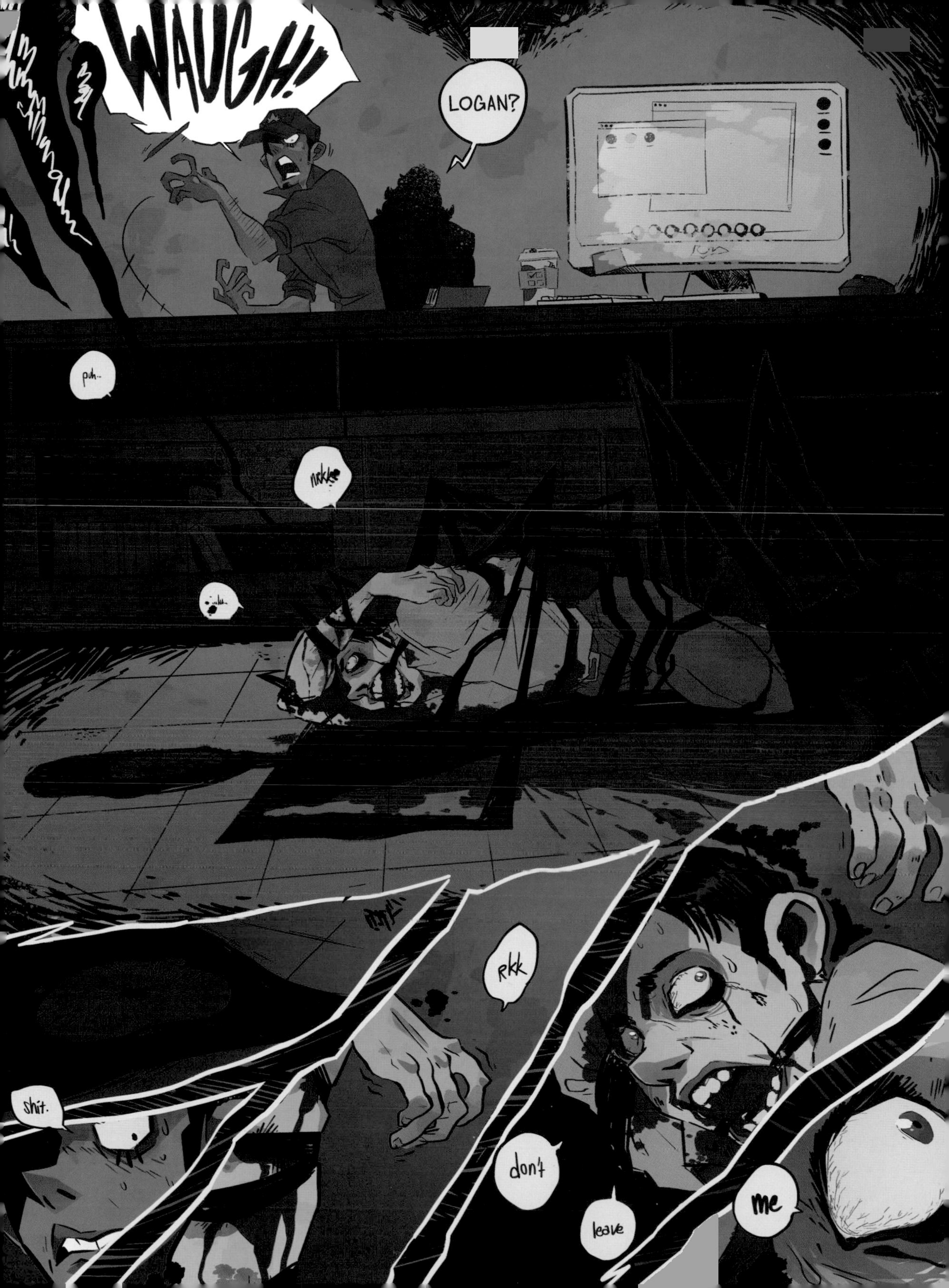
WAUGH!
LOGAN?
puh..
nrkk
rkk
shit.
don't
leave
me

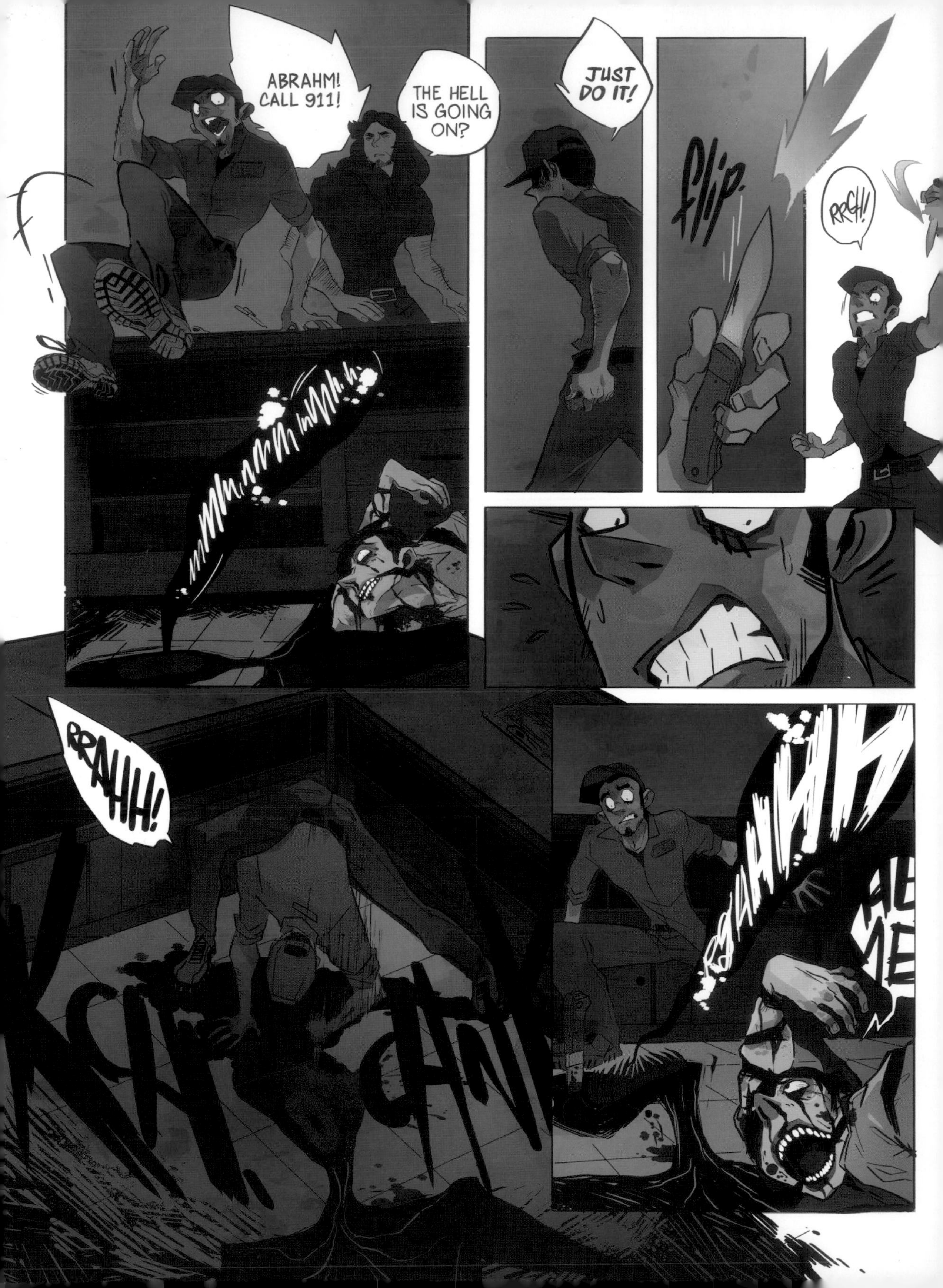
ABRAHM! CALL 911!
THE HELL IS GOING ON?
JUST DO IT!
flip
RRGH!
RRAHH!

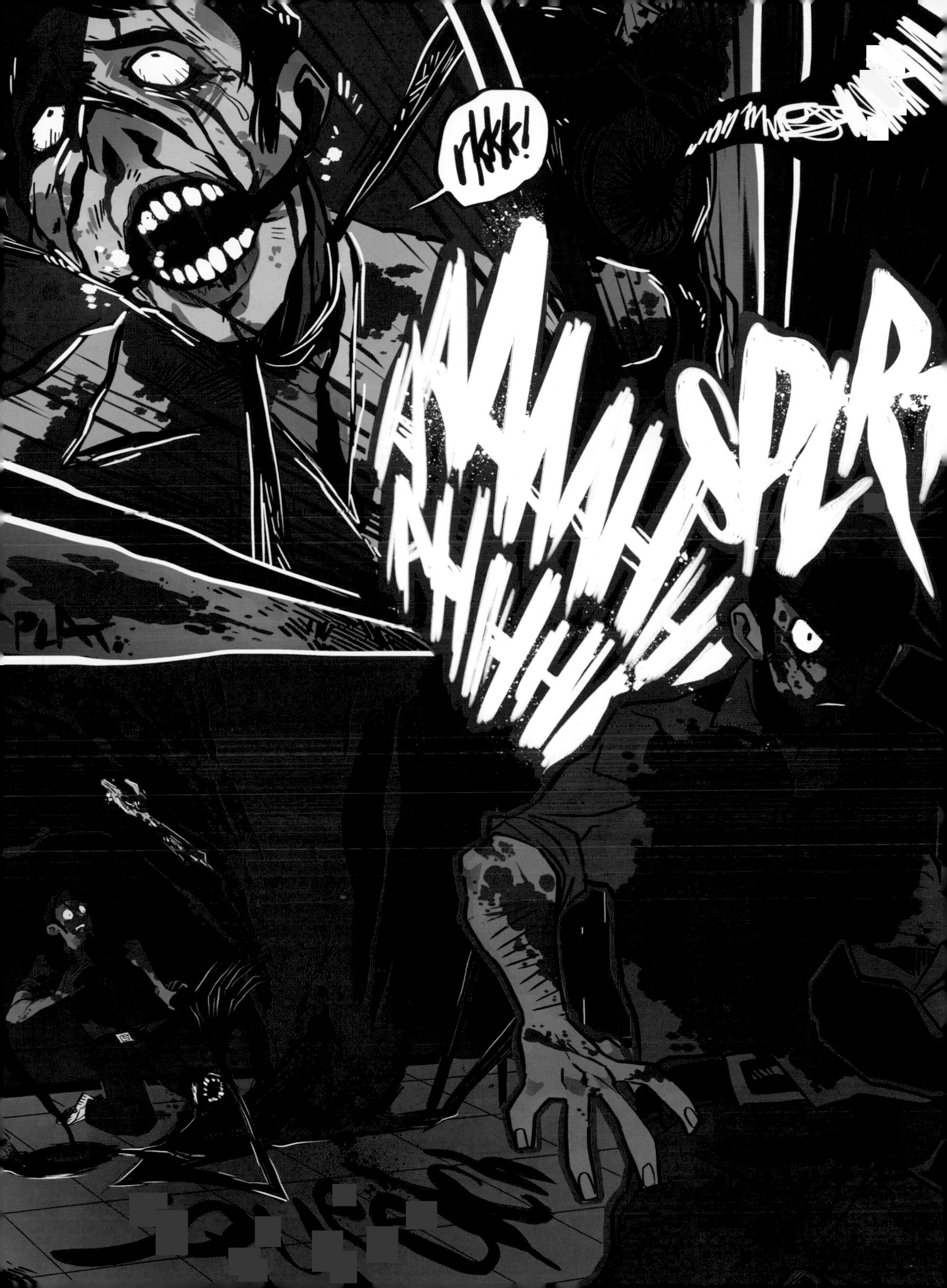
rkkk!

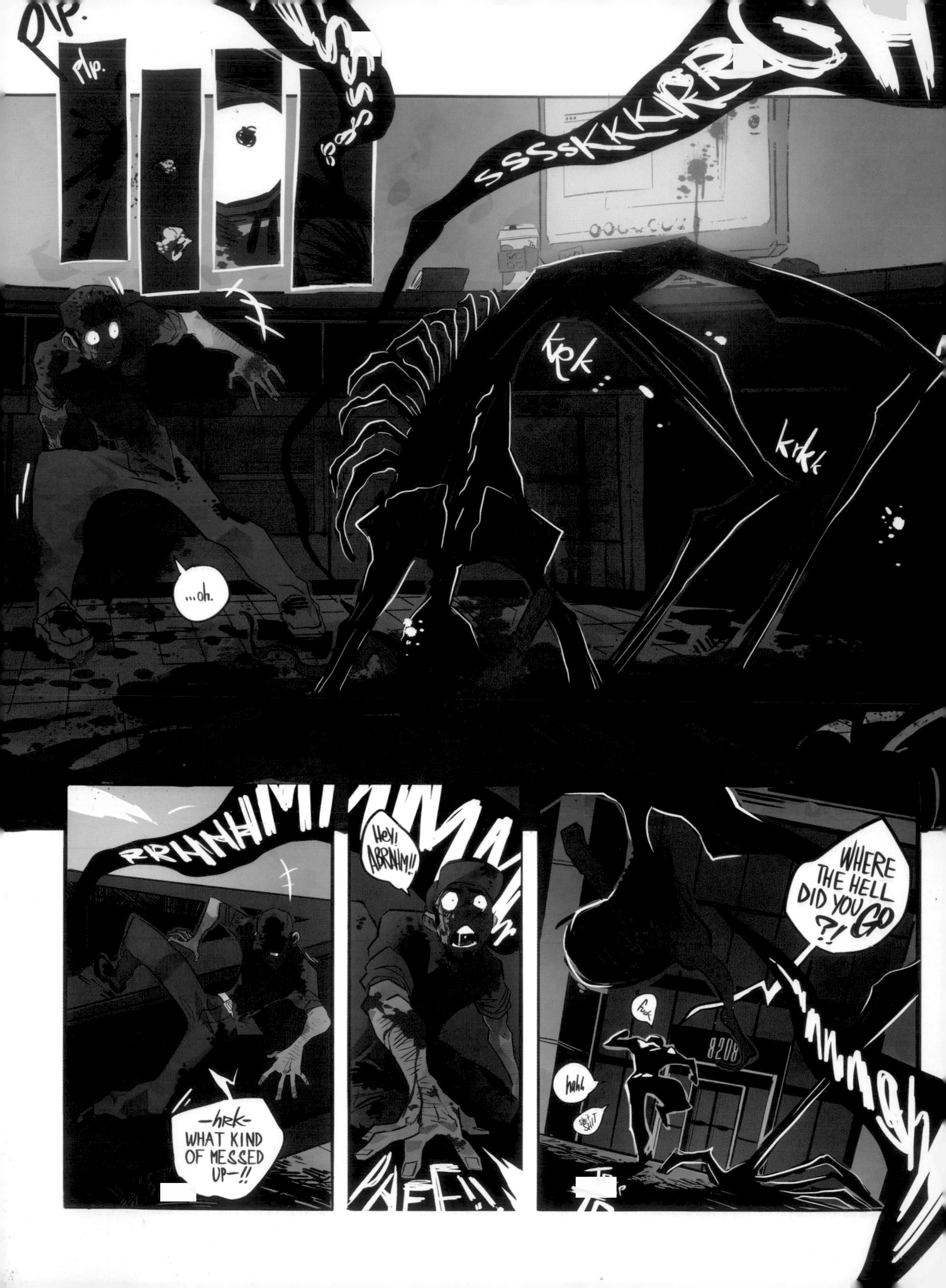

plp.
plp.
SSSSKKKKRR
krk
krkk
...oh.
-hrk- WHAT KIND OF MESSED UP-!!
HEY! ABRHM!!
WHERE THE HELL DID YOU GO?!
fuck
hahh
shit shit
8208

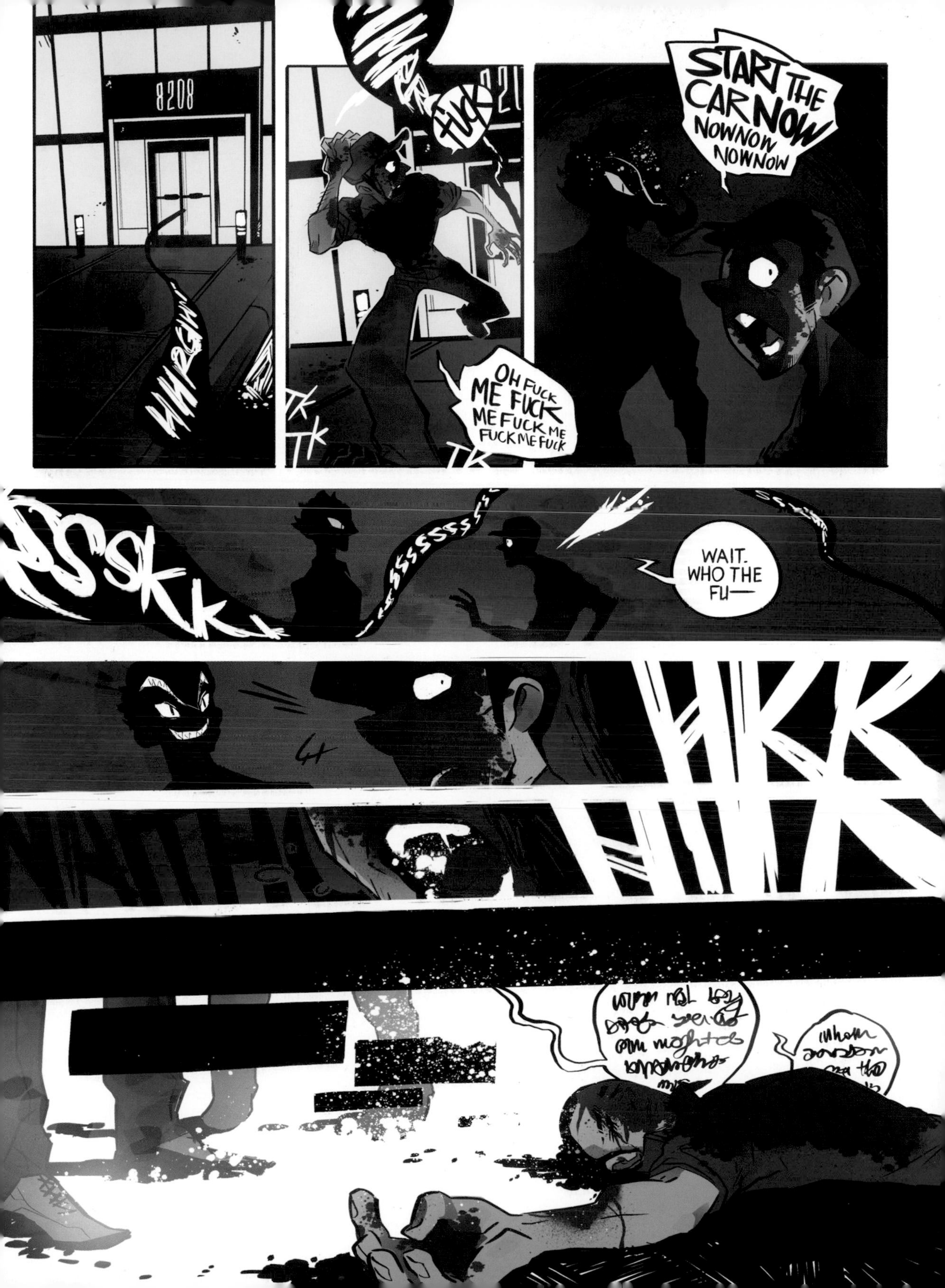
8208
WHRGH
FUCK
OH FUCK ME FUCK ME FUCK ME FUCK ME FUCK
TK
TK
START THE CAR NOW NOWNOW NOWNOW
SSKK
WAIT. WHO THE FU—
HRK

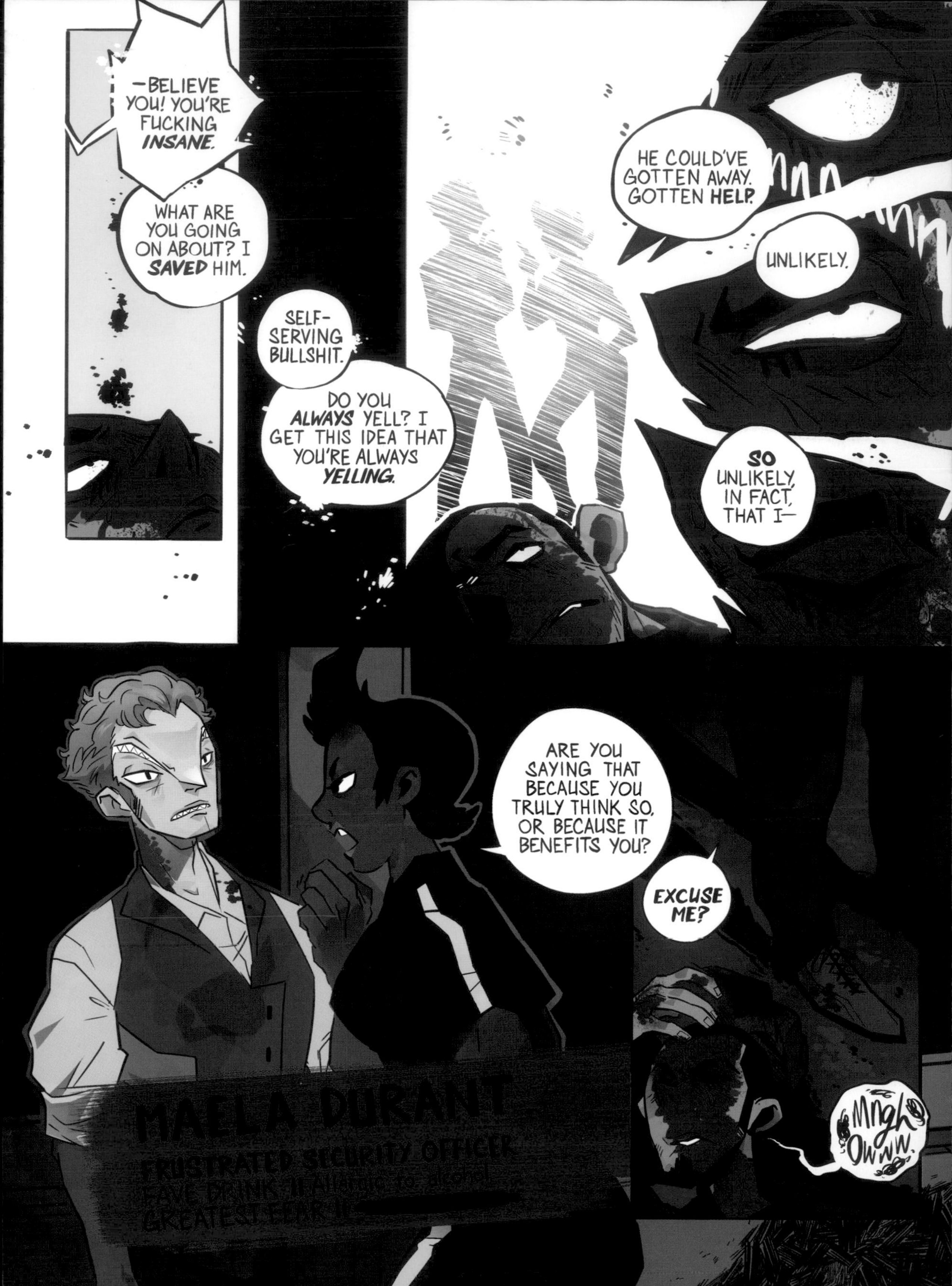
—BELIEVE YOU! YOU'RE FUCKING INSANE.
WHAT ARE YOU GOING ON ABOUT? I SAVED HIM.
SELF-SERVING BULLSHIT.
DO YOU ALWAYS YELL? I GET THIS IDEA THAT YOU'RE ALWAYS YELLING.
HE COULD'VE GOTTEN AWAY. GOTTEN HELP.
UNLIKELY.
SO UNLIKELY, IN FACT, THAT I—
ARE YOU SAYING THAT BECAUSE YOU TRULY THINK SO, OR BECAUSE IT BENEFITS YOU?
EXCUSE ME?
MAELA DURANT
FRUSTRATED SECURITY OFFICER
FAVE DRINK // Allergic to alcohol
GREATEST FEAR // [redacted]
Mngh
Owww.

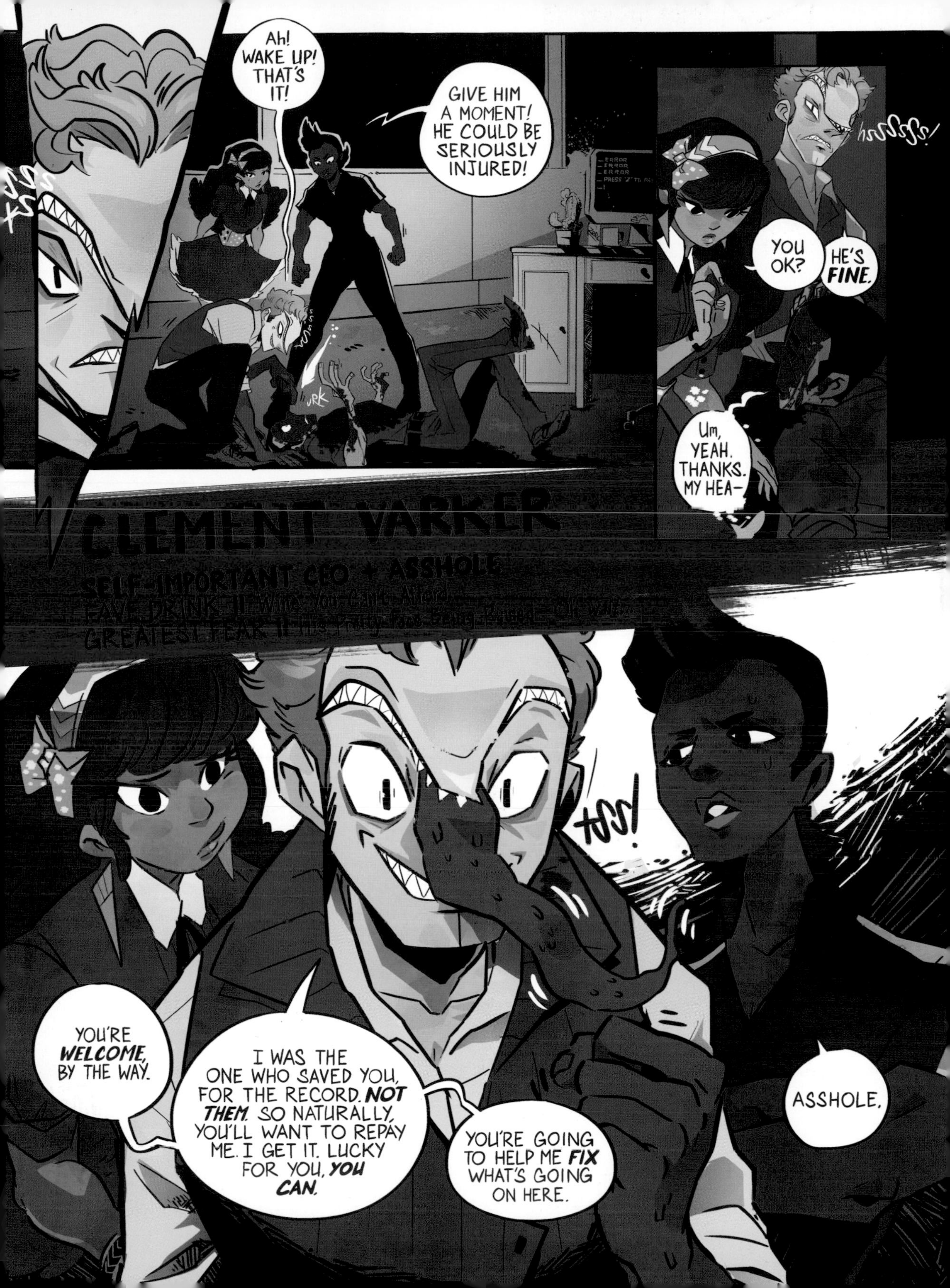

AH! WAKE UP! THAT'S IT!
GIVE HIM A MOMENT! HE COULD BE SERIOUSLY INJURED!
URK
ERROR
ERROR
ERROR
hssssss!
YOU OK?
HE'S FINE.
Um, YEAH. THANKS. MY HEA–
CLEMENT VARKER
SELF-IMPORTANT CEO + ASSHOLE
FAVE DRINK :: Wine You Can't Afford
GREATEST FEAR ::
tssss!
YOU'RE WELCOME, BY THE WAY.
I WAS THE ONE WHO SAVED YOU, FOR THE RECORD. NOT THEM. SO NATURALLY, YOU'LL WANT TO REPAY ME. I GET IT. LUCKY FOR YOU, YOU CAN.
YOU'RE GOING TO HELP ME FIX WHAT'S GOING ON HERE.
ASSHOLE.

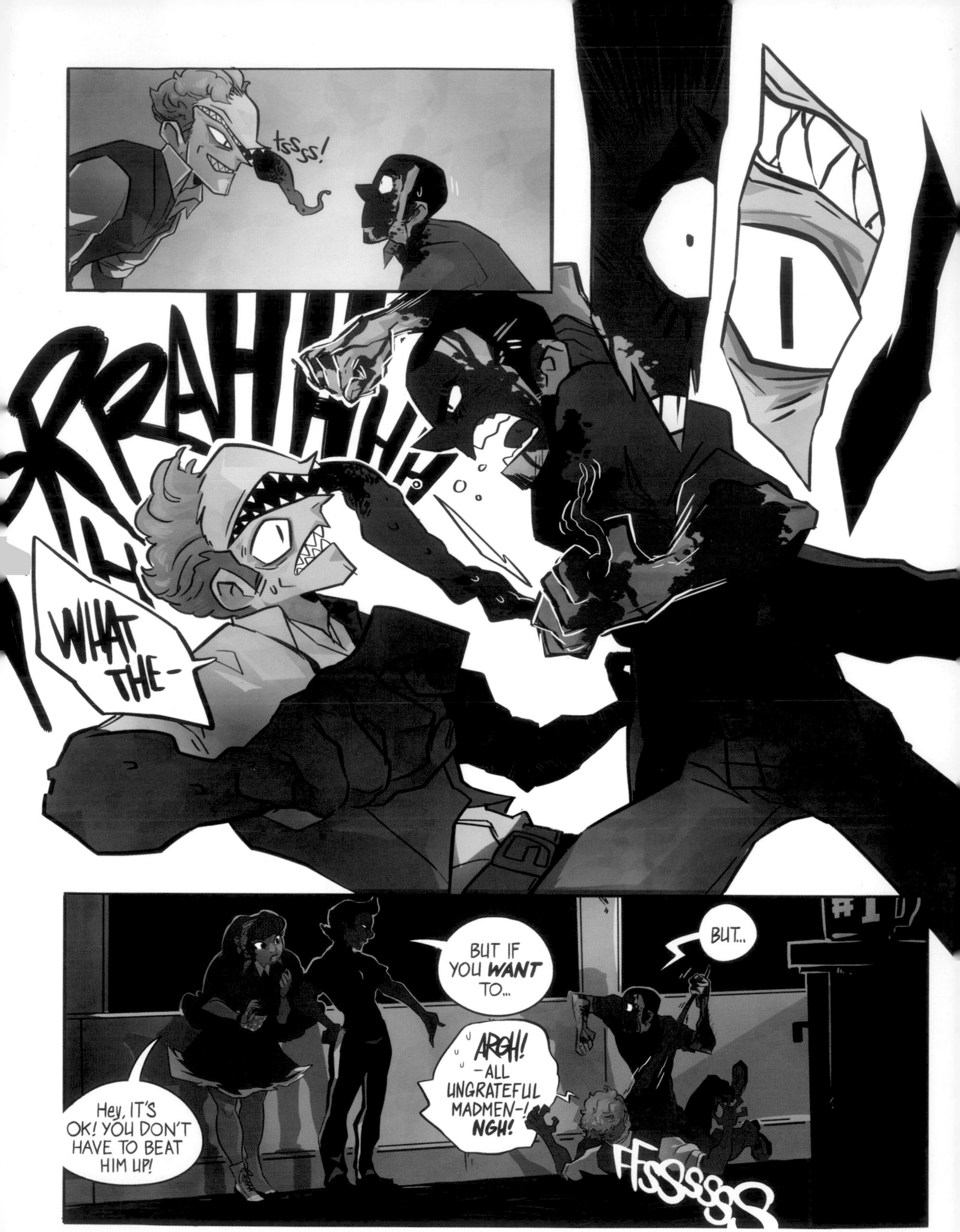
tsssss!
RRAHHHHH
WHAT THE-
BUT...
BUT IF YOU WANT TO...
Hey, IT'S OK! YOU DON'T HAVE TO BEAT HIM UP!
ARGH! -ALL UNGRATEFUL MADMEN-! NGH!
FFSSSSSS

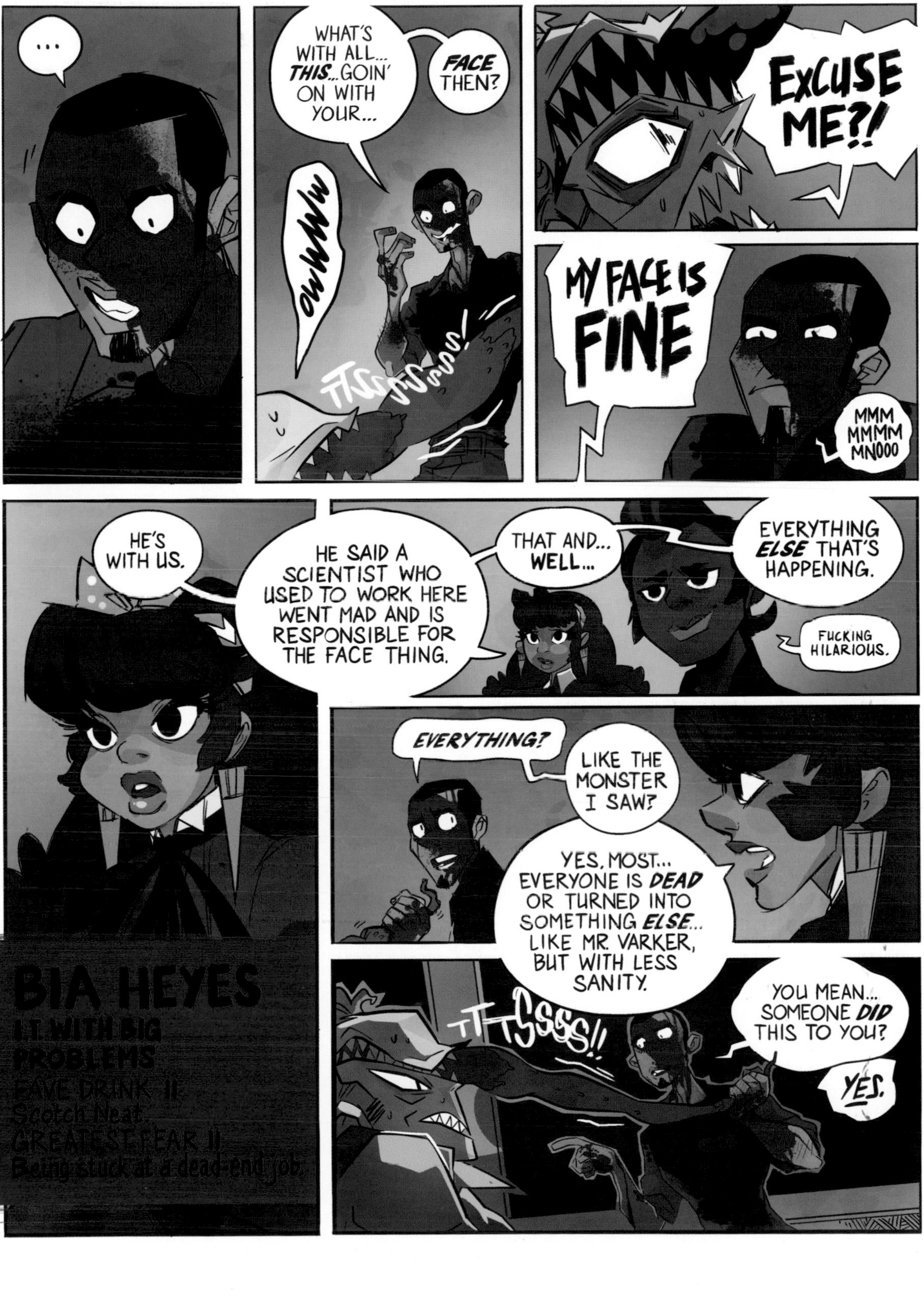
...
WHAT'S WITH ALL... THIS...GOIN' ON WITH YOUR...
FACE THEN?
OWWWW
TTSSSSSSSSS!
EXCUSE ME?!
MY FACE IS FINE
MMM MMMM MNOOO
HE'S WITH US.
HE SAID A SCIENTIST WHO USED TO WORK HERE WENT MAD AND IS RESPONSIBLE FOR THE FACE THING.
THAT AND... WELL...
EVERYTHING ELSE THAT'S HAPPENING.
FUCKING HILARIOUS.
EVERYTHING?
LIKE THE MONSTER I SAW?
YES, MOST... EVERYONE IS DEAD OR TURNED INTO SOMETHING ELSE... LIKE MR. VARKER, BUT WITH LESS SANITY.
TTTSSSS!!
YOU MEAN... SOMEONE DID THIS TO YOU?
YES.
BIA HEYES
I.T. WITH BIG PROBLEMS
FAVE DRINK //
Scotch Neat
GREATEST FEAR //
Being stuck at a dead-end job

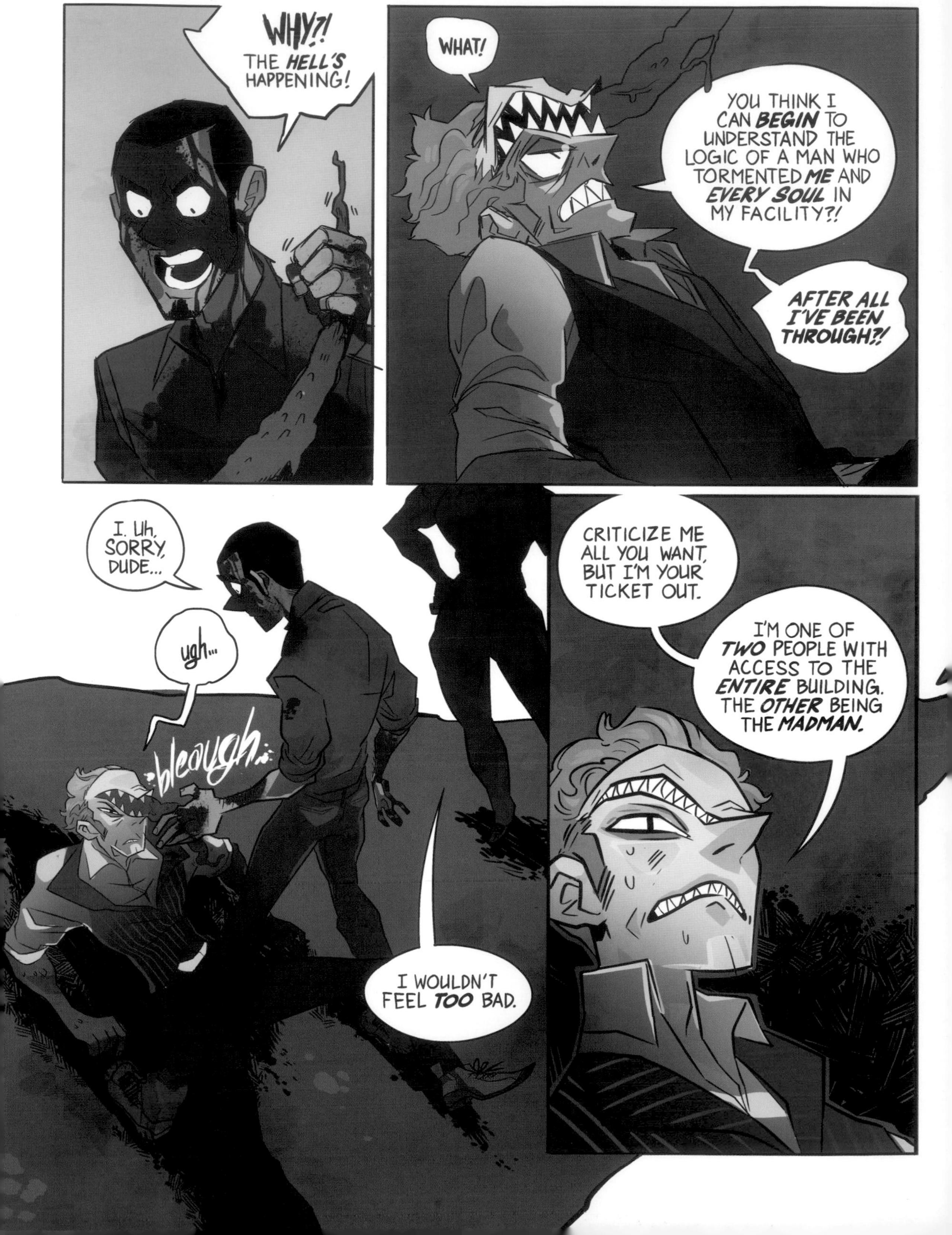
WHY?! THE HELL'S HAPPENING!
WHAT!
YOU THINK I CAN BEGIN TO UNDERSTAND THE LOGIC OF A MAN WHO TORMENTED ME AND EVERY SOUL IN MY FACILITY?!
AFTER ALL I'VE BEEN THROUGH?!
I. Uh, SORRY, DUDE...
ugh...
bleaugh
CRITICIZE ME ALL YOU WANT, BUT I'M YOUR TICKET OUT.
I'M ONE OF TWO PEOPLE WITH ACCESS TO THE ENTIRE BUILDING. THE OTHER BEING THE MADMAN.
I WOULDN'T FEEL TOO BAD.

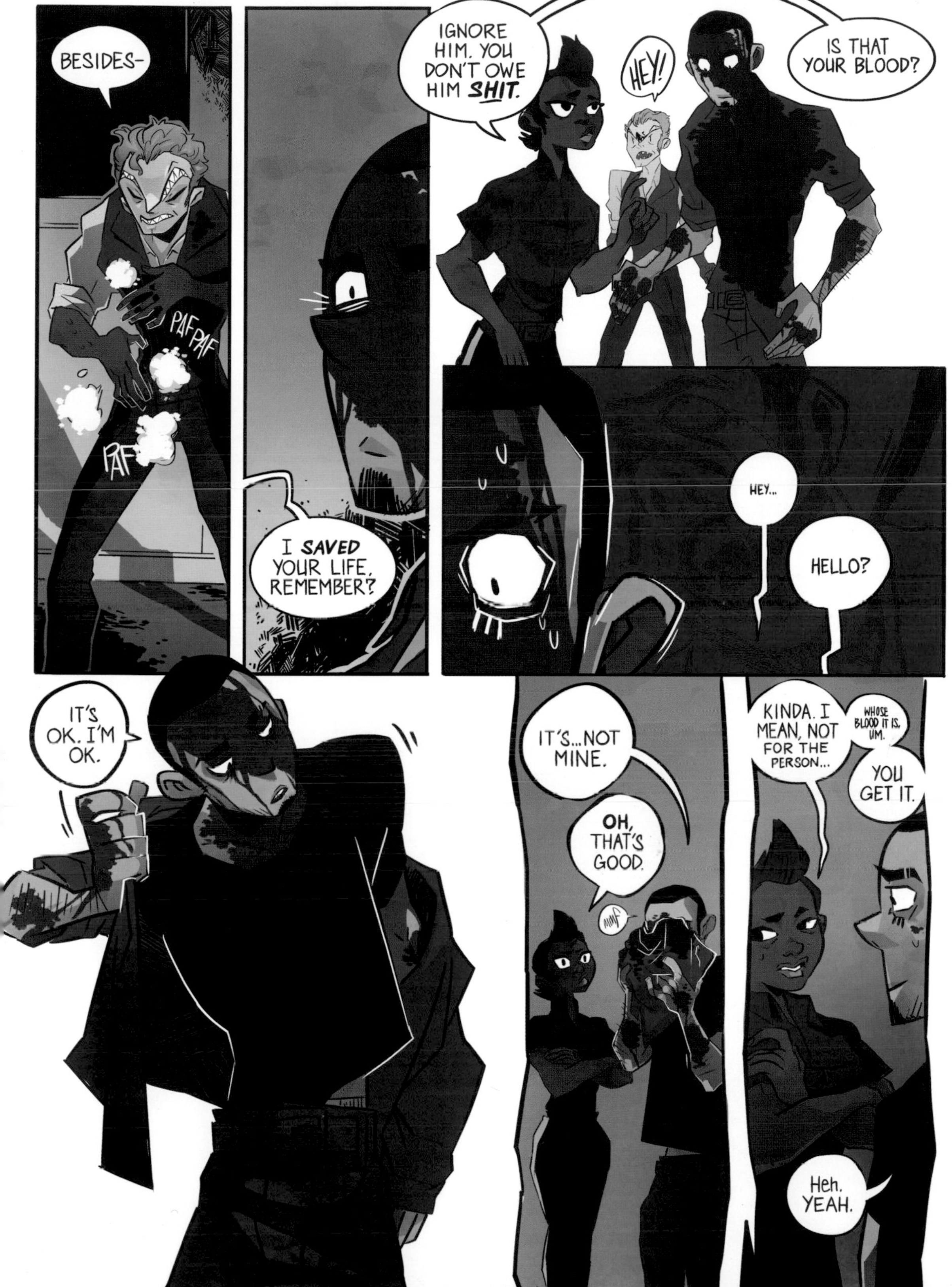
BESIDES-
PAF PAF
PAF
I SAVED YOUR LIFE, REMEMBER?
IGNORE HIM. YOU DON'T OWE HIM SHIT.
HEY!
IS THAT YOUR BLOOD?
HEY...
HELLO?
IT'S OK. I'M OK.
IT'S...NOT MINE.
OH, THAT'S GOOD.
KINDA. I MEAN, NOT FOR THE PERSON...
WHOSE BLOOD IT IS, UM.
YOU GET IT.
Heh. YEAH.

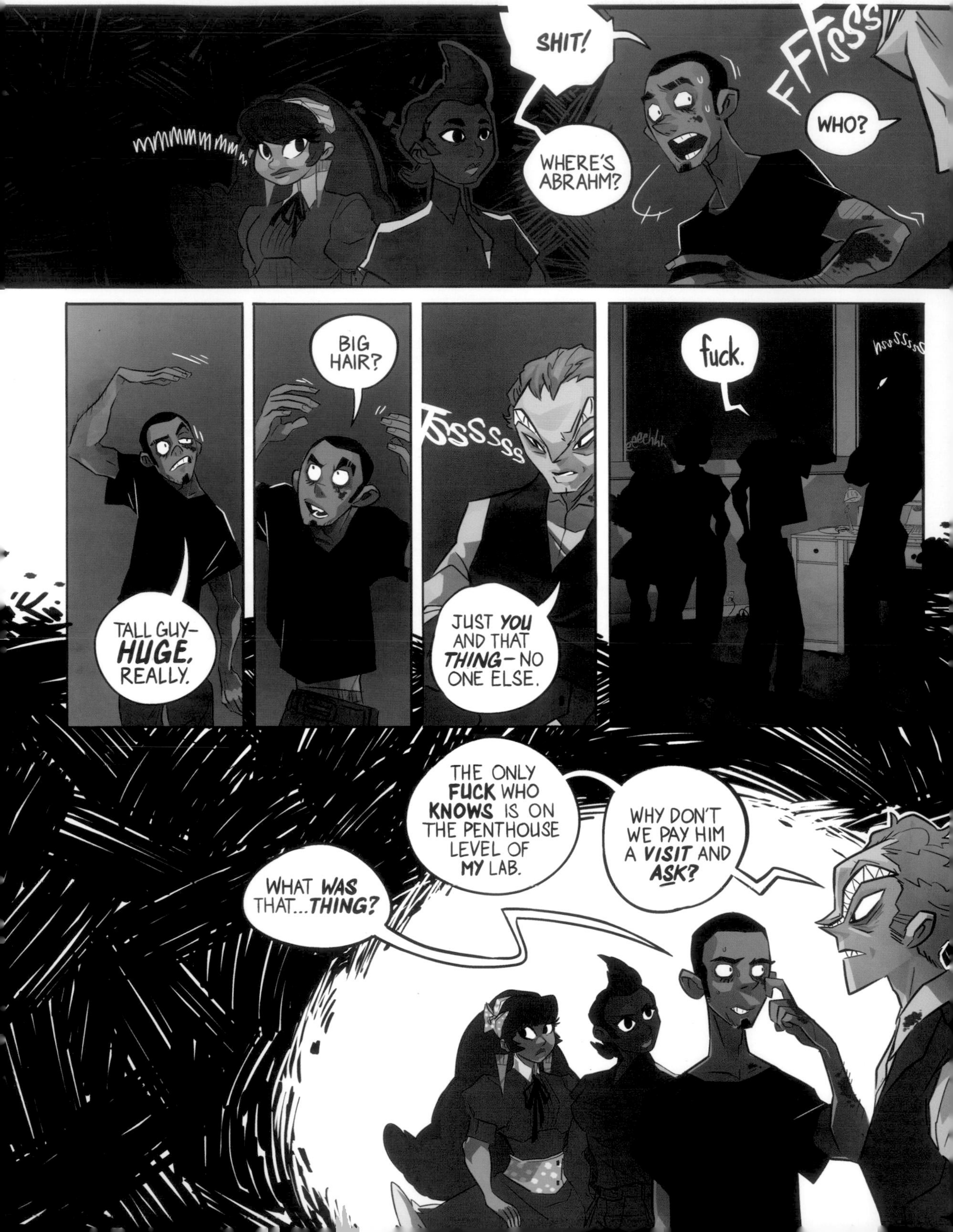

mmmmmmmmmm
SHIT!
WHERE'S ABRAHM?
FFFsss
WHO?
TALL GUY– HUGE, REALLY.
BIG HAIR?
TSSSSSSS
JUST YOU AND THAT THING– NO ONE ELSE.
fuck.
WHAT WAS THAT...THING?
THE ONLY FUCK WHO KNOWS IS ON THE PENTHOUSE LEVEL OF MY LAB.
WHY DON'T WE PAY HIM A VISIT AND ASK?

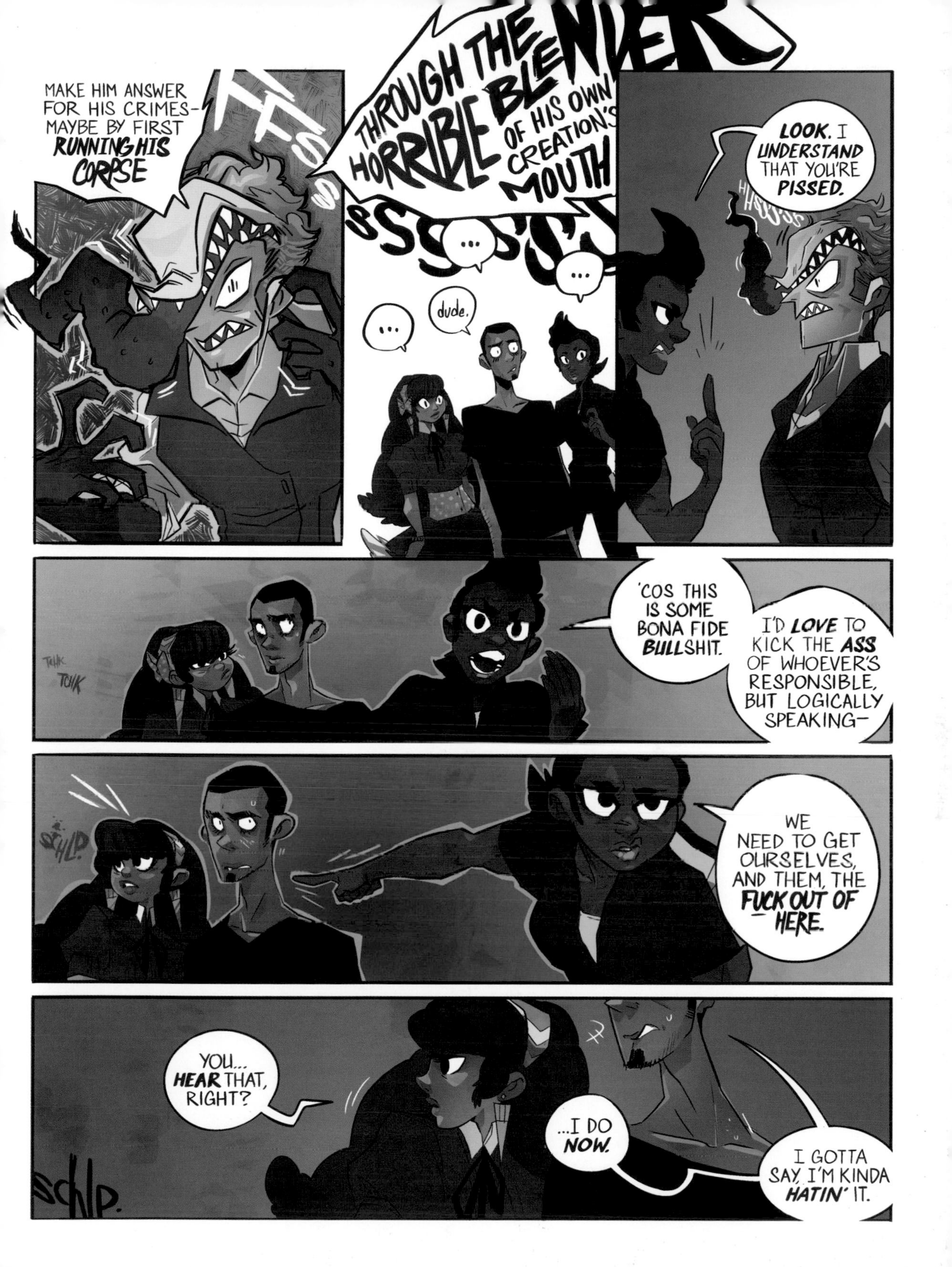

MAKE HIM ANSWER FOR HIS CRIMES- MAYBE BY FIRST RUNNING HIS CORPSE
THROUGH THE HORRIBLE BLENDER OF HIS OWN CREATION'S MOUTH
...
...
dude.
...
LOOK. I UNDERSTAND THAT YOU'RE PISSED.
'COS THIS IS SOME BONA FIDE BULLSHIT.
I'D LOVE TO KICK THE ASS OF WHOEVER'S RESPONSIBLE, BUT LOGICALLY SPEAKING-
TCHK TCHK
SCHLP
WE NEED TO GET OURSELVES, AND THEM, THE FUCK OUT OF HERE.
YOU... HEAR THAT, RIGHT?
...I DO NOW.
I GOTTA SAY, I'M KINDA HATIN' IT.
SCHLP.

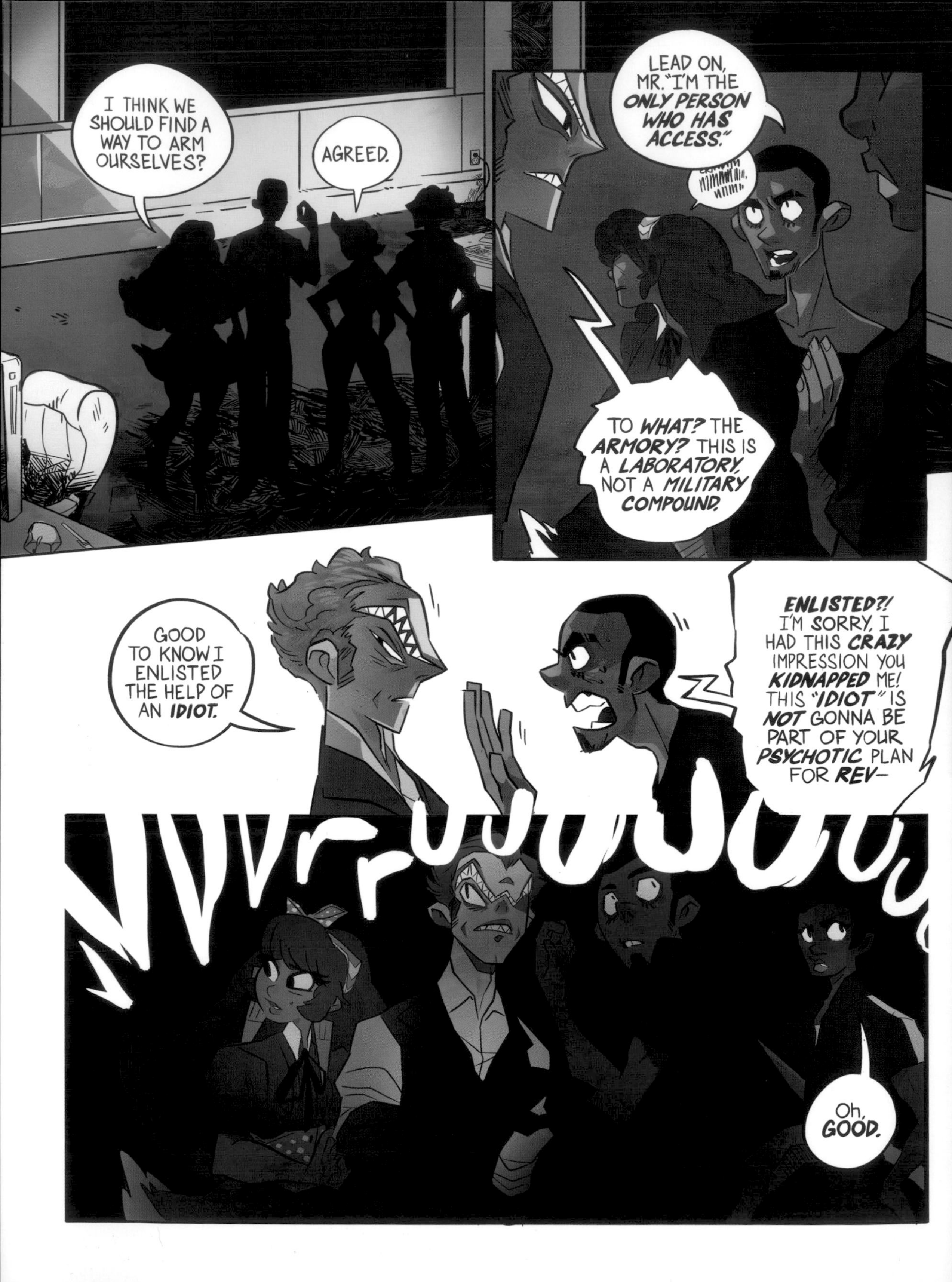
I THINK WE SHOULD FIND A WAY TO ARM OURSELVES?
AGREED.
LEAD ON, MR. "I'M THE *ONLY PERSON WHO HAS ACCESS.*"
TO *WHAT?* THE *ARMORY?* THIS IS A *LABORATORY,* NOT A *MILITARY COMPOUND.*
GOOD TO KNOW I ENLISTED THE HELP OF AN *IDIOT.*
ENLISTED?! I'M SORRY, I HAD THIS *CRAZY* IMPRESSION YOU *KIDNAPPED* ME! THIS *"IDIOT"* IS *NOT* GONNA BE PART OF YOUR *PSYCHOTIC* PLAN FOR *REV—*
VVVrUUUUUUUU
Oh, *GOOD.*

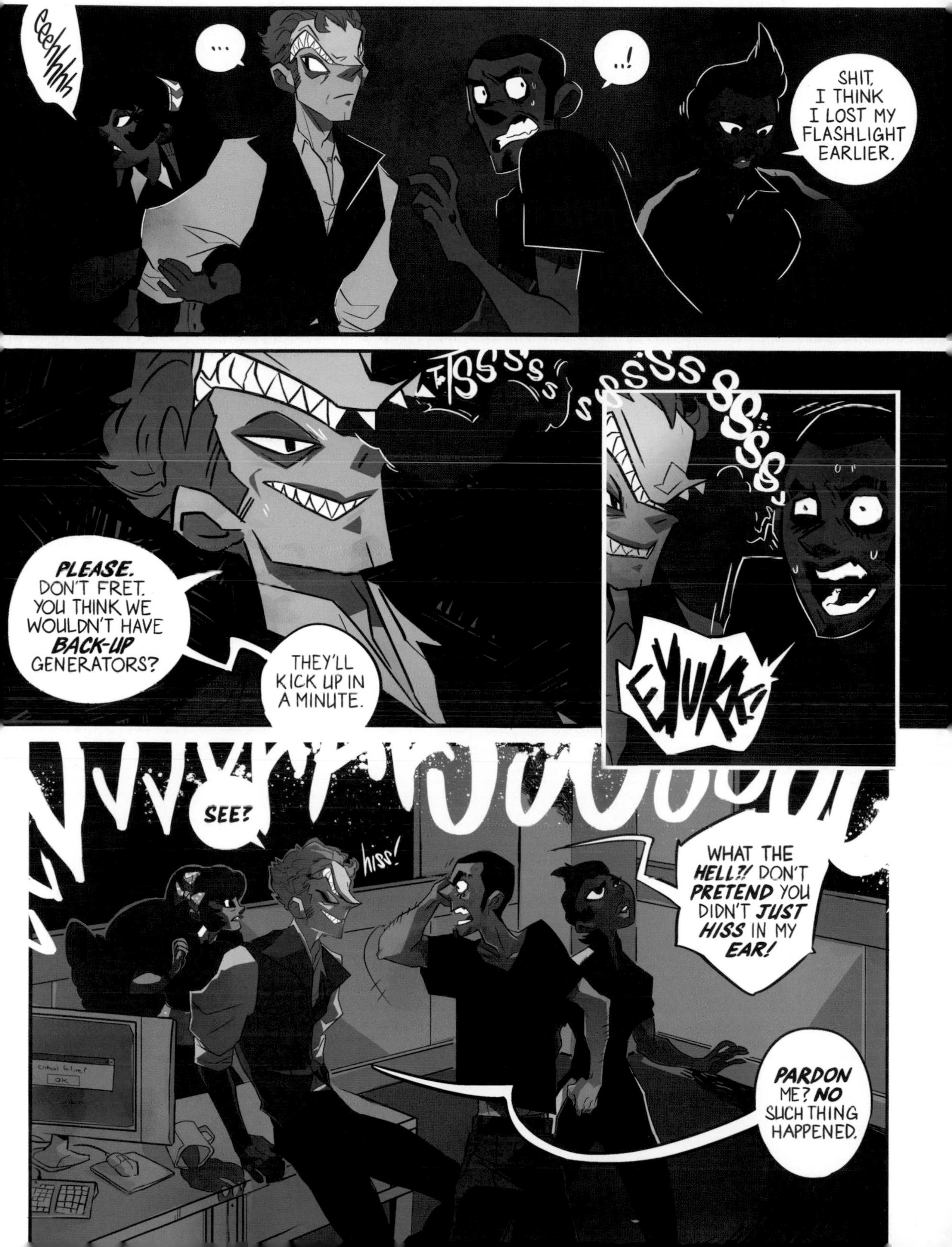
ceehhhh
...
..!
SHIT, I THINK I LOST MY FLASHLIGHT EARLIER.
TSSSSS SSSSSS SSSSSS
PLEASE. DON'T FRET. YOU THINK WE WOULDN'T HAVE BACK-UP GENERATORS?
THEY'LL KICK UP IN A MINUTE.
EYUKK!
SEE?
hiss!
WHAT THE HELL?! DON'T PRETEND YOU DIDN'T JUST HISS IN MY EAR!
PARDON ME? NO SUCH THING HAPPENED.

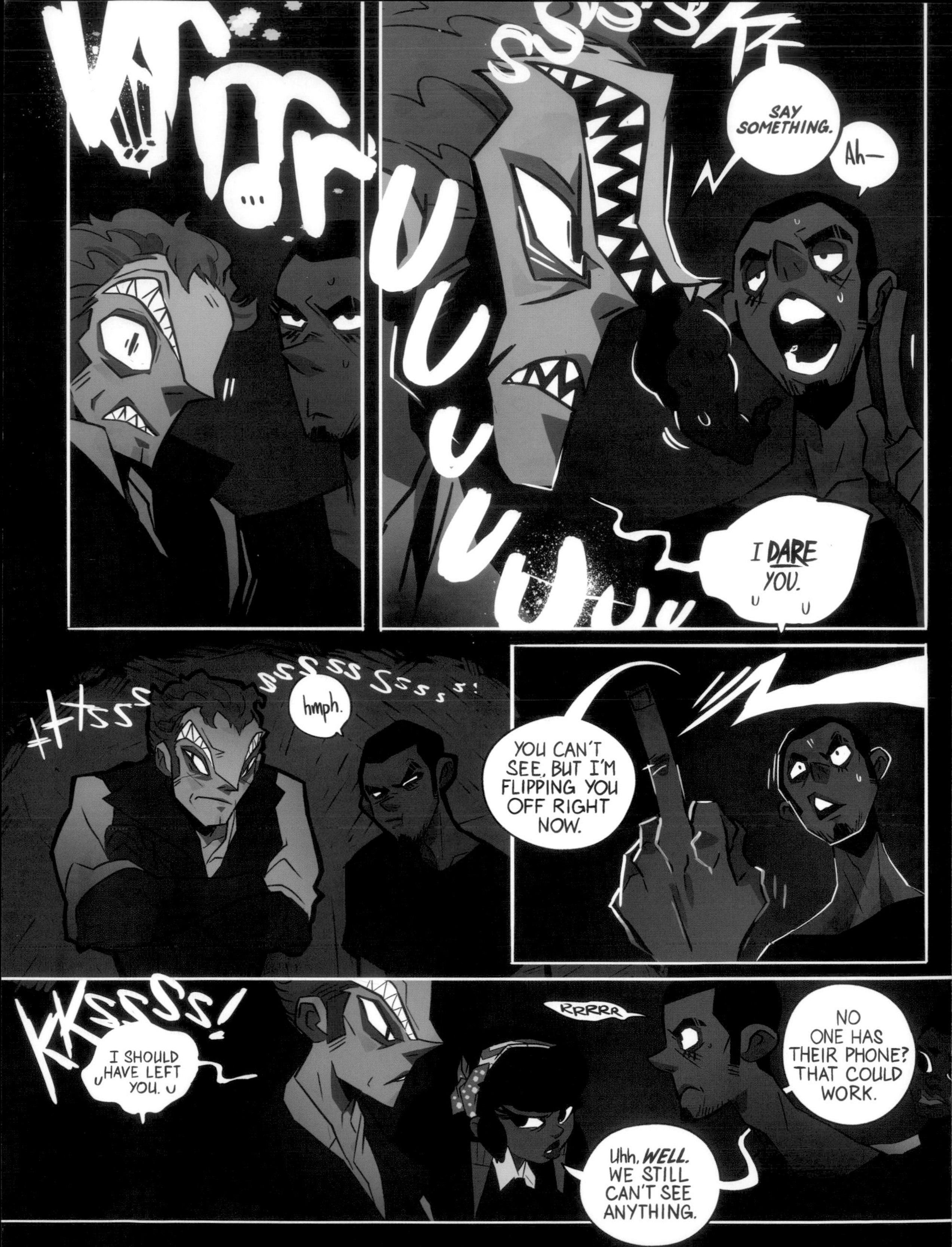
...
SAY SOMETHING.
Ah—
I DARE YOU.
hmph.
YOU CAN'T SEE, BUT I'M FLIPPING YOU OFF RIGHT NOW.
KKSSSS!
I SHOULD HAVE LEFT YOU.
RRRRR
NO ONE HAS THEIR PHONE? THAT COULD WORK.
Uhh, WELL. WE STILL CAN'T SEE ANYTHING.

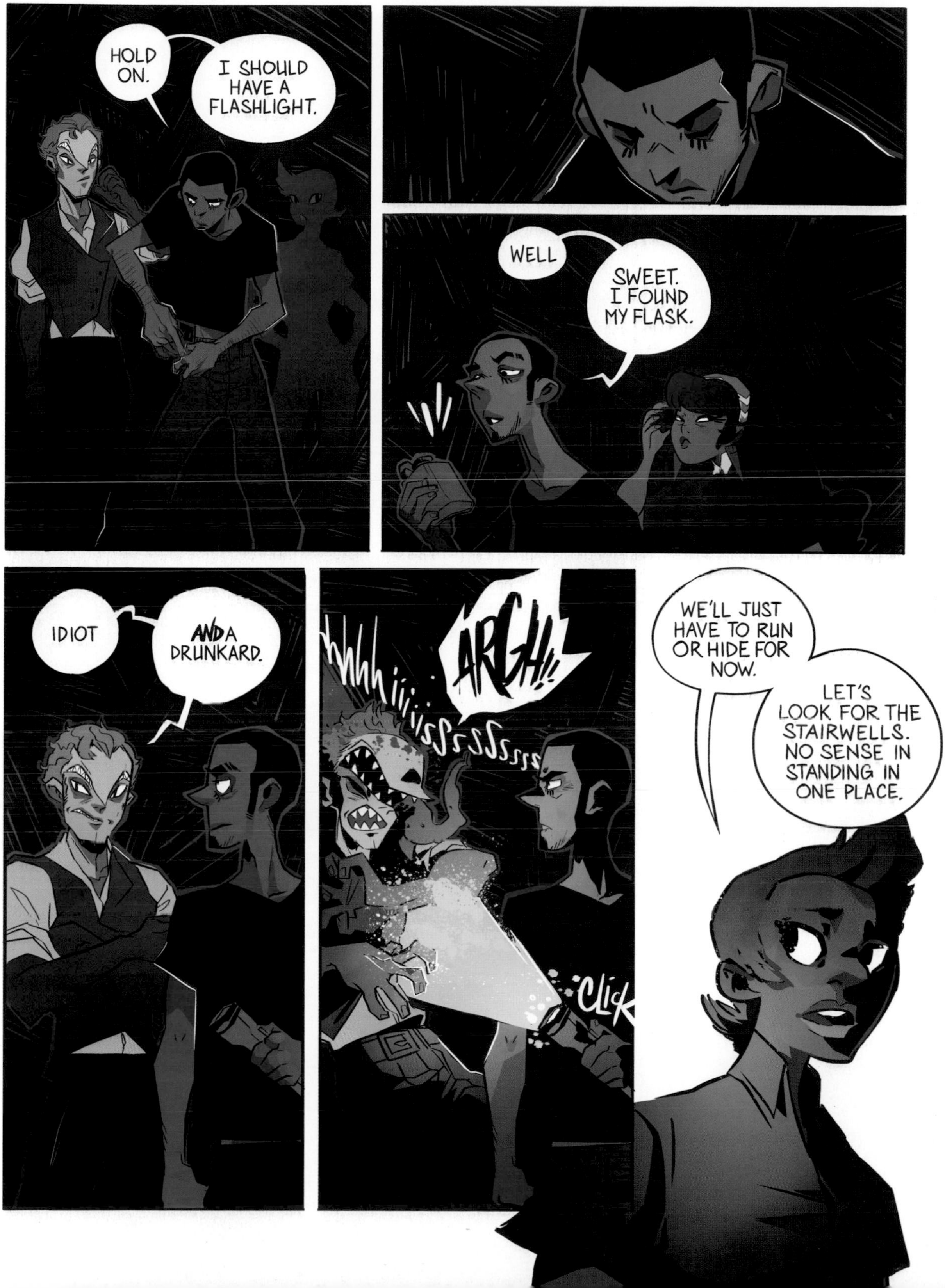
HOLD ON.
I SHOULD HAVE A FLASHLIGHT.
WELL
SWEET. I FOUND MY FLASK.
IDIOT
AND A DRUNKARD.
hhhhiiiissSsSSssss
ARGH!!!
Click
WE'LL JUST HAVE TO RUN OR HIDE FOR NOW.
LET'S LOOK FOR THE STAIRWELLS. NO SENSE IN STANDING IN ONE PLACE.

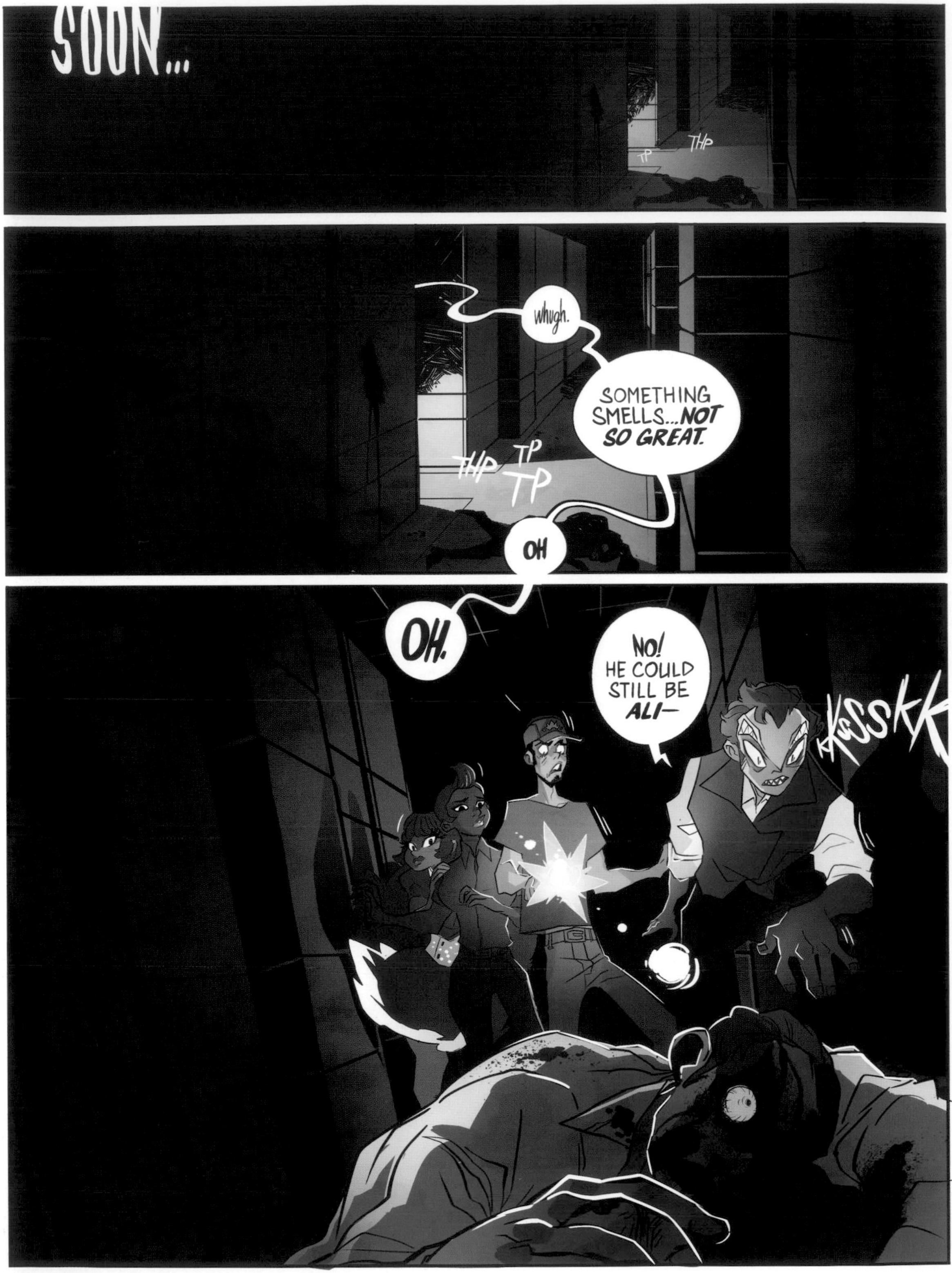
SOON...
TP
THP
whugh.
SOMETHING SMELLS...NOT SO GREAT.
THP TP TP
OH
OH.
NO! HE COULD STILL BE ALI—
KKSSKK

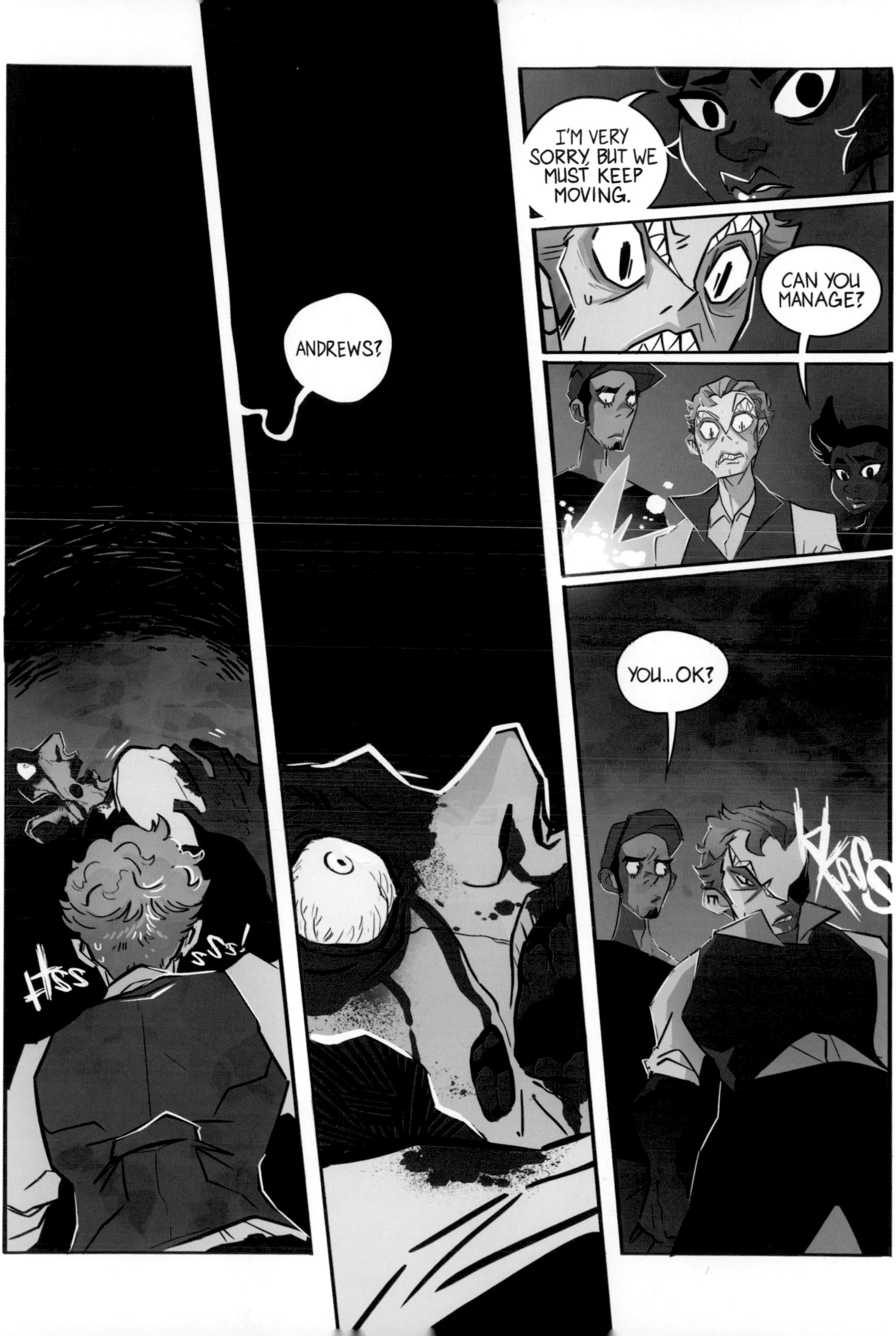
HSS
SSS!
ANDREWS?
I'M VERY SORRY, BUT WE MUST KEEP MOVING.
CAN YOU MANAGE?
YOU...OK?
HSSS

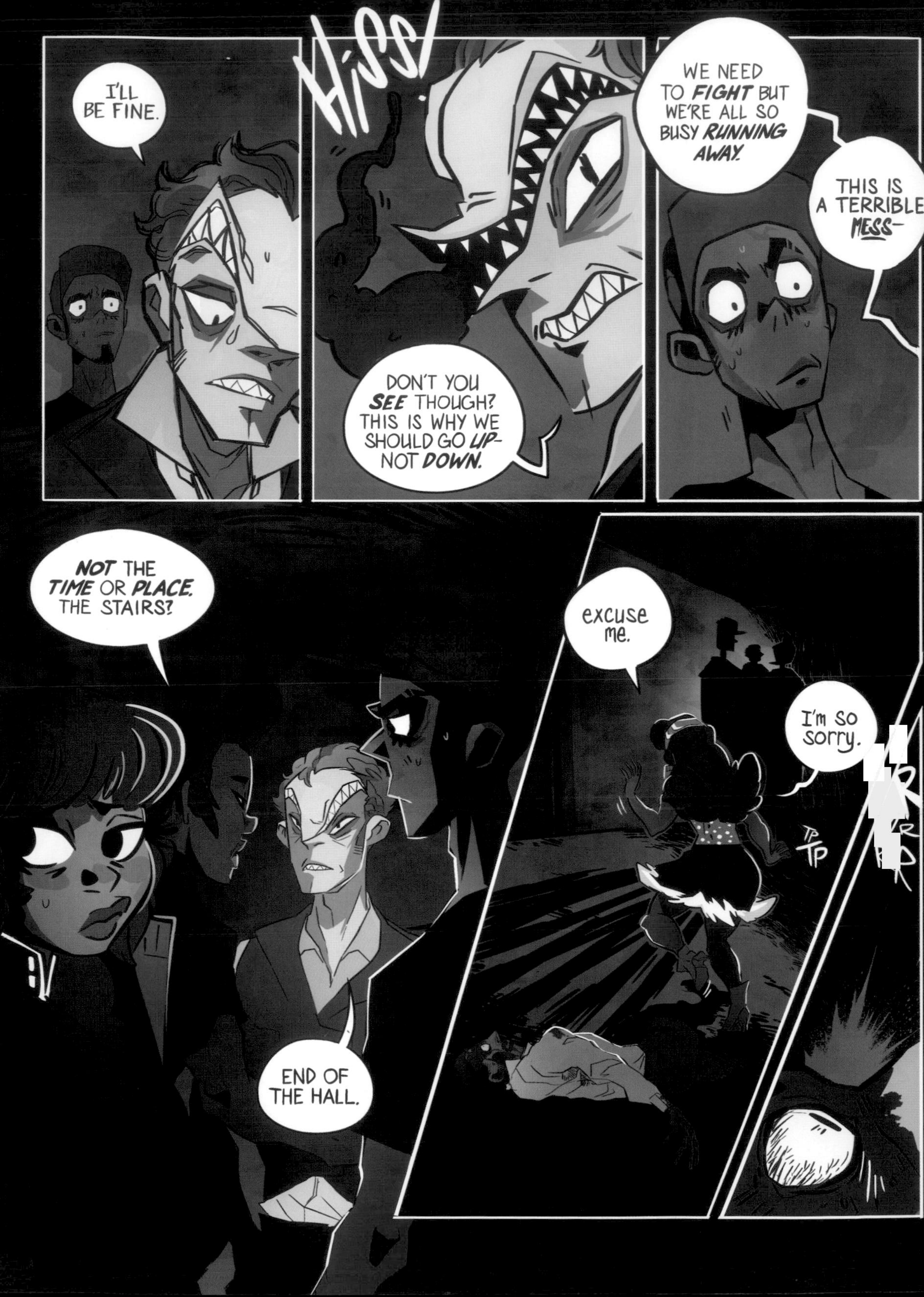
I'LL BE FINE.
HISS!
DON'T YOU SEE THOUGH? THIS IS WHY WE SHOULD GO UP- NOT DOWN.
WE NEED TO FIGHT BUT WE'RE ALL SO BUSY RUNNING AWAY.
THIS IS A TERRIBLE MESS-
NOT THE TIME OR PLACE. THE STAIRS?
END OF THE HALL.
excuse me.
I'm so sorry.
TP TP

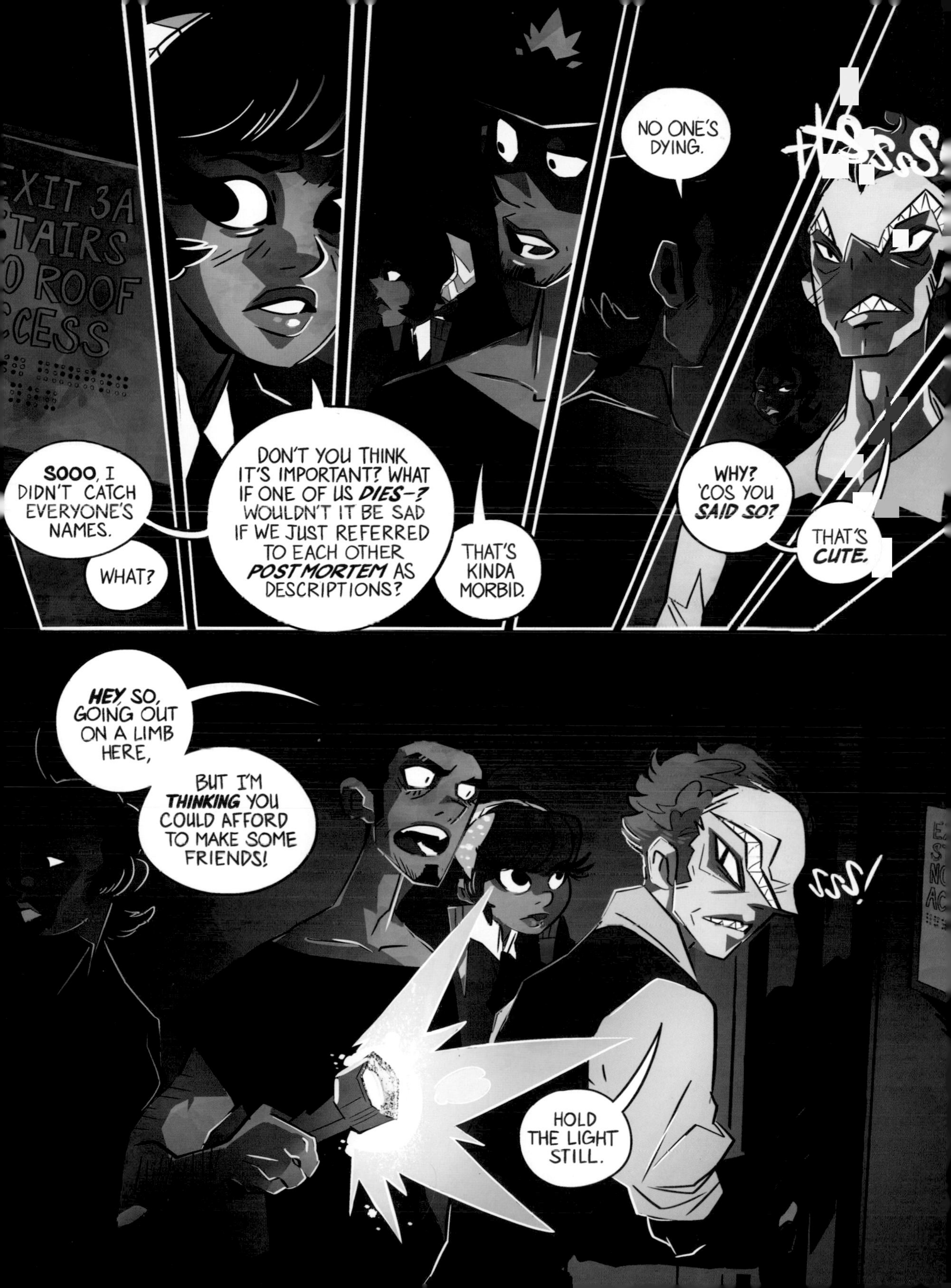
XIT 3A
TAIRS
O ROOF
CESS
SOOO, I DIDN'T CATCH EVERYONE'S NAMES.
WHAT?
DON'T YOU THINK IT'S IMPORTANT? WHAT IF ONE OF US ***DIES*–?** WOULDN'T IT BE SAD IF WE JUST REFERRED TO EACH OTHER ***POST MORTEM*** AS DESCRIPTIONS?
THAT'S KINDA MORBID.
NO ONE'S DYING.
WHY? 'COS YOU ***SAID SO?***
THAT'S ***CUTE.***
HEY, SO, GOING OUT ON A LIMB HERE,
BUT I'M ***THINKING*** YOU COULD AFFORD TO MAKE SOME FRIENDS!
SSS!
HOLD THE LIGHT STILL.

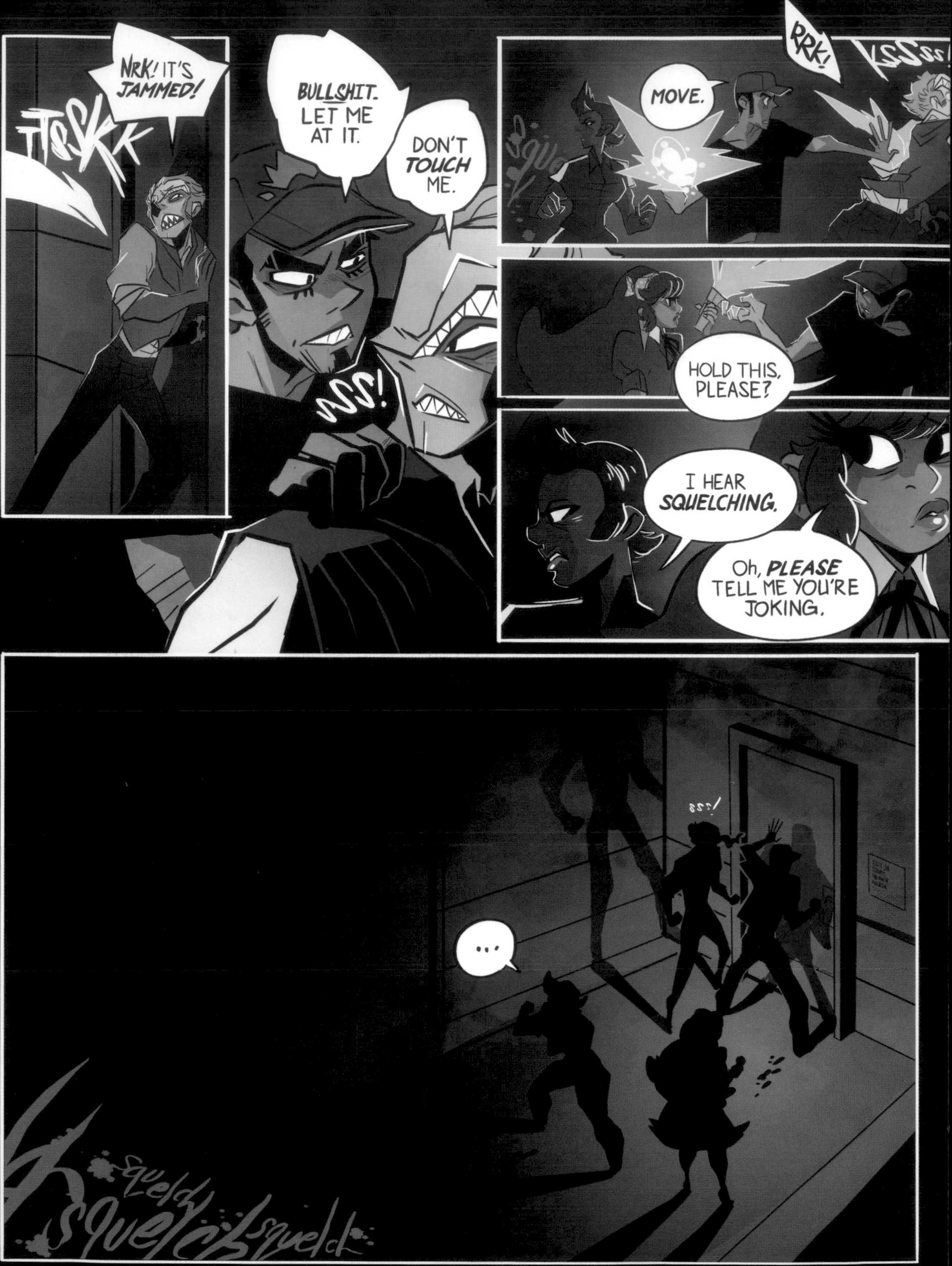

NRK! IT'S JAMMED!
BULLSHIT. LET ME AT IT.
DON'T TOUCH ME.
SS!
RRK!
MOVE.
HOLD THIS, PLEASE?
I HEAR SQUELCHING.
Oh, PLEASE TELL ME YOU'RE JOKING.
...
squelch squelch squelch

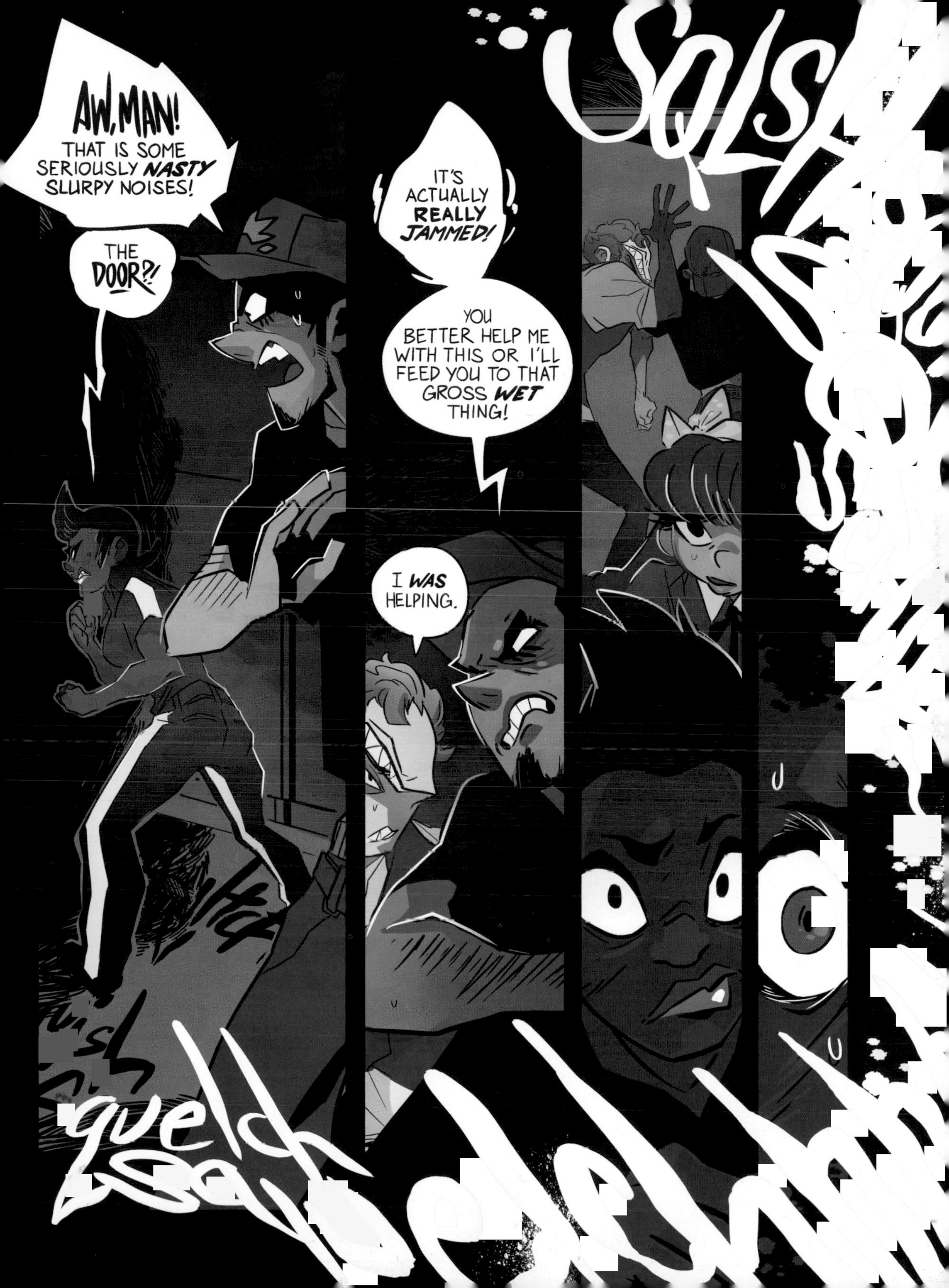
AW, MAN! THAT IS SOME SERIOUSLY NASTY SLURPY NOISES!
THE DOOR?!
IT'S ACTUALLY REALLY JAMMED!
YOU BETTER HELP ME WITH THIS OR I'LL FEED YOU TO THAT GROSS WET THING!
I WAS HELPING.

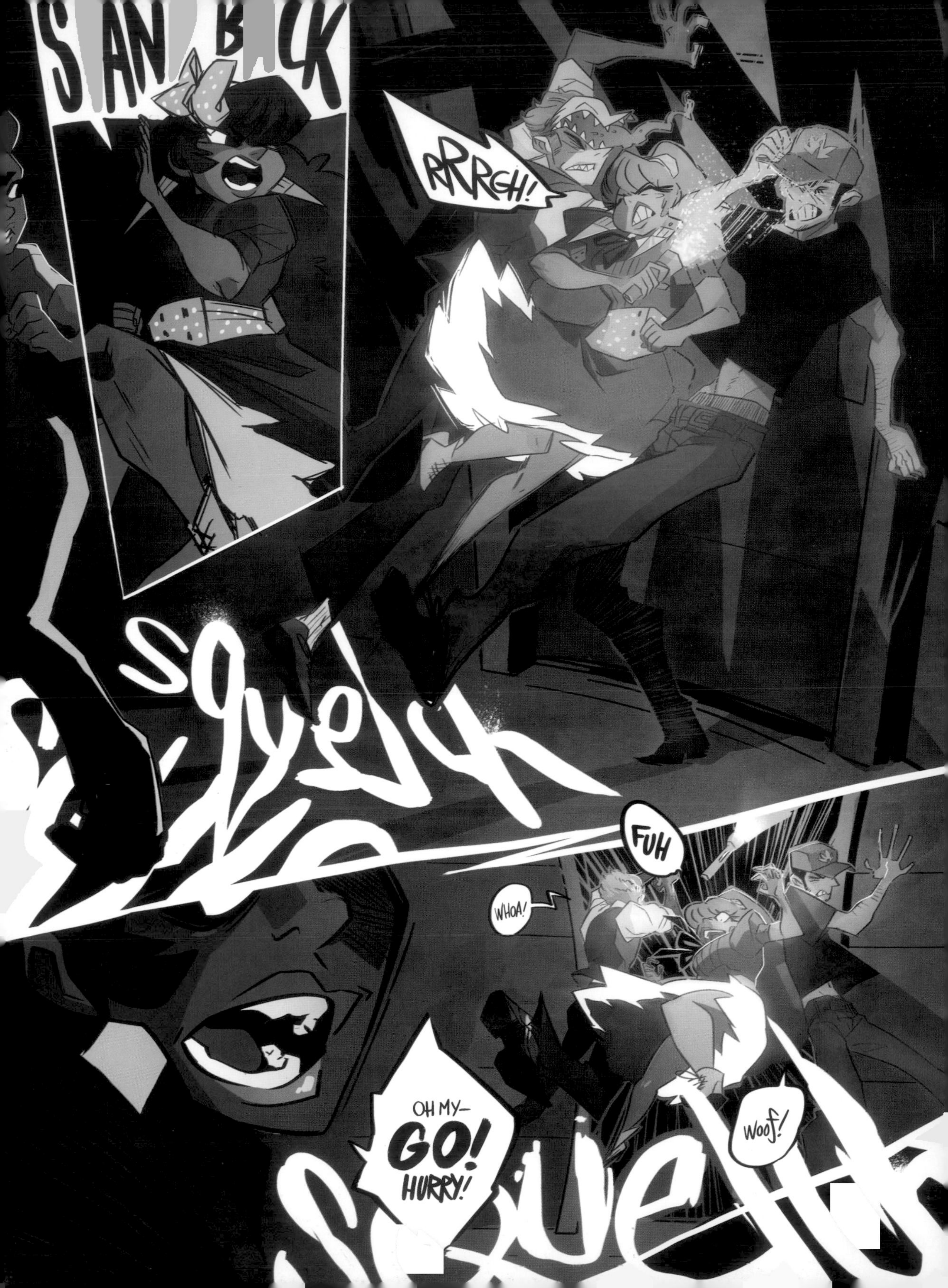
RRRGH!
FUH
WHOA!
OH MY—
GO!
HURRY!
Woof!

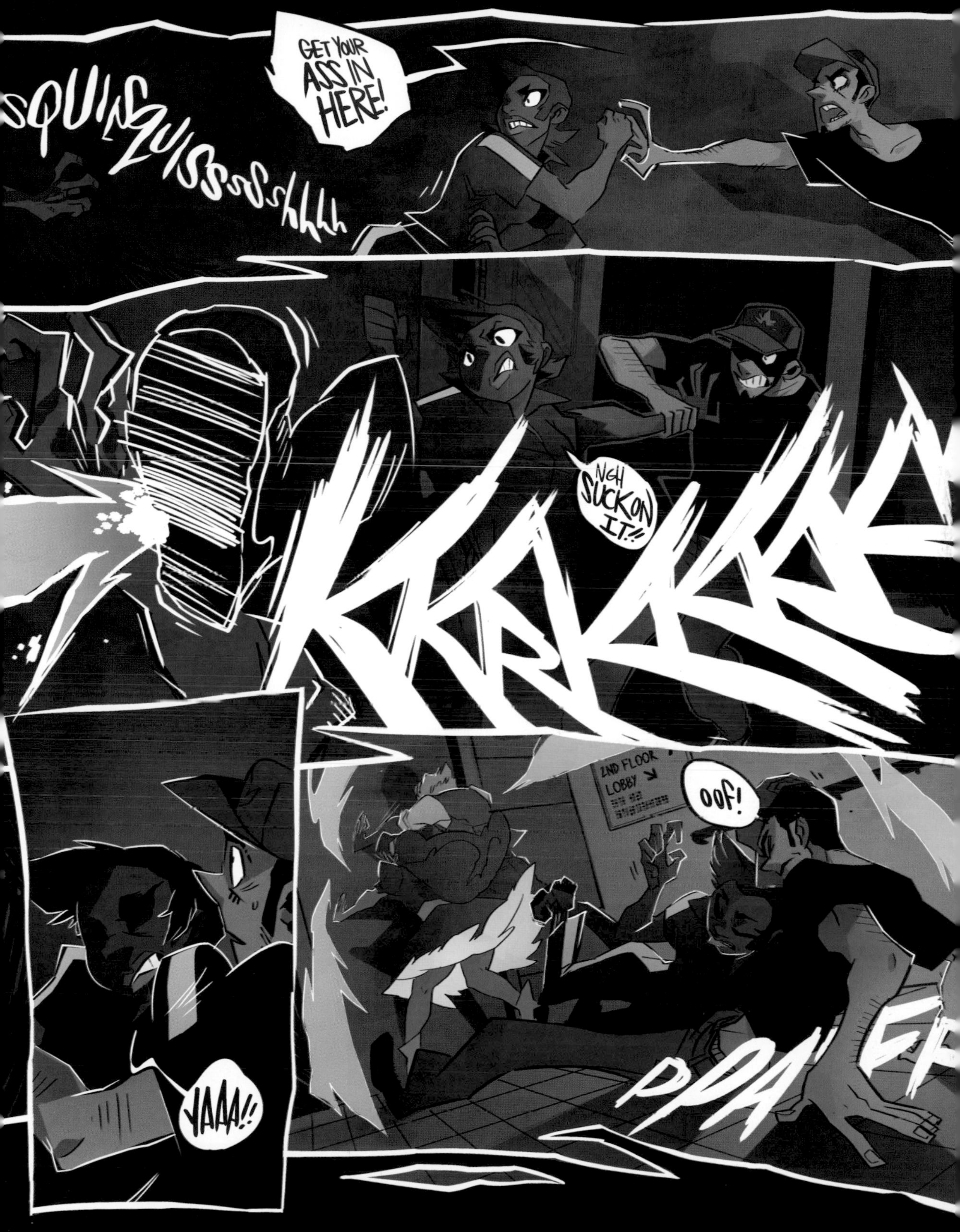
SQUINSQUISSssSShhhh
GET YOUR ASS IN HERE!
NGH SUCK ON IT!!
2ND FLOOR LOBBY
OOF!
YAAA!!

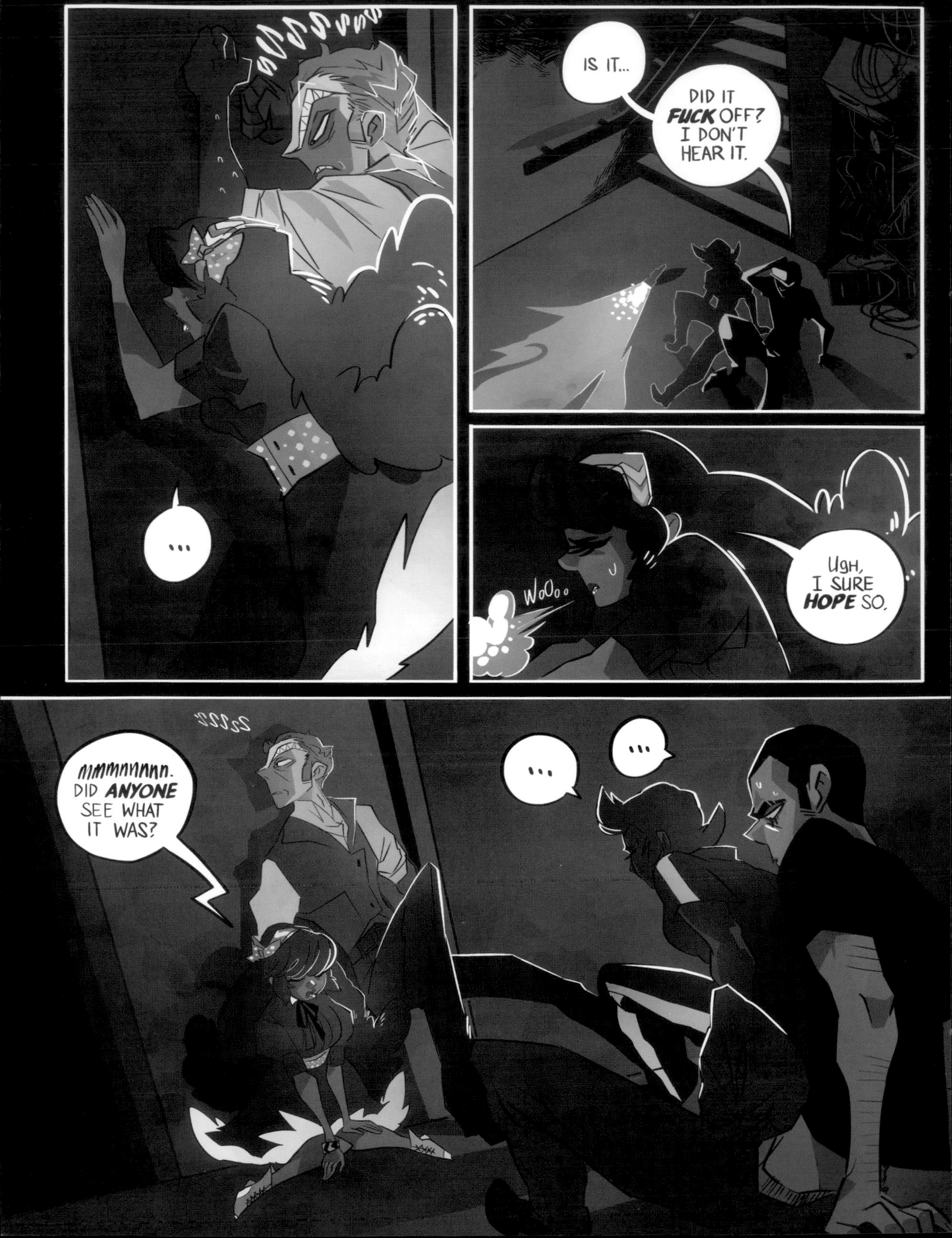

...
IS IT...
DID IT FUCK OFF? I DON'T HEAR IT.
Ugh, I SURE HOPE SO.
WoOoo
SSSsS
mmmnnnnn. DID ANYONE SEE WHAT IT WAS?
...
...

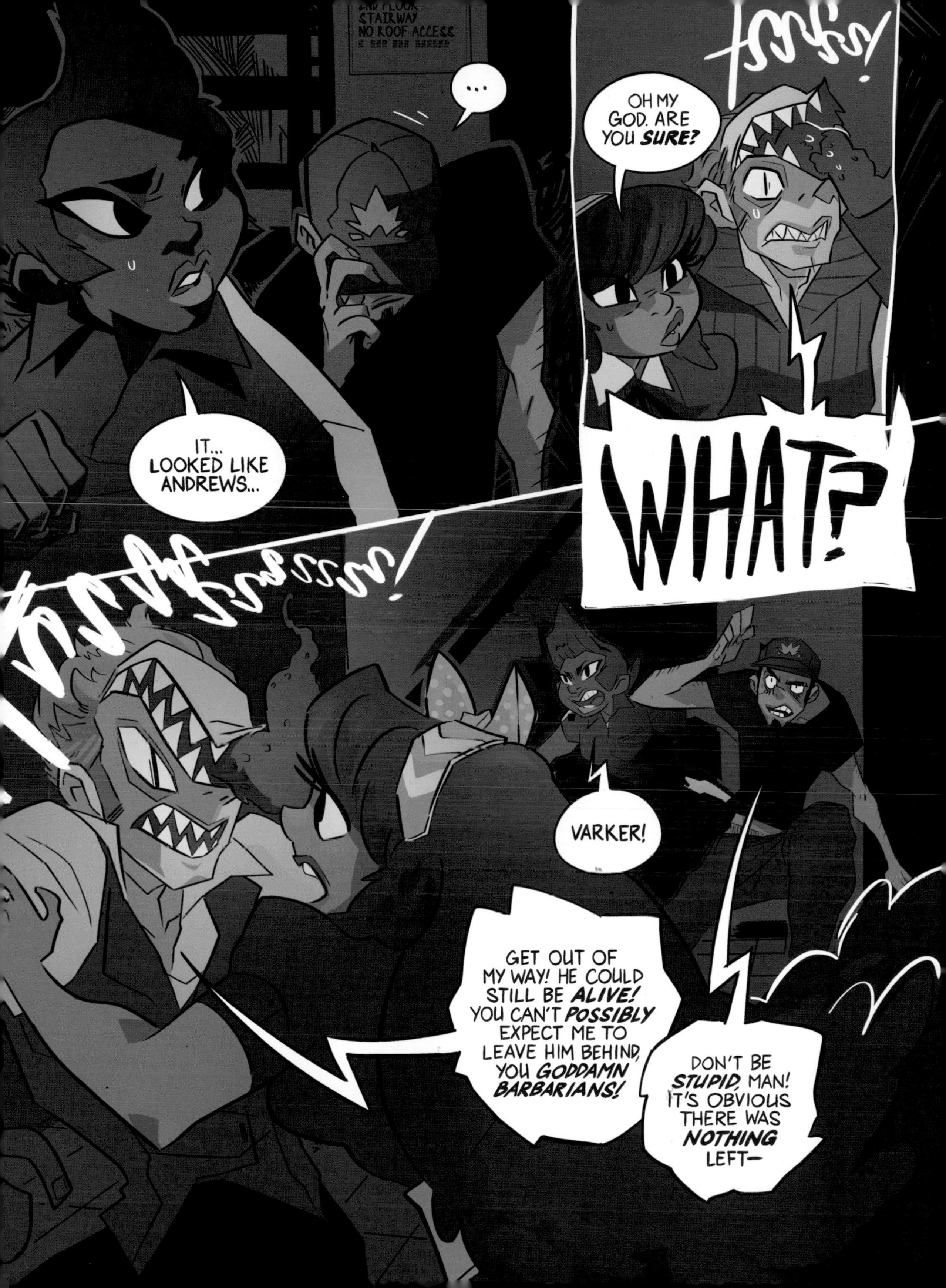

2ND FLOOR
STAIRWAY
NO ROOF ACCESS
...
IT... LOOKED LIKE ANDREWS...
HSSSS!
OH MY GOD. ARE YOU SURE?
WHAT?!
HSSSSSSSSSS!
VARKER!
GET OUT OF MY WAY! HE COULD STILL BE ALIVE! YOU CAN'T POSSIBLY EXPECT ME TO LEAVE HIM BEHIND, YOU GODDAMN BARBARIANS!
DON'T BE STUPID, MAN! IT'S OBVIOUS THERE WAS NOTHING LEFT—

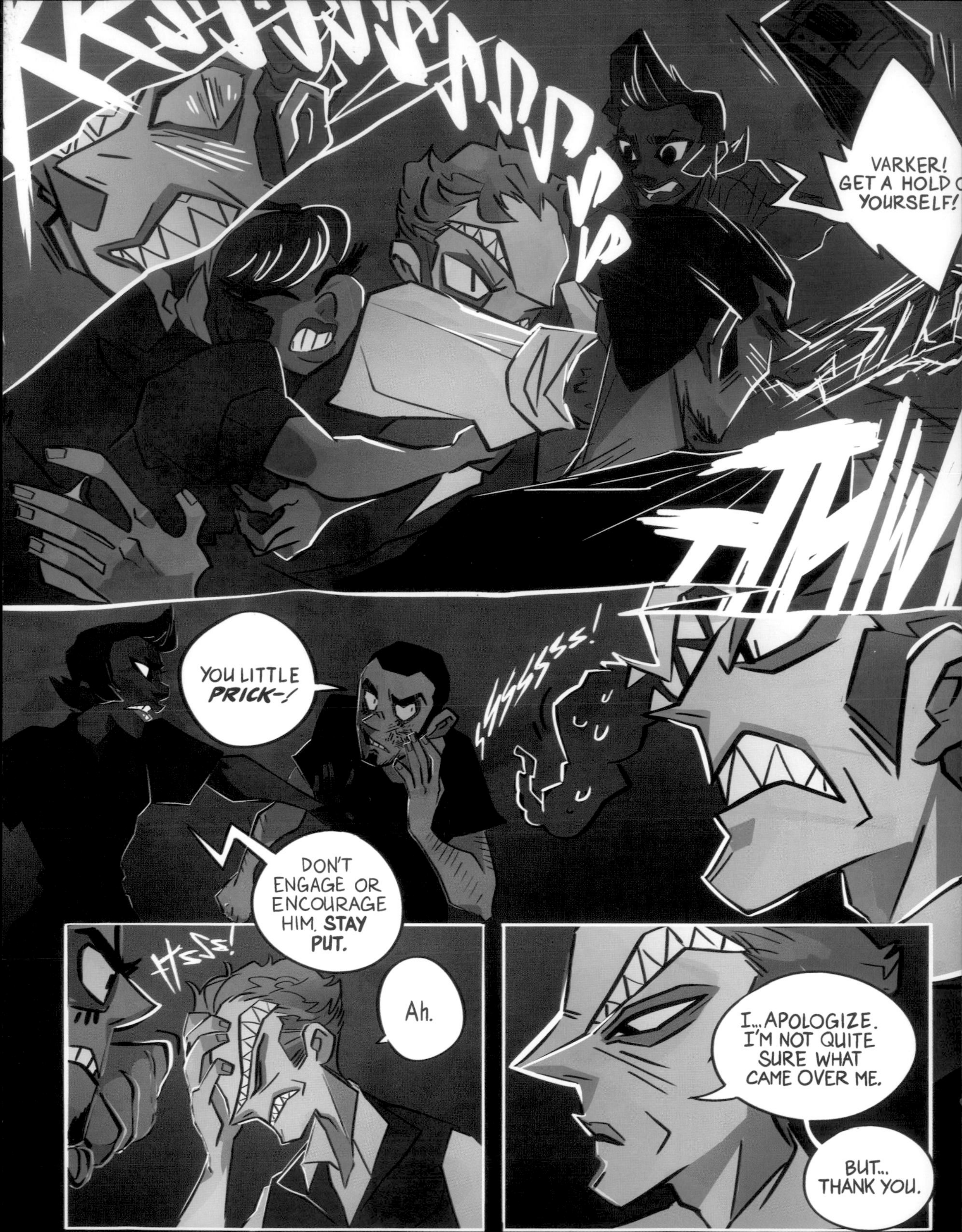
VARKER! GET A HOLD O YOURSELF!
YOU LITTLE PRICK-!
DON'T ENGAGE OR ENCOURAGE HIM. STAY PUT.
Ah.
I... APOLOGIZE. I'M NOT QUITE SURE WHAT CAME OVER ME.
BUT... THANK YOU.

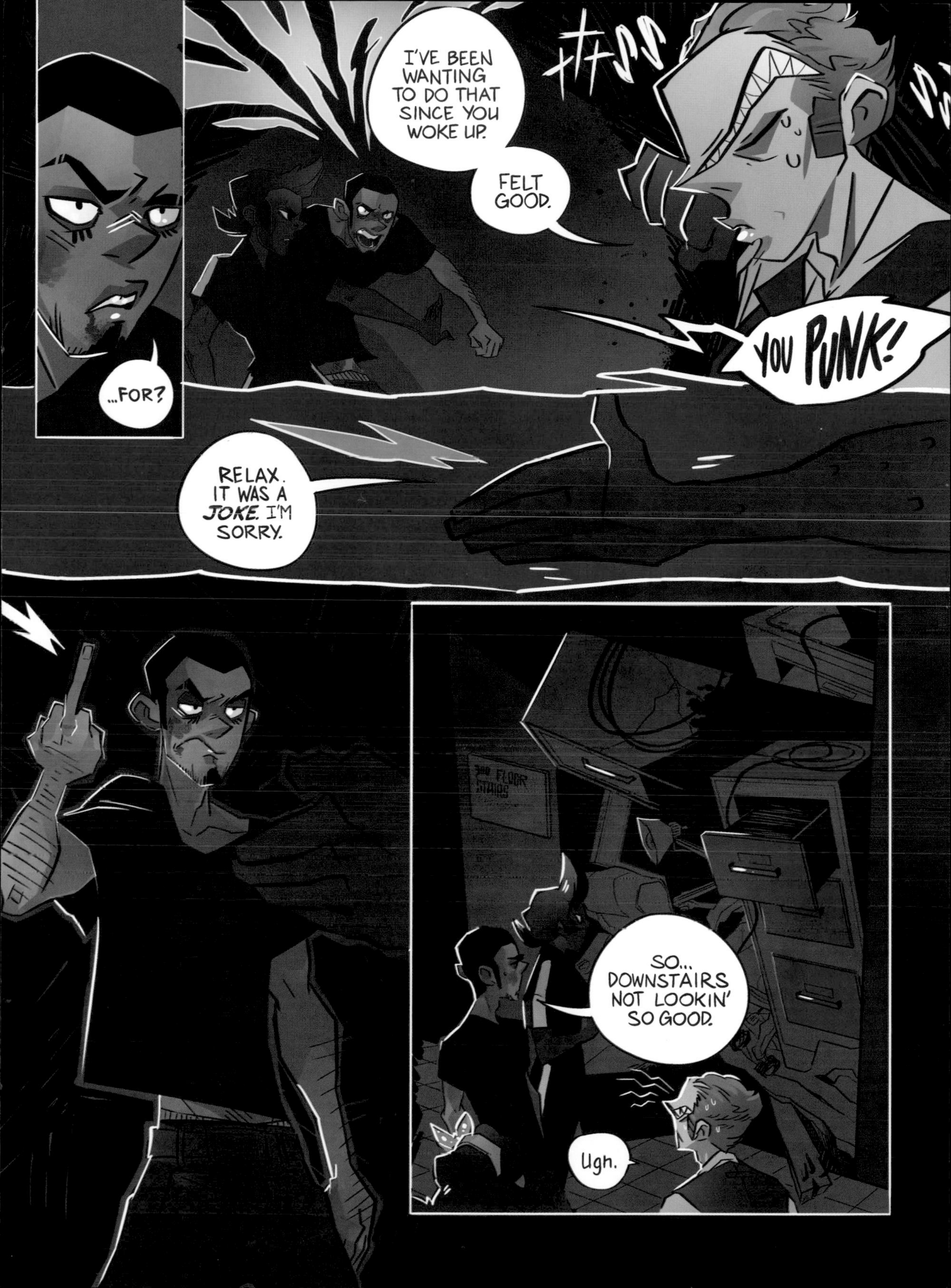
...FOR?
I'VE BEEN WANTING TO DO THAT SINCE YOU WOKE UP.
FELT GOOD.
YOU PUNK!
RELAX. IT WAS A JOKE. I'M SORRY.
SO... DOWNSTAIRS NOT LOOKIN' SO GOOD.
Ugh.

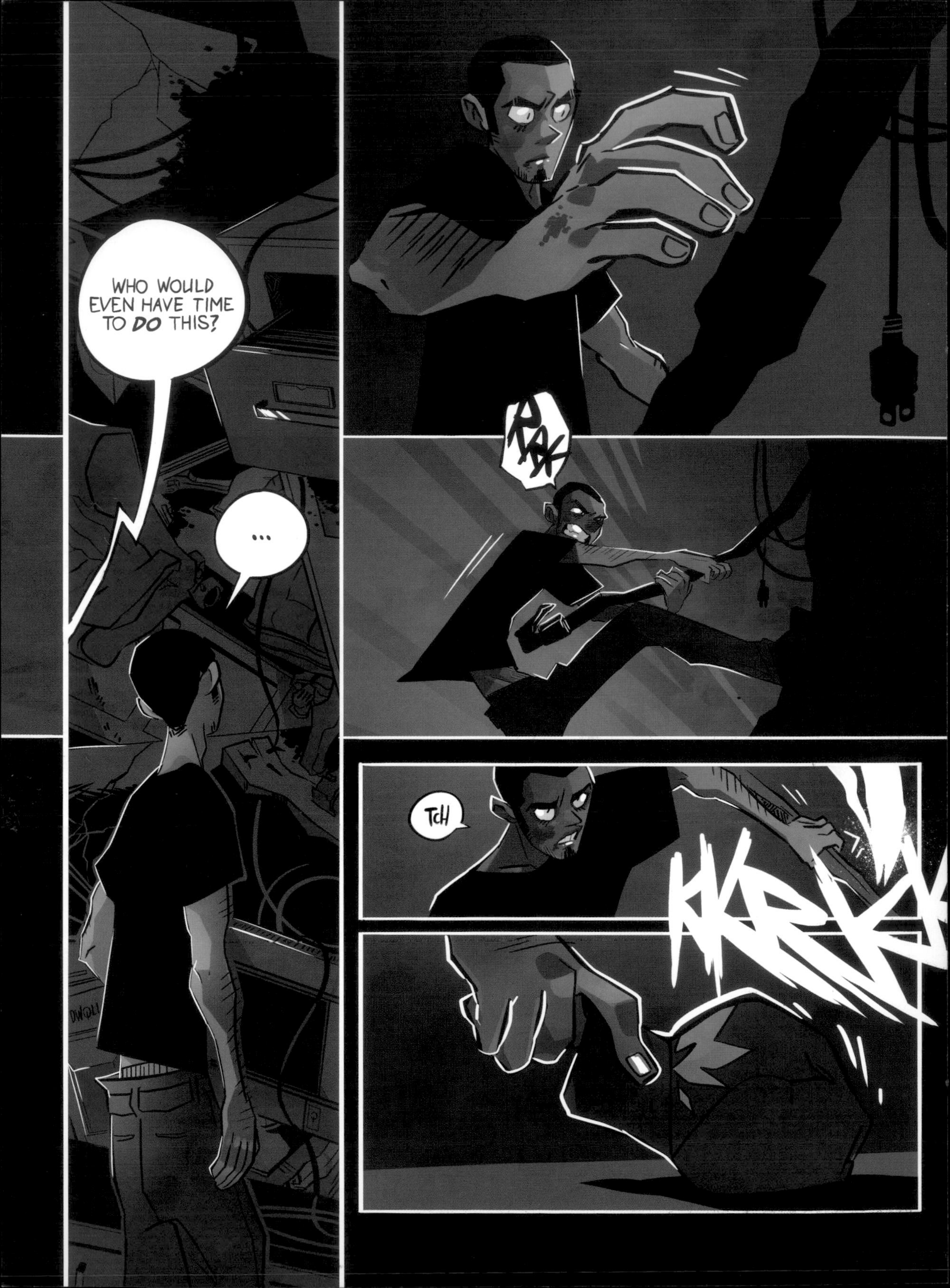
WHO WOULD EVEN HAVE TIME TO **DO** THIS?
...
TCH

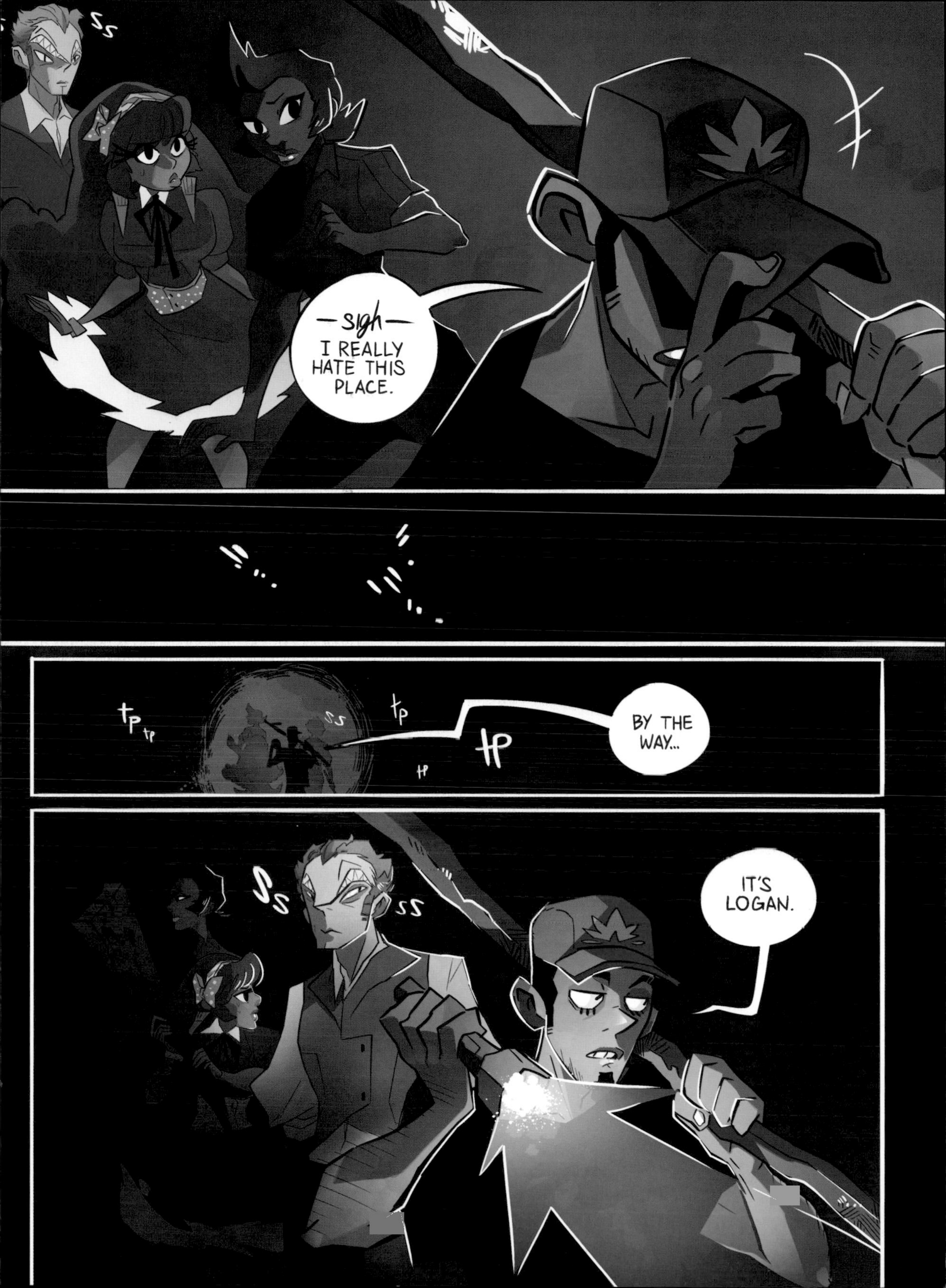

SS
—sigh—
I REALLY HATE THIS PLACE.
tp tp
SS
tp
tp
tp
BY THE WAY...
SS
SS
IT'S LOGAN.

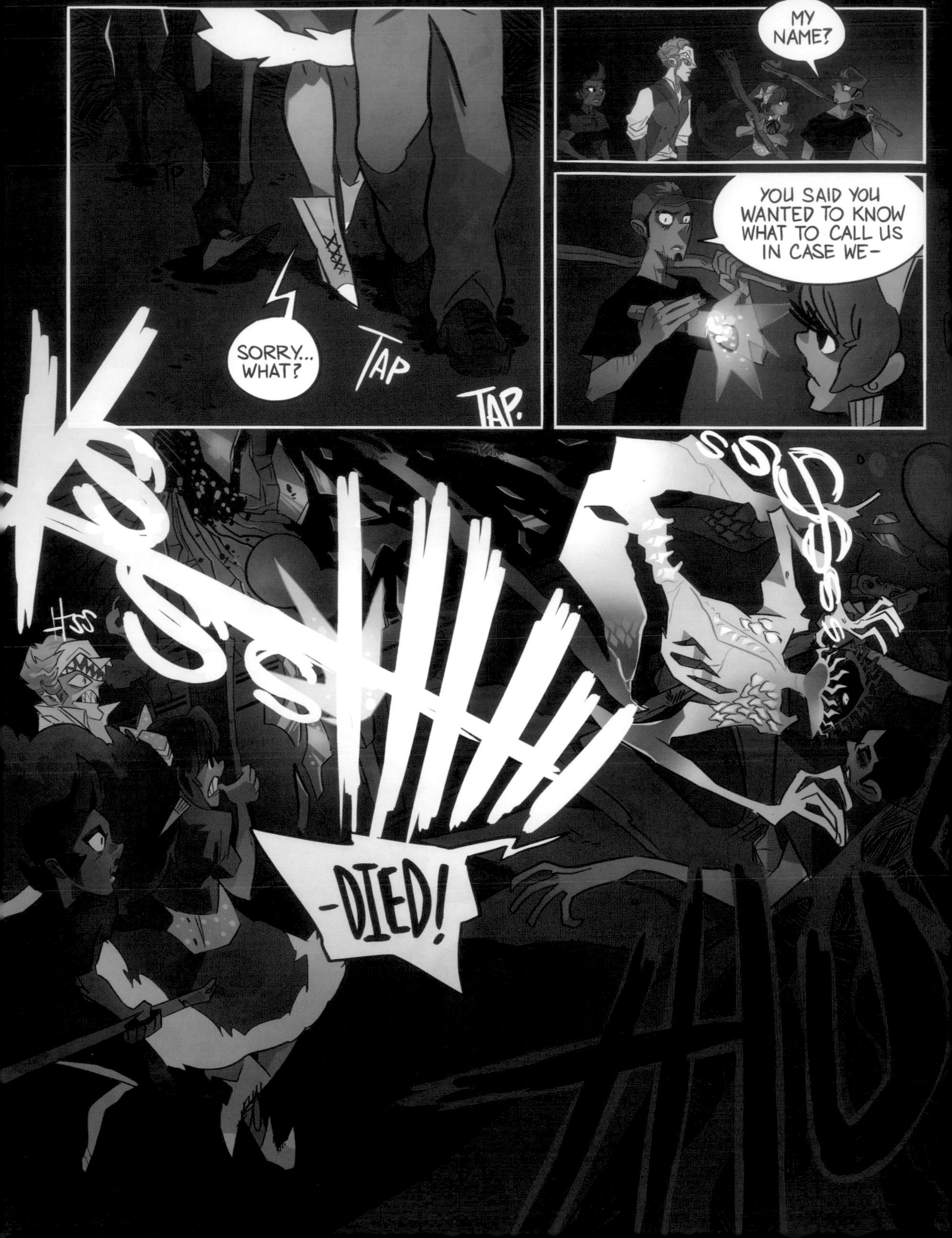

SORRY... WHAT?
TAP
TAP.
MY NAME?
YOU SAID YOU WANTED TO KNOW WHAT TO CALL US IN CASE WE-
-DIED!

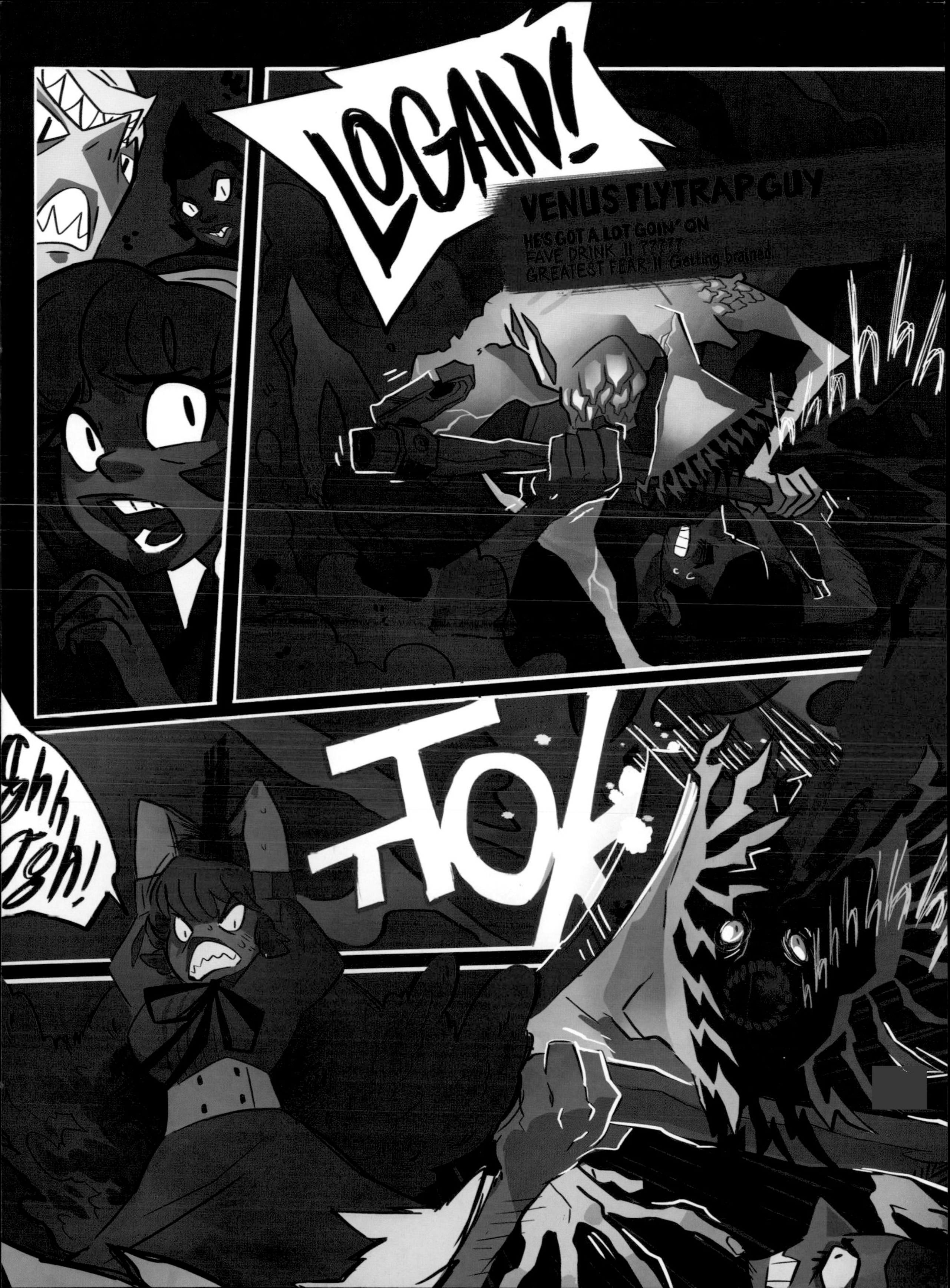
LOGAN!
VENUS FLYTRAP GUY
HE'S GOT A LOT GOIN' ON
FAVE DRINK !! ?????
GREATEST FEAR !! Getting brained.
TOK

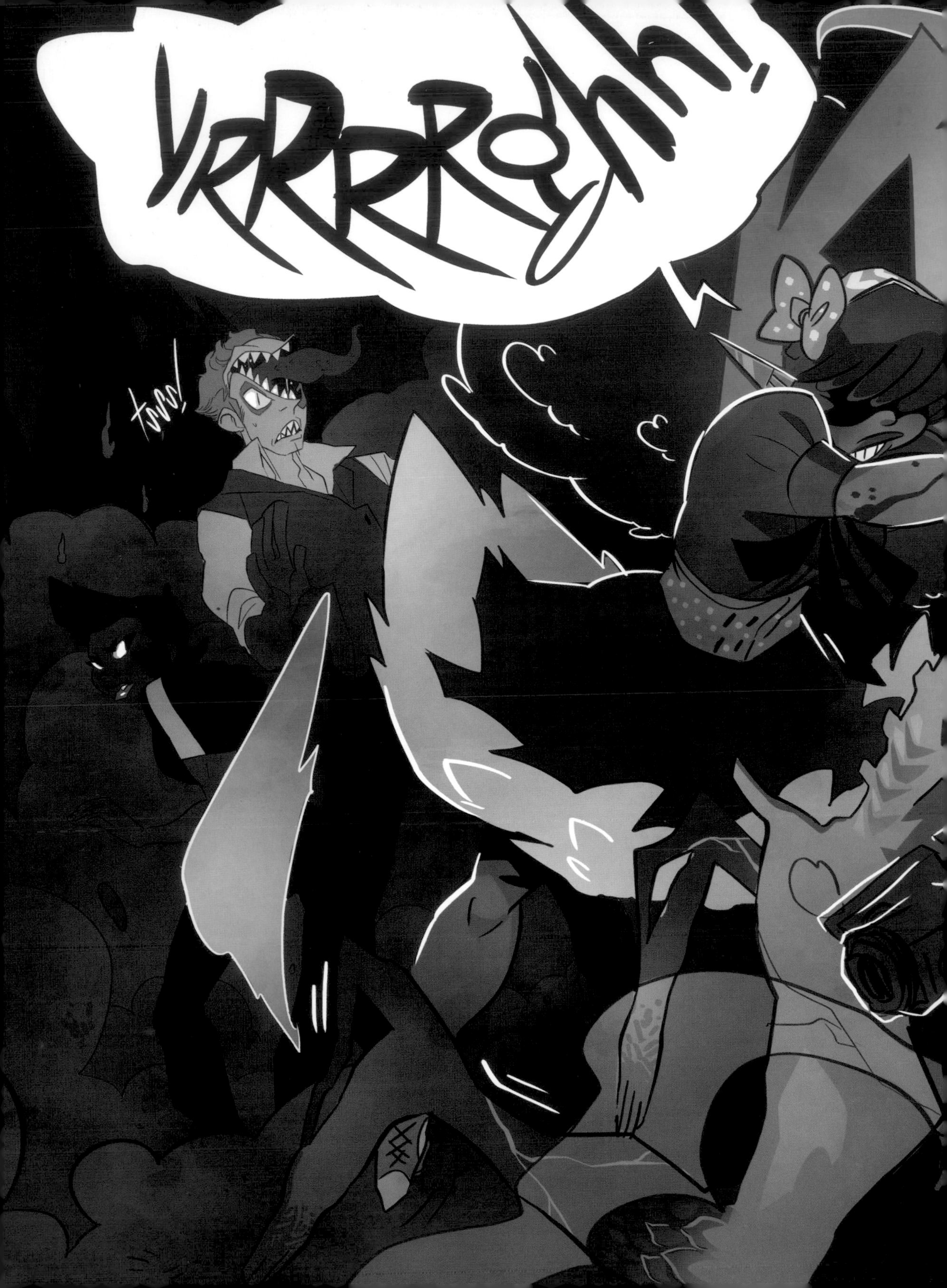
YRRRRaghh!
toss!

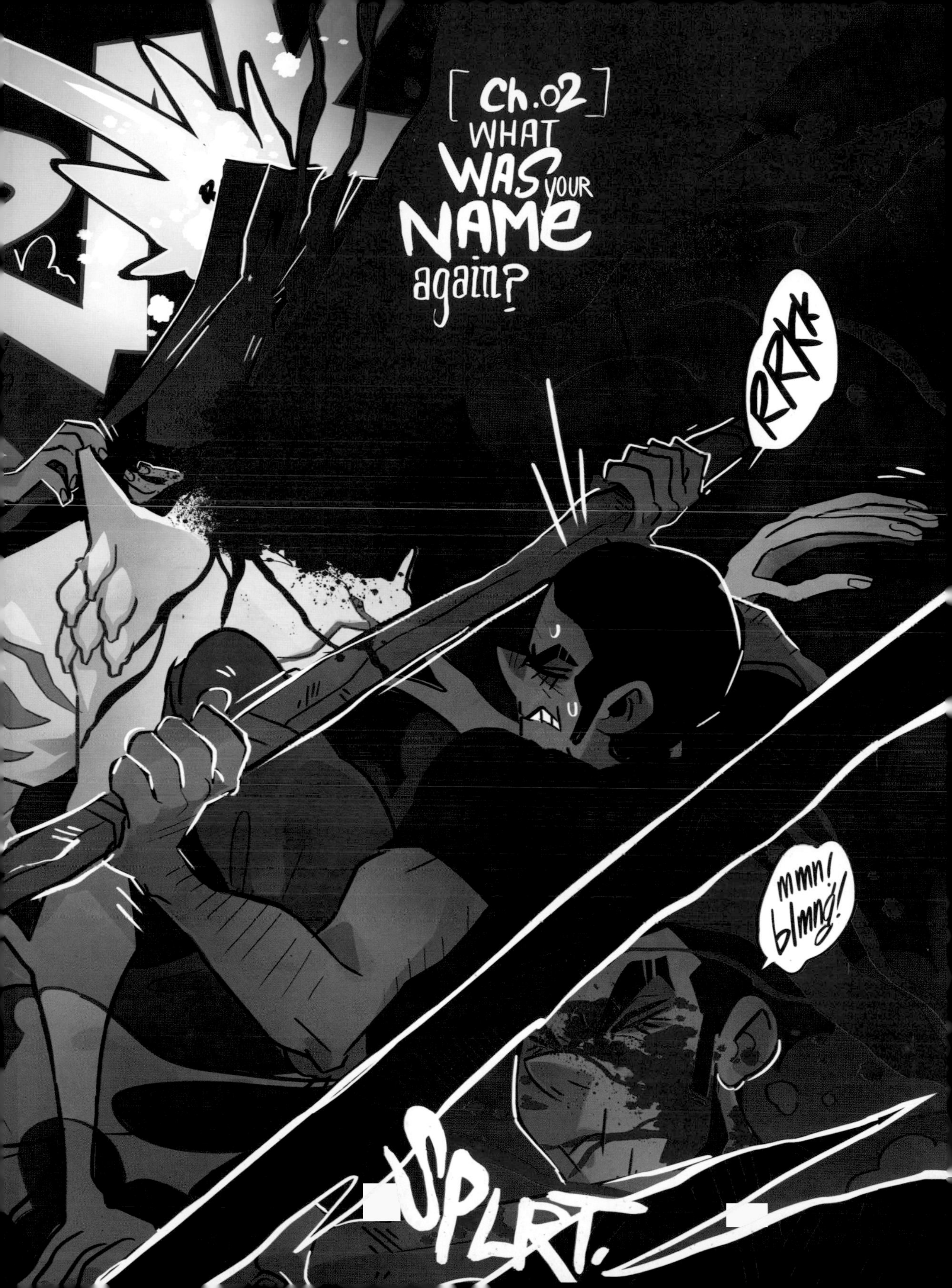
[Ch.02]
WHAT WAS your NAME again?
RRRK
mmn! blmng!
SPLRT.

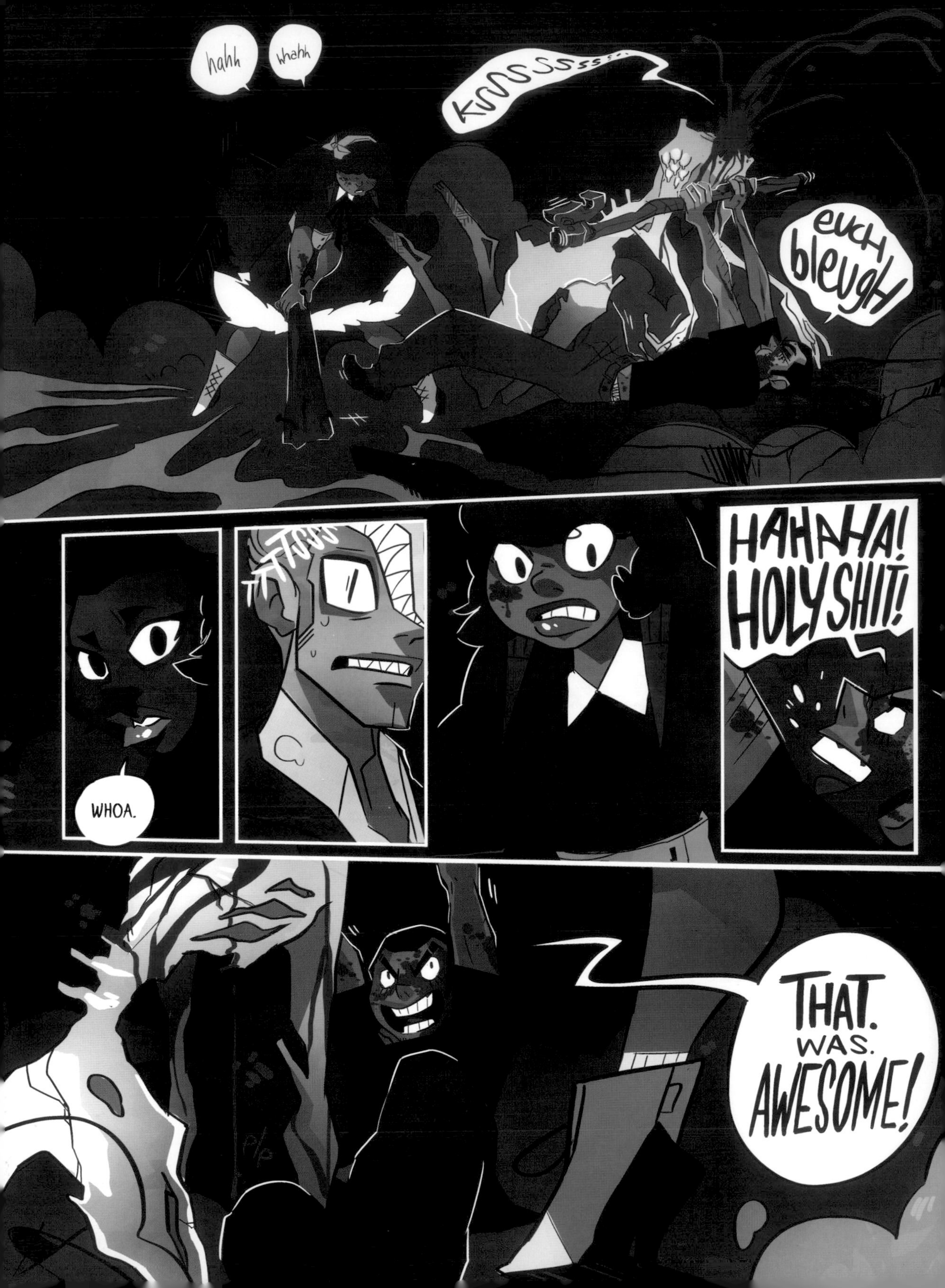
hahh
whahh
euch bleugh
WHOA.
HAHAHA! HOLY SHIT!
THAT. WAS. AWESOME!

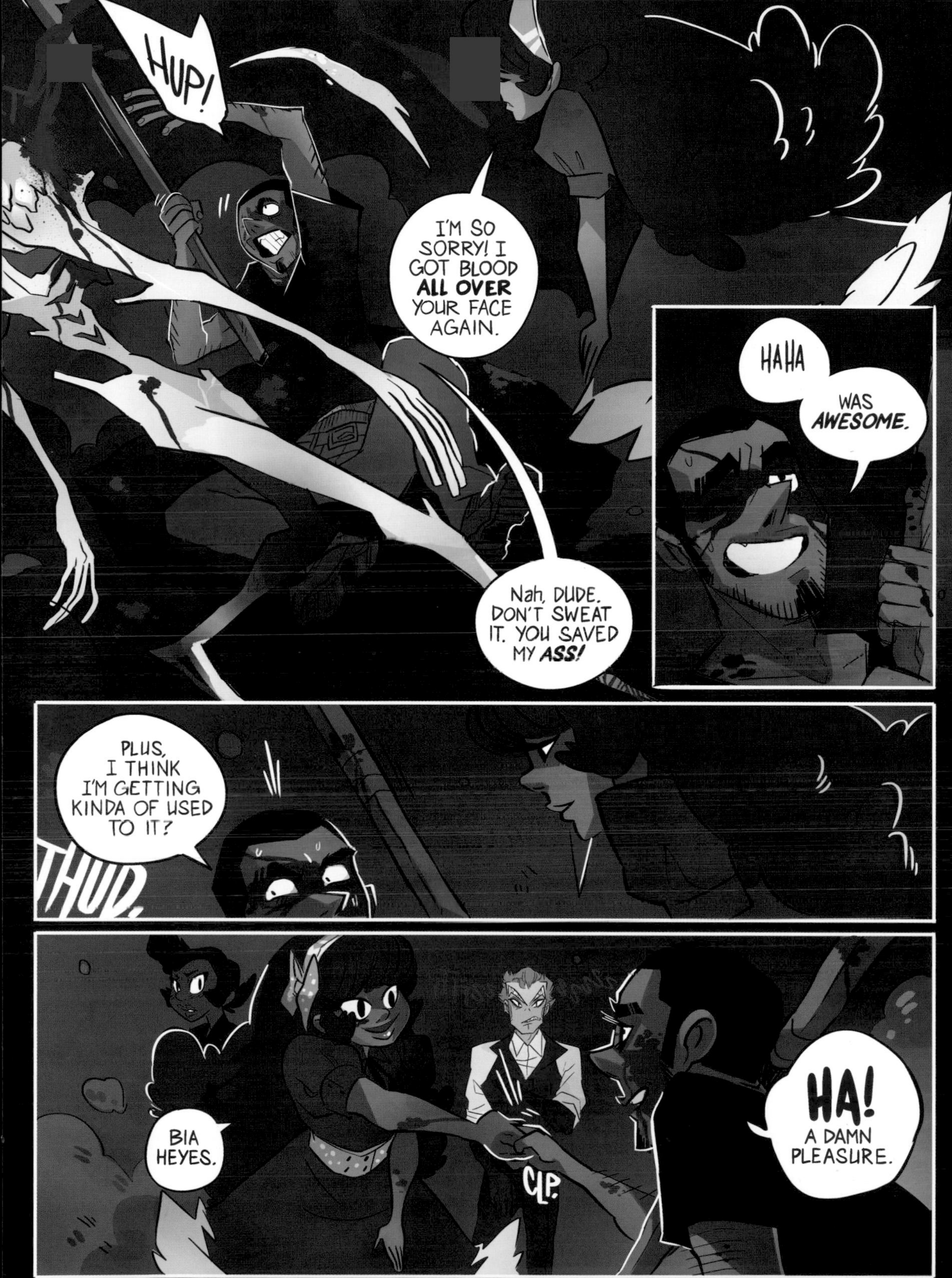
HUP!
I'M SO SORRY! I GOT BLOOD **ALL OVER** YOUR FACE AGAIN.
Nah, DUDE. DON'T SWEAT IT. YOU SAVED MY ***ASS!***
HAHA
WAS ***AWESOME.***
PLUS, I THINK I'M GETTING KINDA OF USED TO IT?
THUD.
BIA HEYES.
CLP.
HA!
A DAMN PLEASURE.

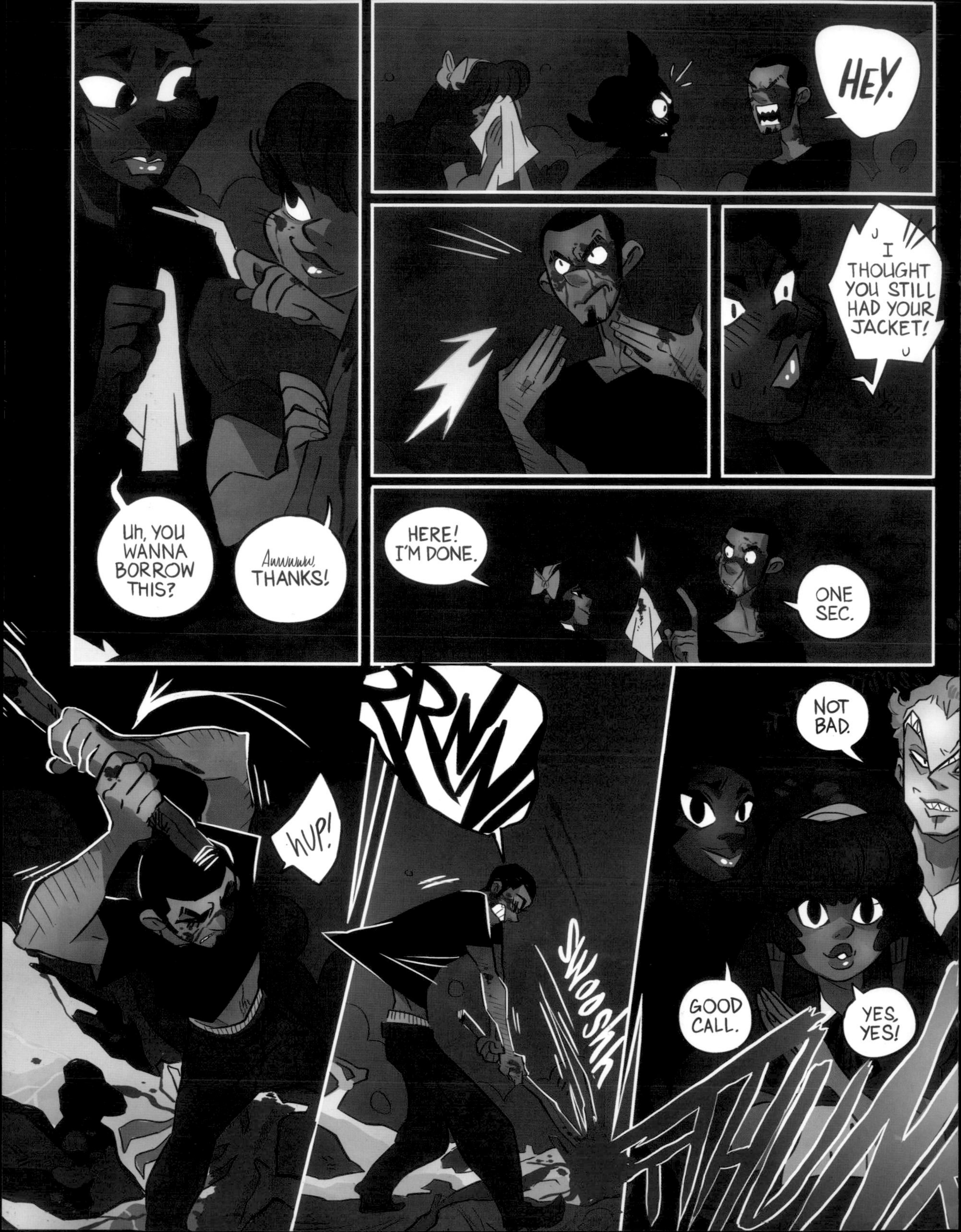

UH, YOU WANNA BORROW THIS?
Awwwww, THANKS!
HEY.
I THOUGHT YOU STILL HAD YOUR JACKET!
HERE! I'M DONE.
ONE SEC.
HUP!
SWOOSHH
NOT BAD.
GOOD CALL.
YES, YES!
THUNK

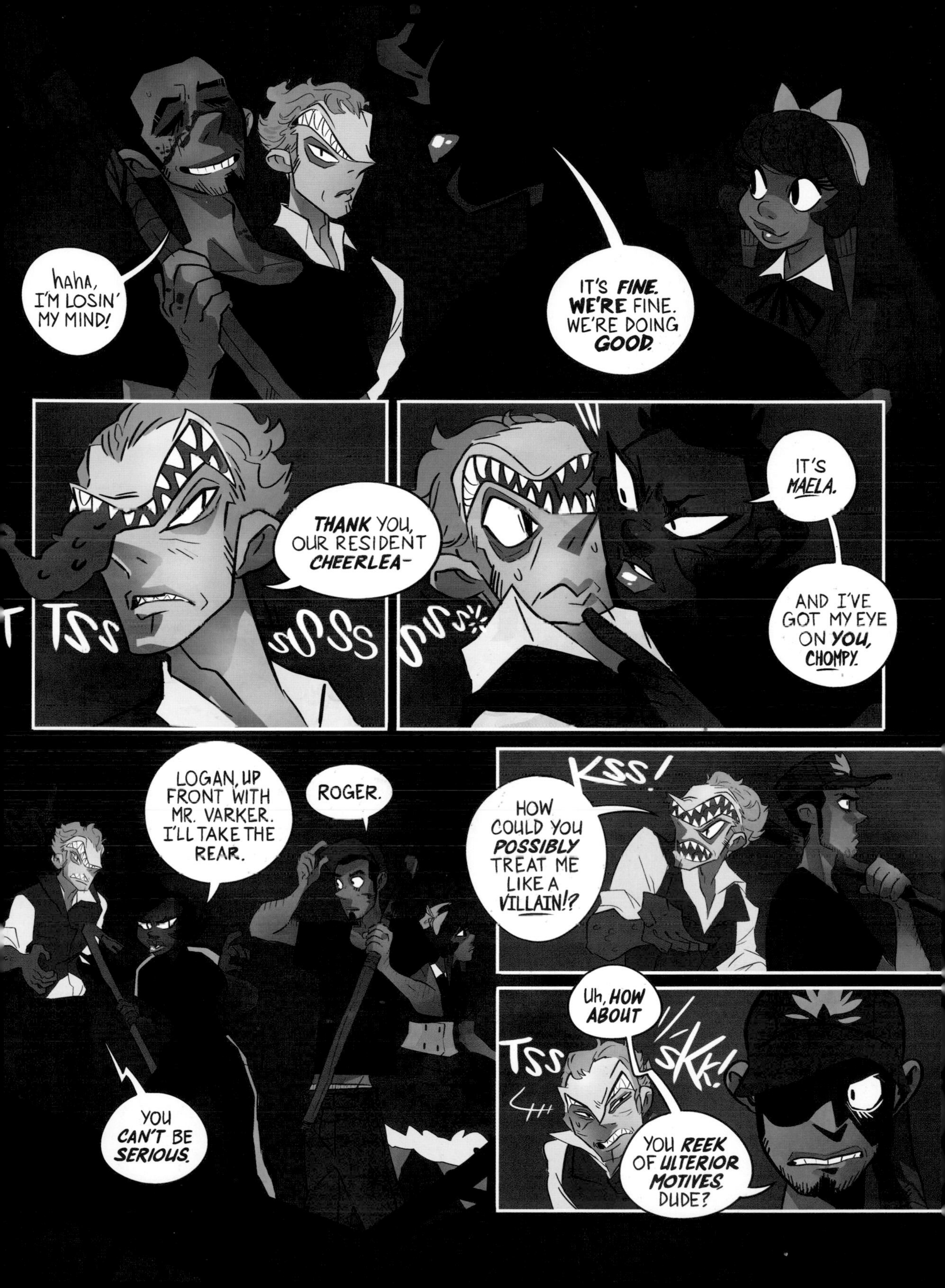
haha, I'M LOSIN' MY MIND!
IT'S FINE. WE'RE FINE. WE'RE DOING GOOD.
THANK YOU, OUR RESIDENT CHEERLEA-
TSS
SSS
SSS
IT'S MAELA.
AND I'VE GOT MY EYE ON YOU, CHOMPY.
LOGAN, UP FRONT WITH MR. VARKER. I'LL TAKE THE REAR.
ROGER.
YOU CAN'T BE SERIOUS.
KSS!
HOW COULD YOU POSSIBLY TREAT ME LIKE A VILLAIN!?
Uh, HOW ABOUT
TSS
SKK!
YOU REEK OF ULTERIOR MOTIVES, DUDE?

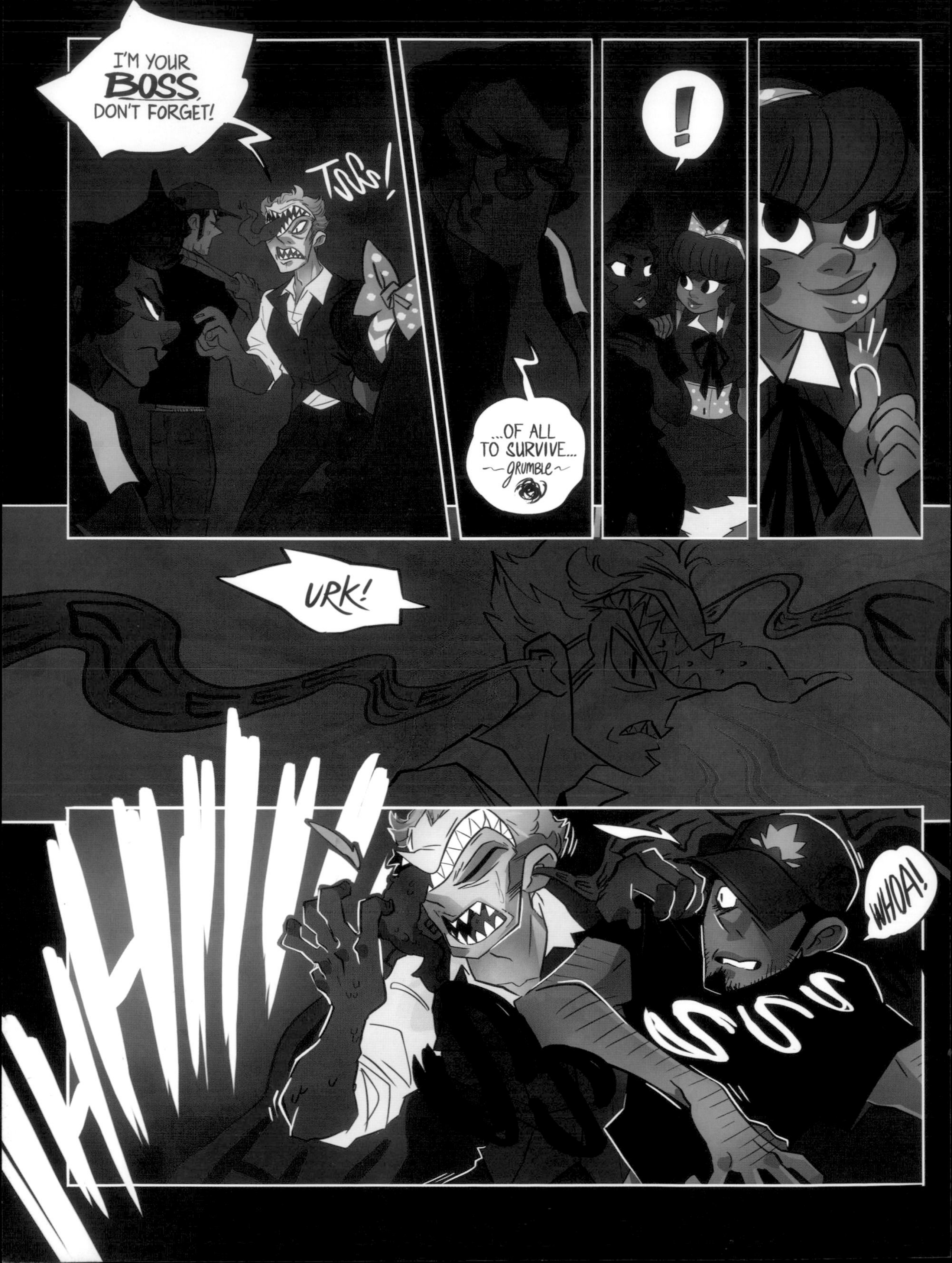
I'M YOUR BOSS, DON'T FORGET!
TSSS!
!
...OF ALL TO SURVIVE... ~grumble~
URK!
WHOA!

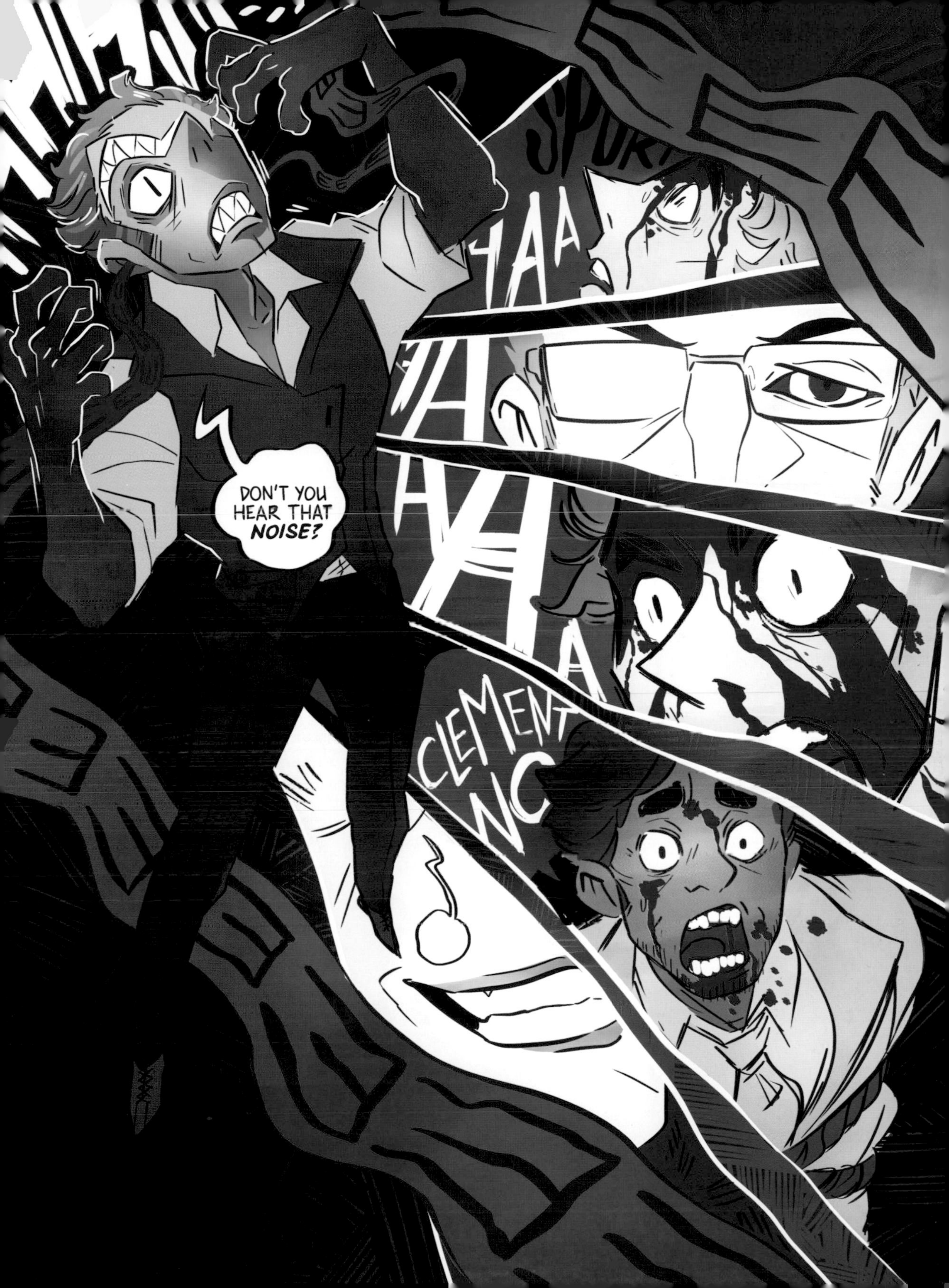
SPURT
DON'T YOU HEAR THAT *NOISE?*
CLEMENT
NO

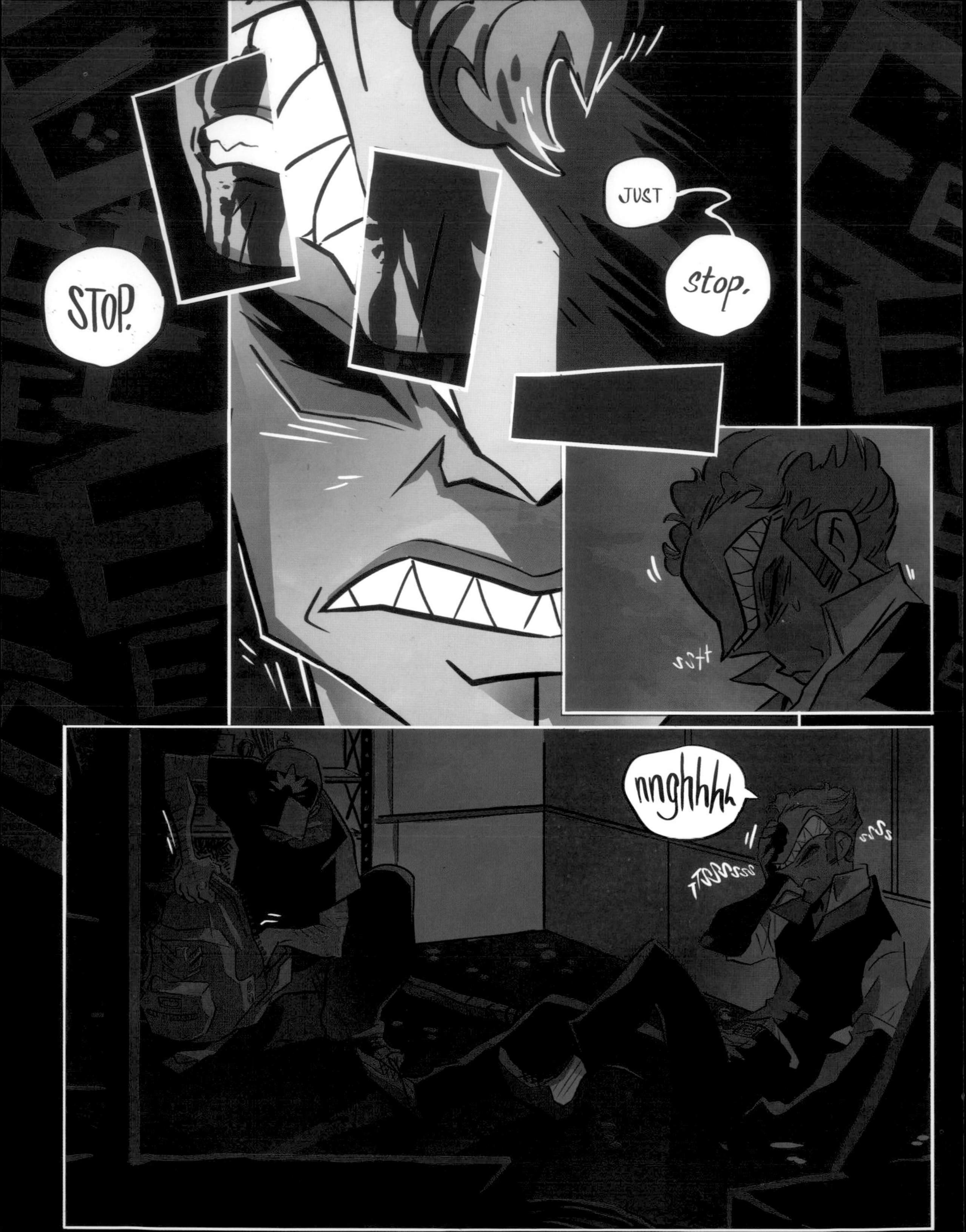
STOP.
JUST
stop.
nnghhhh

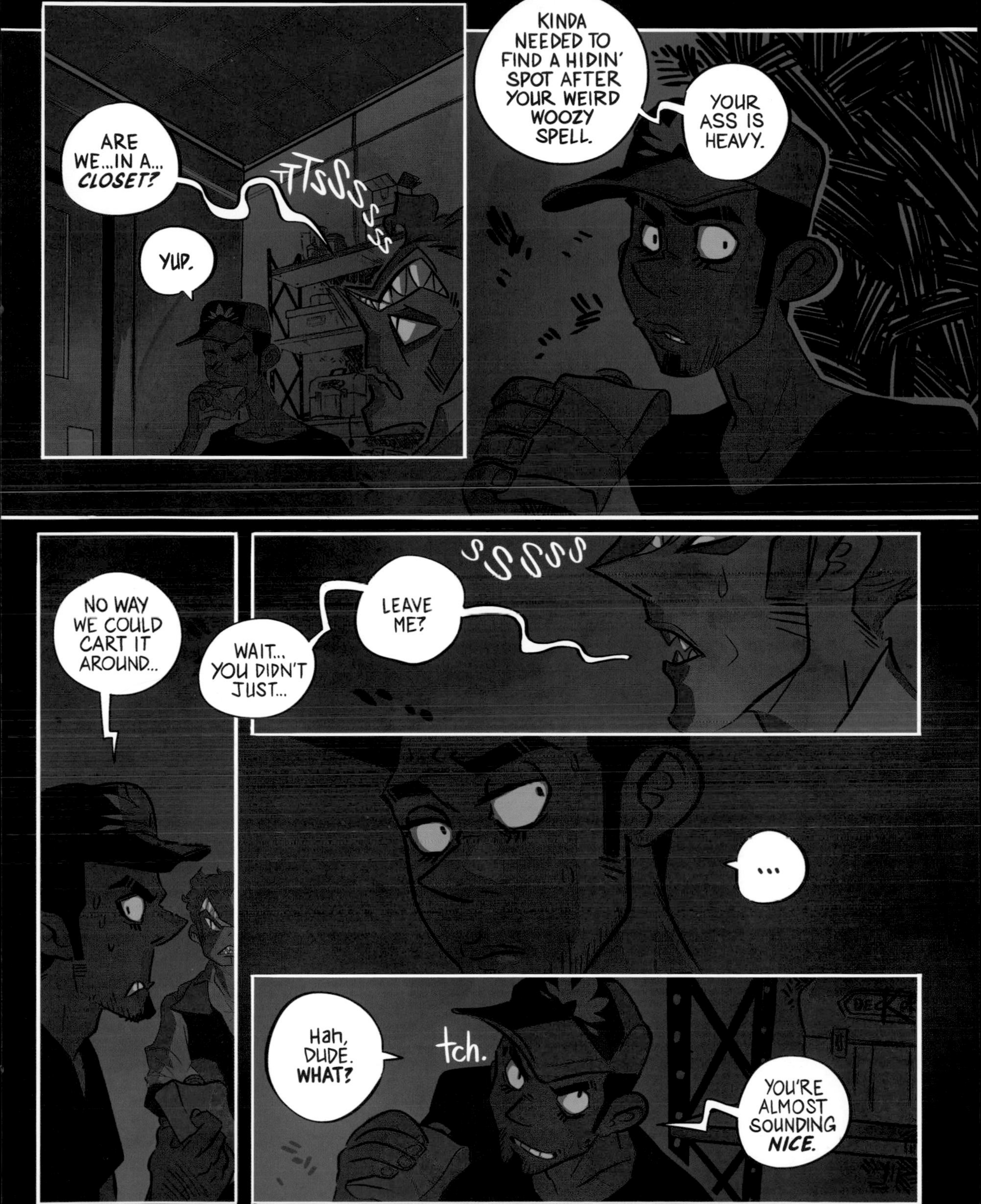
ARE WE...IN A... CLOSET?
TTTSSSSSS
YUP.
KINDA NEEDED TO FIND A HIDIN' SPOT AFTER YOUR WEIRD WOOZY SPELL.
YOUR ASS IS HEAVY.
SSSSS
WAIT... YOU DIDN'T JUST...
LEAVE ME?
NO WAY WE COULD CART IT AROUND...
...
tch.
Hah, DUDE. WHAT?
YOU'RE ALMOST SOUNDING NICE.

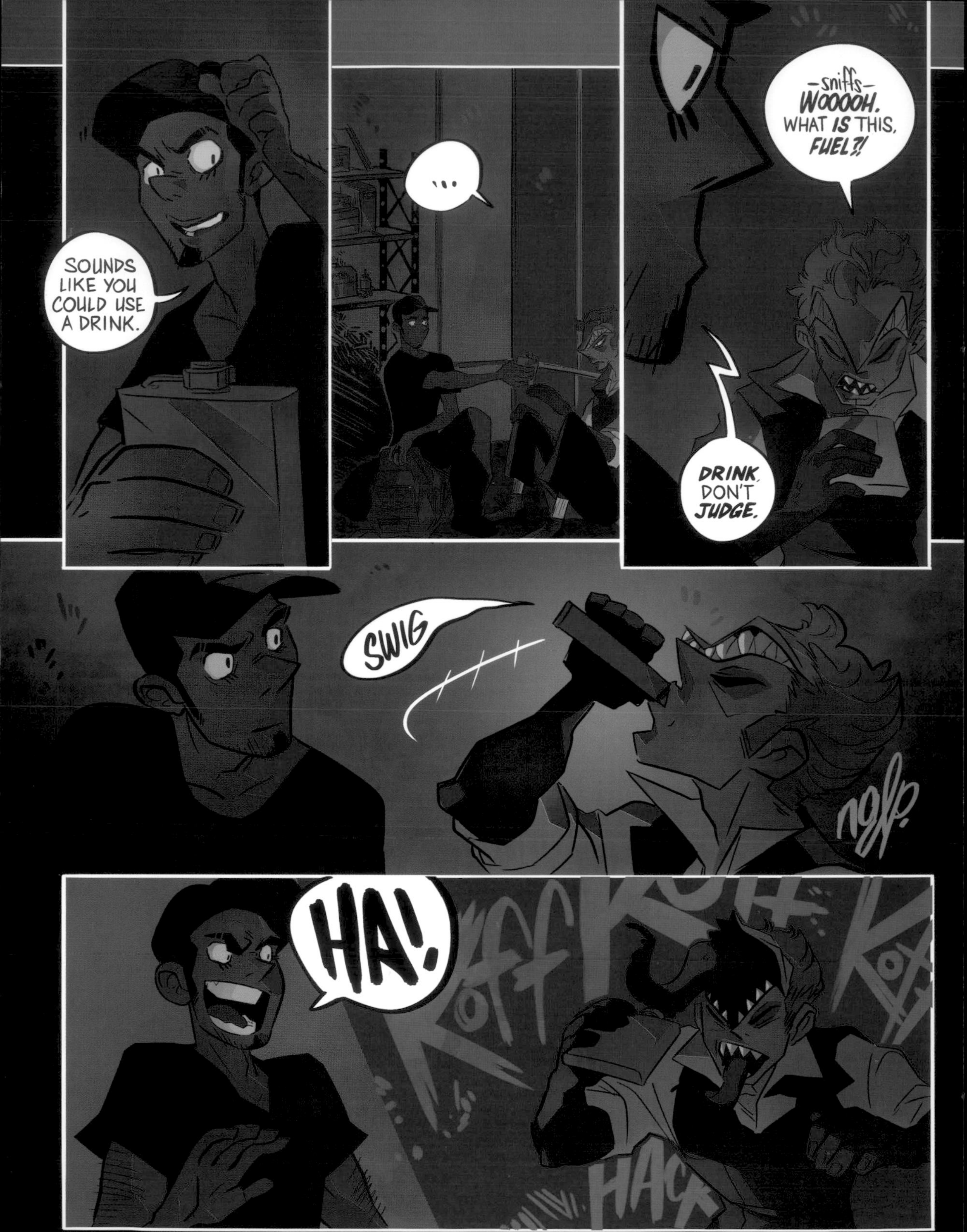
SOUNDS LIKE YOU COULD USE A DRINK.
...
-sniffs- WOOOOH. WHAT IS THIS, FUEL?!
DRINK, DON'T JUDGE.
SWIG
ngh
HA!
HACK

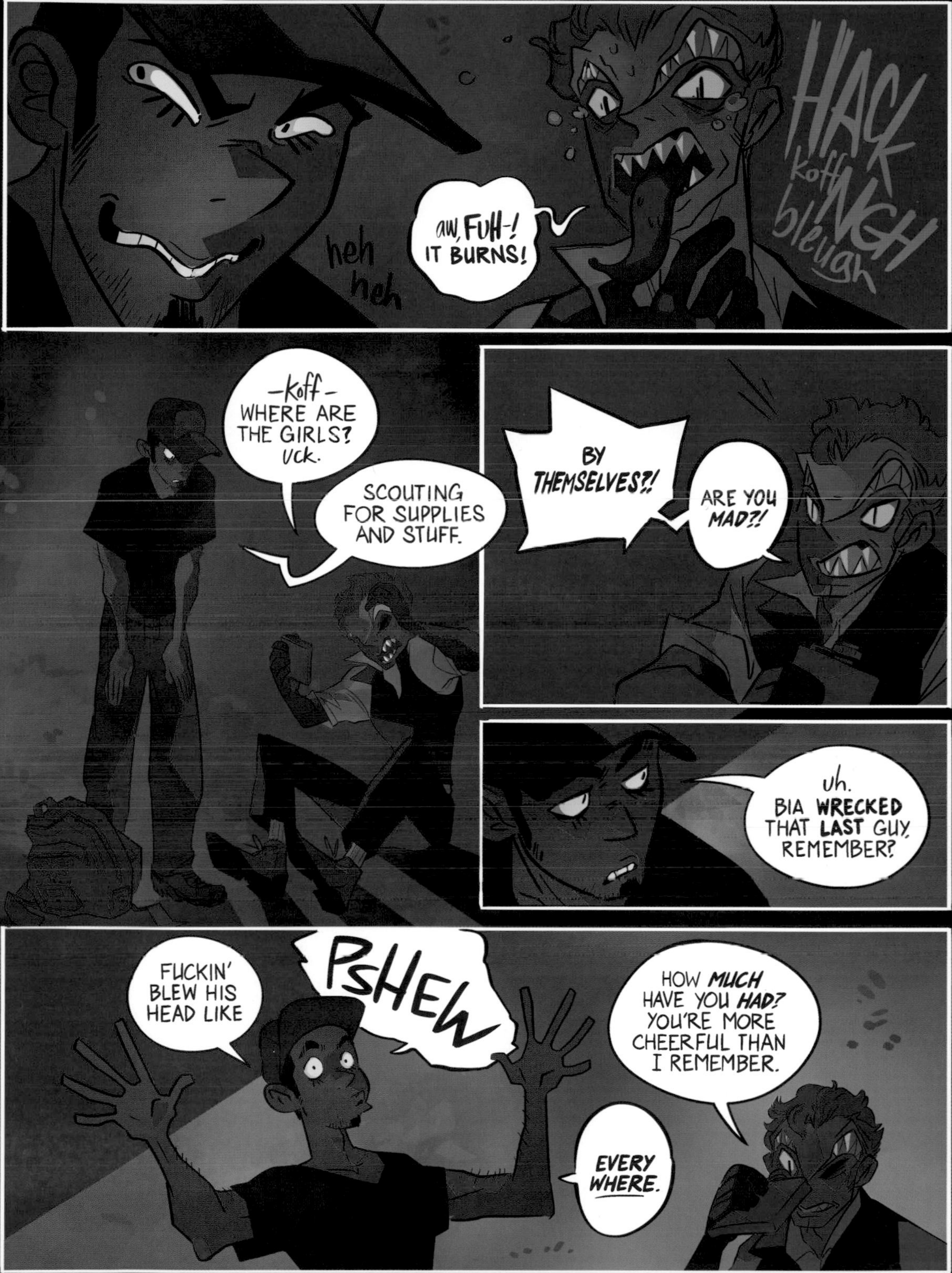
HACK koff NGH bleugh
heh heh
aw, FUH-! IT BURNS!
-koff- WHERE ARE THE GIRLS? UCK.
SCOUTING FOR SUPPLIES AND STUFF.
BY THEMSELVES?!
ARE YOU MAD?!
UH. BIA WRECKED THAT LAST GUY, REMEMBER?
FUCKIN' BLEW HIS HEAD LIKE
PSHEW
HOW MUCH HAVE YOU HAD? YOU'RE MORE CHEERFUL THAN I REMEMBER.
EVERY WHERE.

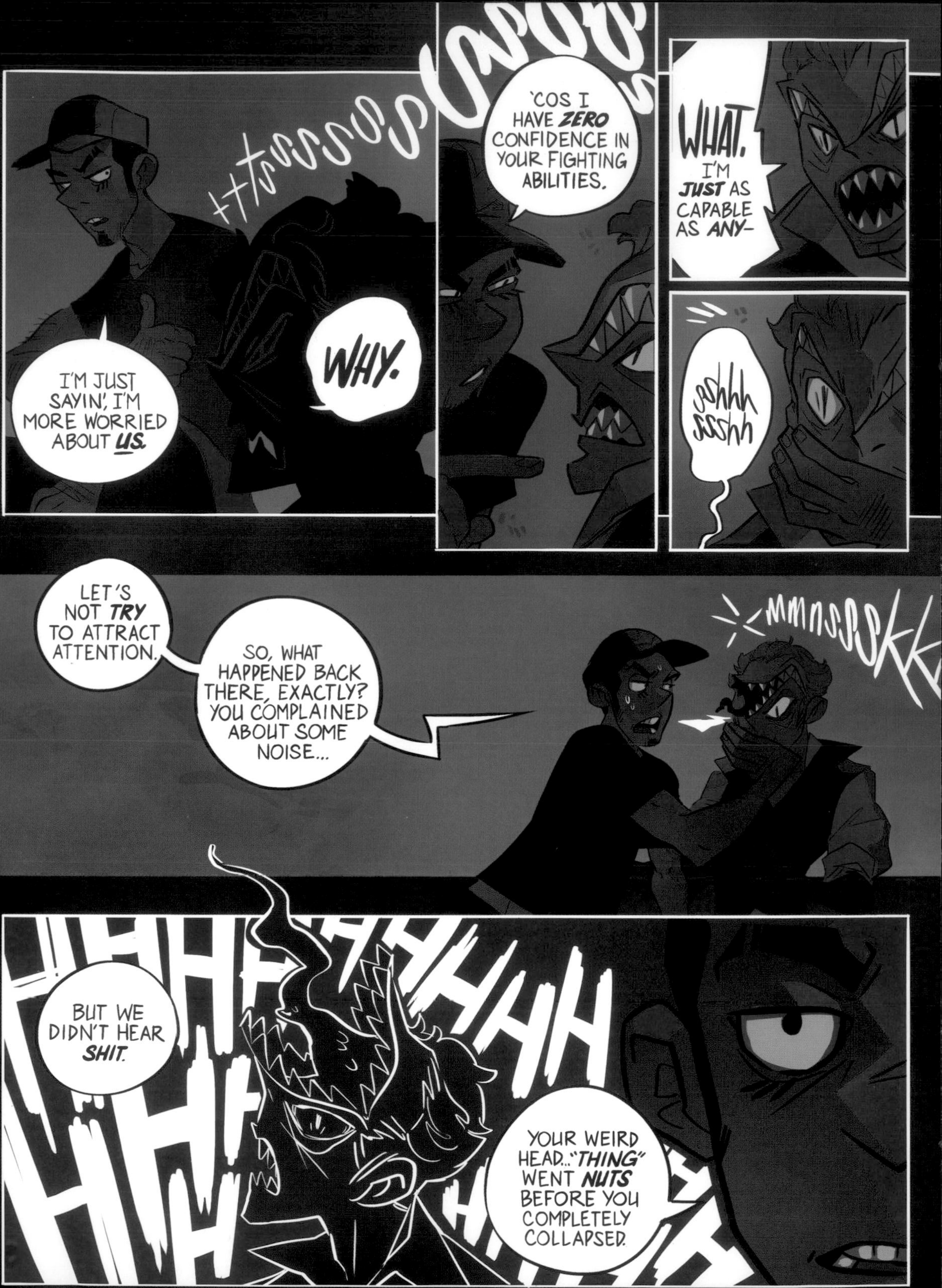

I'M JUST SAYIN', I'M MORE WORRIED ABOUT US.
WHY.
'COS I HAVE ZERO CONFIDENCE IN YOUR FIGHTING ABILITIES.
WHAT. I'M JUST AS CAPABLE AS ANY-
sshhh ssshh
LET'S NOT TRY TO ATTRACT ATTENTION.
SO, WHAT HAPPENED BACK THERE, EXACTLY? YOU COMPLAINED ABOUT SOME NOISE...
MMNSSSKK
BUT WE DIDN'T HEAR SHIT.
YOUR WEIRD HEAD..."THING" WENT NUTS BEFORE YOU COMPLETELY COLLAPSED.

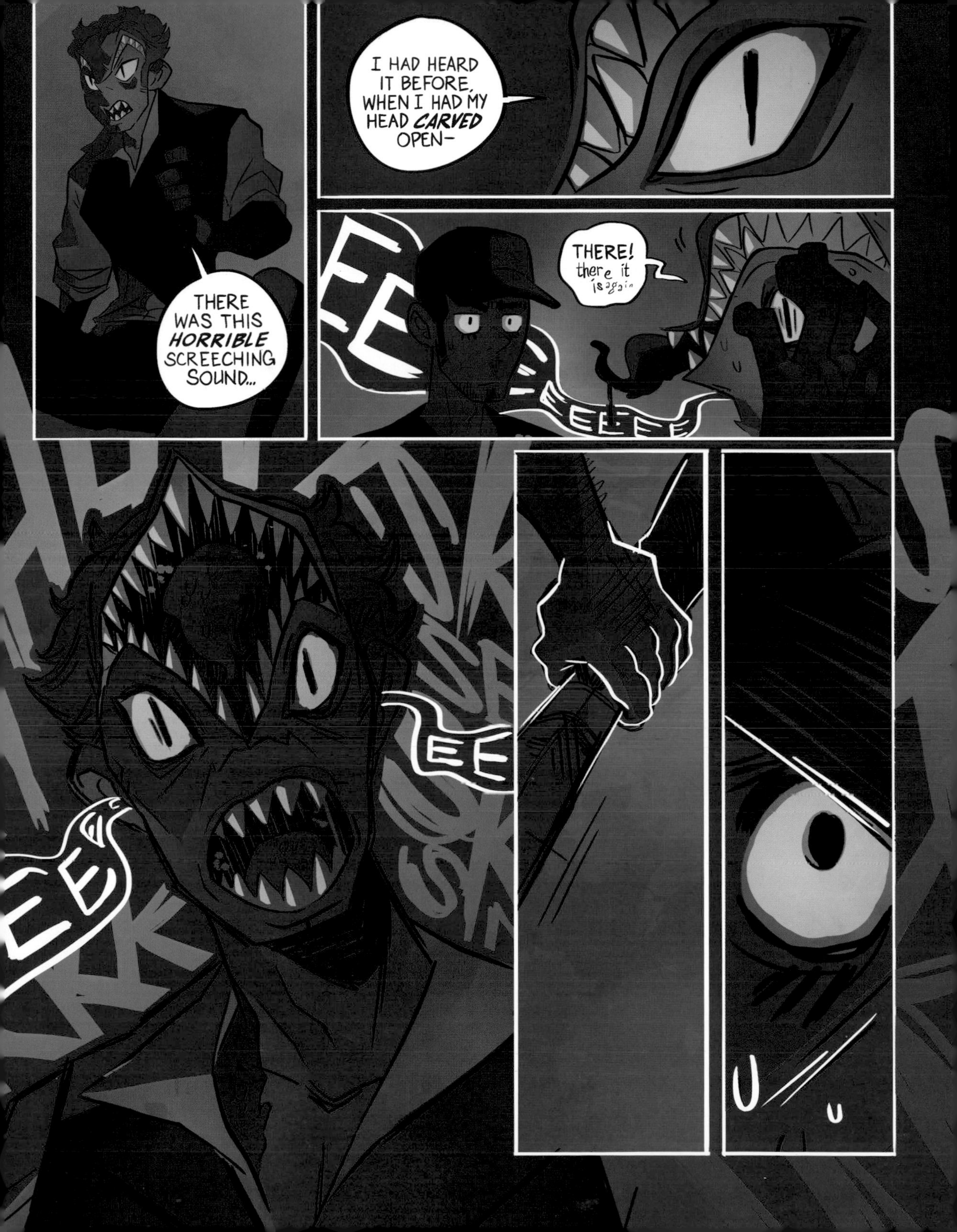
THERE WAS THIS HORRIBLE SCREECHING SOUND...
I HAD HEARD IT BEFORE, WHEN I HAD MY HEAD CARVED OPEN-
EEEEEEEE
THERE! there it is again
EE
EE
U
u

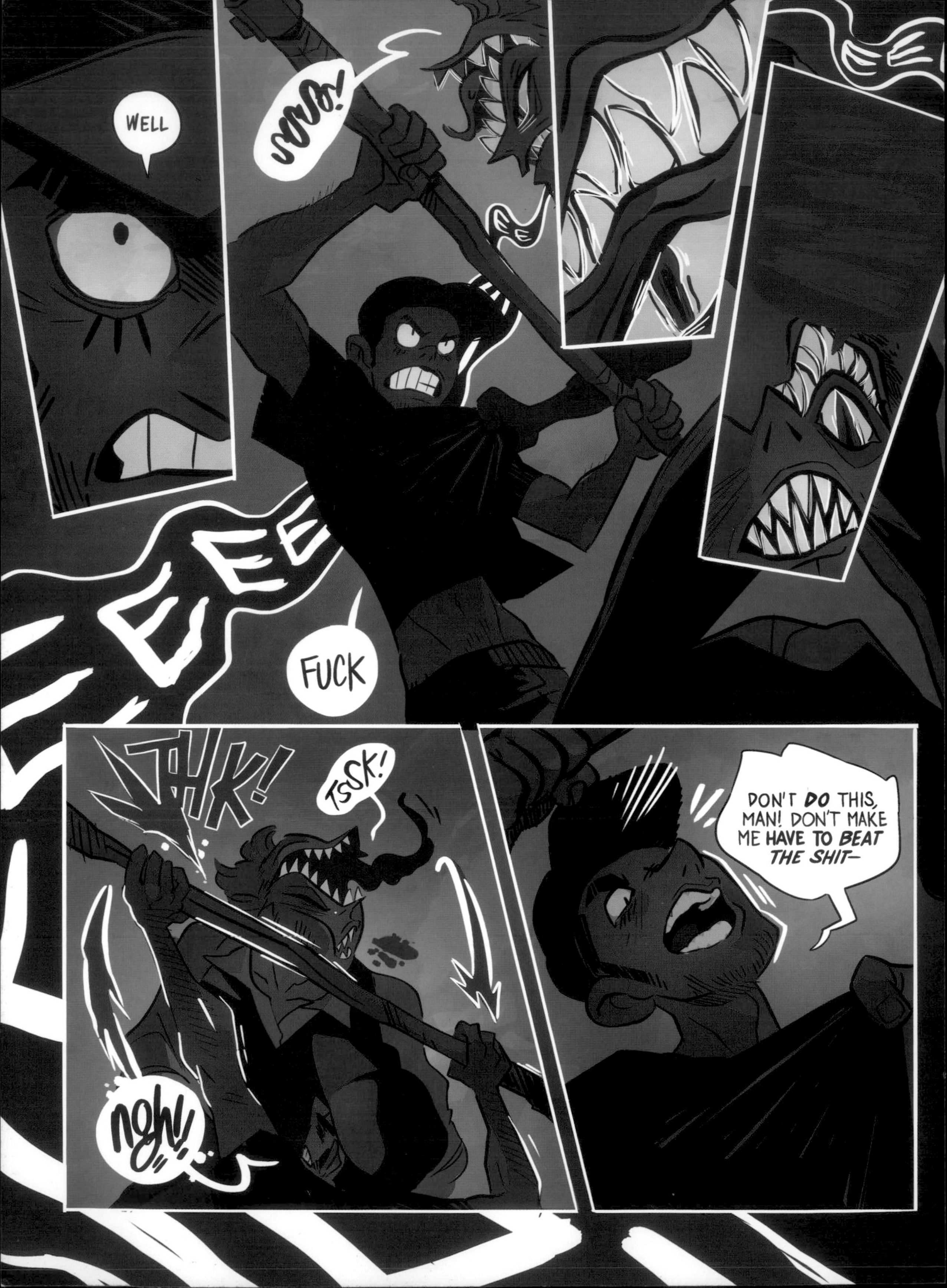
WELL
SOOO!
FUCK
THK!
TSSK!
DON'T DO THIS, MAN! DON'T MAKE ME HAVE TO BEAT THE SHIT–
NGH!!

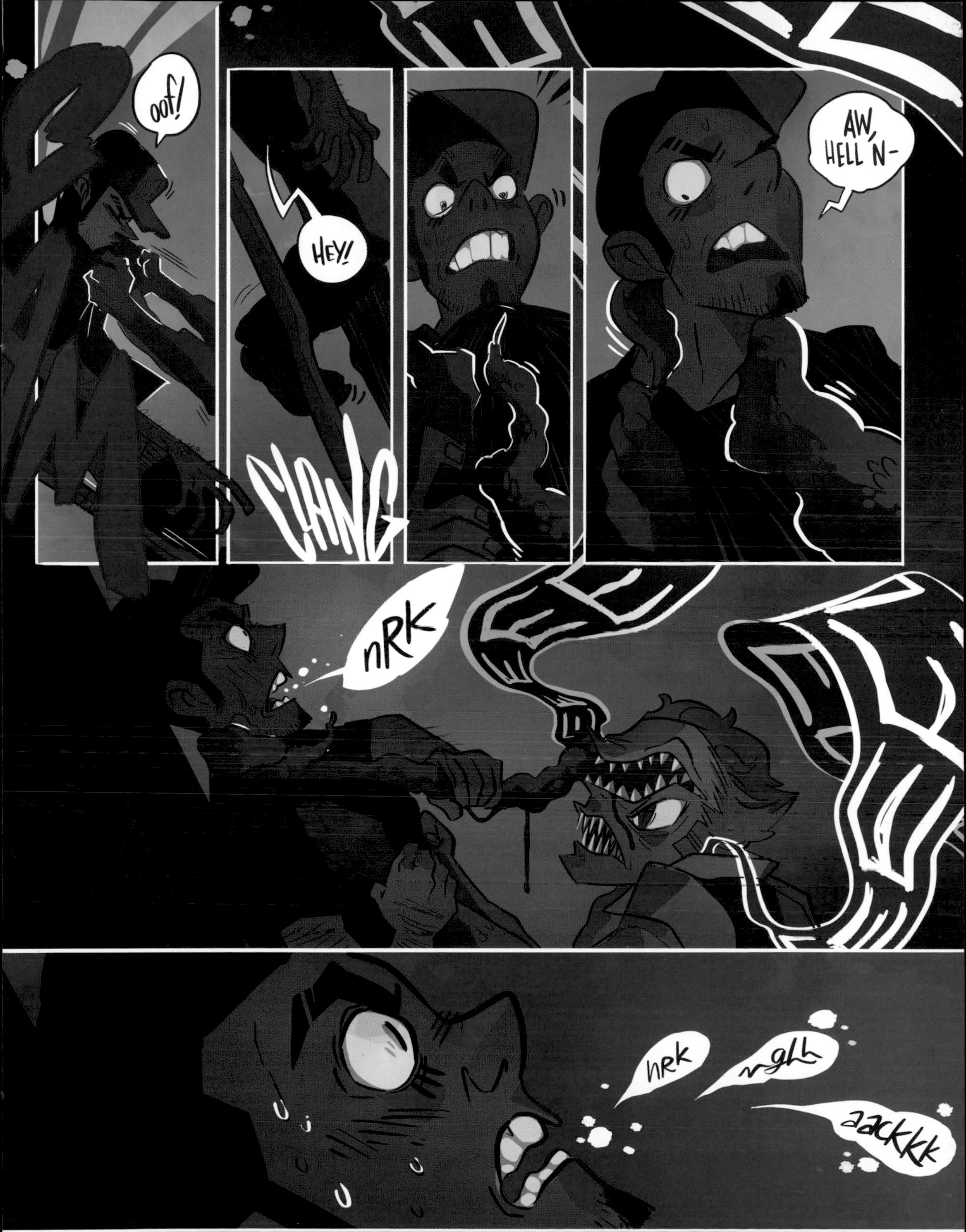
oof!
HEY!
CLANG
AW, HELL N-
nRK
hRK
nghh
aackkk

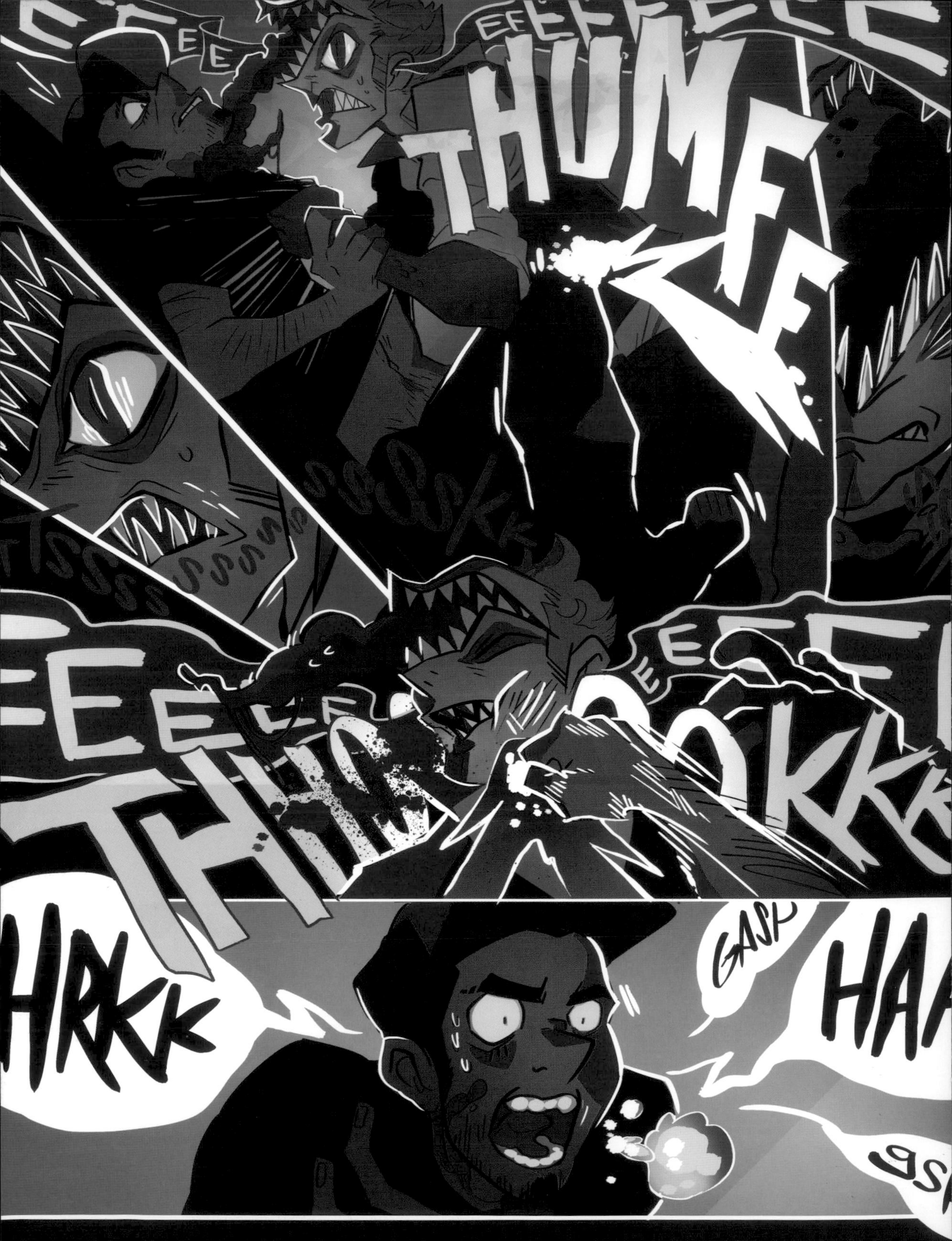
EEEE
THUMF
SSSSSKK
TSSSSSS
EEEE
THOOKKK
HRKKK
GASK
HAA

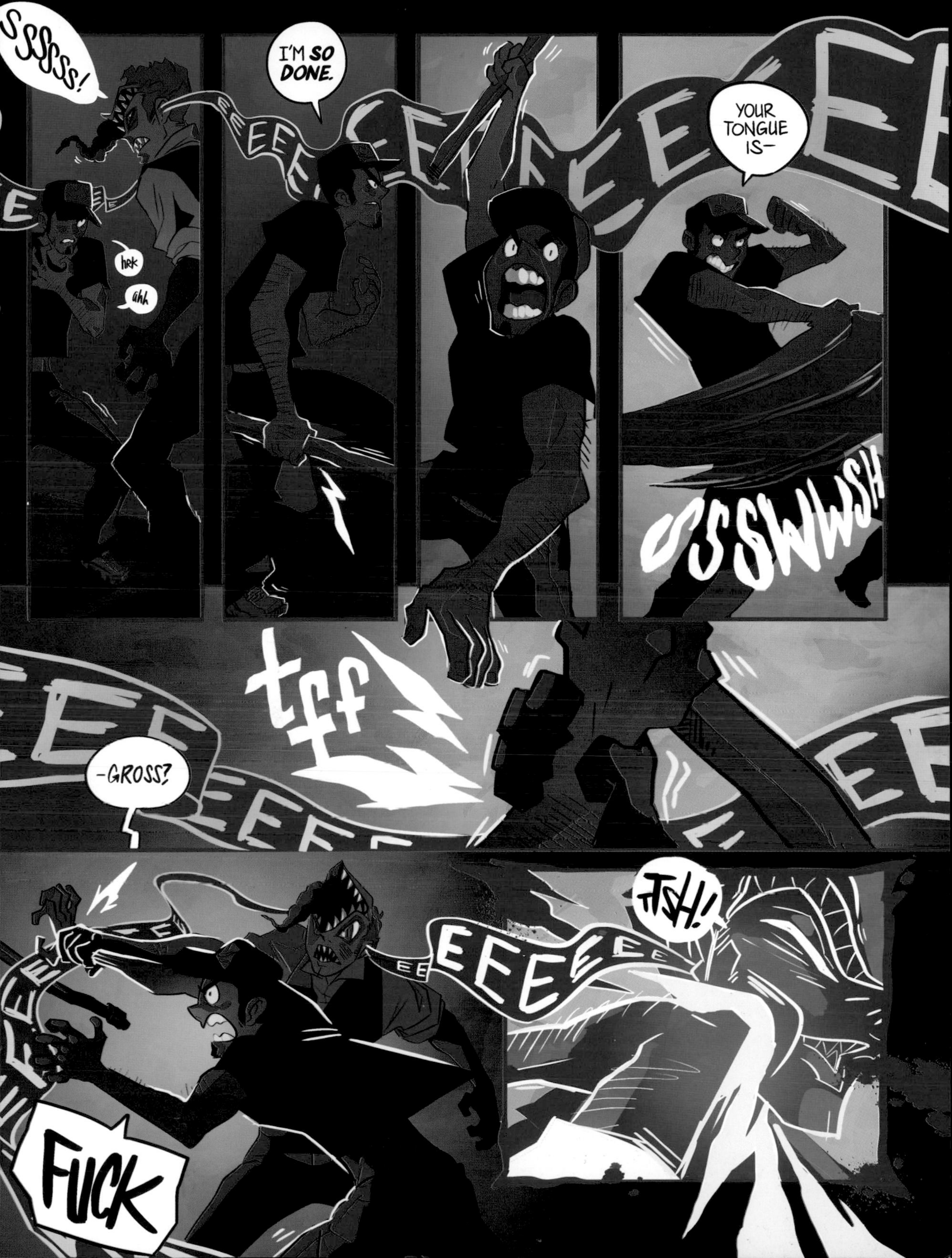
SSSSSS!
hrk
ahh
I'M SO DONE.
YOUR TONGUE IS—
SSWWSH
tff
-GROSS?
TSH!
FUCK

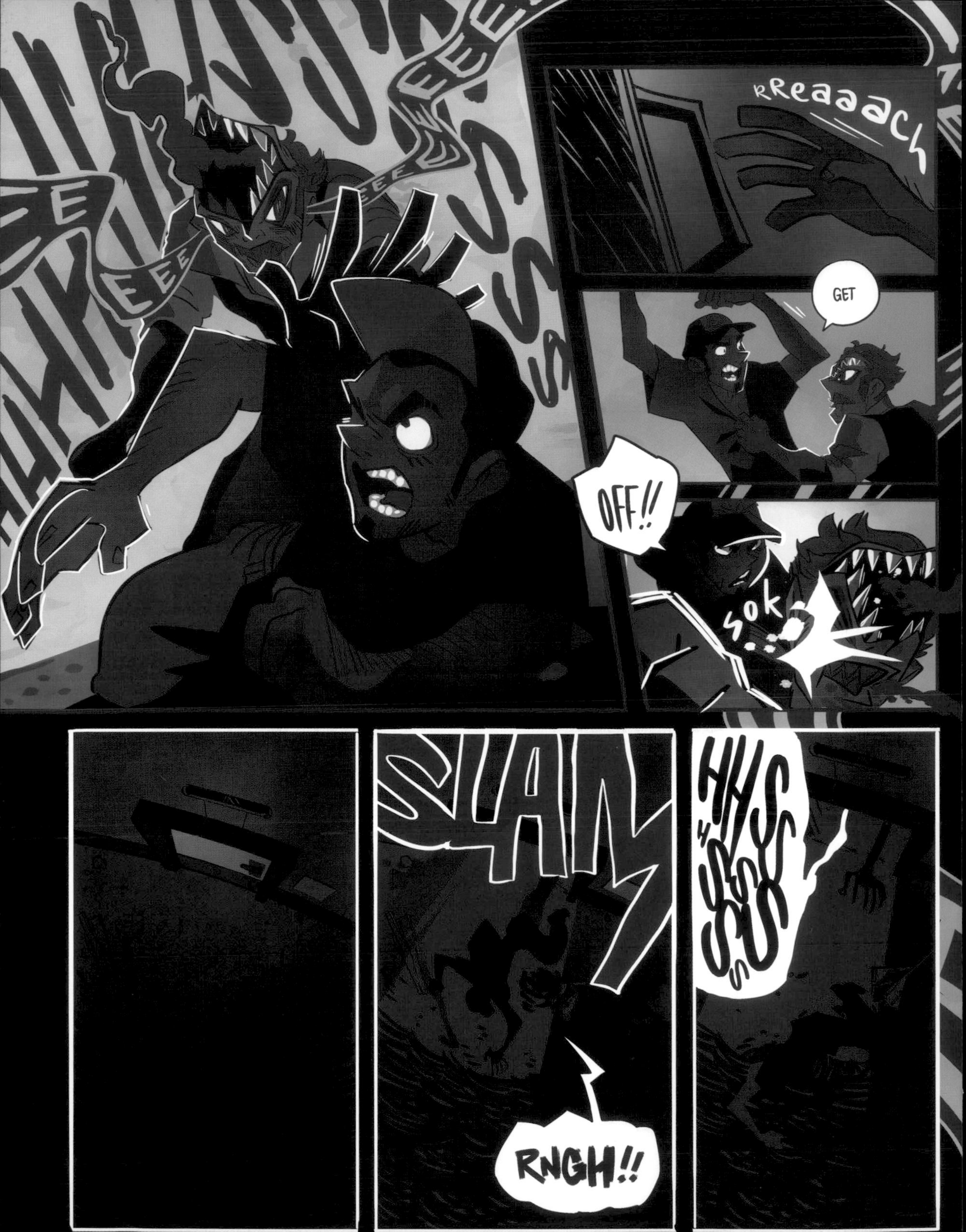
kReaaaach
GET
OFF!!
SOK
SLAM
RNGH!!

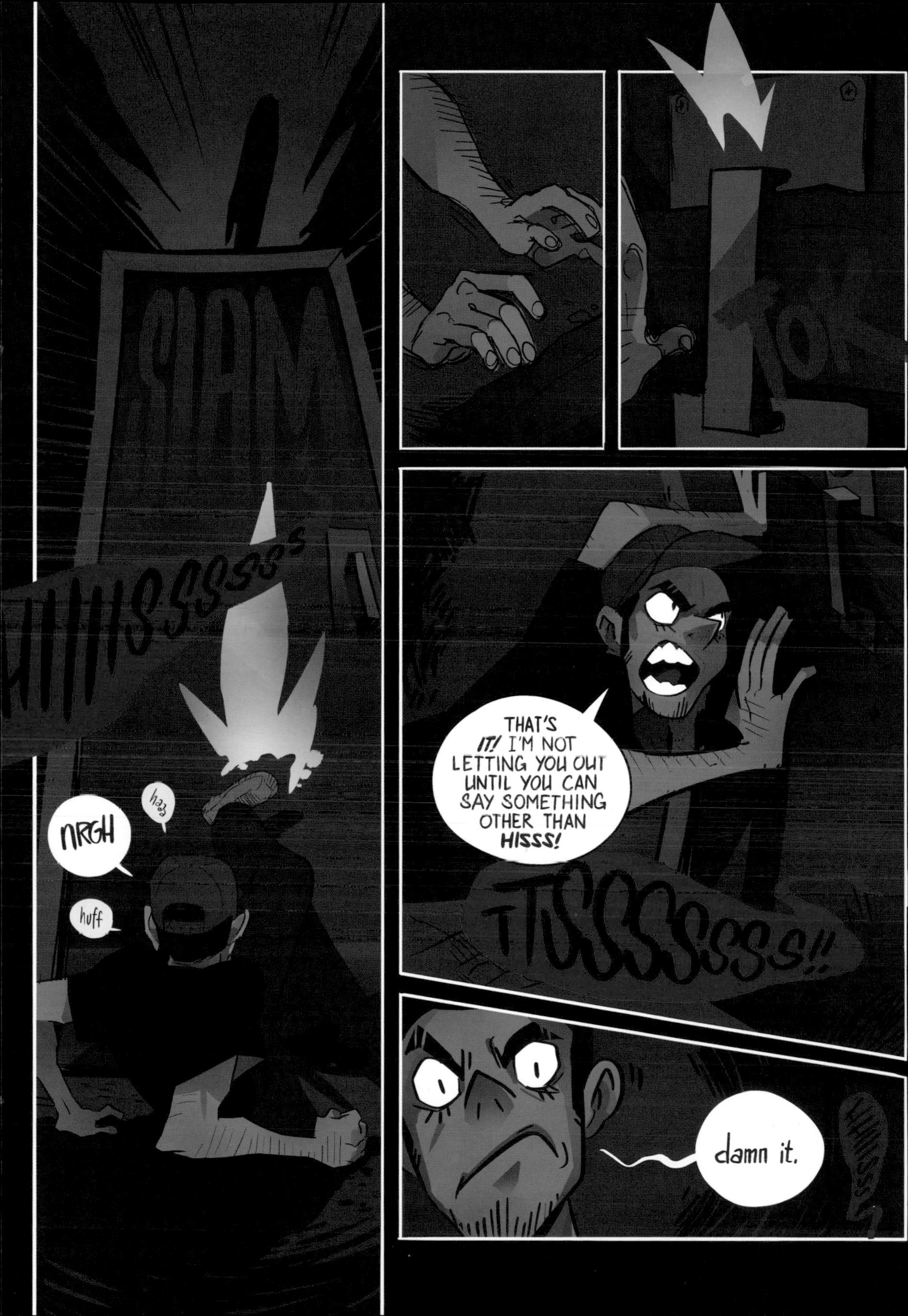
SLAM
HHHHSSSSSSS
haa
NRGH
huff
THAT'S *IT!* I'M NOT LETTING YOU OUT UNTIL YOU CAN SAY SOMETHING OTHER THAN **HISSS!**
TTSSSSSSSS!!
damn it.

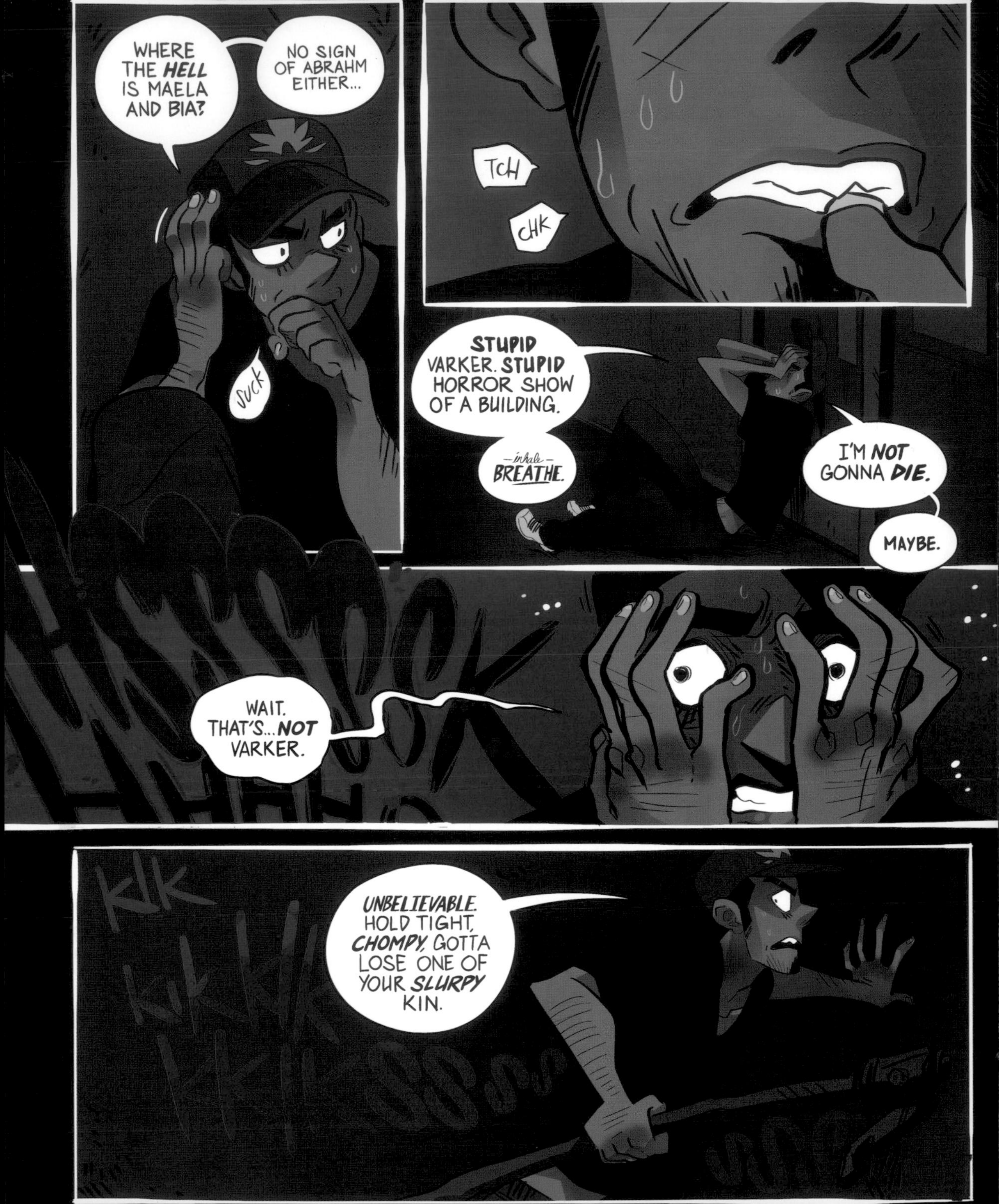
WHERE THE HELL IS MAELA AND BIA?
NO SIGN OF ABRAHM EITHER...
SUCK
TCH
CHK
STUPID VARKER. STUPID HORROR SHOW OF A BUILDING.
-inhale- BREATHE.
I'M NOT GONNA DIE.
MAYBE.
WAIT. THAT'S...NOT VARKER.
KJK
UNBELIEVABLE. HOLD TIGHT, CHOMPY, GOTTA LOSE ONE OF YOUR SLURPY KIN.

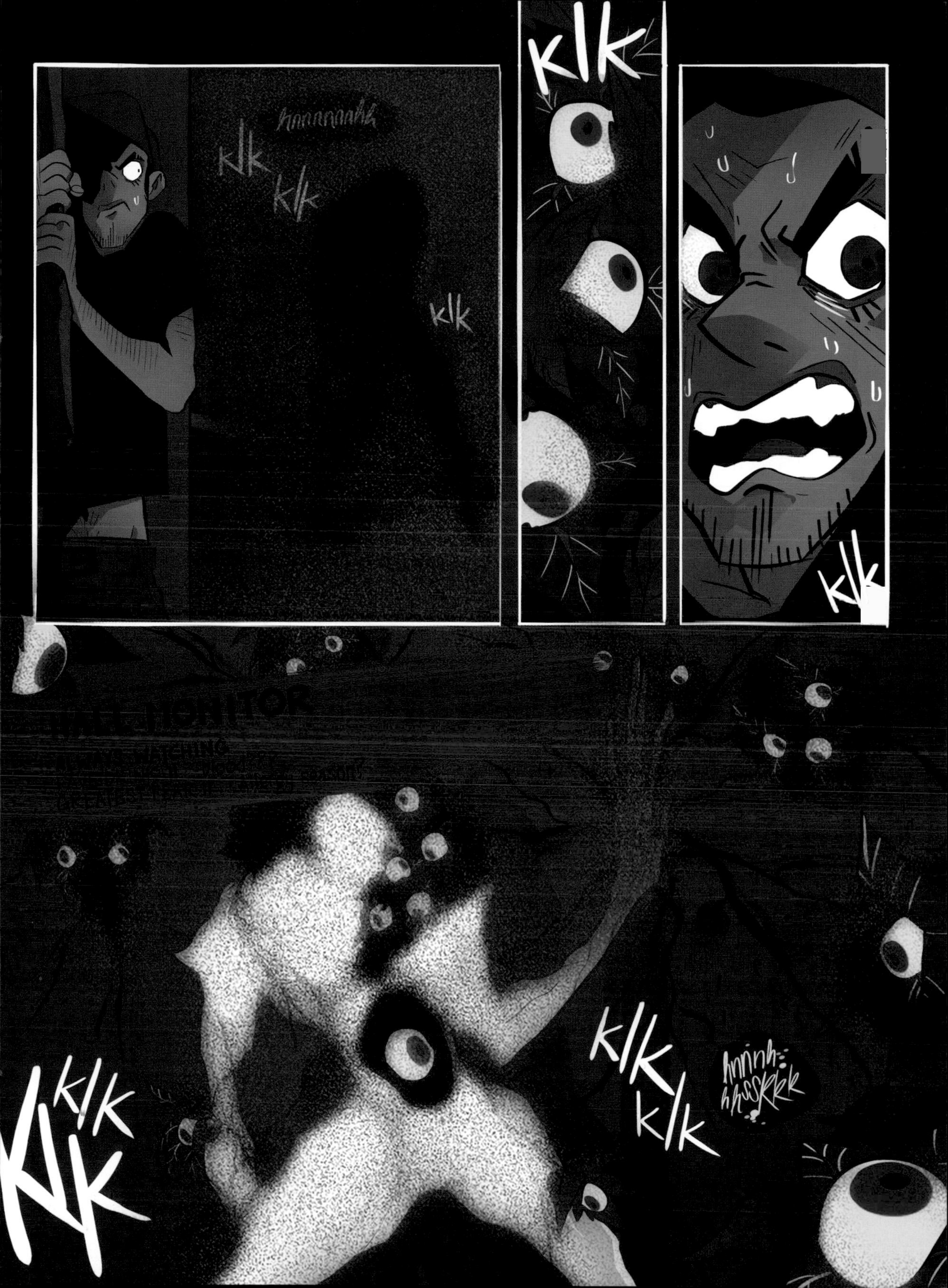
hnnnnnnhh
klk
klk
klk
KLK
klk
MONITOR
KLK
klk
klk
klk
hnnnh-hhssrkk

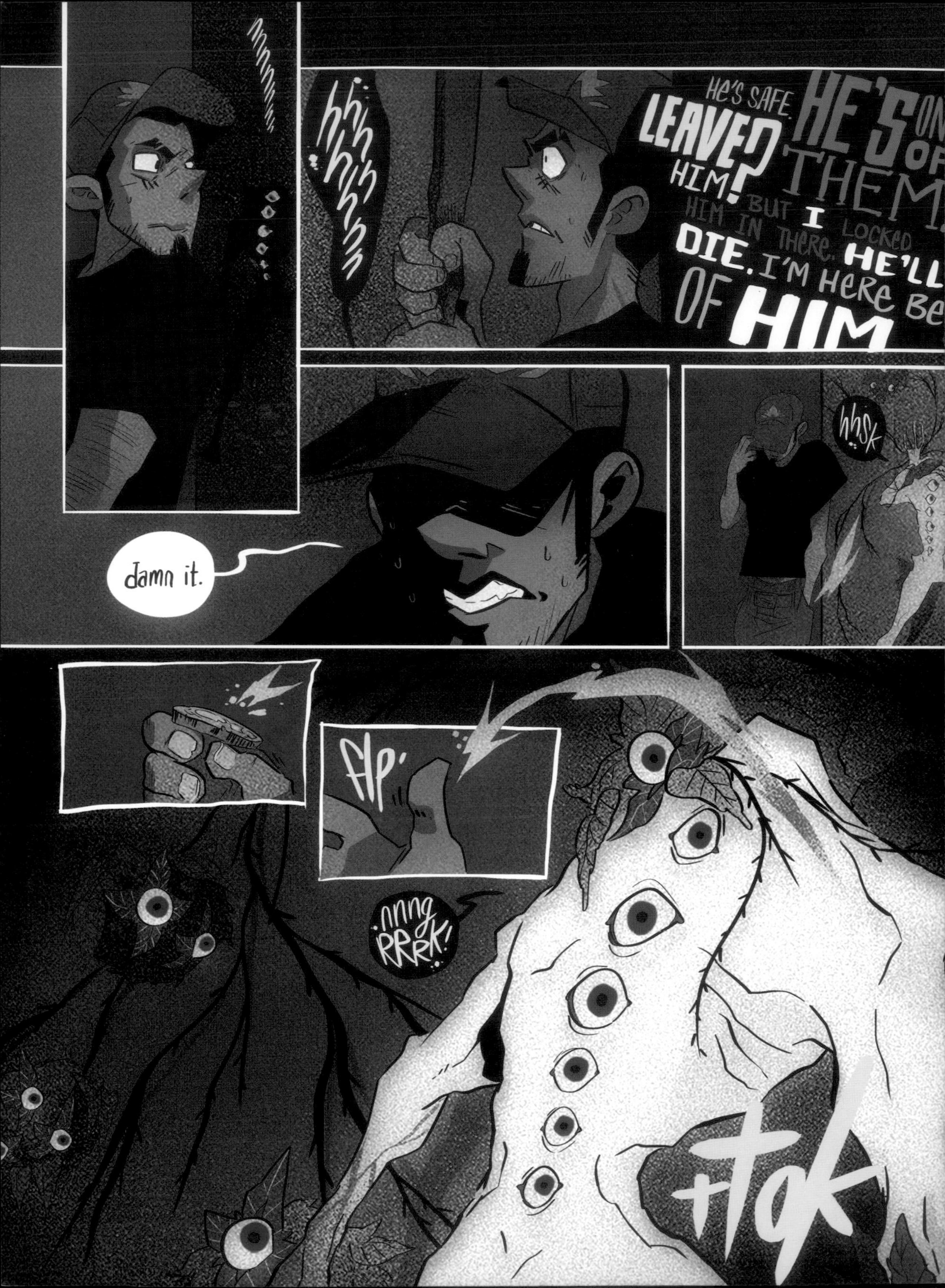
hhhhhhhh
hhhhhhhhh
HE'S SAFE.
HE'S ON
OF
THEM
LEAVE?
HIM!
BUT I
LOCKED
HIM IN THERE.
HE'LL
DIE.
I'M HERE BE
OF HIM
damn it.
hhsk
flp'
nnng RRRK!
ttok

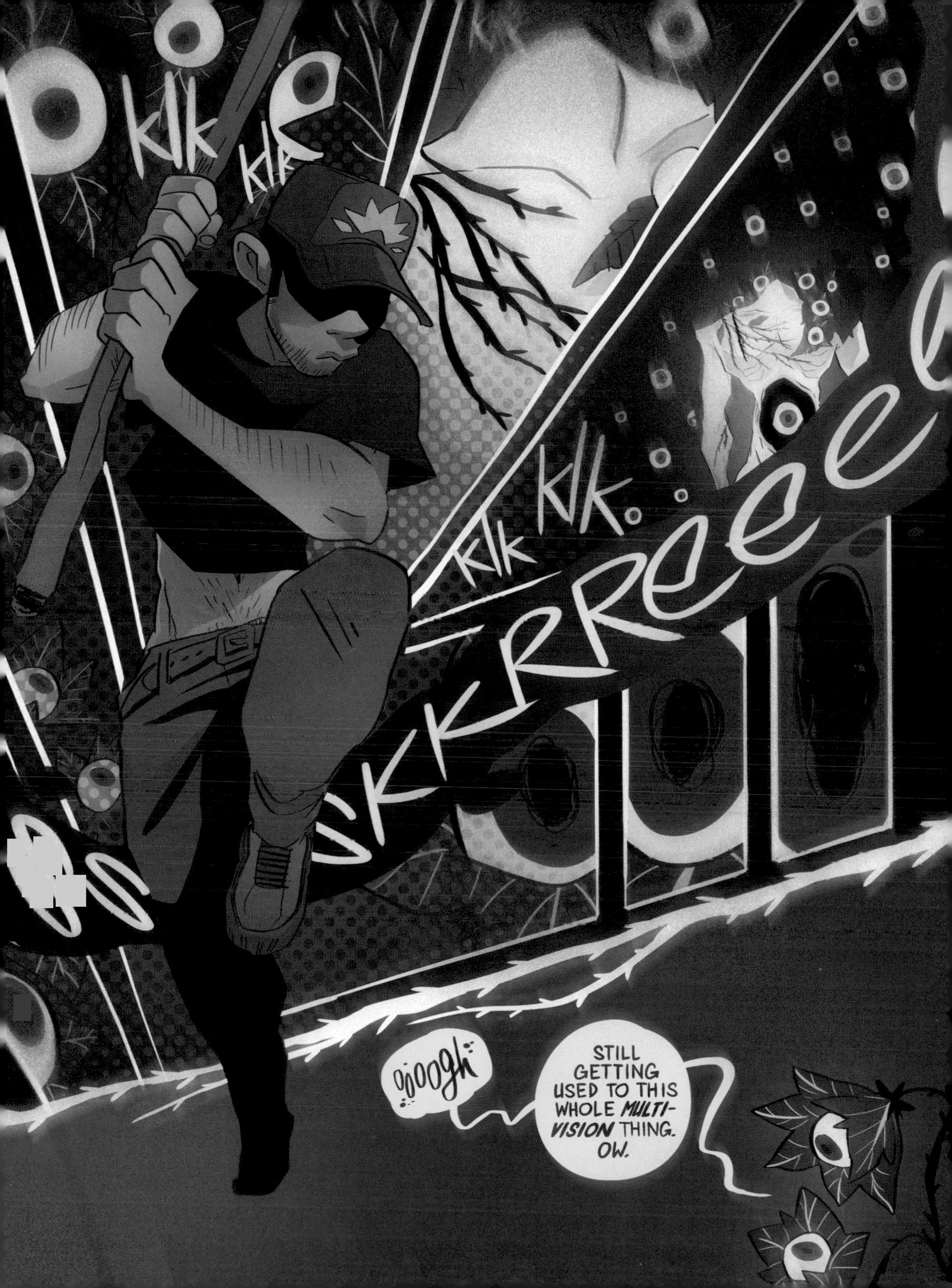
klk
klk
klk klk.
KKRReee
STILL GETTING USED TO THIS WHOLE *MULTI-VISION* THING. OW.

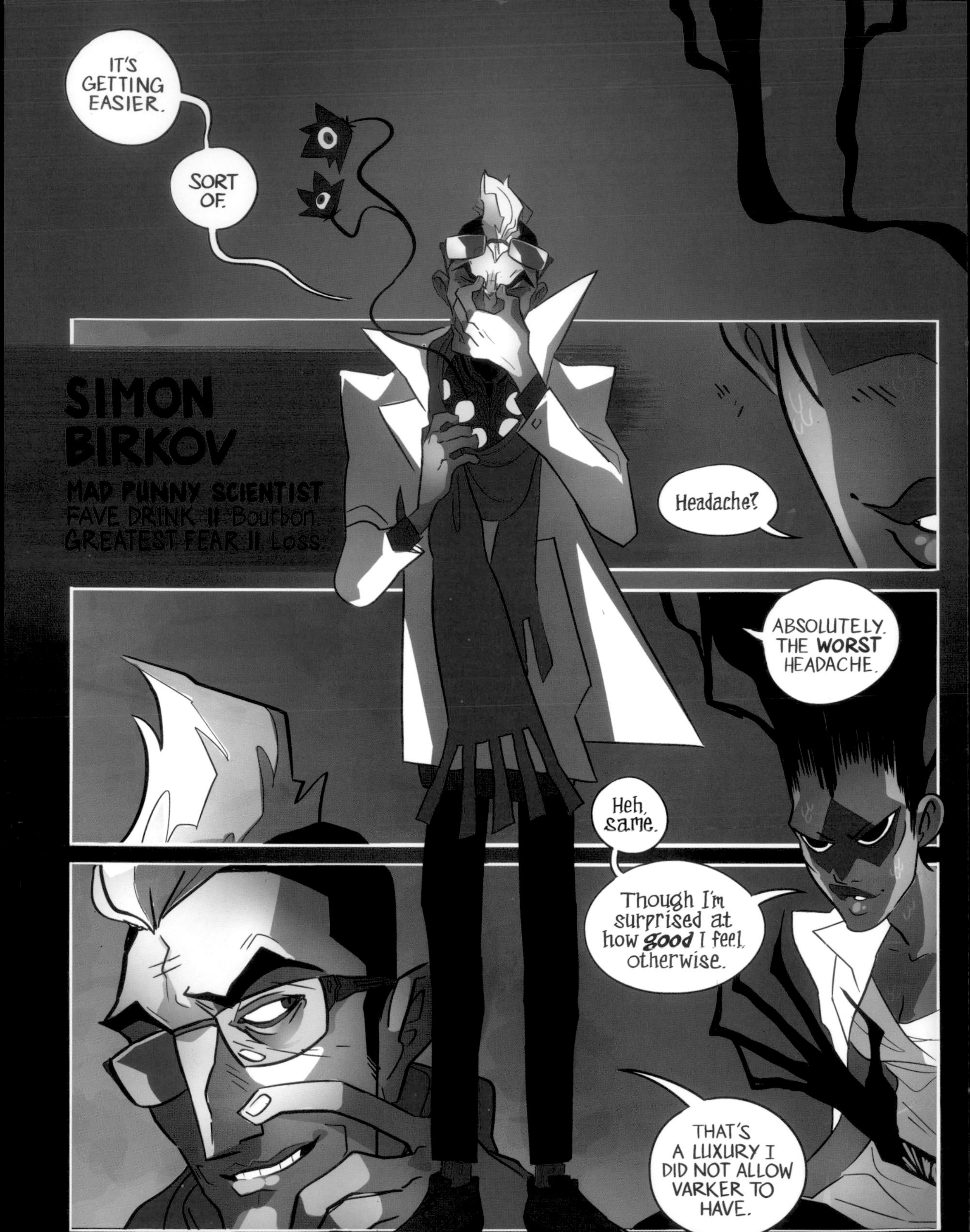
IT'S GETTING EASIER.
SORT OF.
SIMON BIRKOV
MAD PUNNY SCIENTIST
FAVE DRINK :: Bourbon.
GREATEST FEAR :: Loss.
Headache?
ABSOLUTELY. THE WORST HEADACHE.
Heh, same.
Though I'm surprised at how good I feel, otherwise.
THAT'S A LUXURY I DID NOT ALLOW VARKER TO HAVE.

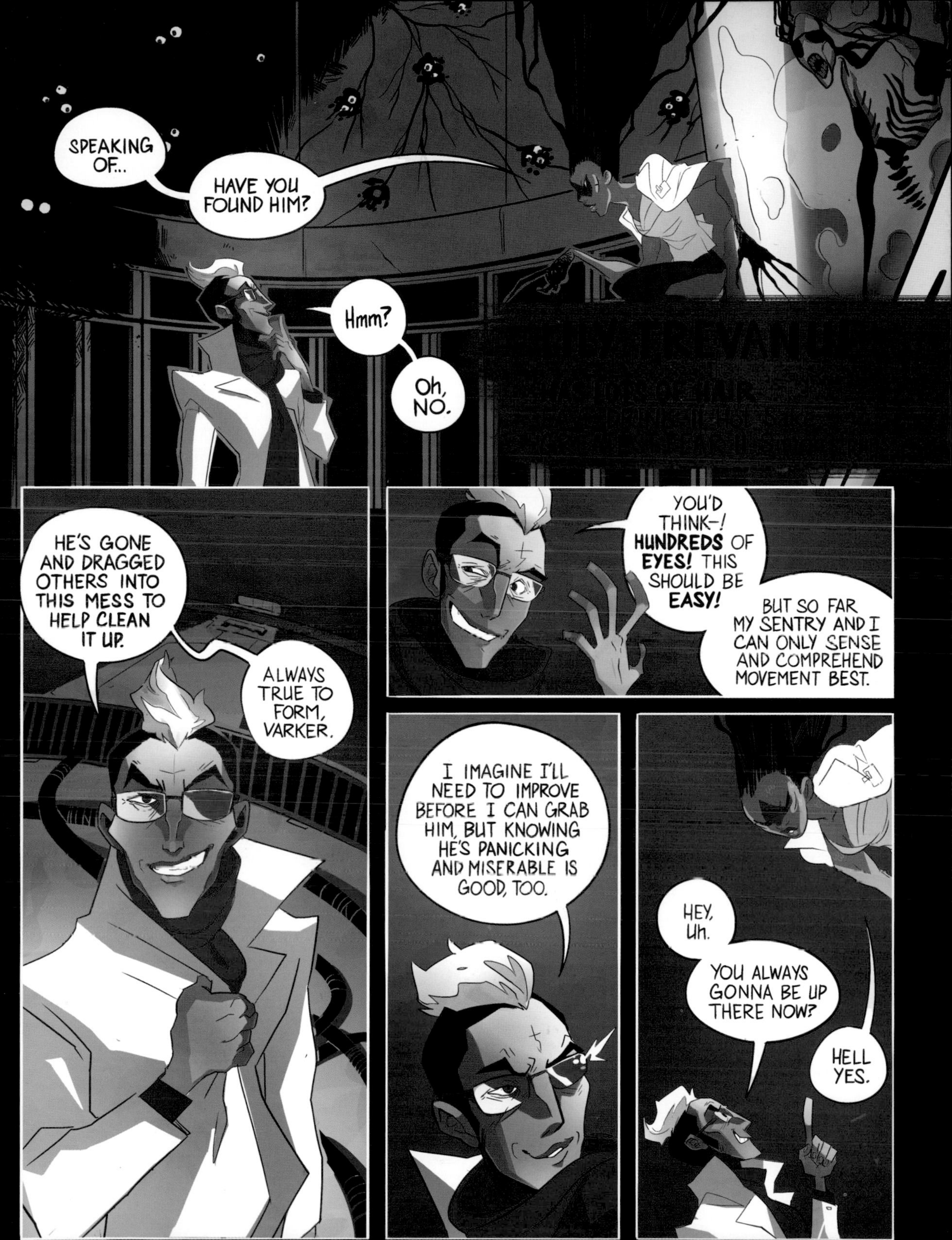
SPEAKING OF...
HAVE YOU FOUND HIM?
Hmm?
Oh, NO.
HE'S GONE AND DRAGGED OTHERS INTO THIS MESS TO HELP CLEAN IT UP.
ALWAYS TRUE TO FORM, VARKER.
YOU'D THINK—! HUNDREDS OF EYES! THIS SHOULD BE EASY!
BUT SO FAR MY SENTRY AND I CAN ONLY SENSE AND COMPREHEND MOVEMENT BEST.
I IMAGINE I'LL NEED TO IMPROVE BEFORE I CAN GRAB HIM, BUT KNOWING HE'S PANICKING AND MISERABLE IS GOOD, TOO.
HEY, Uh.
YOU ALWAYS GONNA BE UP THERE NOW?
HELL YES.

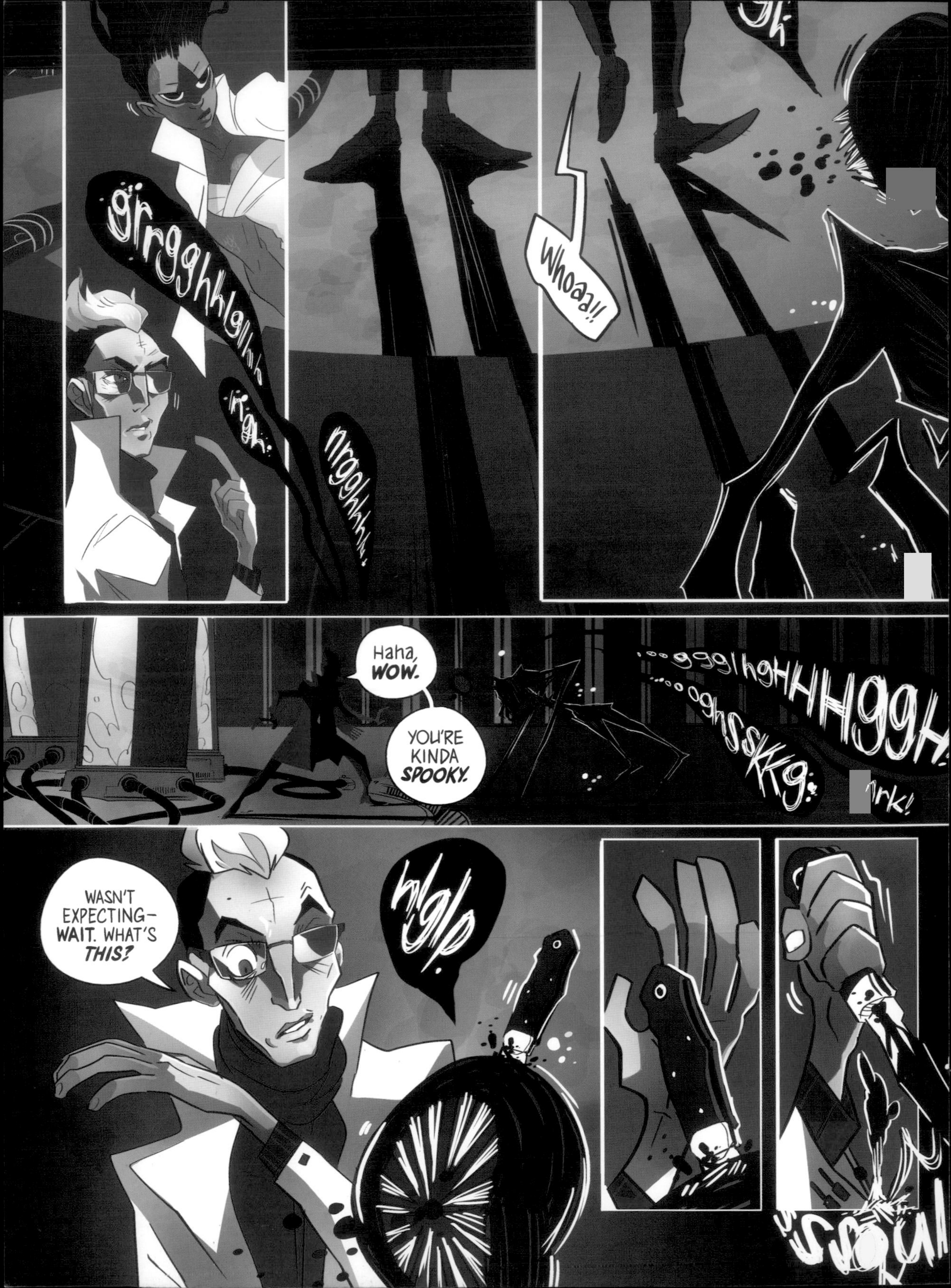
Whoaa!!
Haha, WOW.
YOU'RE KINDA SPOOKY.
rk!
WASN'T EXPECTING— WAIT. WHAT'S THIS?

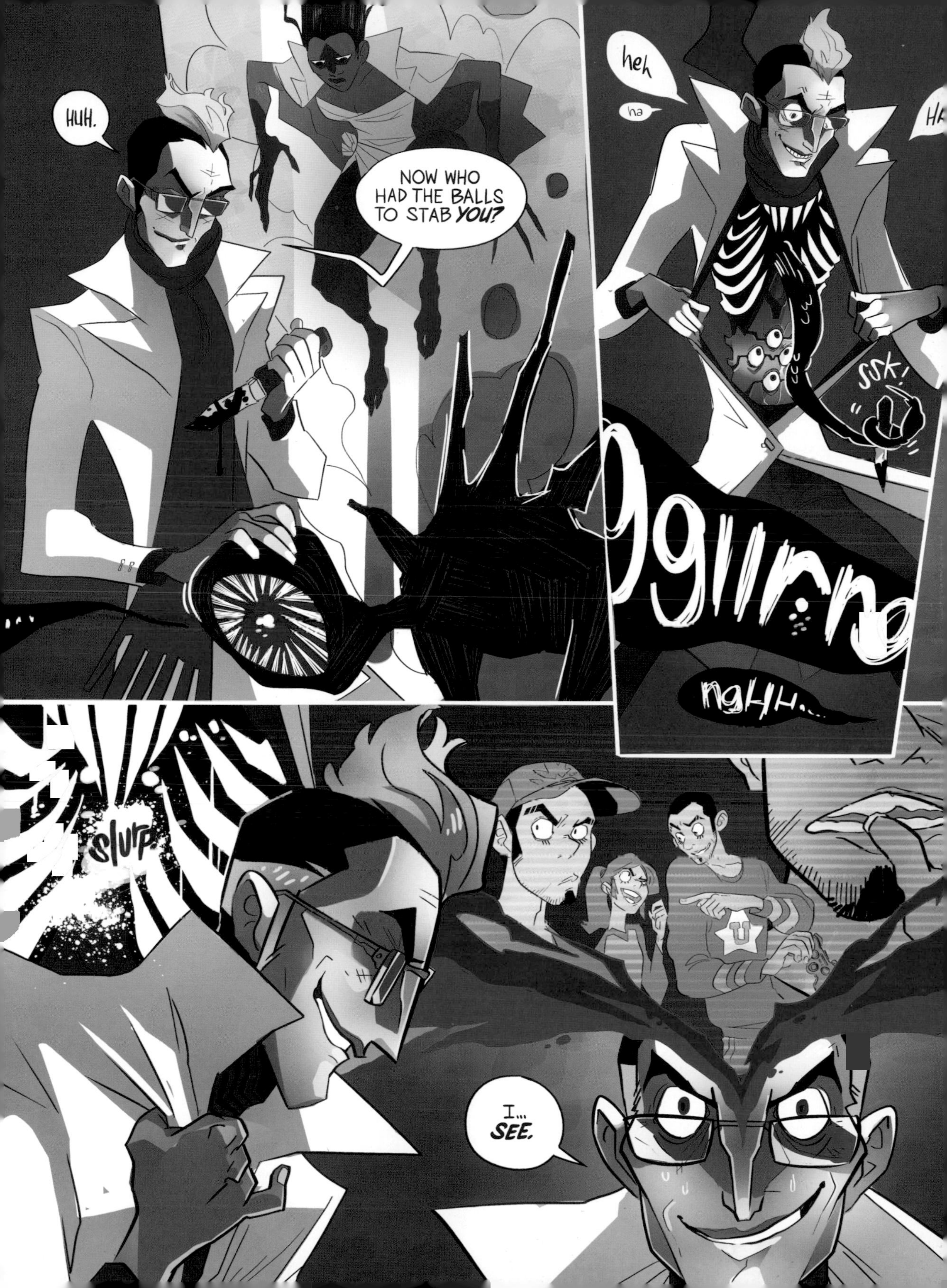
HUH.
NOW WHO HAD THE BALLS TO STAB *YOU?*
heh
ha
SSK!
ggllrrn
nghh...
slurp
I... *SEE.*

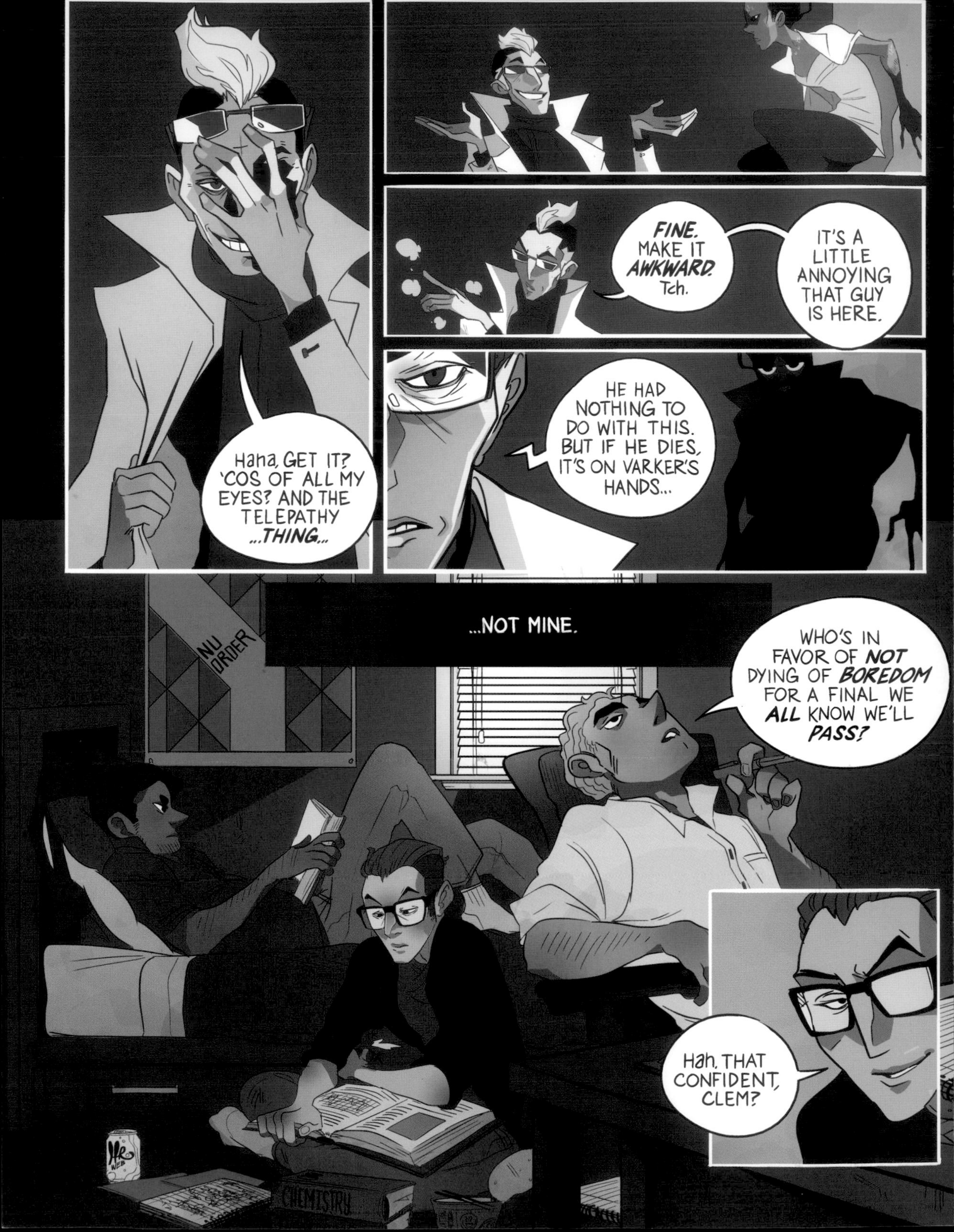
Haha, GET IT? 'COS OF ALL MY EYES? AND THE TELEPATHY ...THING...
FINE. MAKE IT AWKWARD. Tch.
IT'S A LITTLE ANNOYING THAT GUY IS HERE.
HE HAD NOTHING TO DO WITH THIS. BUT IF HE DIES, IT'S ON VARKER'S HANDS...
...NOT MINE.
NU ORDER
WHO'S IN FAVOR OF NOT DYING OF BOREDOM FOR A FINAL WE ALL KNOW WE'LL PASS?
Hah. THAT CONFIDENT, CLEM?
CHEMISTRY

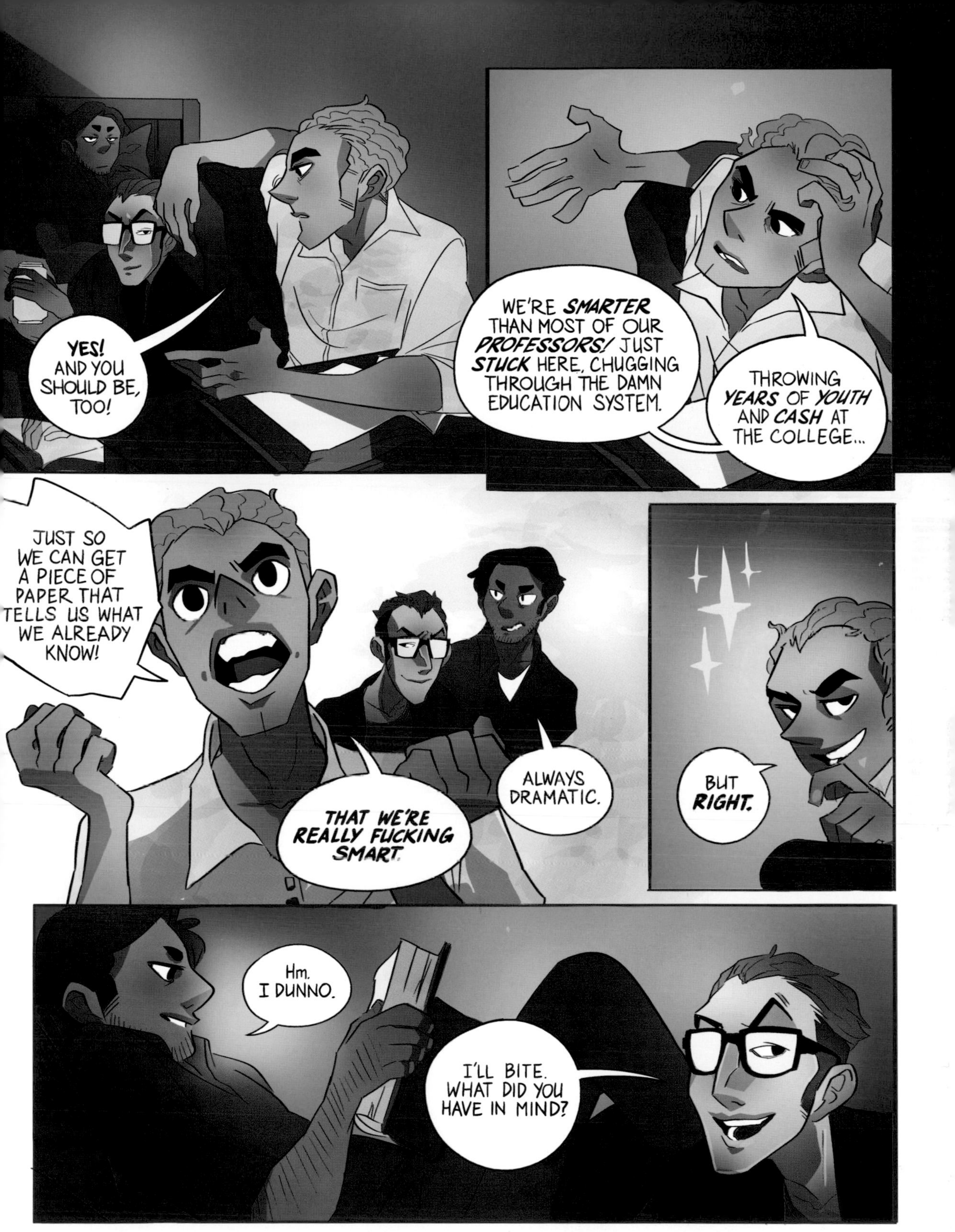

YES! AND YOU SHOULD BE, TOO!
WE'RE **SMARTER** THAN MOST OF OUR **PROFESSORS!** JUST **STUCK** HERE, CHUGGING THROUGH THE DAMN EDUCATION SYSTEM.
THROWING **YEARS** OF **YOUTH** AND **CASH** AT THE COLLEGE...
JUST SO WE CAN GET A PIECE OF PAPER THAT TELLS US WHAT WE ALREADY KNOW!
THAT WE'RE REALLY FUCKING SMART.
ALWAYS DRAMATIC.
BUT **RIGHT.**
Hm. I DUNNO.
I'LL BITE. WHAT DID YOU HAVE IN MIND?

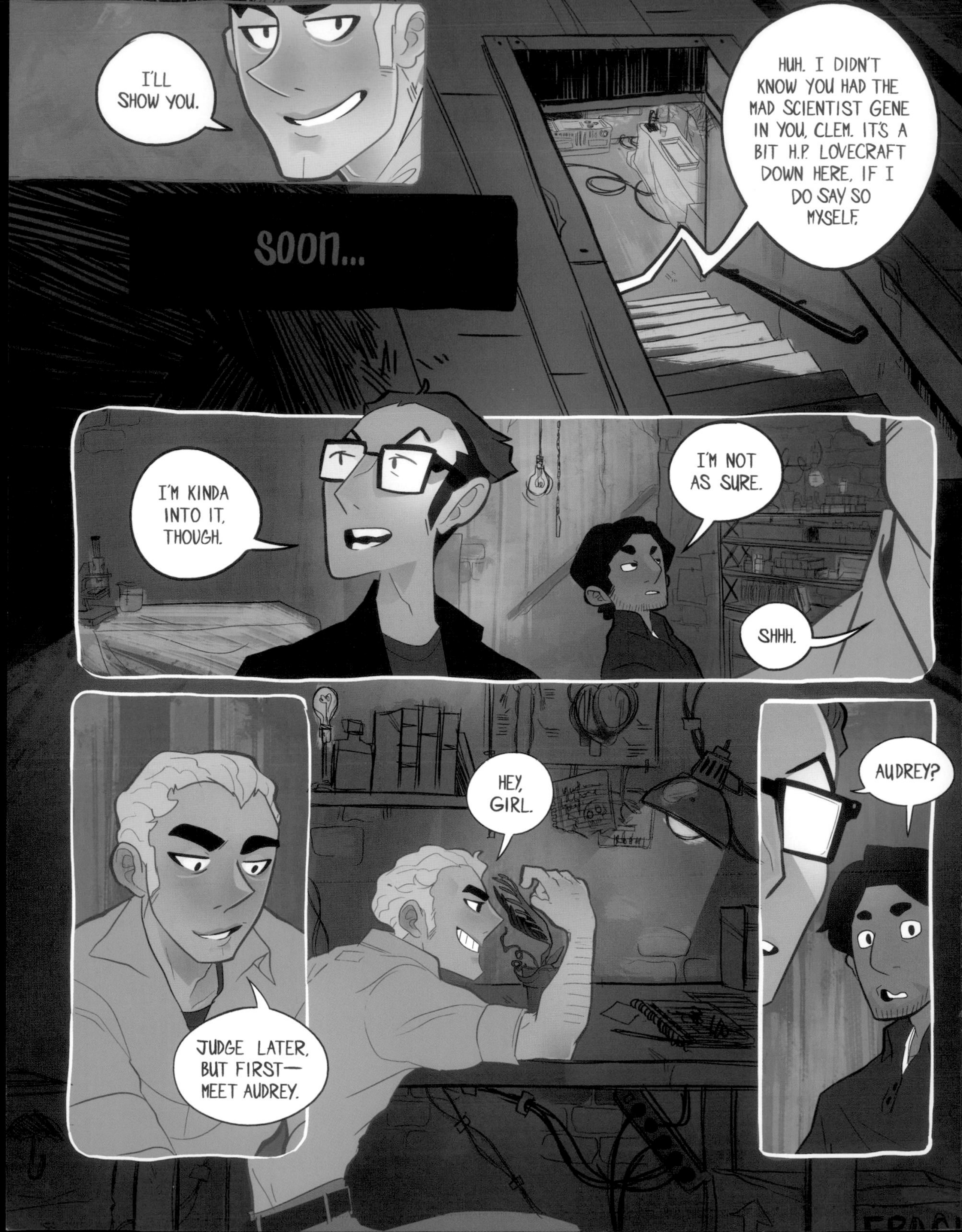
I'LL SHOW YOU.
soon...
HUH. I DIDN'T KNOW YOU HAD THE MAD SCIENTIST GENE IN YOU, CLEM. IT'S A BIT H.P. LOVECRAFT DOWN HERE, IF I DO SAY SO MYSELF.
I'M KINDA INTO IT, THOUGH.
I'M NOT AS SURE.
SHHH.
JUDGE LATER, BUT FIRST— MEET AUDREY.
HEY, GIRL.
AUDREY?

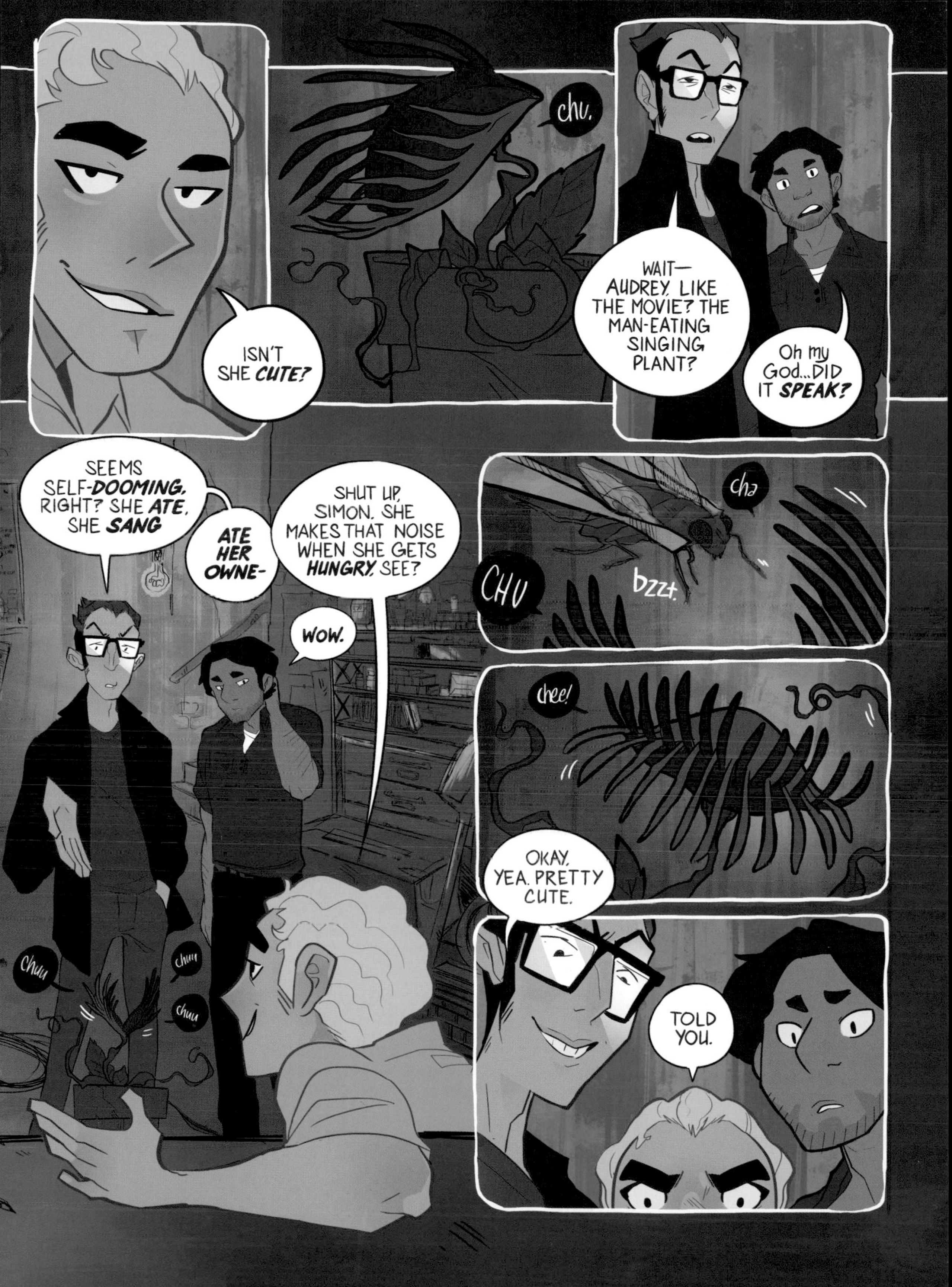
ISN'T SHE *CUTE?*
chu.
WAIT— AUDREY, LIKE THE MOVIE? THE MAN-EATING SINGING PLANT?
Oh my God...DID IT *SPEAK?*
SEEMS SELF-*DOOMING,* RIGHT? SHE *ATE*, SHE *SANG*
ATE HER OWNE-
SHUT UP, SIMON. SHE MAKES THAT NOISE WHEN SHE GETS *HUNGRY,* SEE?
WOW.
chuu
chuu
chuu
cha
CHU
bzzt.
chee!
OKAY, YEA. PRETTY CUTE.
TOLD YOU.

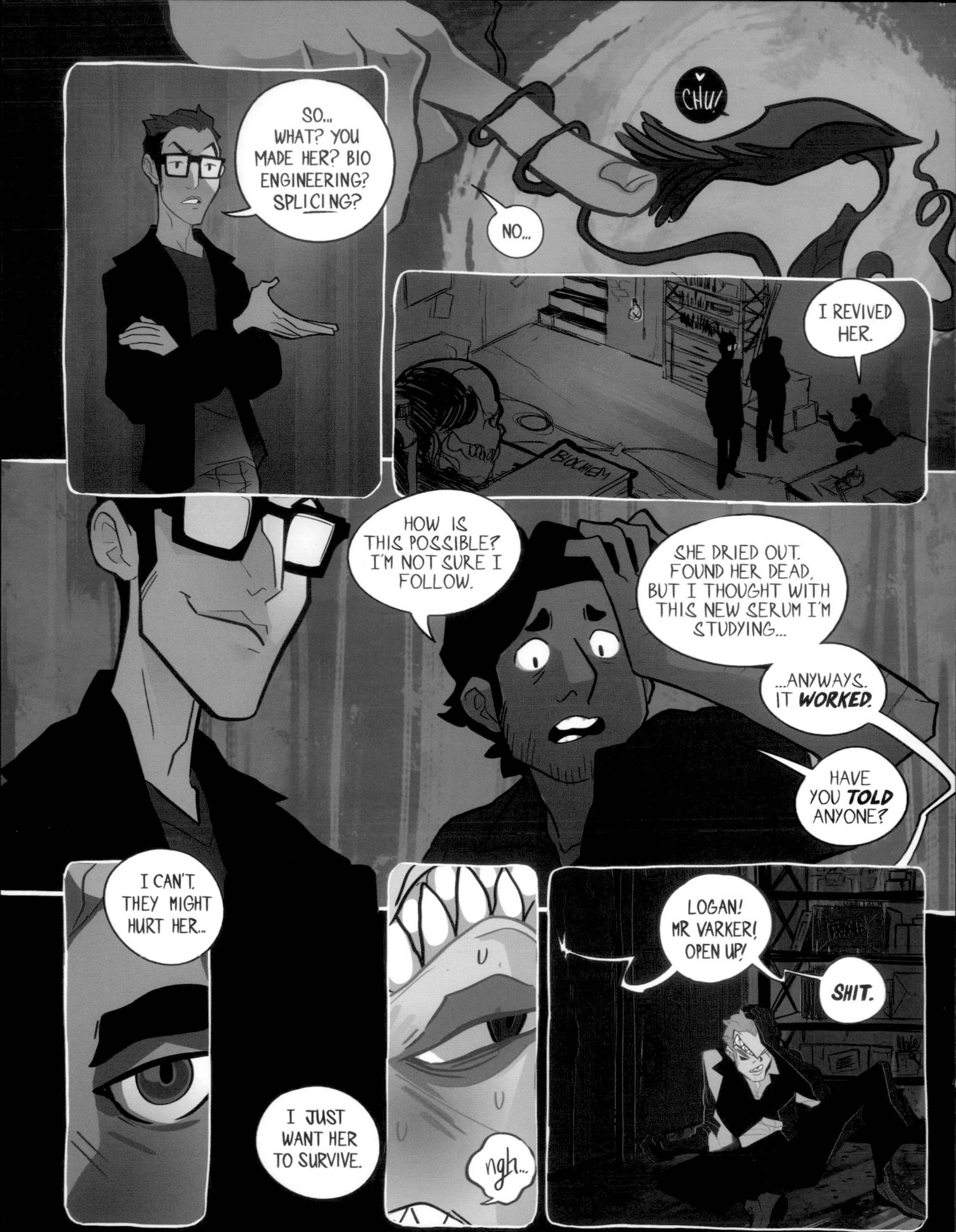
SO... WHAT? YOU MADE HER? BIO ENGINEERING? SPLICING?
CHU!
NO...
I REVIVED HER.
BIOCHEM
HOW IS THIS POSSIBLE? I'M NOT SURE I FOLLOW.
SHE DRIED OUT. FOUND HER DEAD, BUT I THOUGHT WITH THIS NEW SERUM I'M STUDYING...
...ANYWAYS. IT WORKED.
HAVE YOU TOLD ANYONE?
I CAN'T. THEY MIGHT HURT HER...
I JUST WANT HER TO SURVIVE.
ngh...
LOGAN! MR VARKER! OPEN UP!
SHIT.

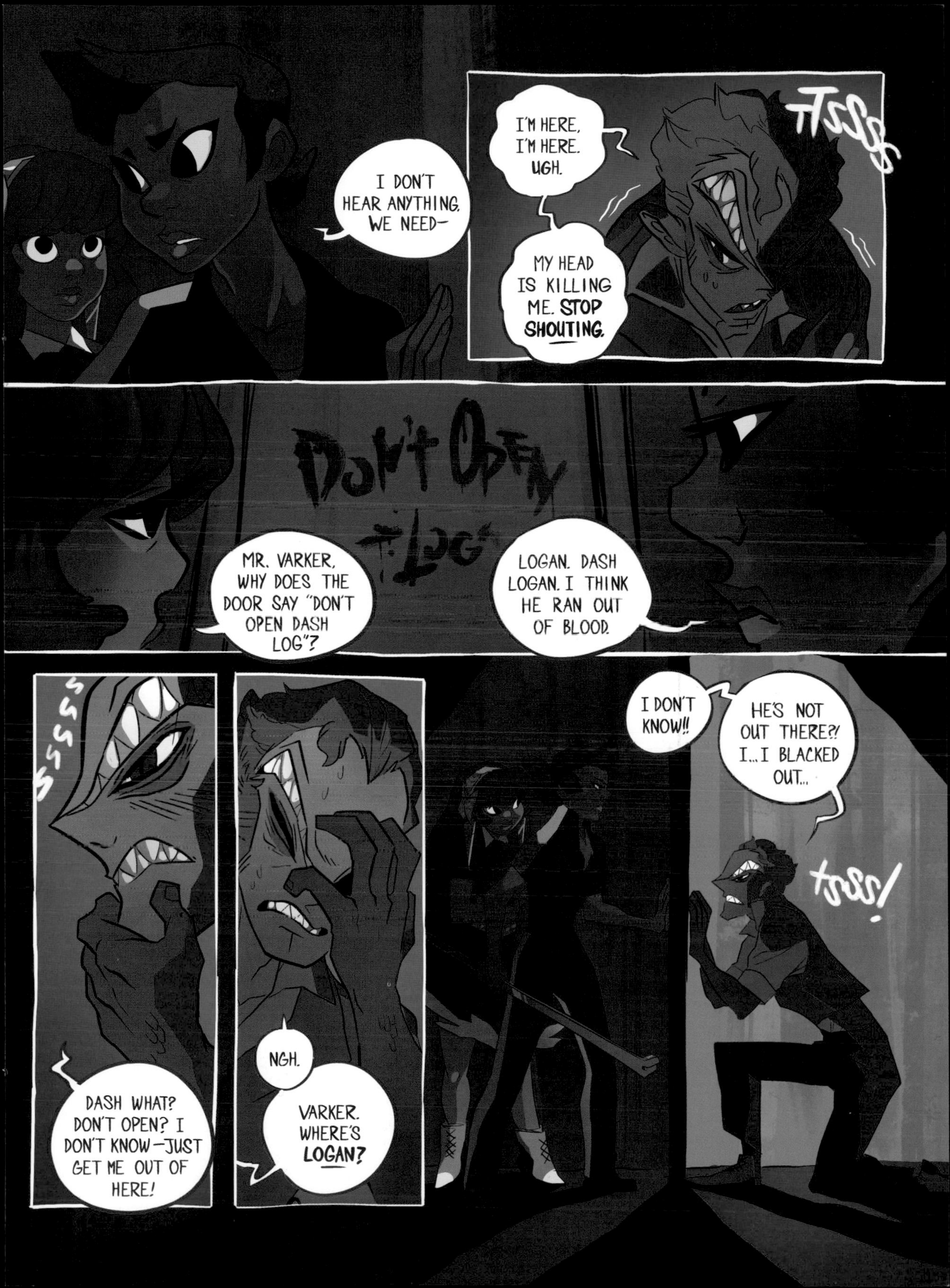

I DON'T HEAR ANYTHING. WE NEED—
I'M HERE, I'M HERE. UGH.
MY HEAD IS KILLING ME. STOP SHOUTING.
TTSSSS
DON'T OPEN T. LOG
MR. VARKER, WHY DOES THE DOOR SAY "DON'T OPEN DASH LOG"?
LOGAN. DASH LOGAN. I THINK HE RAN OUT OF BLOOD.
SSSSS
DASH WHAT? DON'T OPEN? I DON'T KNOW—JUST GET ME OUT OF HERE!
NGH.
VARKER. WHERE'S LOGAN?
I DON'T KNOW!!
HE'S NOT OUT THERE?! I... I BLACKED OUT...
TSSS!

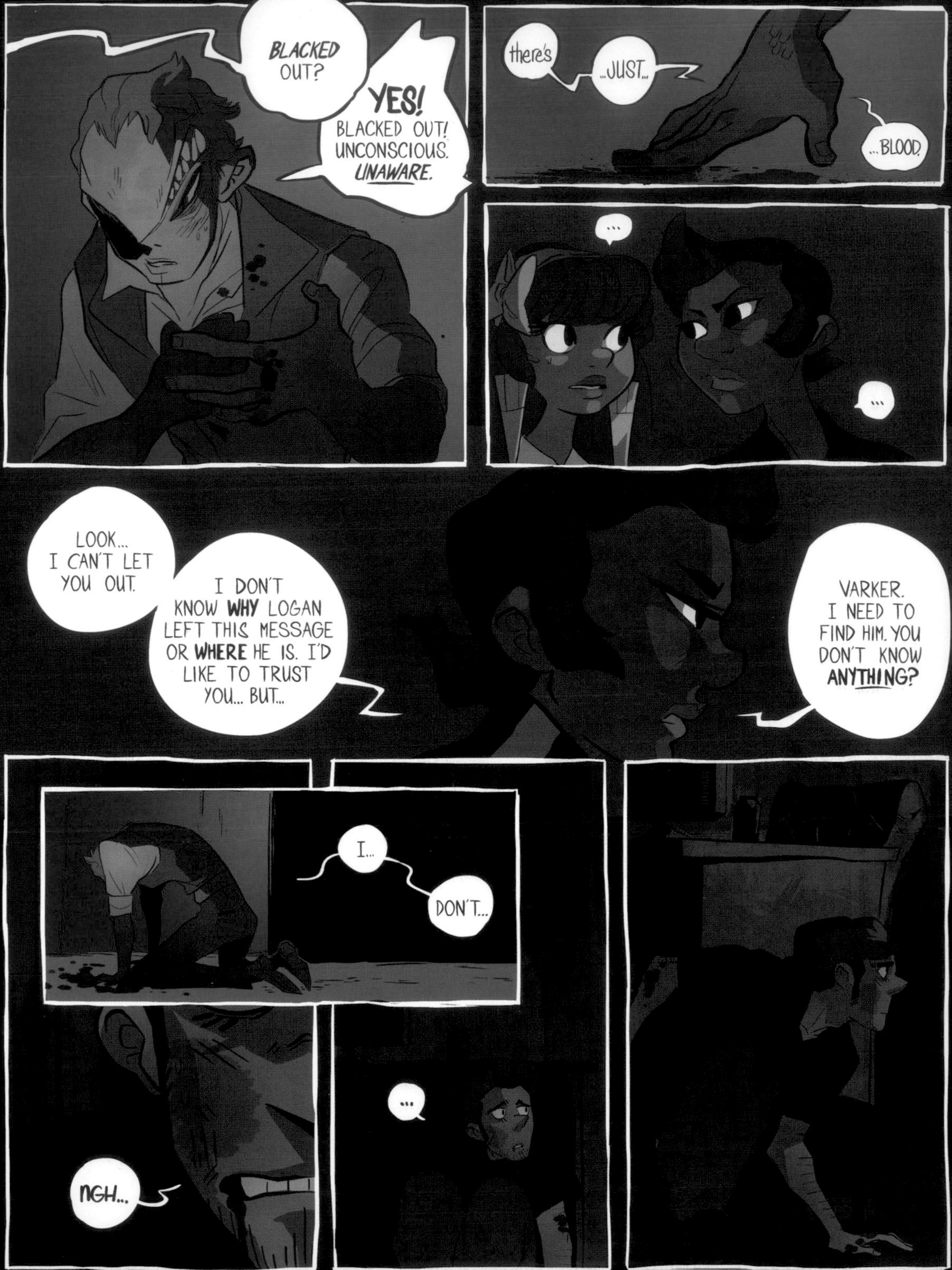
BLACKED OUT?
YES! BLACKED OUT! UNCONSCIOUS. UNAWARE.
there's
...JUST...
...BLOOD.
...
...
LOOK... I CAN'T LET YOU OUT.
I DON'T KNOW WHY LOGAN LEFT THIS MESSAGE OR WHERE HE IS. I'D LIKE TO TRUST YOU... BUT...
VARKER. I NEED TO FIND HIM. YOU DON'T KNOW ANYTHING?
I...
DON'T...
NGH...
...

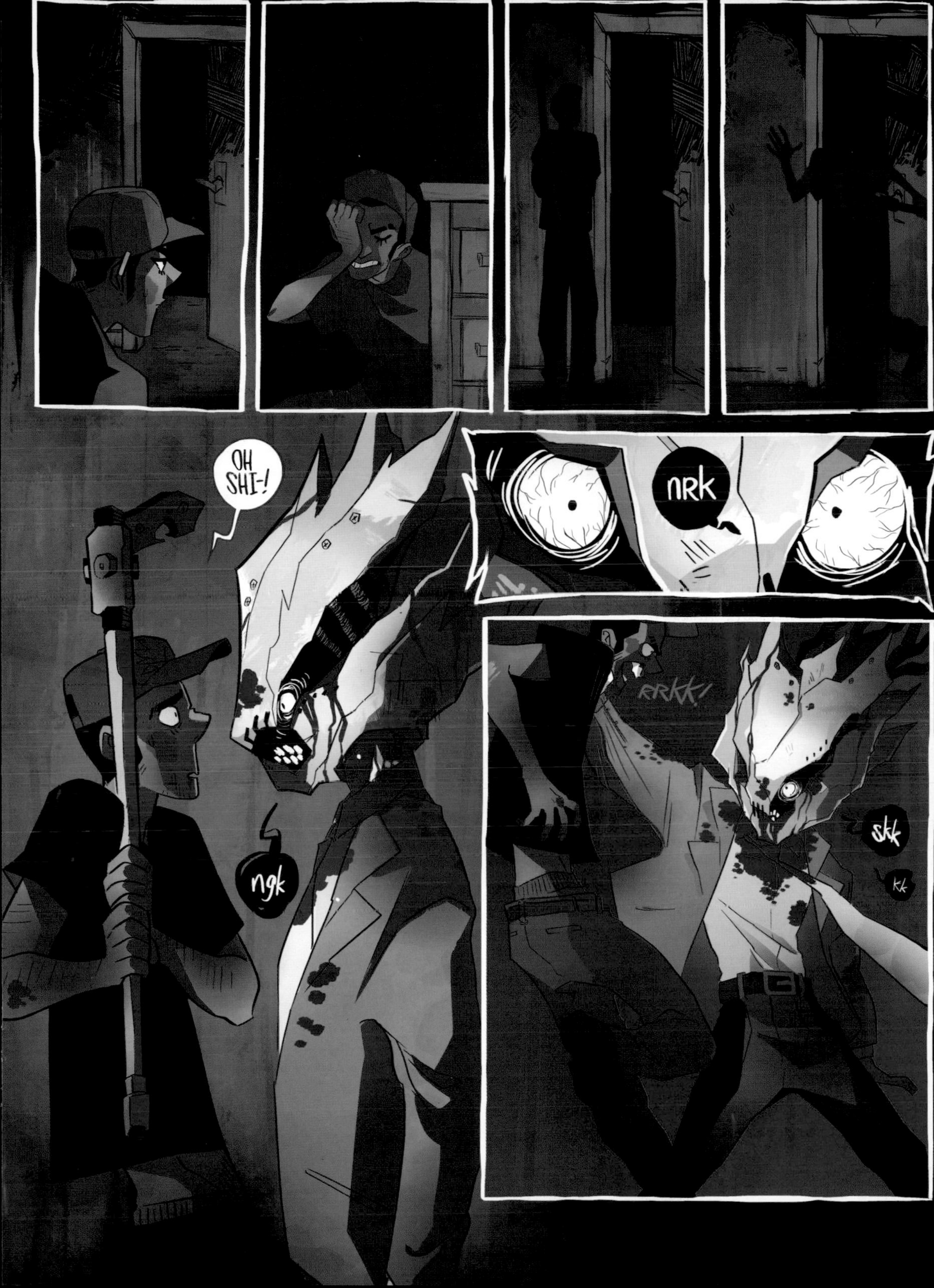

OH SHI-!
ngk
nRK
RRKK!
skk
kk

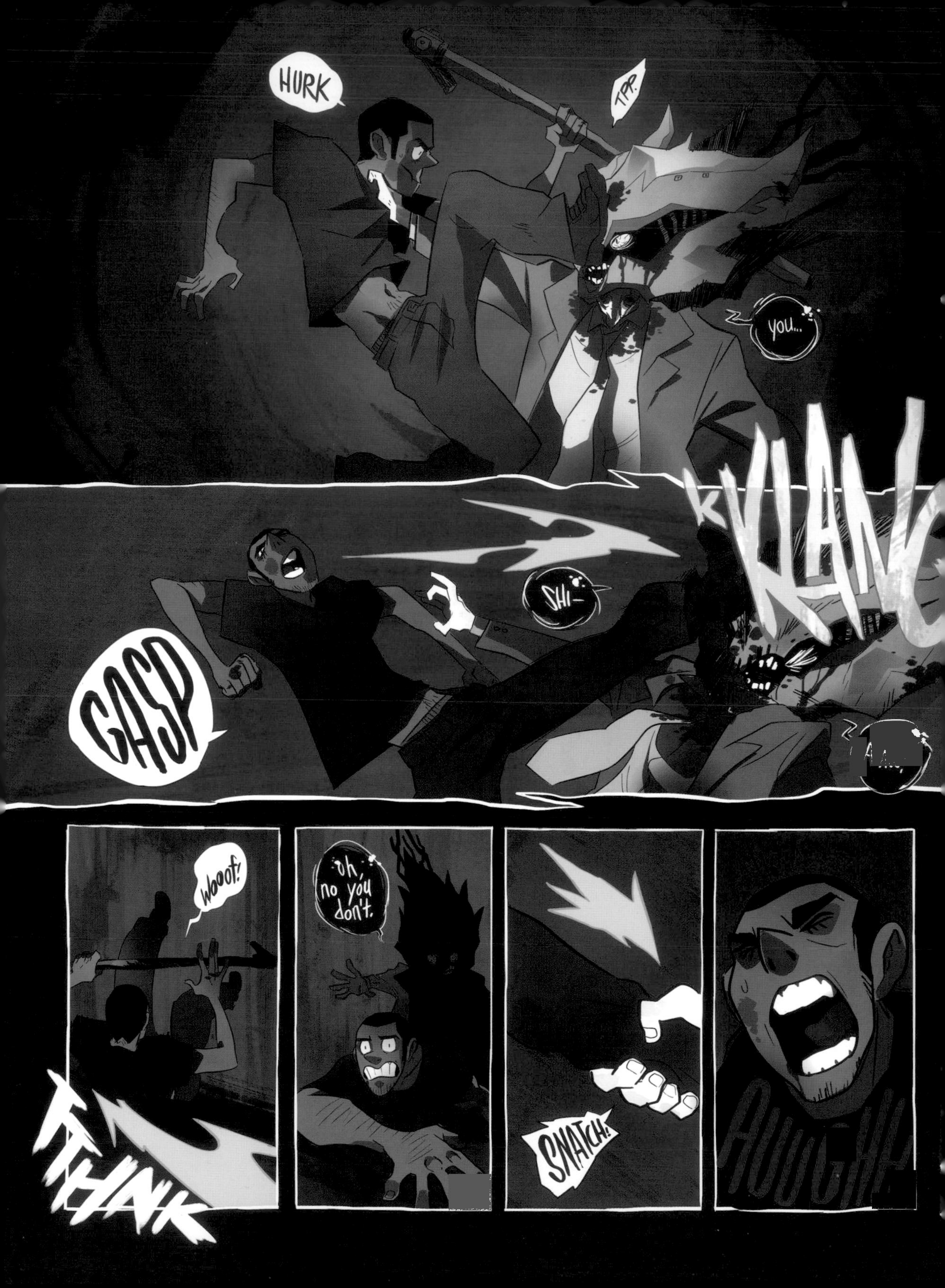
HURK
TPP.
you...
KLANG
SHI-
GASP
wooof!
oh, no you don't.
THUNK
SNATCH!

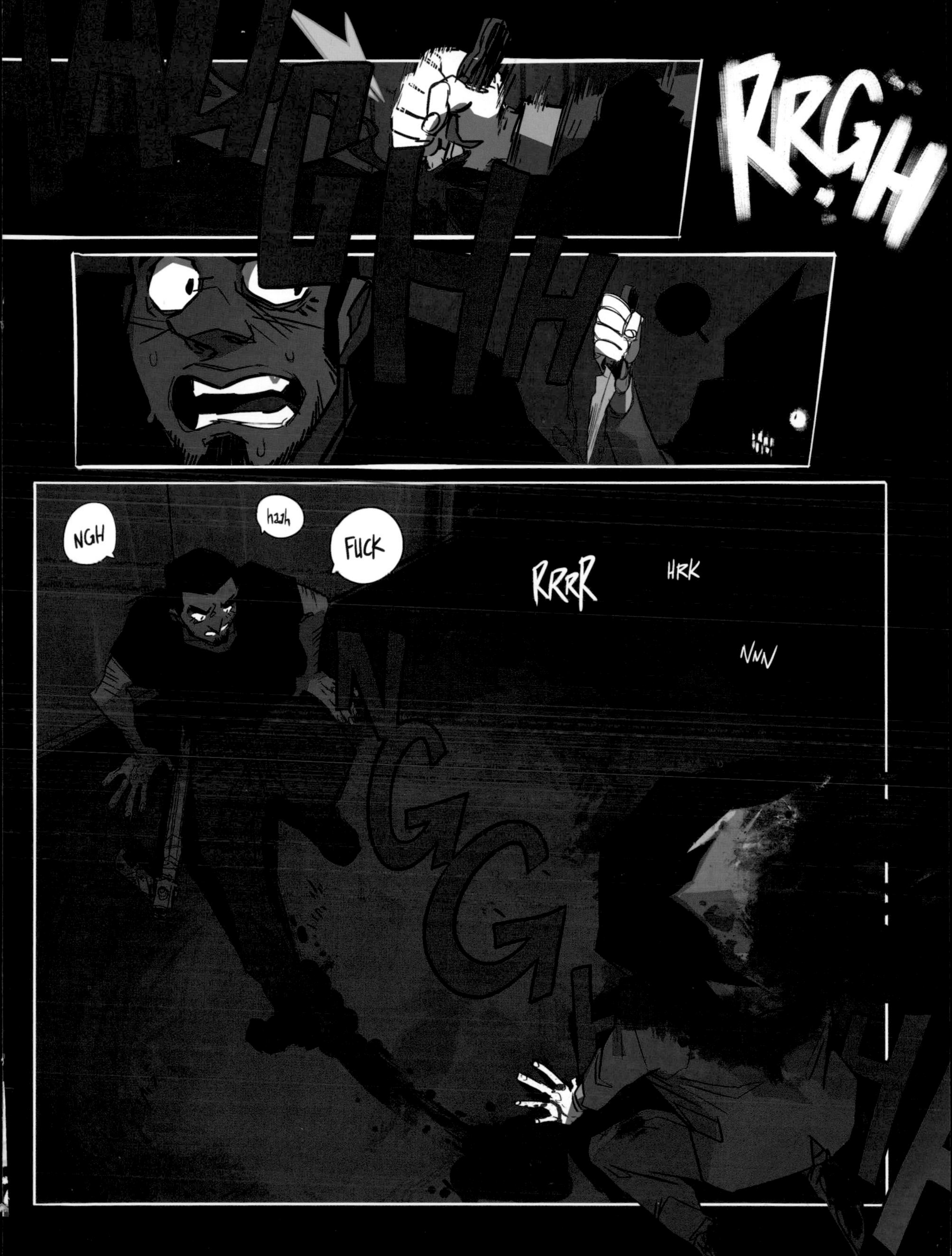
RRGH
NGH
hah
FUCK
RRRR
HRK
NNN

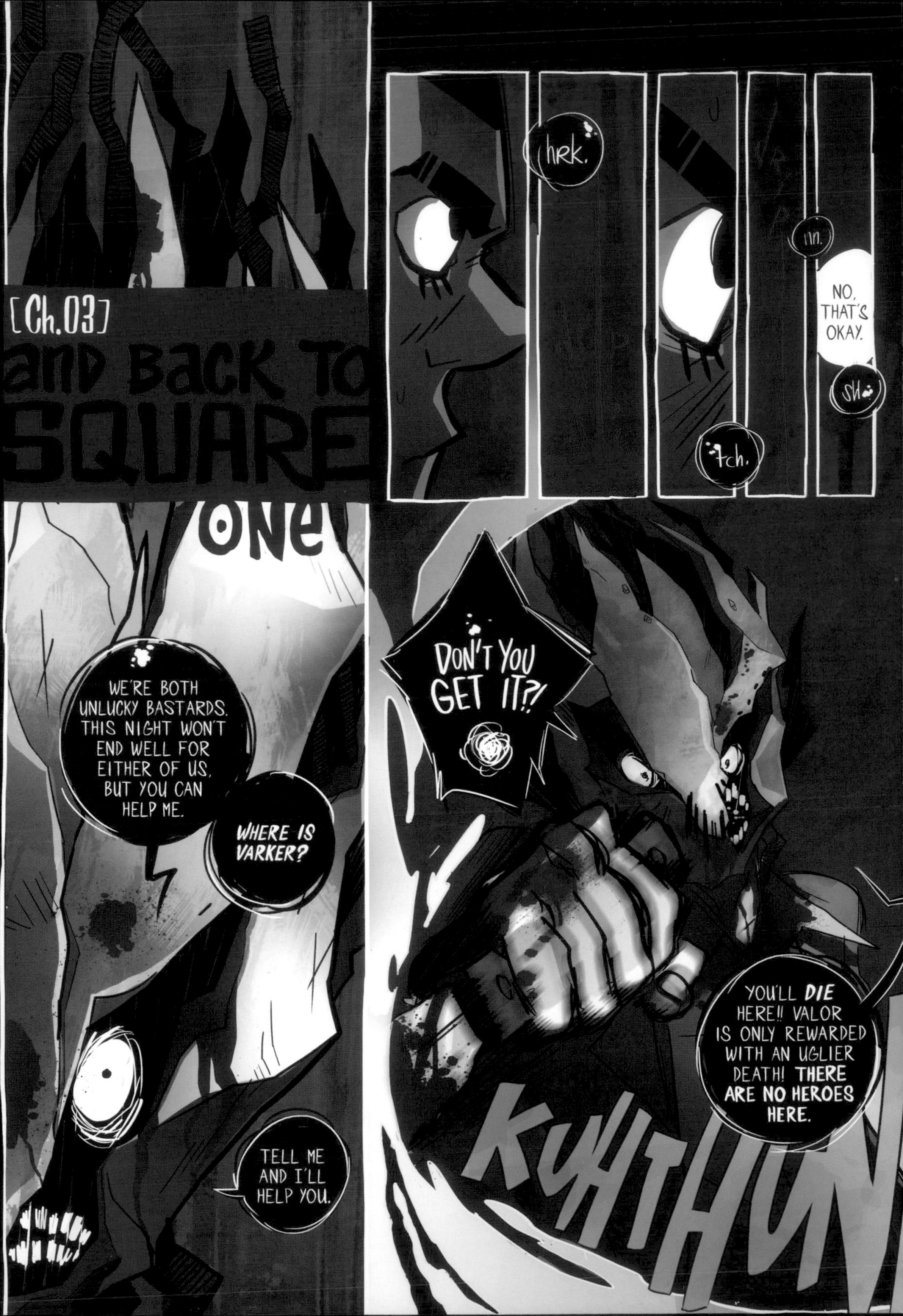
[Ch.03]
and Back to
SQUARE
ONE
hrk.
nn.
NO, THAT'S OKAY.
tch.
sh
WE'RE BOTH UNLUCKY BASTARDS. THIS NIGHT WON'T END WELL FOR EITHER OF US, BUT YOU CAN HELP ME.
WHERE IS VARKER?
TELL ME AND I'LL HELP YOU.
DON'T YOU GET IT?!
YOU'LL DIE HERE!! VALOR IS ONLY REWARDED WITH AN UGLIER DEATH! THERE ARE NO HEROES HERE.
KUHTHUN

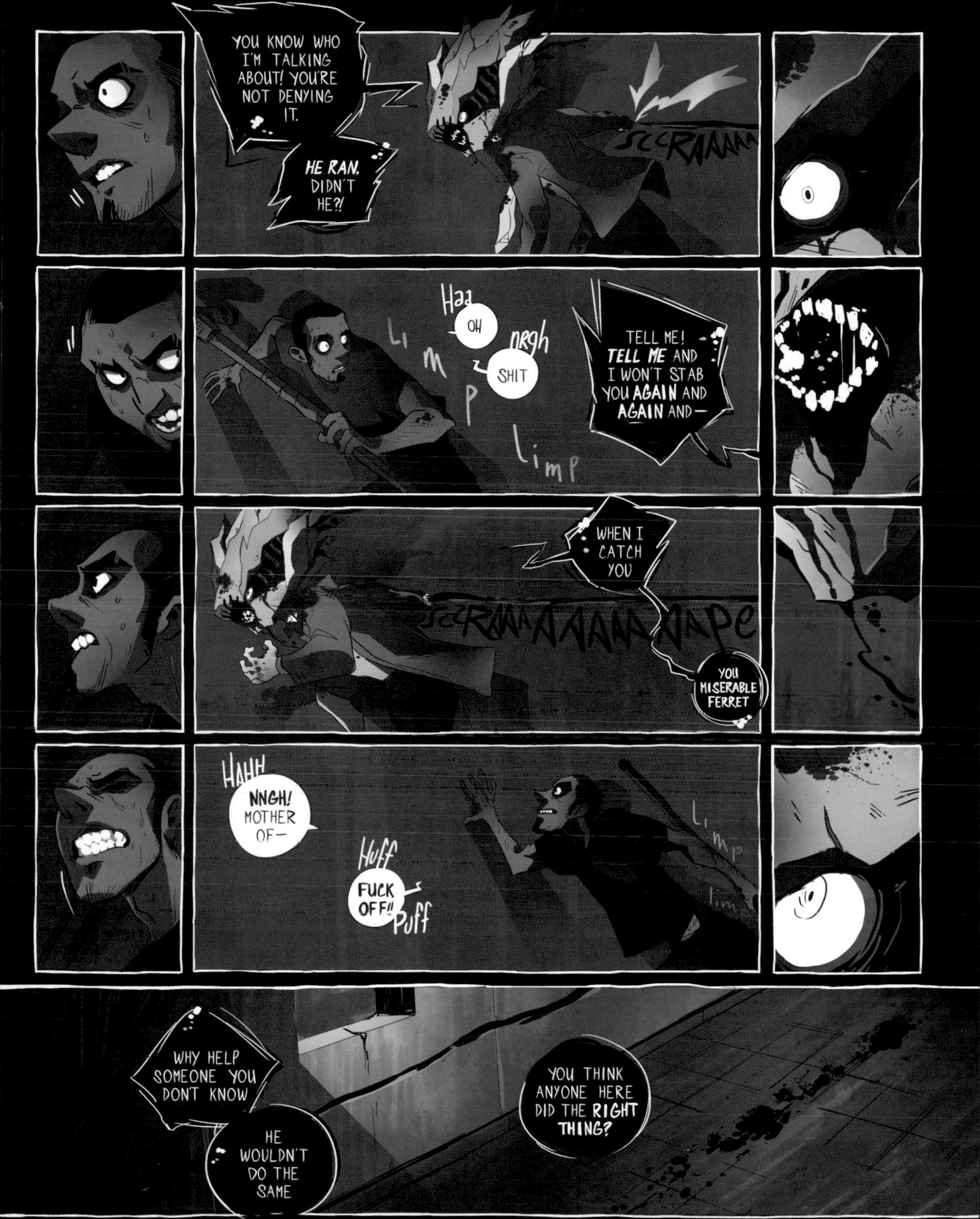

YOU KNOW WHO I'M TALKING ABOUT! YOU'RE NOT DENYING IT.
HE RAN, DIDN'T HE?!
SCCRAAAAA
Haa
OH
nrgh
SHIT
Limp
Limp
TELL ME! TELL ME AND I WON'T STAB YOU AGAIN AND AGAIN AND—
WHEN I CATCH YOU
SCCRAAAAAAAAAAAPE
YOU MISERABLE FERRET
HAHH
NNGH! MOTHER OF—
Huff
FUCK OFF!!
Puff
Limp
WHY HELP SOMEONE YOU DON'T KNOW
HE WOULDN'T DO THE SAME
YOU THINK ANYONE HERE DID THE RIGHT THING?

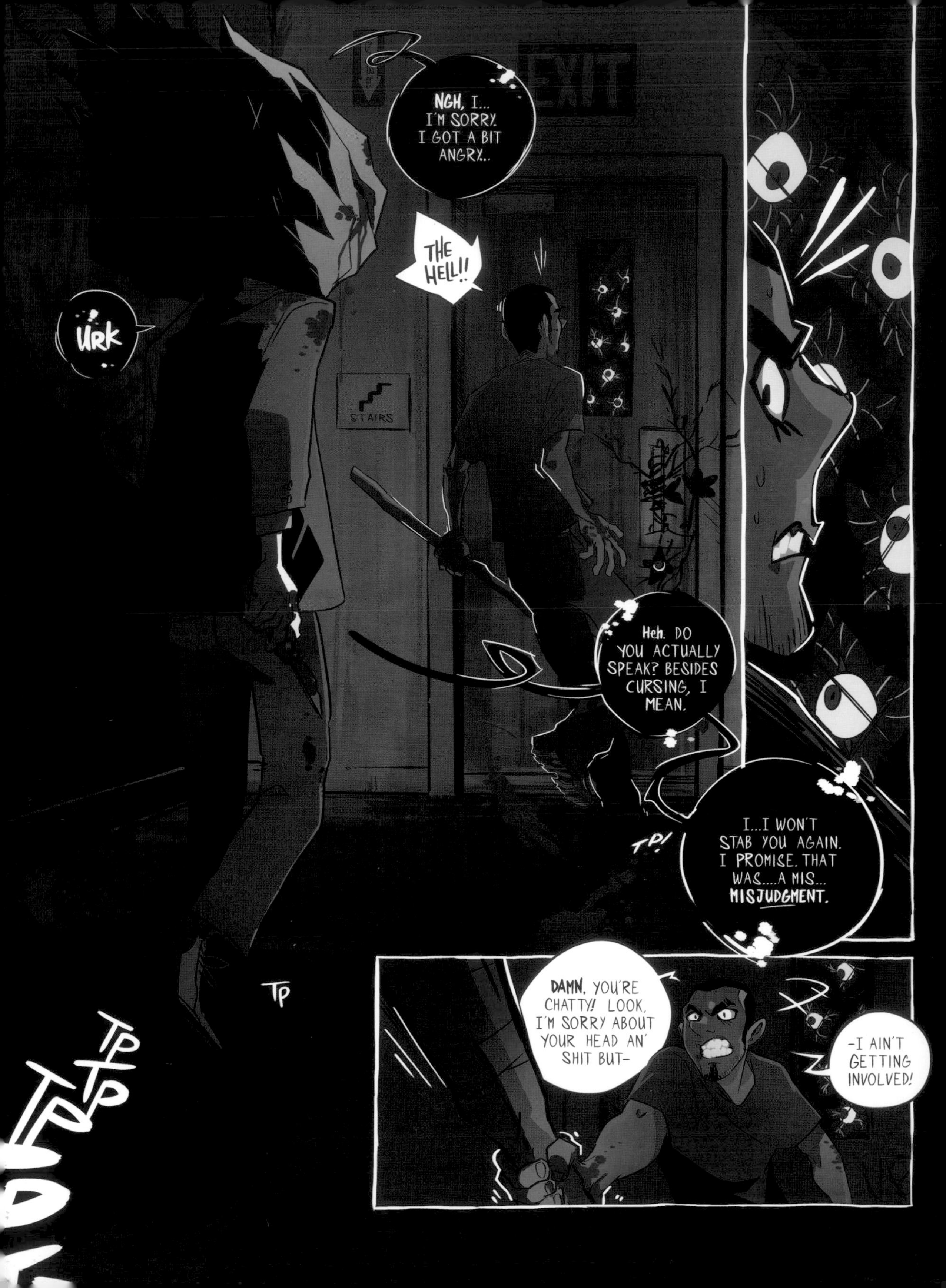

NGH, I... I'M SORRY. I GOT A BIT ANGRY...
EXIT
THE HELL!!
URK
STAIRS
Heh. DO YOU ACTUALLY SPEAK? BESIDES CURSING, I MEAN.
TP!
I...I WON'T STAB YOU AGAIN. I PROMISE. THAT WAS....A MIS... MISJUDGMENT.
TP
TP TP TP
DAMN, YOU'RE CHATTY! LOOK, I'M SORRY ABOUT YOUR HEAD AN' SHIT BUT-
-I AIN'T GETTING INVOLVED!

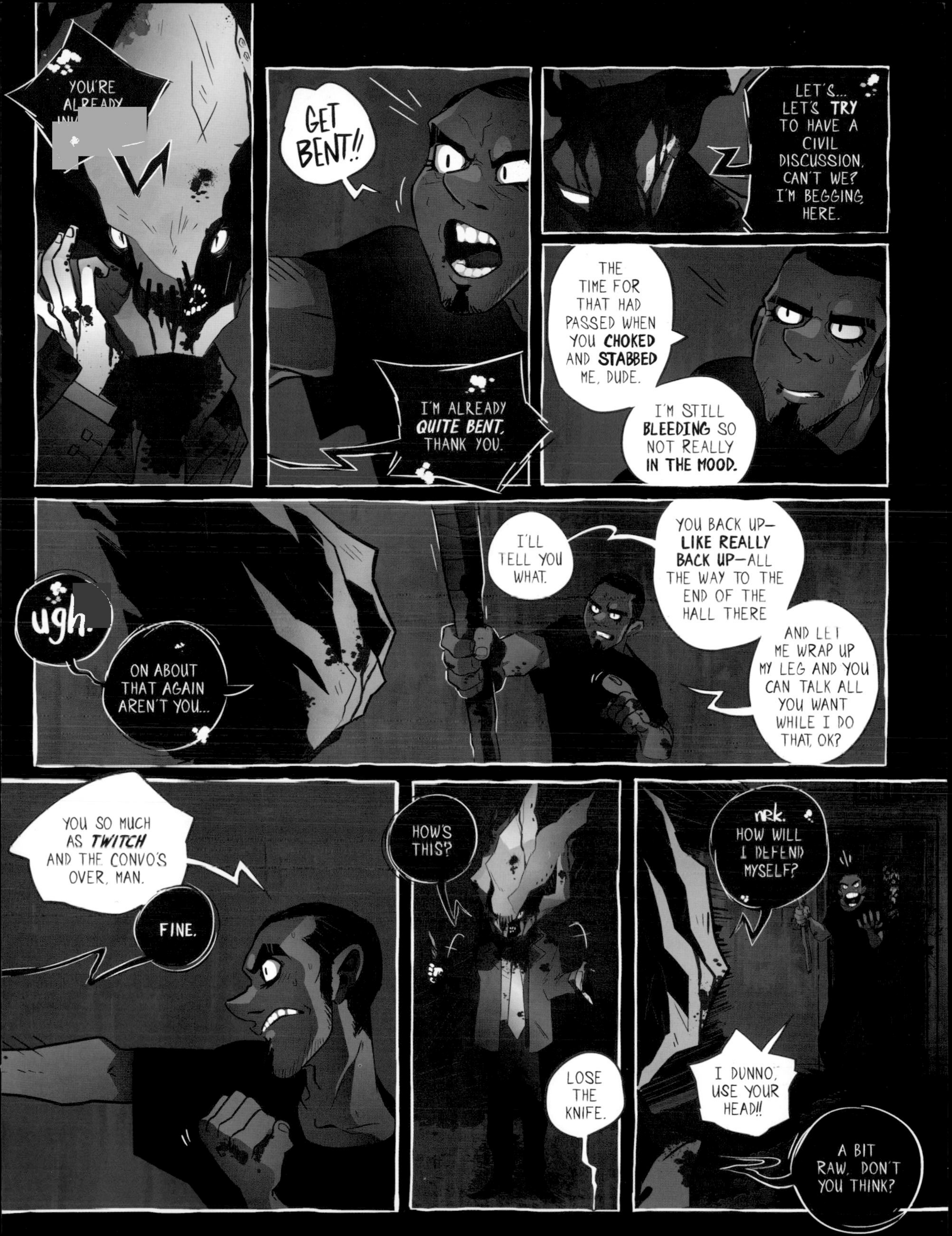
YOU'RE ALREADY
GET BENT!!
I'M ALREADY QUITE BENT, THANK YOU.
LET'S... LET'S TRY TO HAVE A CIVIL DISCUSSION, CAN'T WE? I'M BEGGING HERE.
THE TIME FOR THAT HAD PASSED WHEN YOU CHOKED AND STABBED ME, DUDE.
I'M STILL BLEEDING SO NOT REALLY IN THE MOOD.
ugh.
ON ABOUT THAT AGAIN AREN'T YOU...
I'LL TELL YOU WHAT.
YOU BACK UP—LIKE REALLY BACK UP—ALL THE WAY TO THE END OF THE HALL THERE
AND LET ME WRAP UP MY LEG AND YOU CAN TALK ALL YOU WANT WHILE I DO THAT, OK?
YOU SO MUCH AS TWITCH AND THE CONVO'S OVER, MAN.
FINE.
HOW'S THIS?
LOSE THE KNIFE.
nrk. HOW WILL I DEFEND MYSELF?
I DUNNO, USE YOUR HEAD!!
A BIT RAW, DON'T YOU THINK?

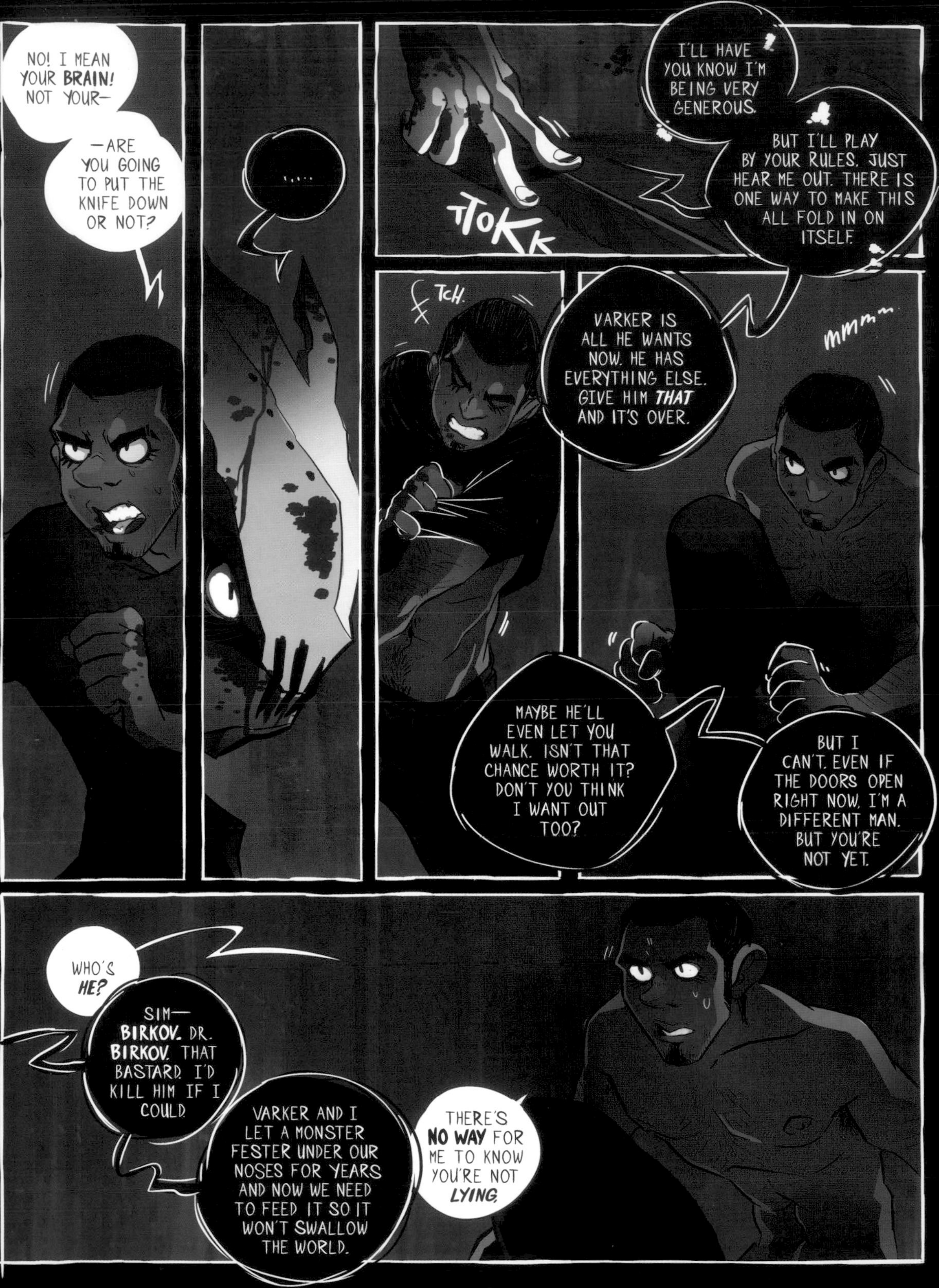

NO! I MEAN YOUR BRAIN! NOT YOUR—
—ARE YOU GOING TO PUT THE KNIFE DOWN OR NOT?
.....
I'LL HAVE YOU KNOW I'M BEING VERY GENEROUS.
BUT I'LL PLAY BY YOUR RULES. JUST HEAR ME OUT. THERE IS ONE WAY TO MAKE THIS ALL FOLD IN ON ITSELF.
TTOKK
TCH.
VARKER IS ALL HE WANTS NOW. HE HAS EVERYTHING ELSE. GIVE HIM THAT AND IT'S OVER.
MMMM
MAYBE HE'LL EVEN LET YOU WALK. ISN'T THAT CHANCE WORTH IT? DON'T YOU THINK I WANT OUT TOO?
BUT I CAN'T. EVEN IF THE DOORS OPEN RIGHT NOW, I'M A DIFFERENT MAN. BUT YOU'RE NOT YET.
WHO'S HE?
SIM— BIRKOV. DR. BIRKOV. THAT BASTARD. I'D KILL HIM IF I COULD.
VARKER AND I LET A MONSTER FESTER UNDER OUR NOSES FOR YEARS AND NOW WE NEED TO FEED IT SO IT WON'T SWALLOW THE WORLD.
THERE'S NO WAY FOR ME TO KNOW YOU'RE NOT LYING.

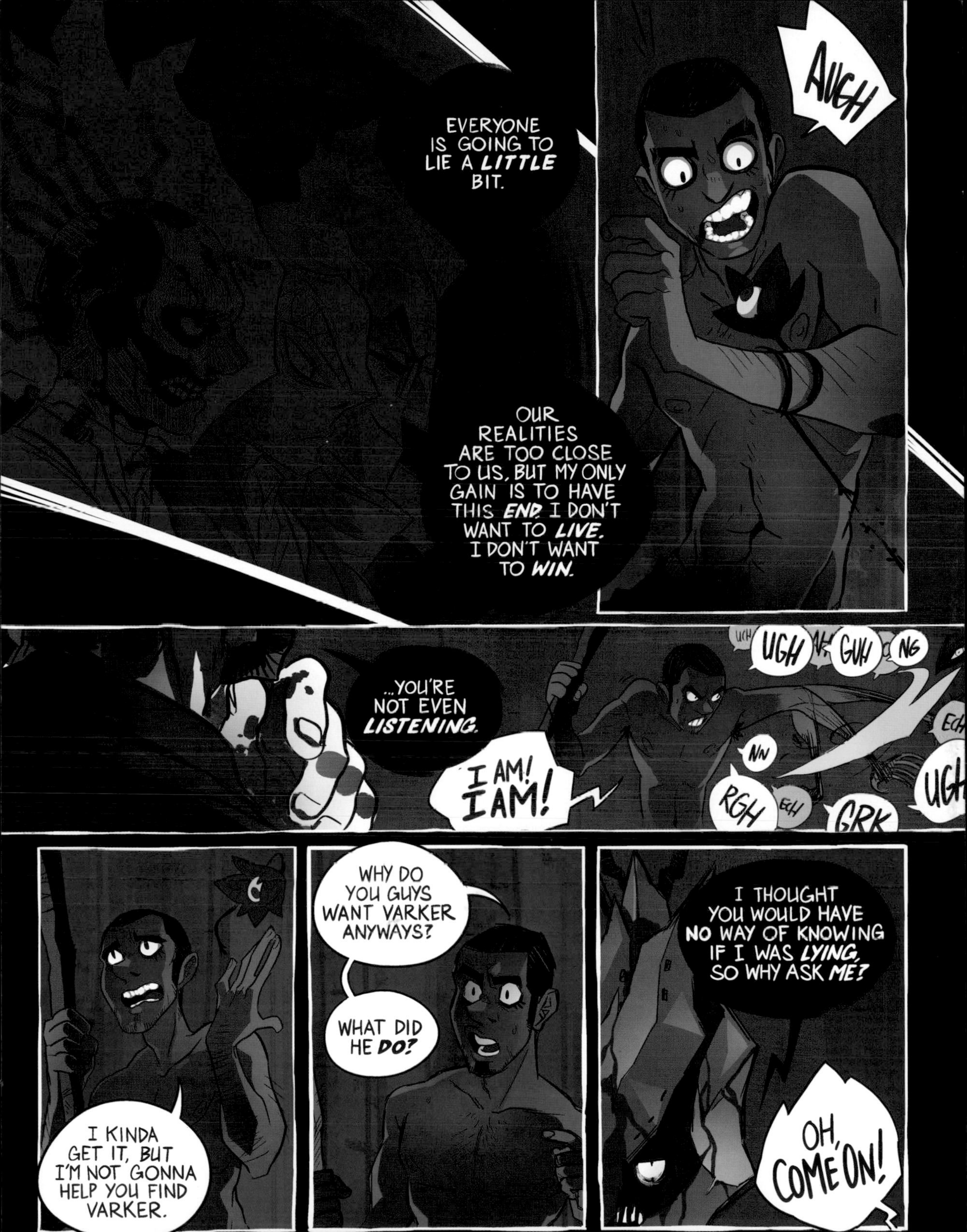

EVERYONE IS GOING TO LIE A LITTLE BIT.
AUGH
OUR REALITIES ARE TOO CLOSE TO US, BUT MY ONLY GAIN IS TO HAVE THIS END. I DON'T WANT TO LIVE. I DON'T WANT TO WIN.
...YOU'RE NOT EVEN LISTENING.
I AM! I AM!
UGH
GUH
NG
ECH
NN
RGH
ECH
GRK
UGH
I KINDA GET IT, BUT I'M NOT GONNA HELP YOU FIND VARKER.
WHY DO YOU GUYS WANT VARKER ANYWAYS?
WHAT DID HE DO?
I THOUGHT YOU WOULD HAVE NO WAY OF KNOWING IF I WAS LYING, SO WHY ASK ME?
OH, COME ON!

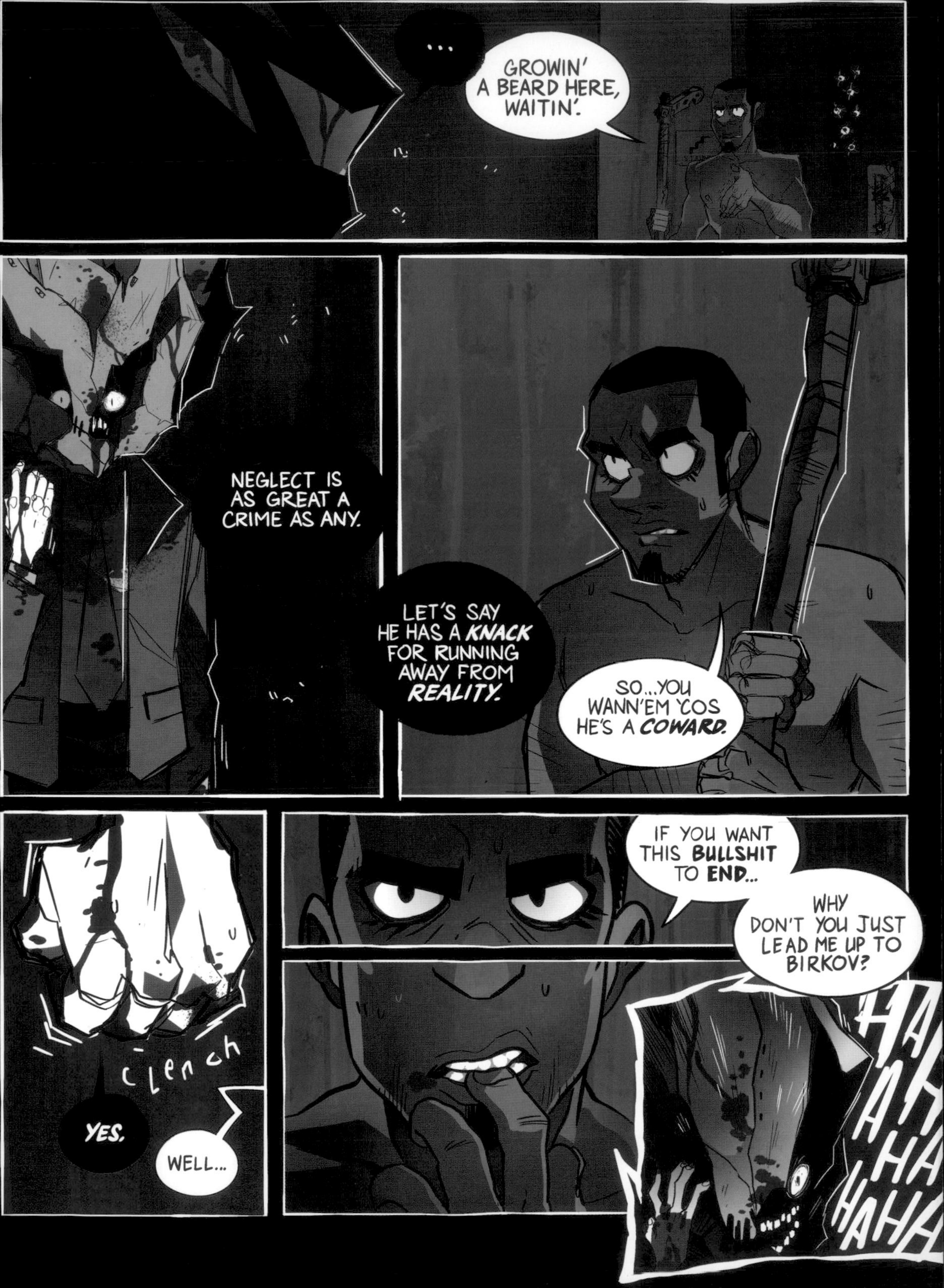
...
GROWIN' A BEARD HERE, WAITIN'.
NEGLECT IS AS GREAT A CRIME AS ANY.
LET'S SAY HE HAS A KNACK FOR RUNNING AWAY FROM REALITY.
SO...YOU WANN'EM 'COS HE'S A COWARD.
clench
YES.
WELL...
IF YOU WANT THIS BULLSHIT TO END...
WHY DON'T YOU JUST LEAD ME UP TO BIRKOV?
HAHAHAHAHAHAHA

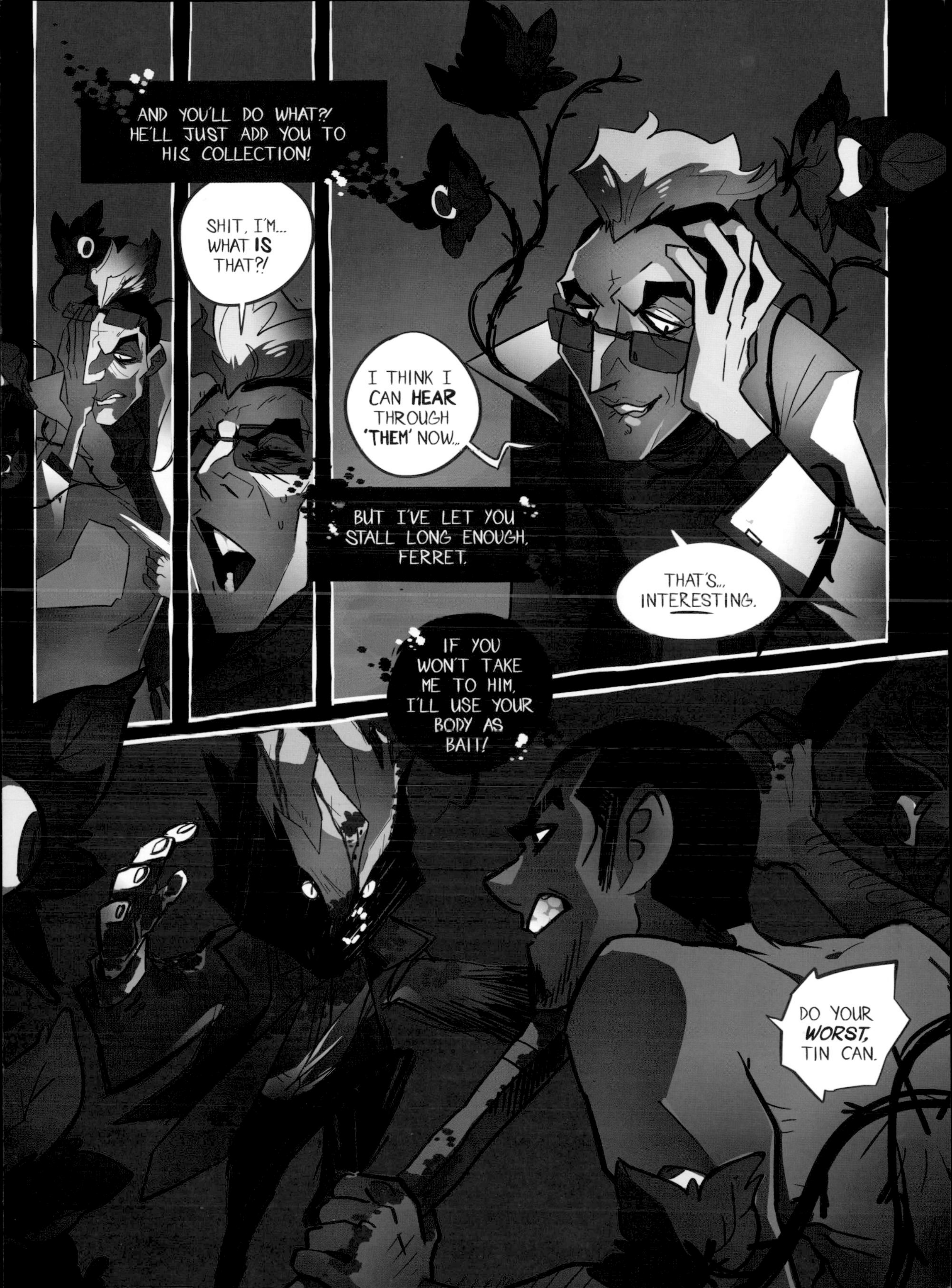
AND YOU'LL DO WHAT?! HE'LL JUST ADD YOU TO HIS COLLECTION!
SHIT, I'M... WHAT IS THAT?!
I THINK I CAN HEAR THROUGH 'THEM' NOW...
BUT I'VE LET YOU STALL LONG ENOUGH, FERRET.
THAT'S... INTERESTING.
IF YOU WON'T TAKE ME TO HIM, I'LL USE YOUR BODY AS BAIT!
DO YOUR WORST, TIN CAN.

GREAT.

THEY LEFT ME, ALONE WITH MY THOUGHTS.

tto!

COULDN'T ASK FOR A BETTER SCENARIO, REALLY.

I *LOOOVE* TO STEW IN GUILT AND REGRET.

SSSS!

Uck! MY SKIN FEELS AWFUL!

IT'S LIKE BEING TOUCHED BY A WARM SCALY SNA—huh?

HISS

klk:

tssy?

klk

HELLO.

I'VE SEEN *YOU* BEFORE, UNDER SIMON'S SCARF...

BIRKOV! THAT YOU? CAN YOU SEE ME?

klk

SSSt!

tt#JSSSJJSSSJSSSS

OKAY, WHAT IF...

I SAID YOU WERE A HACK SCIENTIST THAT IS **UNINSPIRED, SLOPPY,** AND HAD THE **WORST** GRADES OUT OF **ALL** OF US?!

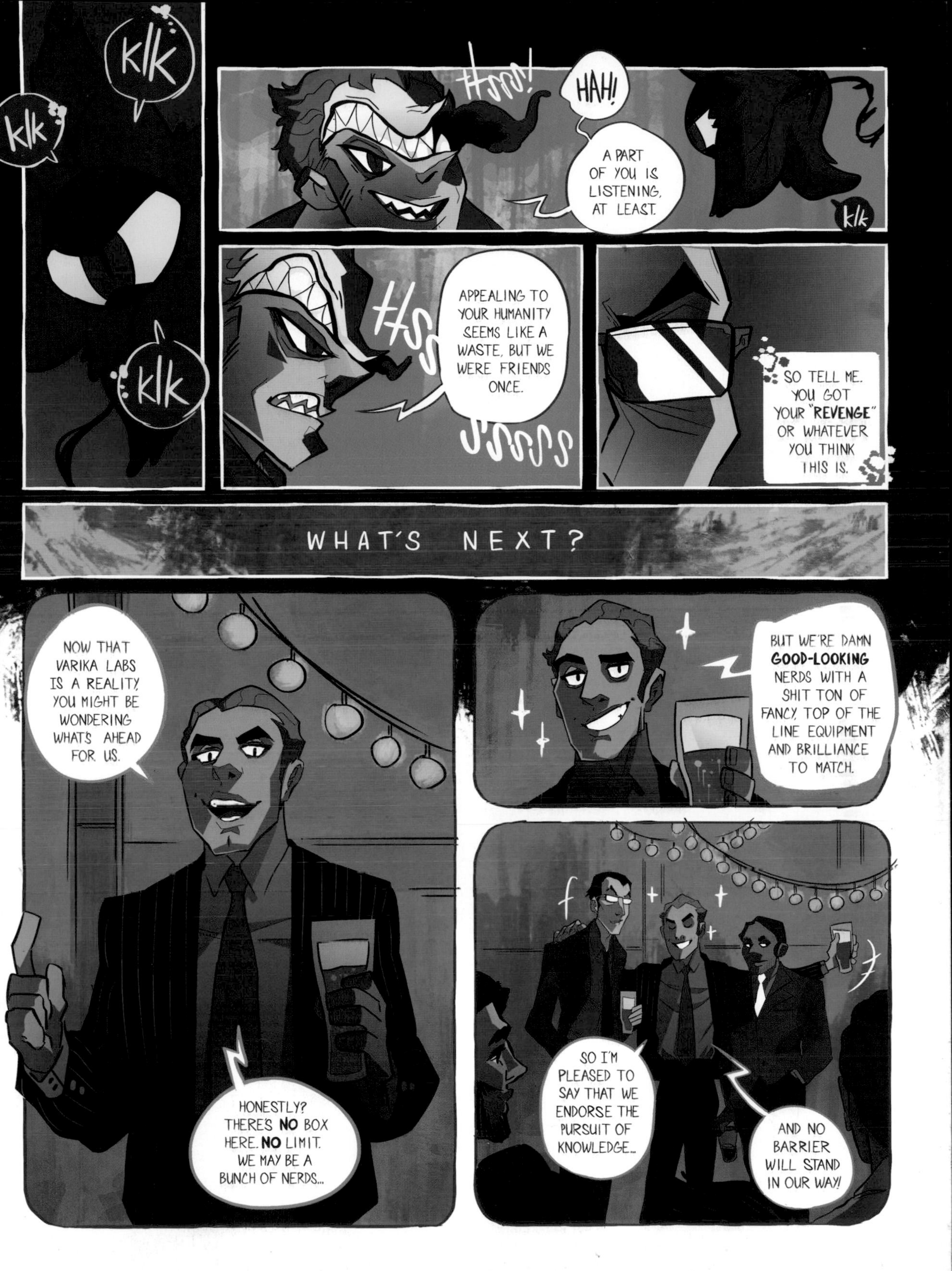
klk
klk
HAH!
A PART OF YOU IS LISTENING, AT LEAST.
klk
klk
APPEALING TO YOUR HUMANITY SEEMS LIKE A WASTE, BUT WE WERE FRIENDS ONCE.
SO TELL ME. YOU GOT YOUR "REVENGE" OR WHATEVER YOU THINK THIS IS.
WHAT'S NEXT?
NOW THAT VARIKA LABS IS A REALITY, YOU MIGHT BE WONDERING WHAT'S AHEAD FOR US.
HONESTLY? THERE'S NO BOX HERE. NO LIMIT. WE MAY BE A BUNCH OF NERDS...
BUT WE'RE DAMN GOOD-LOOKING NERDS WITH A SHIT TON OF FANCY, TOP OF THE LINE EQUIPMENT AND BRILLIANCE TO MATCH.
SO I'M PLEASED TO SAY THAT WE ENDORSE THE PURSUIT OF KNOWLEDGE...
AND NO BARRIER WILL STAND IN OUR WAY!

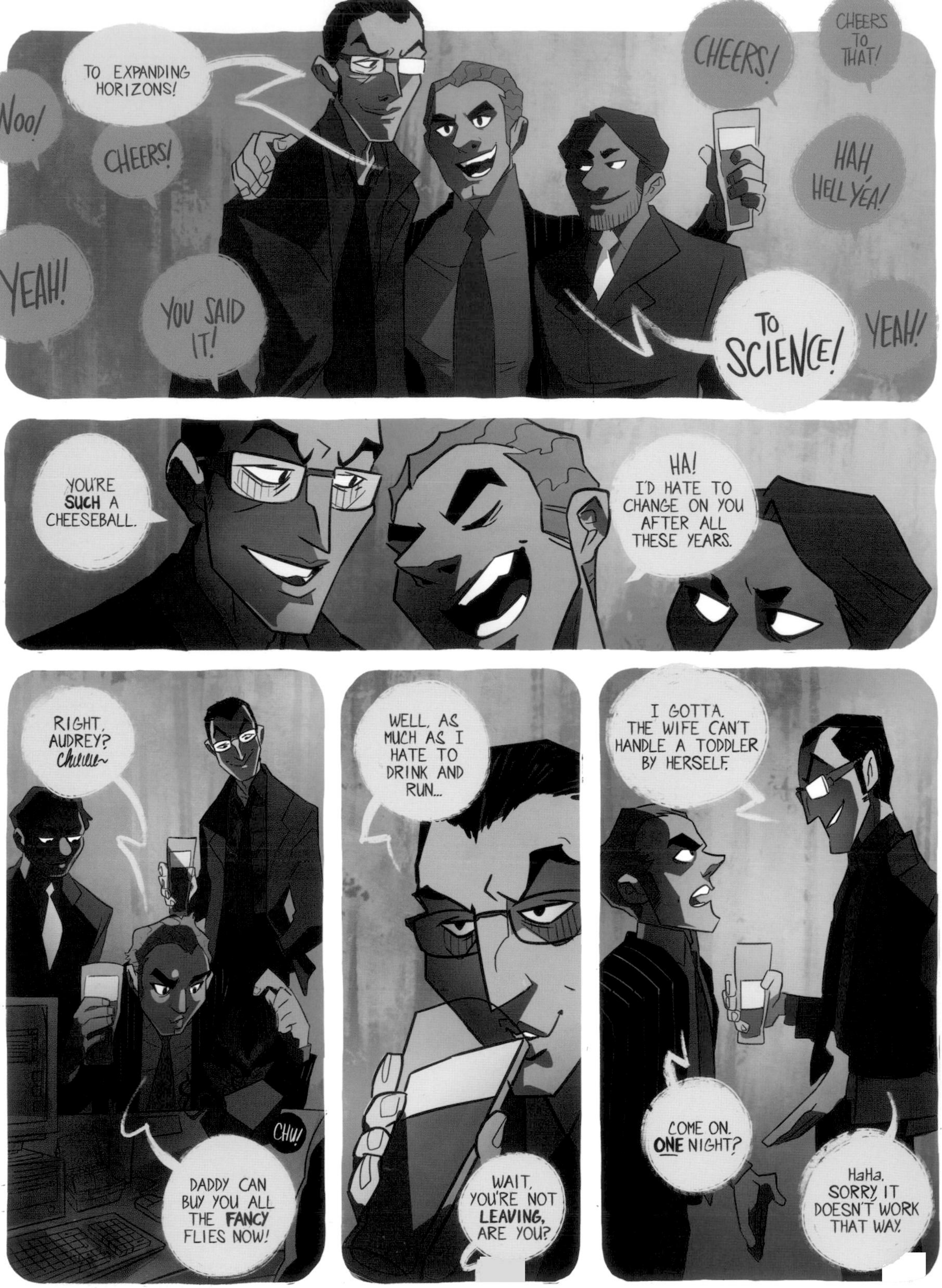

TO EXPANDING HORIZONS!
Woo!
CHEERS!
YEAH!
YOU SAID IT!
CHEERS!
CHEERS TO THAT!
HAH, HELL YEA!
TO SCIENCE!
YEAH!
YOU'RE SUCH A CHEESEBALL.
HA! I'D HATE TO CHANGE ON YOU AFTER ALL THESE YEARS.
RIGHT, AUDREY? Chuuu~
CHU!
DADDY CAN BUY YOU ALL THE FANCY FLIES NOW!
WELL, AS MUCH AS I HATE TO DRINK AND RUN...
WAIT, YOU'RE NOT LEAVING, ARE YOU?
I GOTTA. THE WIFE CAN'T HANDLE A TODDLER BY HERSELF.
COME ON. ONE NIGHT?
HaHa. SORRY, IT DOESN'T WORK THAT WAY.

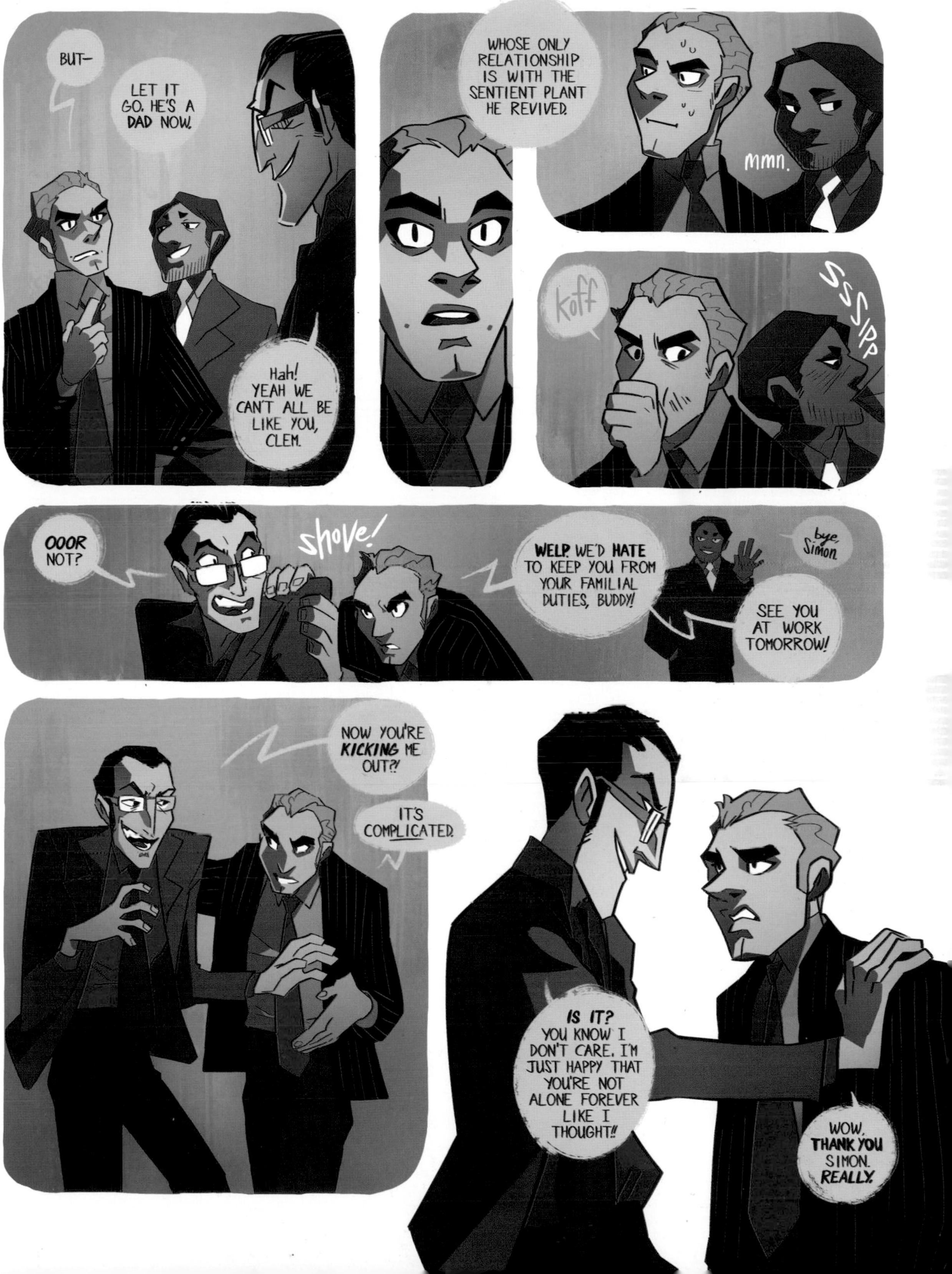

BUT-
LET IT GO. HE'S A DAD NOW.
Hah! YEAH WE CAN'T ALL BE LIKE YOU, CLEM.
WHOSE ONLY RELATIONSHIP IS WITH THE SENTIENT PLANT HE REVIVED.
mmn.
koff
SSSIPP
OOOR NOT?
shove!
WELP. WE'D HATE TO KEEP YOU FROM YOUR FAMILIAL DUTIES, BUDDY!
bye, Simon
SEE YOU AT WORK TOMORROW!
NOW YOU'RE KICKING ME OUT?!
IT'S COMPLICATED.
IS IT? YOU KNOW I DON'T CARE. I'M JUST HAPPY THAT YOU'RE NOT ALONE FOREVER LIKE I THOUGHT!!
WOW. THANK YOU SIMON. REALLY.

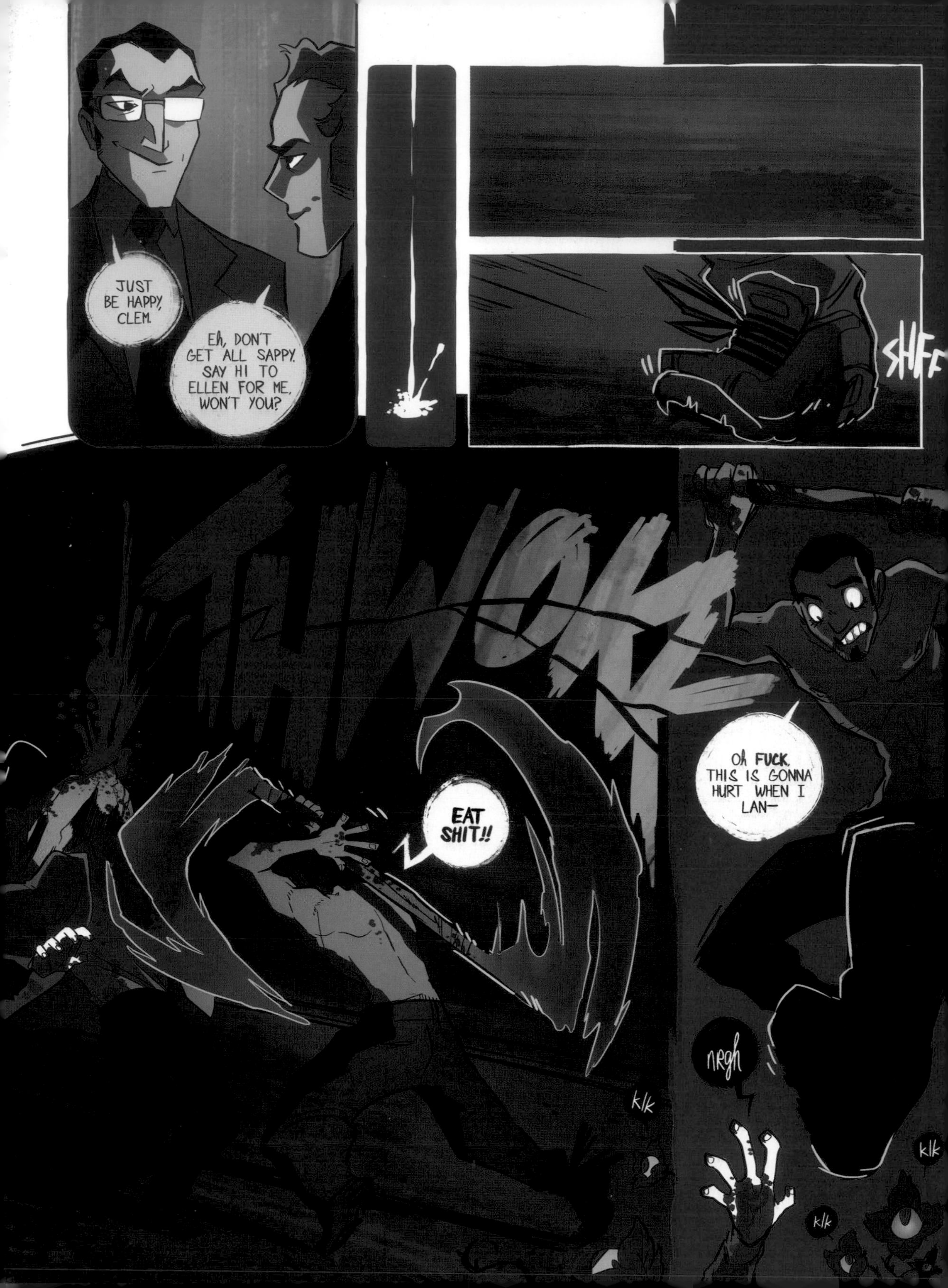
JUST BE HAPPY, CLEM.
Eh, DON'T GET ALL SAPPY. SAY HI TO ELLEN FOR ME, WON'T YOU?
SHFF
THWOK
EAT SHIT!!
Oh FUCK, THIS IS GONNA HURT WHEN I LAN—
nrgh
klk
klk
klk

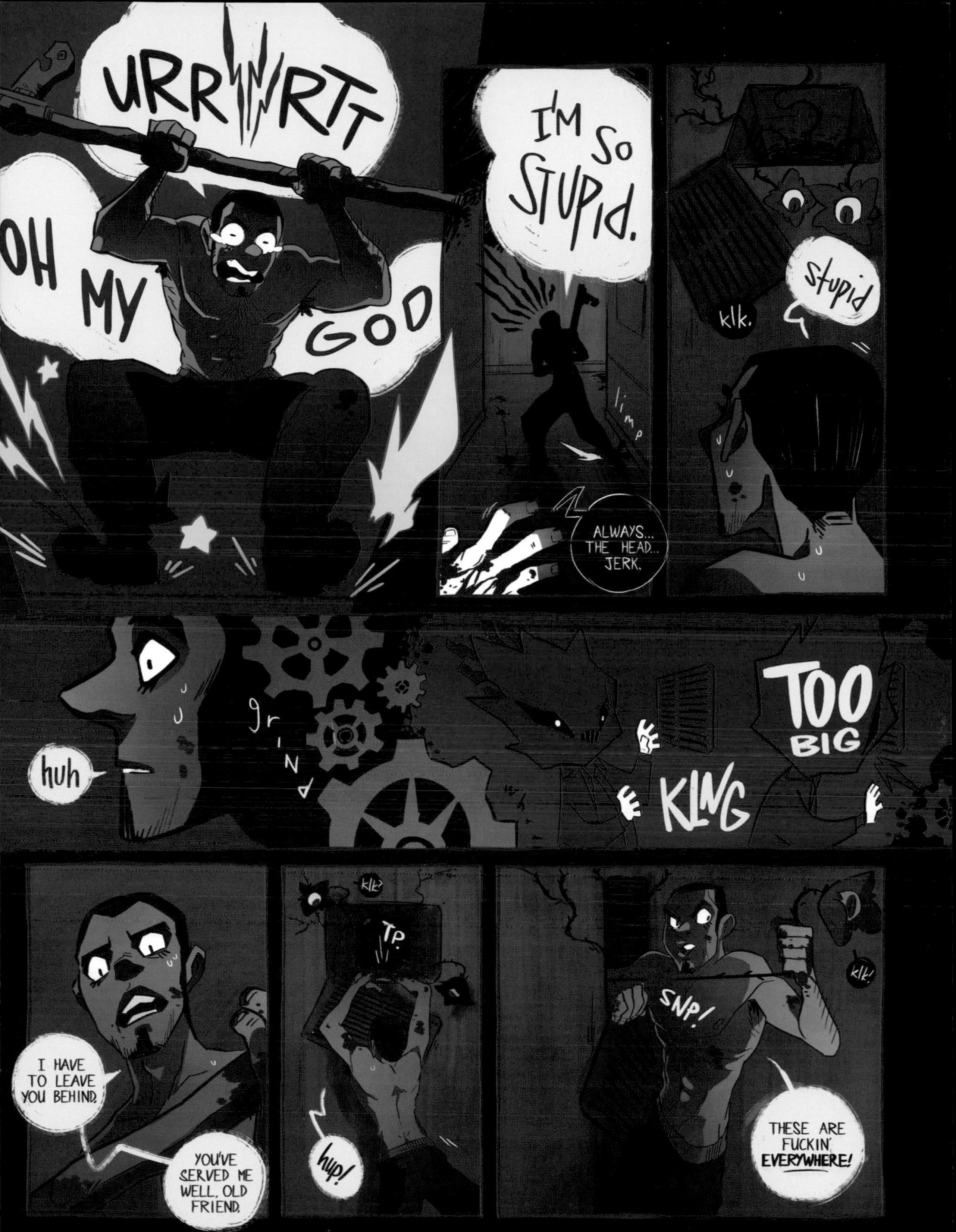
URRRRRTT
OH MY GOD
I'M SO STUPID.
limp
ALWAYS... THE HEAD... JERK.
klk.
stupid
huh
grind
TOO BIG
KLNG
I HAVE TO LEAVE YOU BEHIND.
YOU'VE SERVED ME WELL, OLD FRIEND.
klk?
TP.
hup!
klk!
SNP!
THESE ARE FUCKIN' EVERYWHERE!

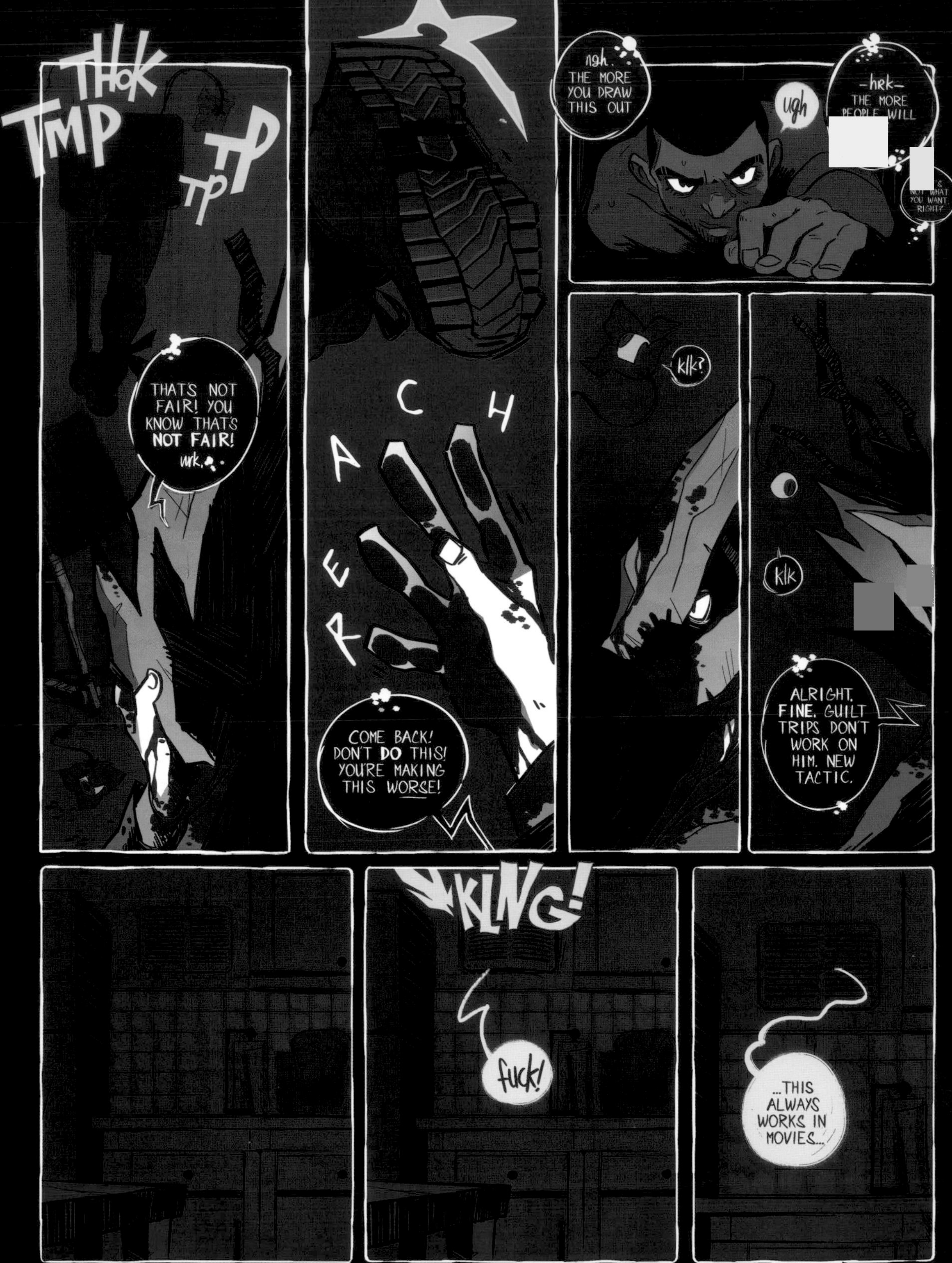
THOK
TMP
TP
TP
THAT'S NOT FAIR! YOU KNOW THAT'S **NOT FAIR!**
urk.
ACH
COME BACK! DON'T **DO** THIS! YOU'RE MAKING THIS WORSE!
ngh. THE MORE YOU DRAW THIS OUT
ugh
-hrk- THE MORE PEOPLE WILL
NOT WHAT YOU WANT, RIGHT?
klk?
klk
ALRIGHT, **FINE.** GUILT TRIPS DON'T WORK ON HIM. NEW TACTIC.
KLING!
fuck!
...THIS ALWAYS WORKS IN MOVIES...

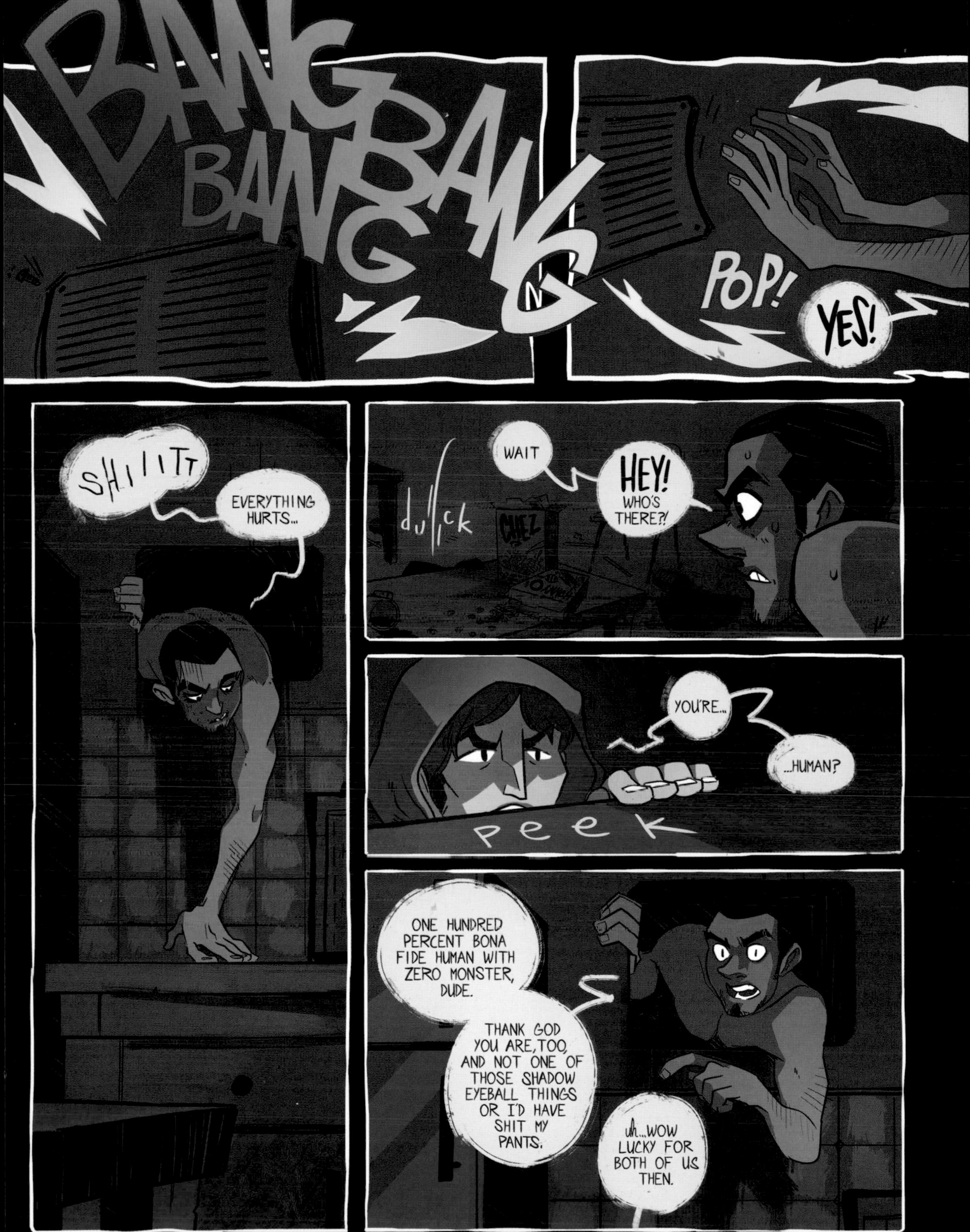
BANG BANG BANG BANG
POP!
YES!
SHIIITT
EVERYTHING HURTS...
WAIT
HEY! WHO'S THERE?!
YOU'RE...
...HUMAN?
peek
ONE HUNDRED PERCENT BONA FIDE HUMAN WITH ZERO MONSTER, DUDE.
THANK GOD YOU ARE, TOO, AND NOT ONE OF THOSE SHADOW EYEBALL THINGS OR I'D HAVE SHIT MY PANTS.
uh...WOW LUCKY FOR BOTH OF US THEN.

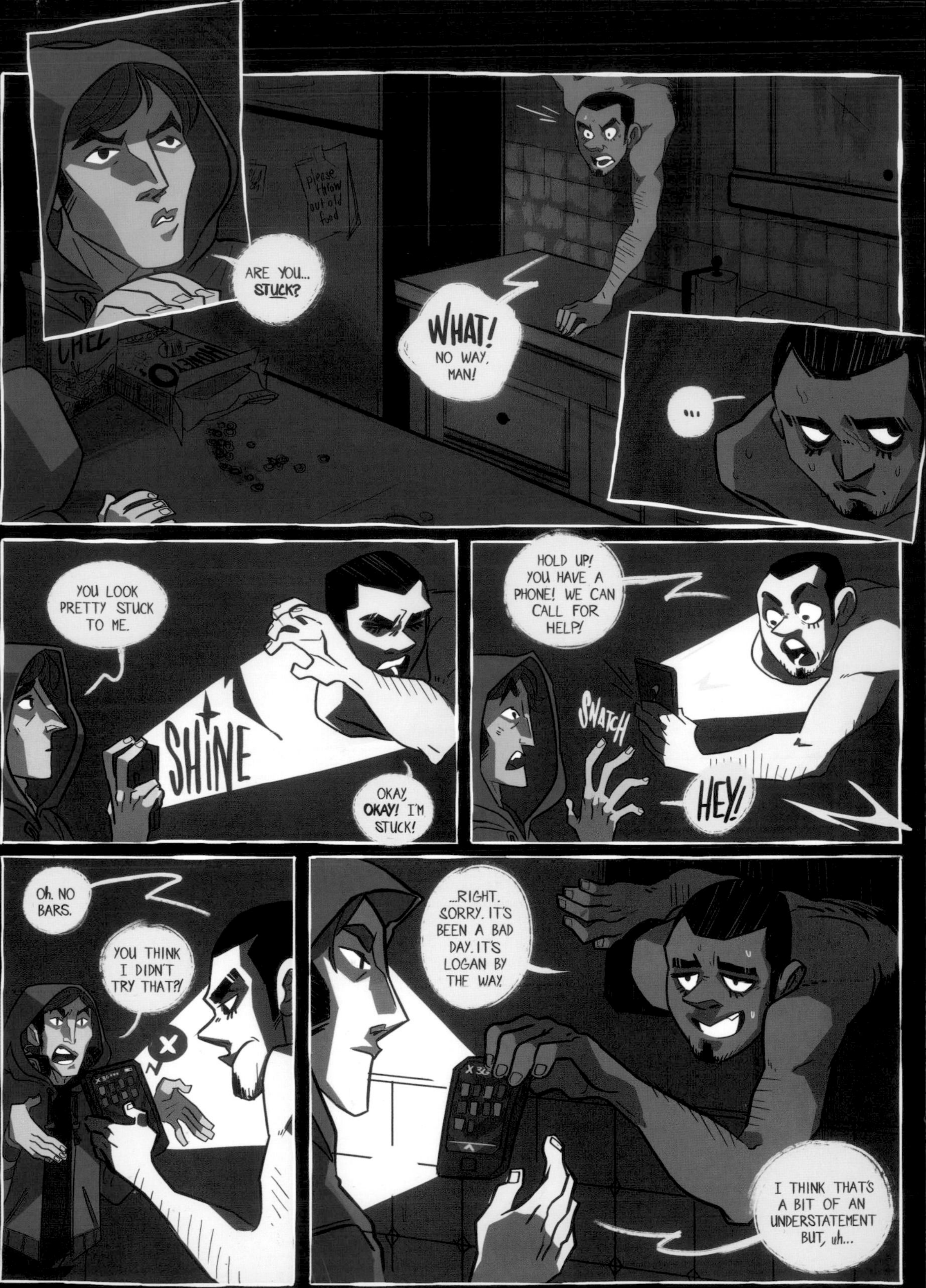
please throw out old food
ARE YOU... STUCK?
WHAT! NO WAY, MAN!
...
YOU LOOK PRETTY STUCK TO ME.
SHINE
OKAY, OKAY! I'M STUCK!
HOLD UP! YOU HAVE A PHONE! WE CAN CALL FOR HELP!
SNATCH
HEY!
Oh. NO BARS.
YOU THINK I DIDN'T TRY THAT?!
...RIGHT. SORRY. IT'S BEEN A BAD DAY. IT'S LOGAN BY THE WAY.
I THINK THAT'S A BIT OF AN UNDERSTATEMENT BUT, uh...

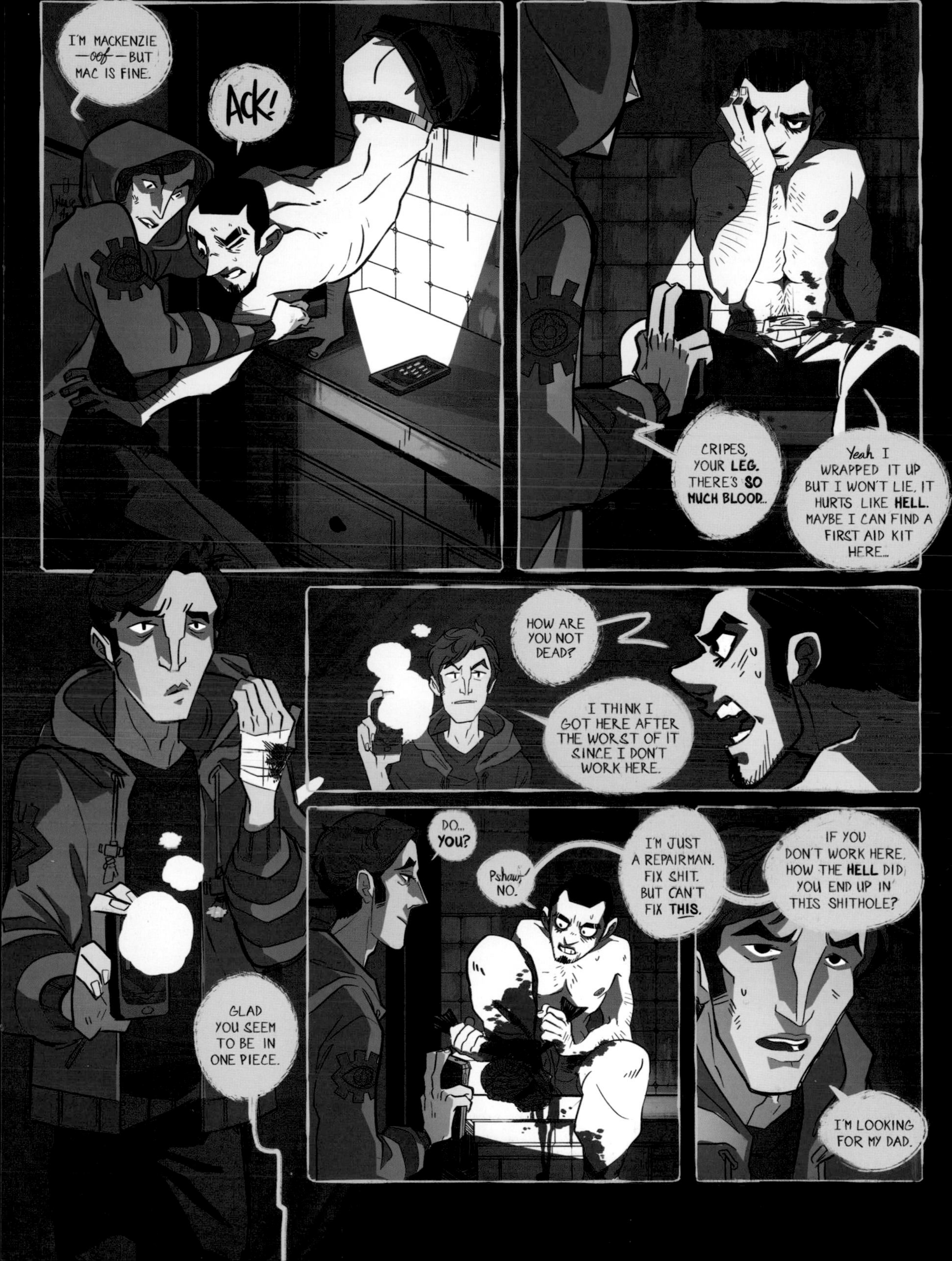

I'M MACKENZIE —oof— BUT MAC IS FINE.
ACK!
CRIPES, YOUR LEG. THERE'S SO MUCH BLOOD...
Yeah. I WRAPPED IT UP BUT I WON'T LIE, IT HURTS LIKE HELL. MAYBE I CAN FIND A FIRST AID KIT HERE...
GLAD YOU SEEM TO BE IN ONE PIECE.
HOW ARE YOU NOT DEAD?
I THINK I GOT HERE AFTER THE WORST OF IT SINCE I DON'T WORK HERE.
DO... YOU?
Pshaw, NO.
I'M JUST A REPAIRMAN. FIX SHIT. BUT CAN'T FIX THIS.
IF YOU DON'T WORK HERE, HOW THE HELL DID YOU END UP IN THIS SHITHOLE?
I'M LOOKING FOR MY DAD.

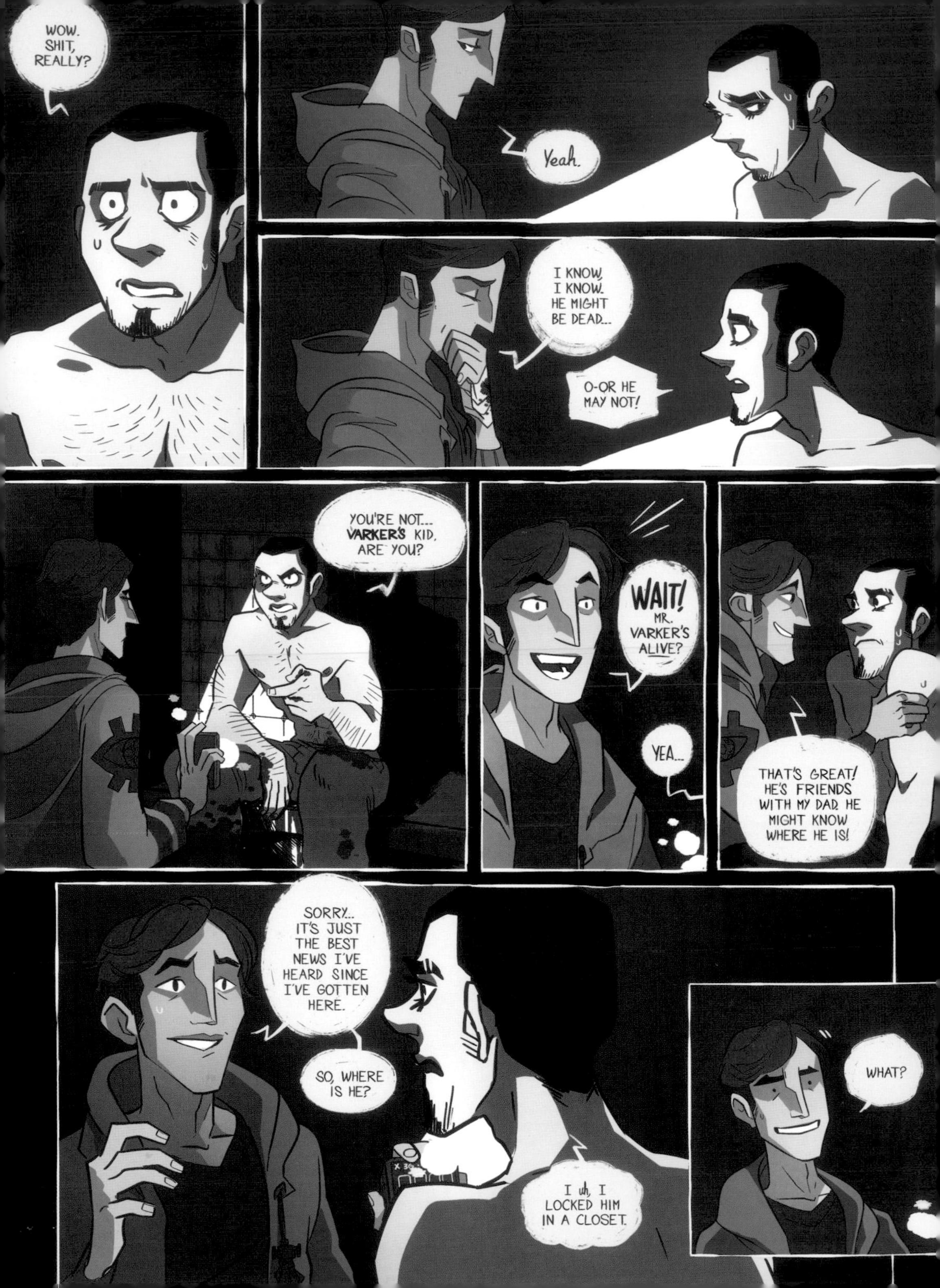
WOW. SHIT, REALLY?
Yeah.
I KNOW, I KNOW. HE MIGHT BE DEAD...
O-OR HE MAY NOT!
YOU'RE NOT... VARKER'S KID, ARE YOU?
WAIT! MR. VARKER'S ALIVE?
YEA...
THAT'S GREAT! HE'S FRIENDS WITH MY DAD. HE MIGHT KNOW WHERE HE IS!
SORRY... IT'S JUST THE BEST NEWS I'VE HEARD SINCE I'VE GOTTEN HERE.
SO, WHERE IS HE?
I uh, I LOCKED HIM IN A CLOSET.
WHAT?

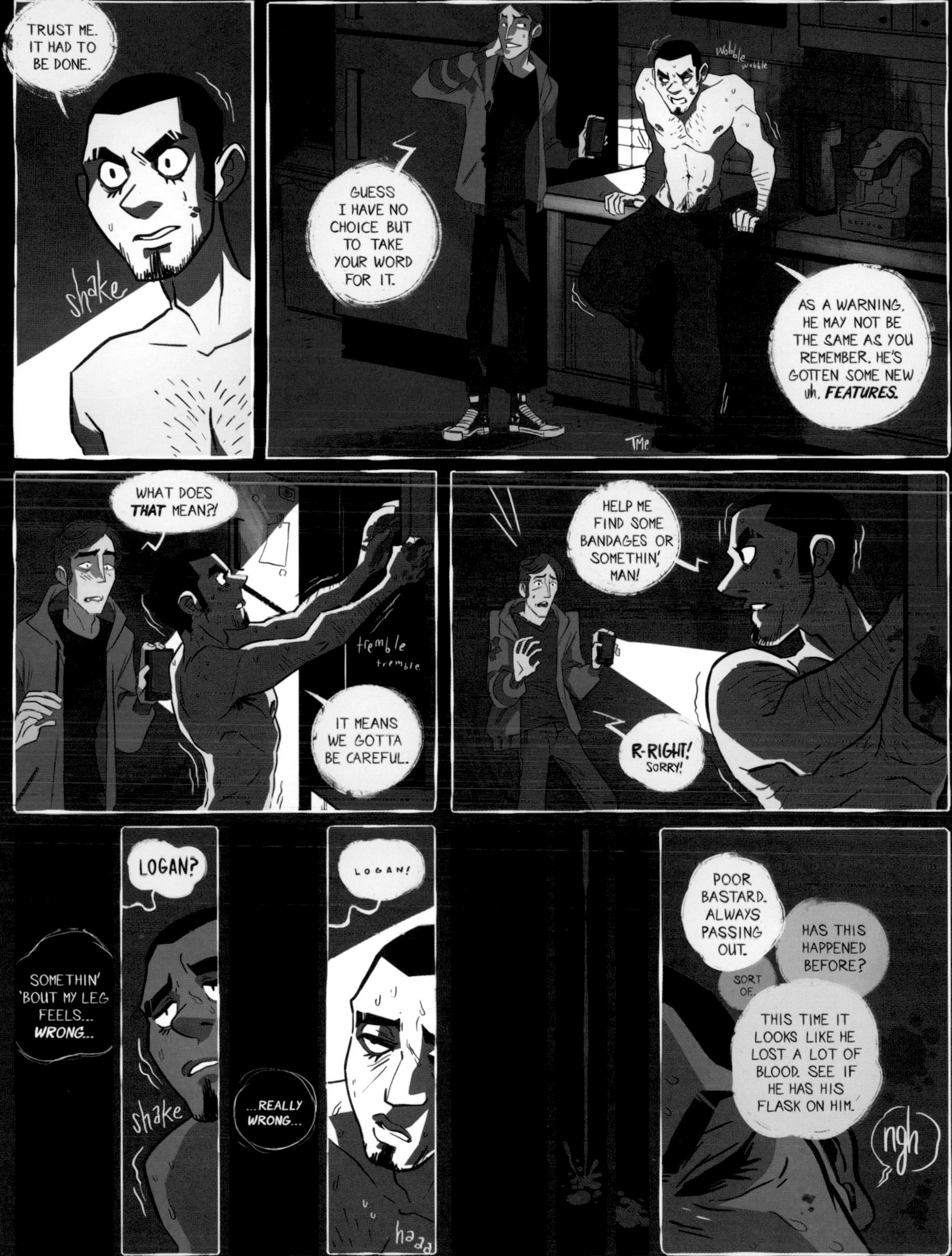
TRUST ME. IT HAD TO BE DONE.
shake
GUESS I HAVE NO CHOICE BUT TO TAKE YOUR WORD FOR IT.
wobble wobble
AS A WARNING, HE MAY NOT BE THE SAME AS YOU REMEMBER. HE'S GOTTEN SOME NEW uh, FEATURES.
WHAT DOES THAT MEAN?!
tremble tremble
IT MEANS WE GOTTA BE CAREFUL.
HELP ME FIND SOME BANDAGES OR SOMETHIN', MAN!
R-RIGHT! SORRY!
SOMETHIN' 'BOUT MY LEG FEELS... WRONG...
LOGAN?
shake
...REALLY WRONG...
LOGAN!
haaa
POOR BASTARD. ALWAYS PASSING OUT.
HAS THIS HAPPENED BEFORE?
SORT OF.
THIS TIME IT LOOKS LIKE HE LOST A LOT OF BLOOD. SEE IF HE HAS HIS FLASK ON HIM.
ngh

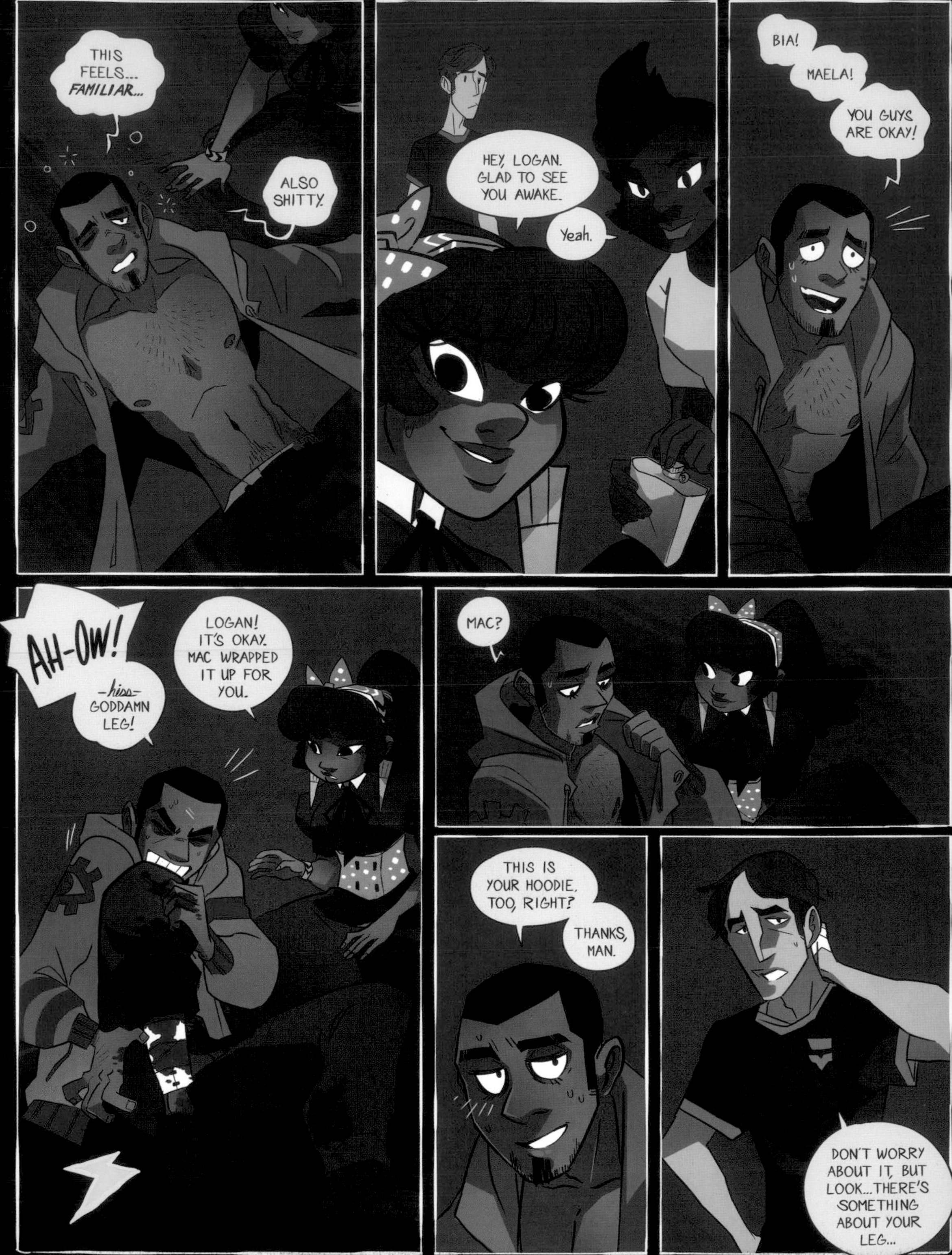

THIS FEELS... FAMILIAR...
ALSO SHITTY.
HEY, LOGAN. GLAD TO SEE YOU AWAKE.
Yeah.
BIA!
MAELA!
YOU GUYS ARE OKAY!
AH-OW!
-hiss- GODDAMN LEG!
LOGAN! IT'S OKAY. MAC WRAPPED IT UP FOR YOU.
MAC?
THIS IS YOUR HOODIE, TOO, RIGHT?
THANKS, MAN.
DON'T WORRY ABOUT IT, BUT LOOK...THERE'S SOMETHING ABOUT YOUR LEG...

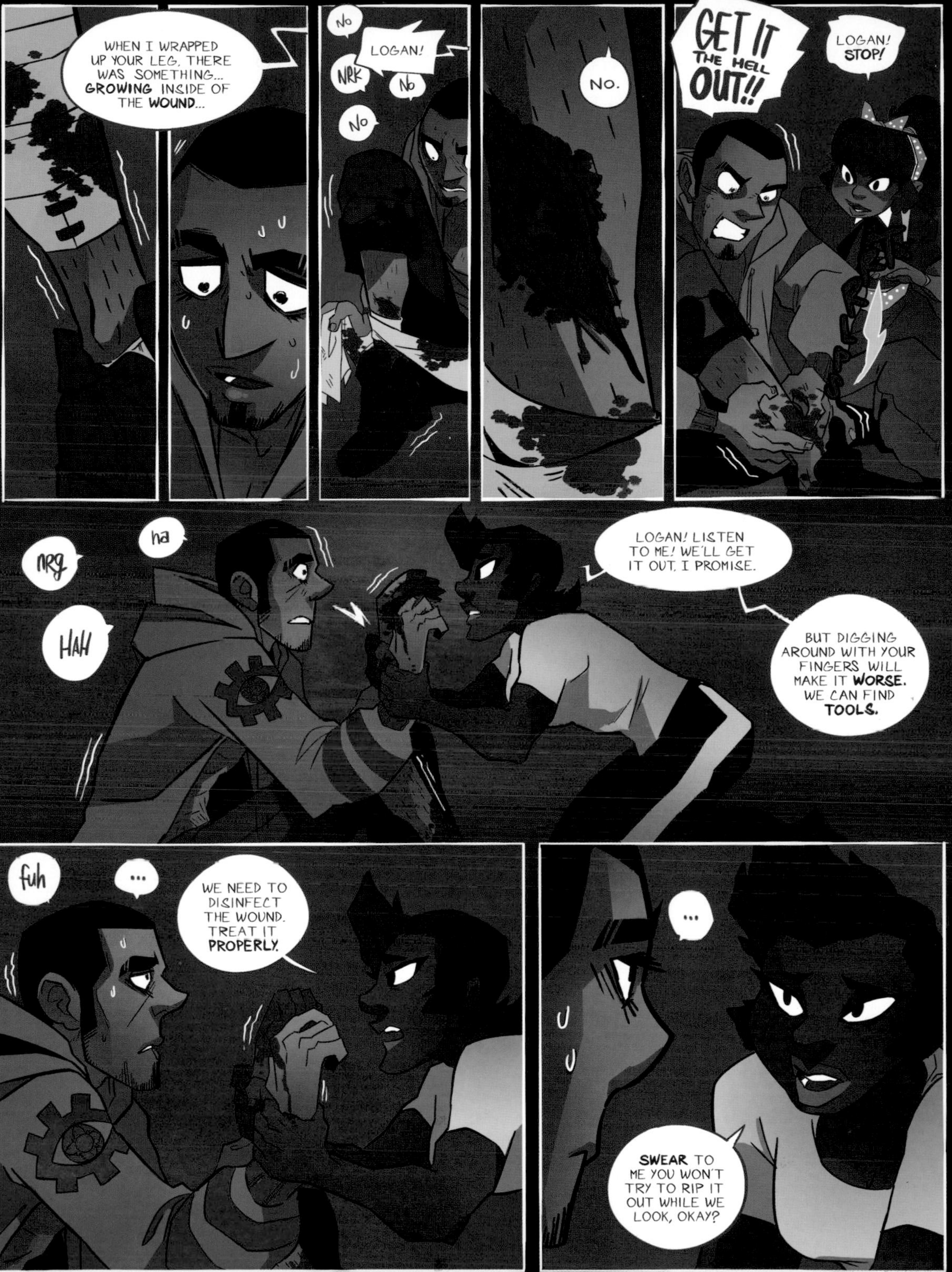

WHEN I WRAPPED UP YOUR LEG, THERE WAS SOMETHING... GROWING INSIDE OF THE WOUND...
No
LOGAN!
NRK
No
No
No.
GET IT THE HELL OUT!!
LOGAN! STOP!
ha
nrg
HAH
LOGAN! LISTEN TO ME! WE'LL GET IT OUT, I PROMISE.
BUT DIGGING AROUND WITH YOUR FINGERS WILL MAKE IT WORSE. WE CAN FIND TOOLS.
fuh
...
WE NEED TO DISINFECT THE WOUND. TREAT IT PROPERLY.
...
SWEAR TO ME YOU WON'T TRY TO RIP IT OUT WHILE WE LOOK, OKAY?

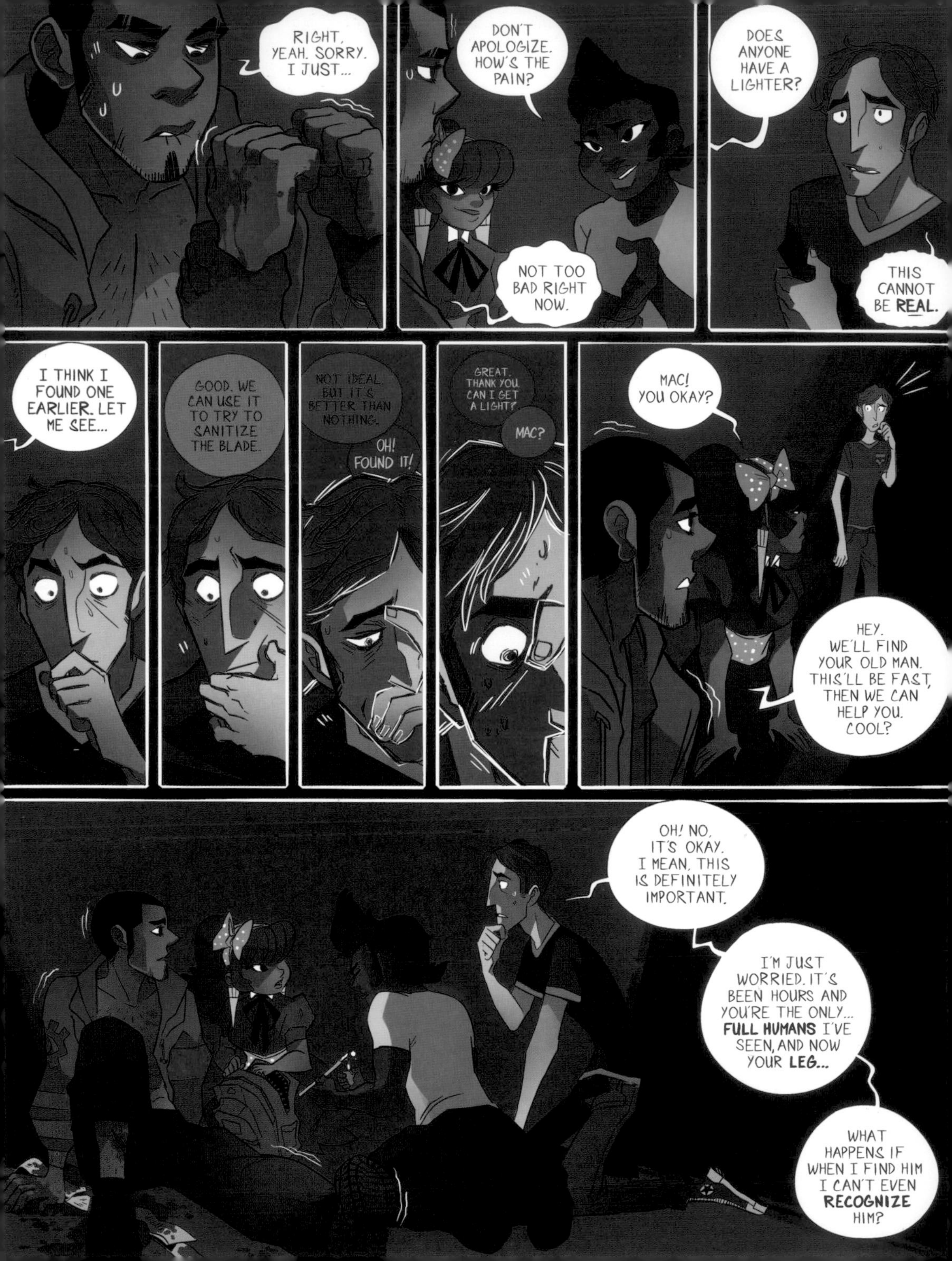
RIGHT, YEAH. SORRY. I JUST...
DON'T APOLOGIZE. HOW'S THE PAIN?
NOT TOO BAD RIGHT NOW.
DOES ANYONE HAVE A LIGHTER?
THIS CANNOT BE REAL.
I THINK I FOUND ONE EARLIER. LET ME SEE...
GOOD. WE CAN USE IT TO TRY TO SANITIZE THE BLADE.
NOT IDEAL. BUT IT'S BETTER THAN NOTHING.
OH! FOUND IT!
GREAT. THANK YOU. CAN I GET A LIGHT?
MAC?
MAC! YOU OKAY?
HEY. WE'LL FIND YOUR OLD MAN. THIS'LL BE FAST, THEN WE CAN HELP YOU. COOL?
OH! NO, IT'S OKAY. I MEAN, THIS IS DEFINITELY IMPORTANT.
I'M JUST WORRIED. IT'S BEEN HOURS AND YOU'RE THE ONLY... FULL HUMANS I'VE SEEN, AND NOW YOUR LEG...
WHAT HAPPENS IF WHEN I FIND HIM I CAN'T EVEN RECOGNIZE HIM?

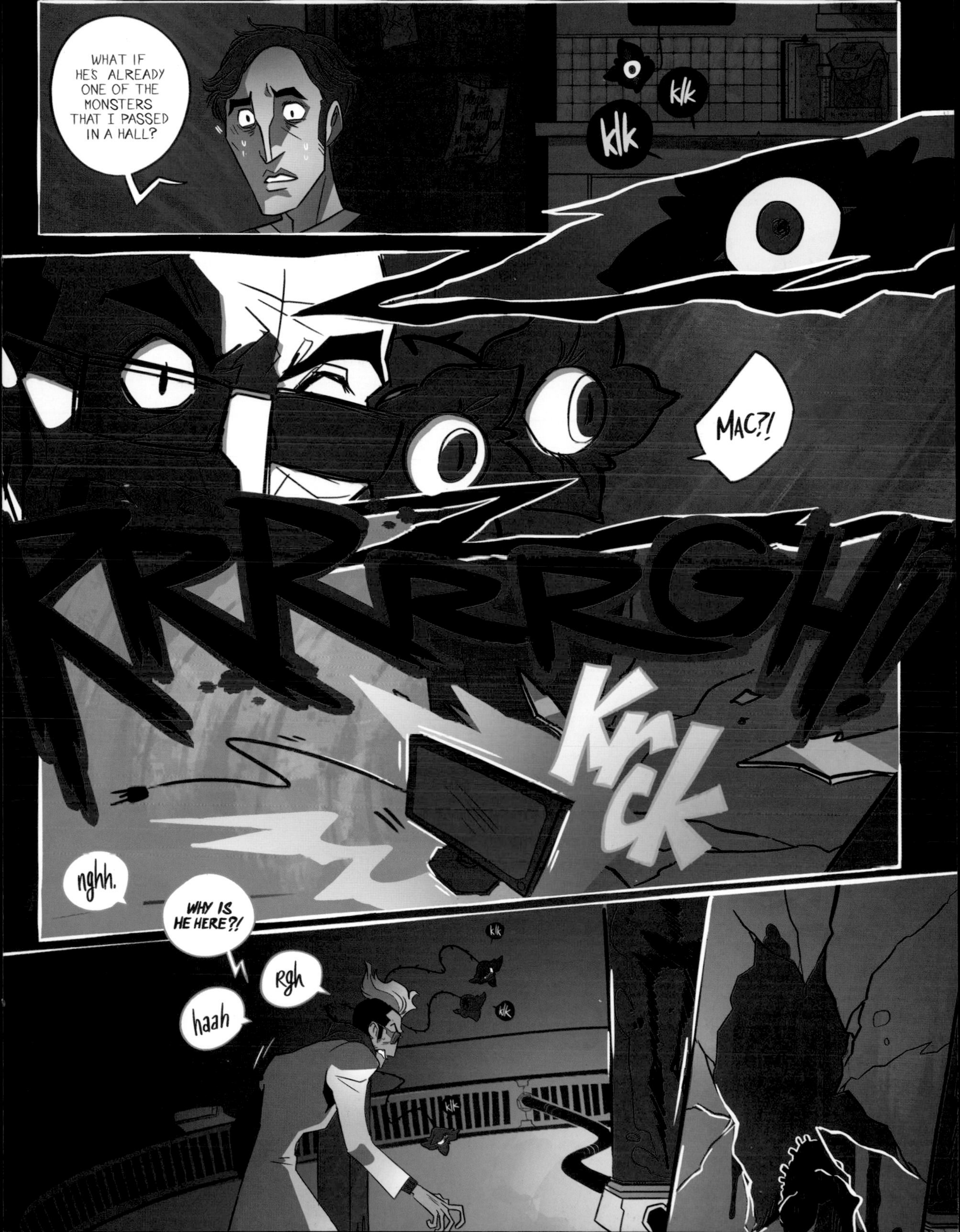
WHAT IF HE'S ALREADY ONE OF THE MONSTERS THAT I PASSED IN A HALL?
klk
klk
MAC?!
KRRRRGH!!
Krrck
nghh.
WHY IS HE HERE?!
Rgh
haah
klk
klk
klk

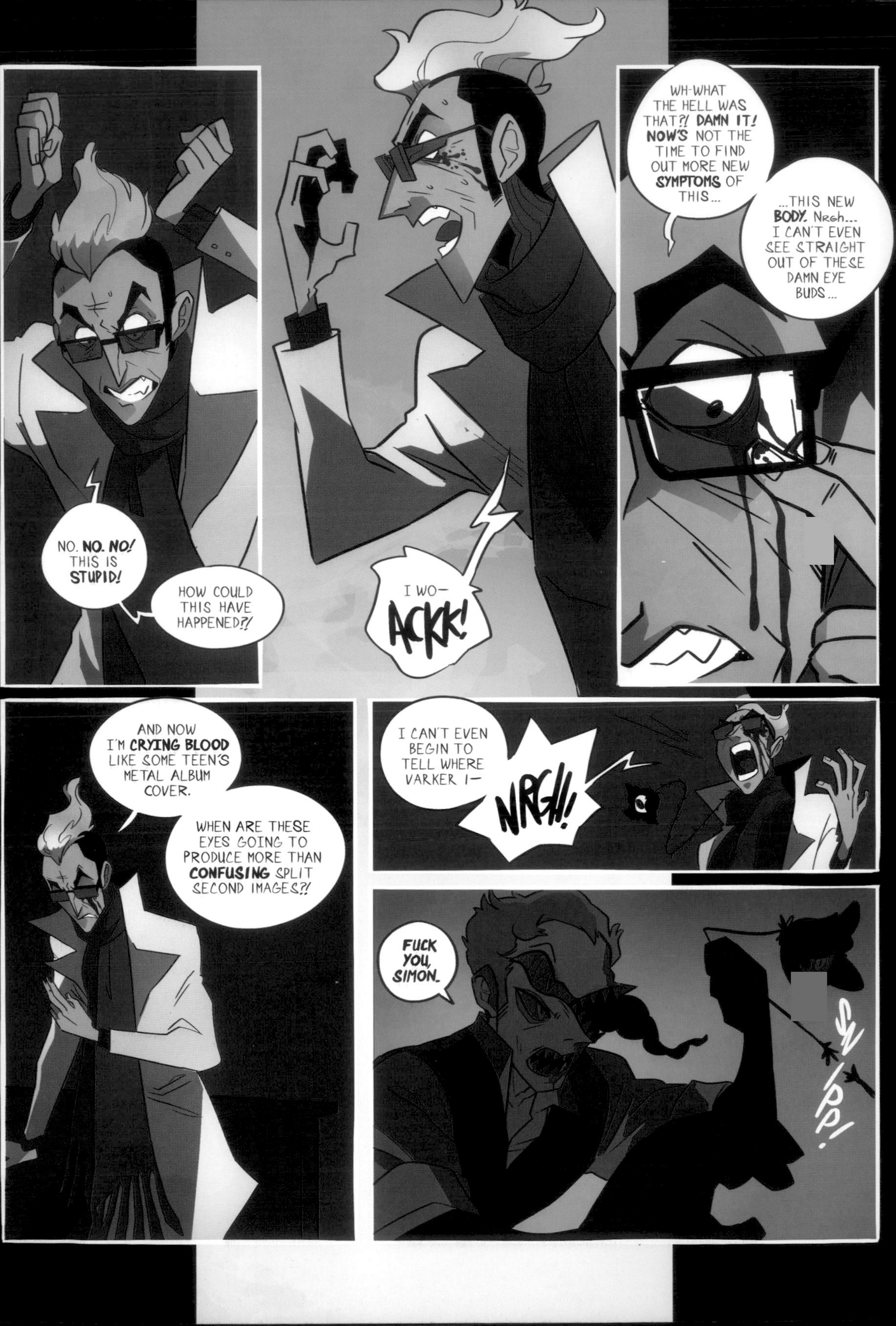

NO. NO. NO! THIS IS STUPID!
HOW COULD THIS HAVE HAPPENED?!
I WO—
ACKK!
WH-WHAT THE HELL WAS THAT?! DAMN IT! NOW'S NOT THE TIME TO FIND OUT MORE NEW SYMPTOMS OF THIS...
...THIS NEW BODY. Nrgh... I CAN'T EVEN SEE STRAIGHT OUT OF THESE DAMN EYE BUDS...
AND NOW I'M CRYING BLOOD LIKE SOME TEEN'S METAL ALBUM COVER.
WHEN ARE THESE EYES GOING TO PRODUCE MORE THAN CONFUSING SPLIT SECOND IMAGES?!
I CAN'T EVEN BEGIN TO TELL WHERE VARKER I—
NRGH!
FUCK YOU, SIMON.
SWIPP!

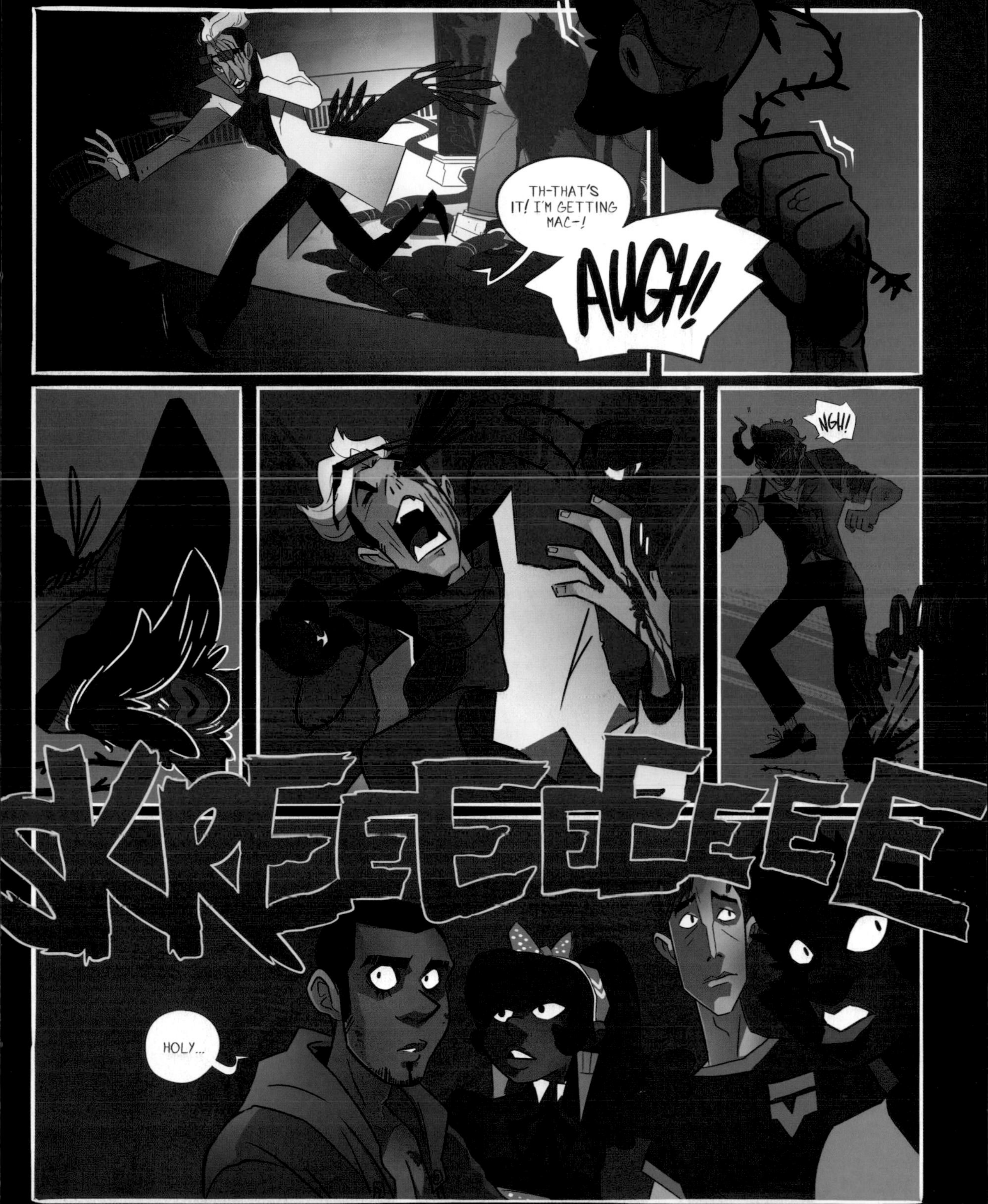
TH-THAT'S IT! I'M GETTING MAC-!
AUGH!
NGH!
SKREEEEEEEEE
HOLY...

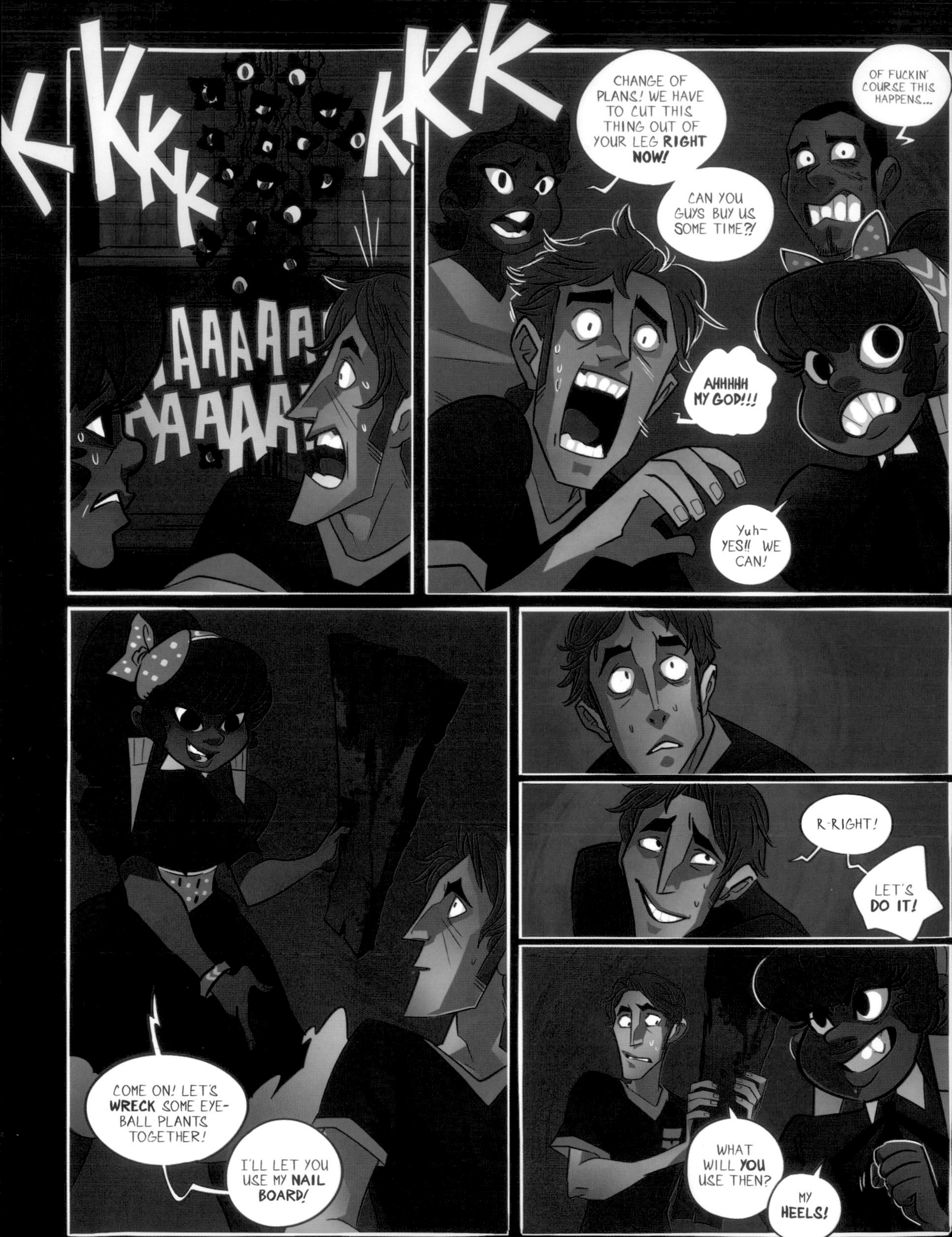
KKKKKKK
AAAAAAA AAAAAR!
CHANGE OF PLANS! WE HAVE TO CUT THIS THING OUT OF YOUR LEG RIGHT NOW!
CAN YOU GUYS BUY US SOME TIME?!
OF FUCKIN' COURSE THIS HAPPENS...
AHHHHH MY GOD!!!
Yuh– YES!! WE CAN!
COME ON! LET'S WRECK SOME EYE-BALL PLANTS TOGETHER!
I'LL LET YOU USE MY NAIL BOARD!
R-RIGHT!
LET'S DO IT!
WHAT WILL YOU USE THEN?
MY HEELS!

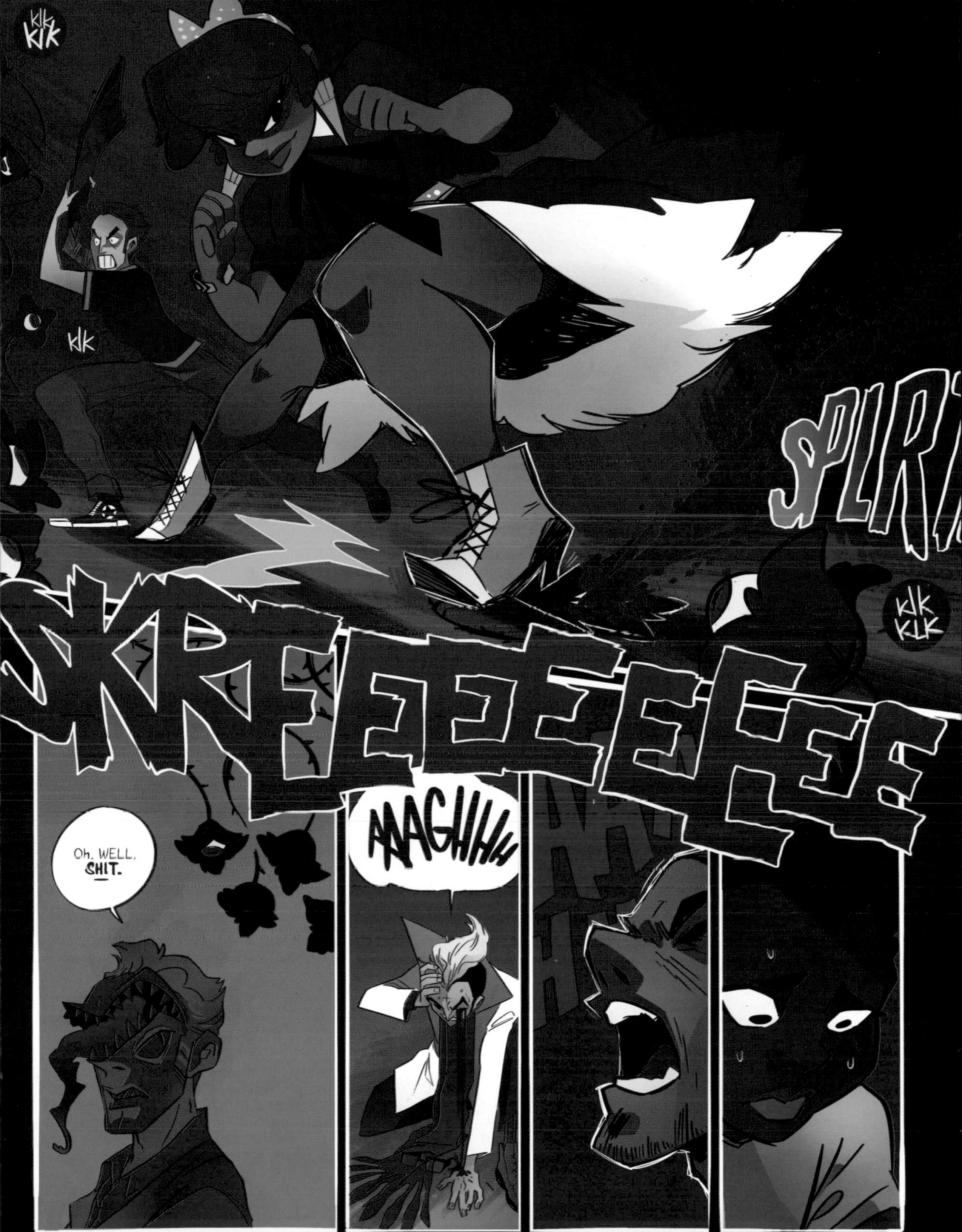
KLK KLK
KLK
SPLRT
KLK KLK
SKREEEEEEEE
Oh. WELL, SHIT.
AAAGHHH

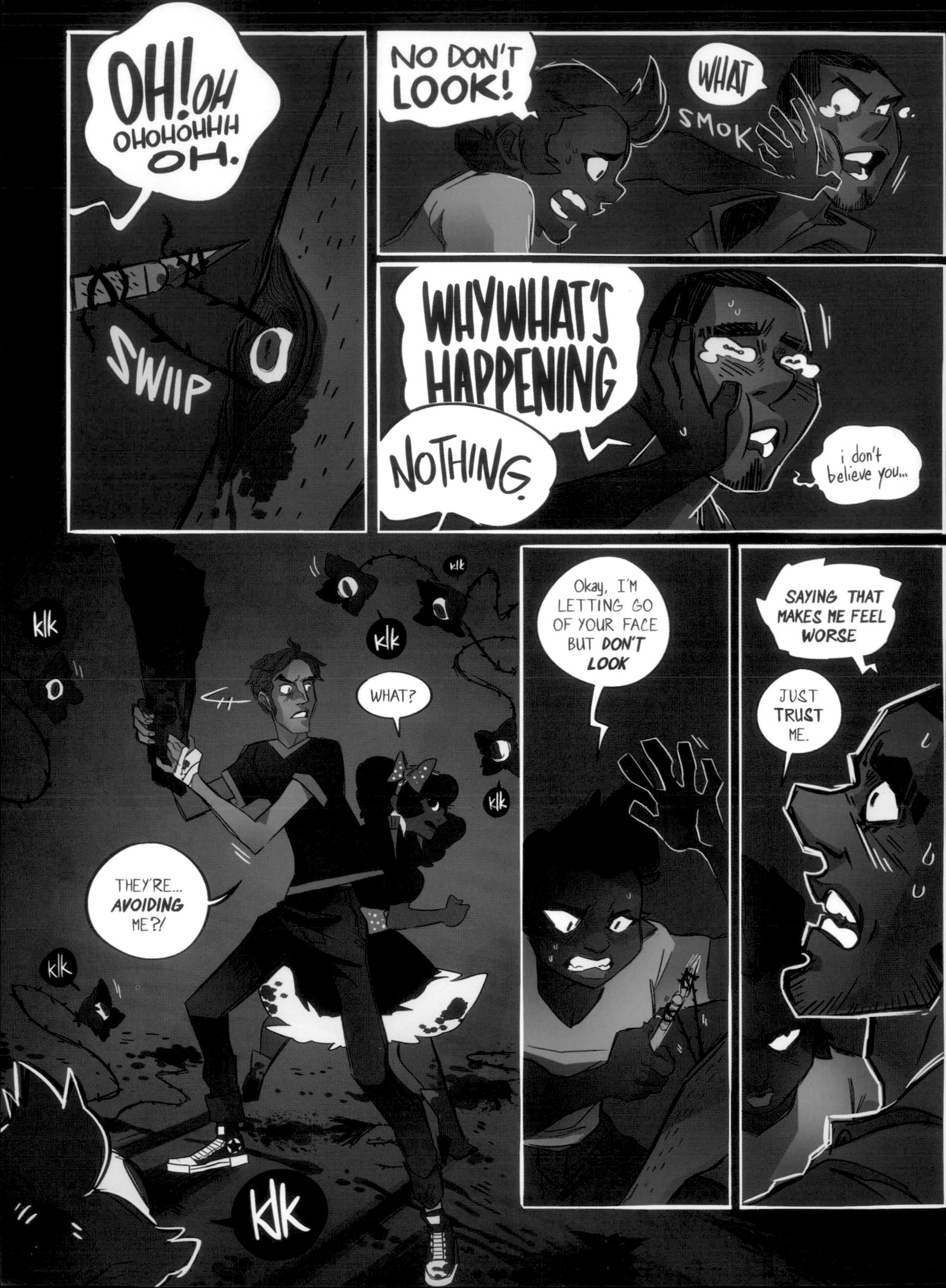
OH! OH OHOHOHHH OH.
SWIIP
NO DON'T LOOK!
WHAT
SMOK
WHY WHAT'S HAPPENING
NOTHING.
i don't believe you...
klk
klk
klk
WHAT?
klk
klk
THEY'RE... AVOIDING ME?!
klk
KLK
Okay, I'M LETTING GO OF YOUR FACE BUT DON'T LOOK
SAYING THAT MAKES ME FEEL WORSE
JUST TRUST ME.

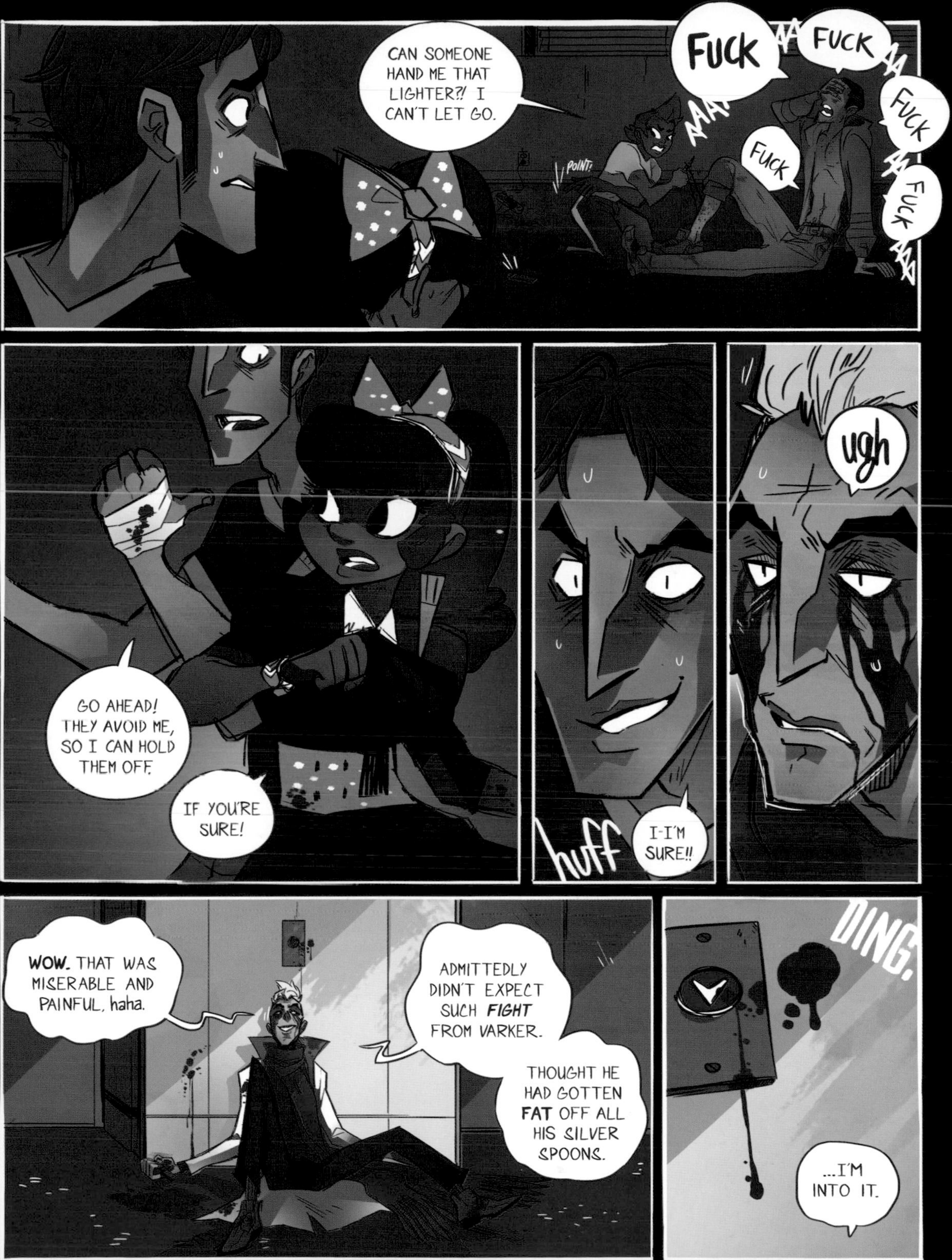
CAN SOMEONE HAND ME THAT LIGHTER?! I CAN'T LET GO.
FUCK
FUCK
FUCK
FUCK
FUCK
POINT!
GO AHEAD! THEY AVOID ME, SO I CAN HOLD THEM OFF.
IF YOU'RE SURE!
huff
I-I'M SURE!!
ugh
WOW. THAT WAS MISERABLE AND PAINFUL, haha.
ADMITTEDLY DIDN'T EXPECT SUCH FIGHT FROM VARKER.
THOUGHT HE HAD GOTTEN FAT OFF ALL HIS SILVER SPOONS.
DING.
...I'M INTO IT.

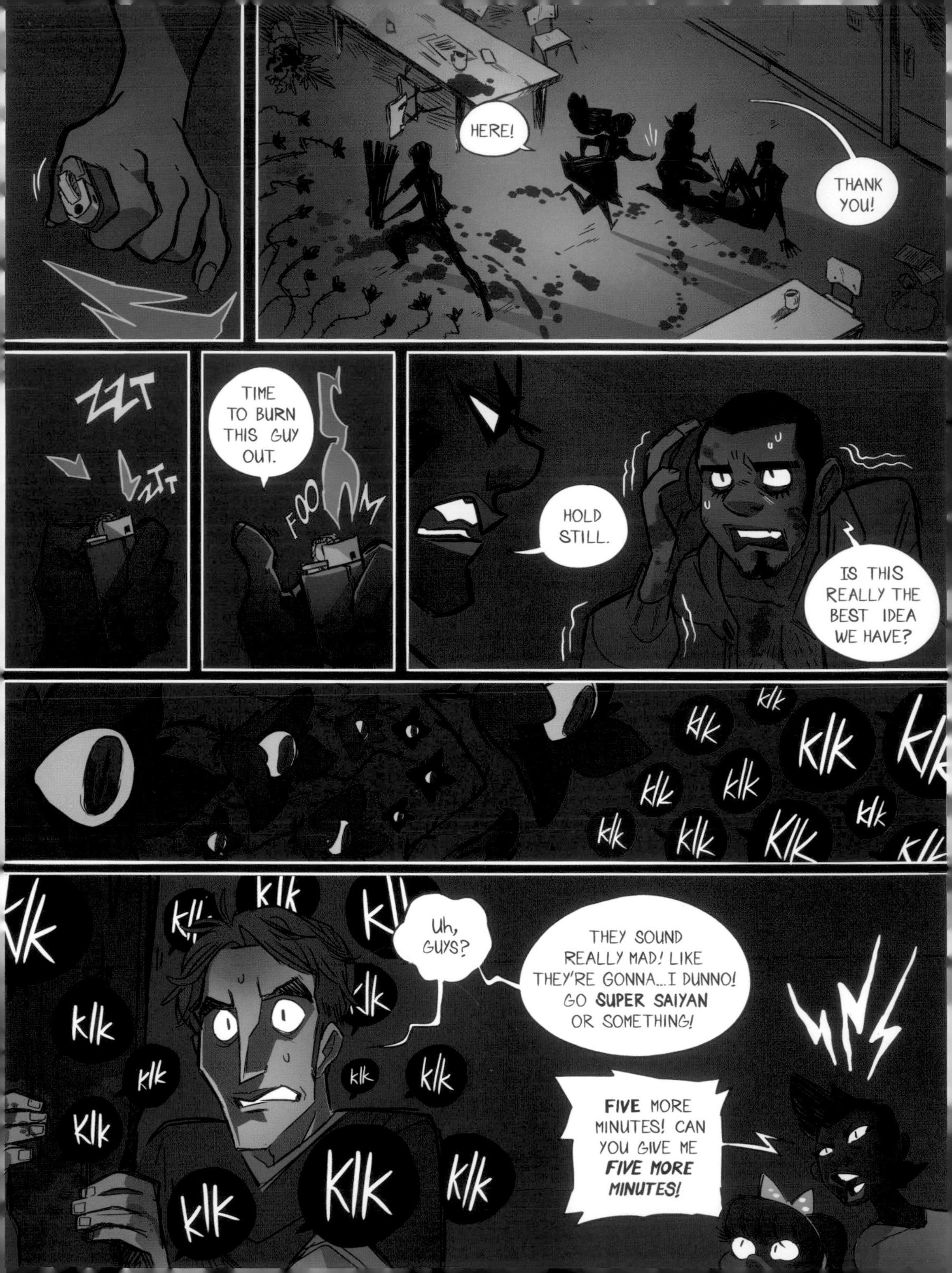
HERE!
THANK YOU!
ZZT
ZZT
TIME TO BURN THIS GUY OUT.
FOOM
HOLD STILL.
IS THIS REALLY THE BEST IDEA WE HAVE?
KLK
Uh, GUYS?
THEY SOUND REALLY MAD! LIKE THEY'RE GONNA...I DUNNO! GO **SUPER SAIYAN** OR SOMETHING!
FIVE MORE MINUTES! CAN YOU GIVE ME ***FIVE MORE MINUTES!***

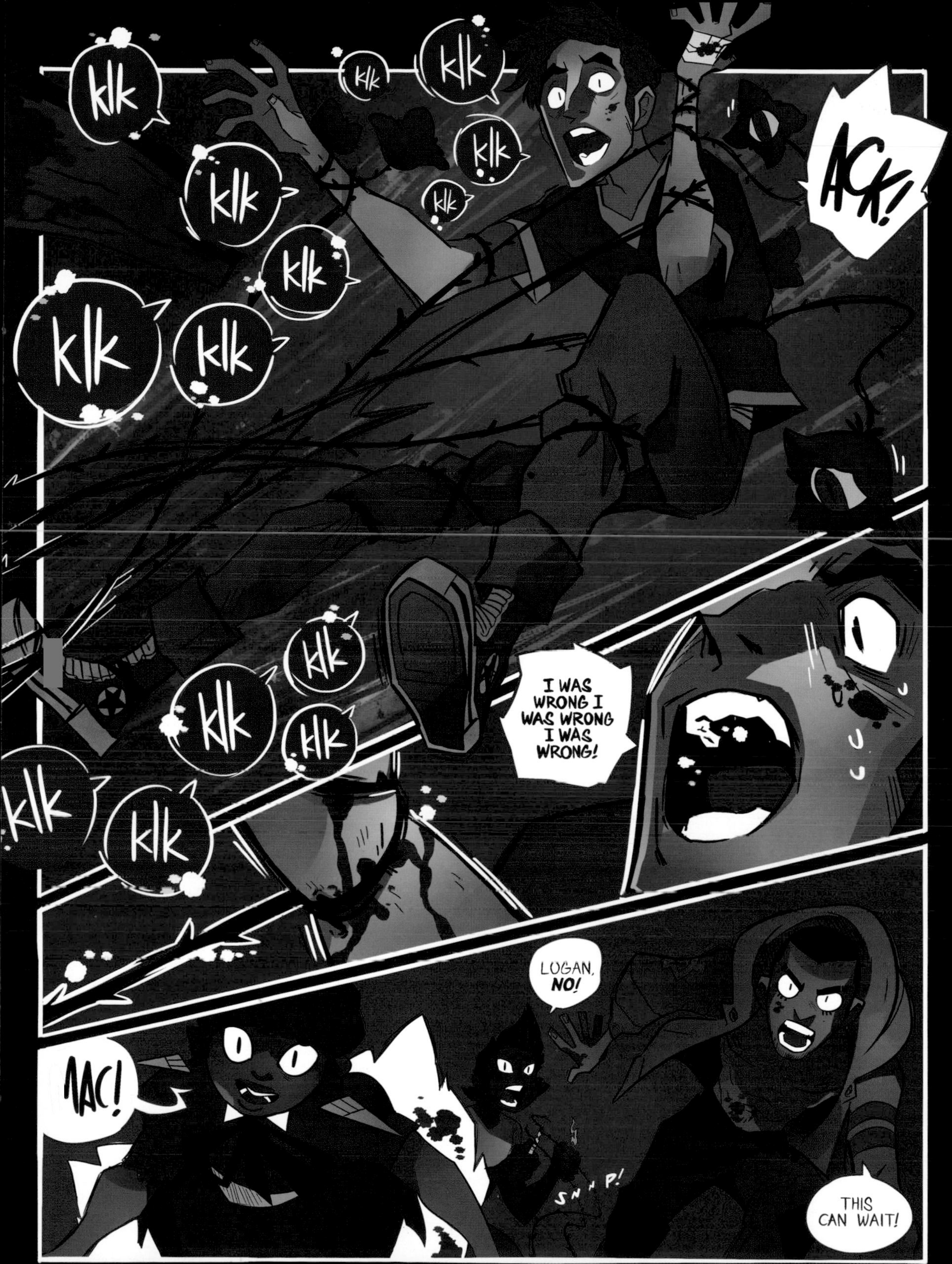
klk
klk
klk
klk
klk
klk
klk
klk
ACK!
klk
klk
klk
klk
klk
I WAS WRONG I WAS WRONG I WAS WRONG!
LOGAN, NO!
MAC!
SNAP!
THIS CAN WAIT!

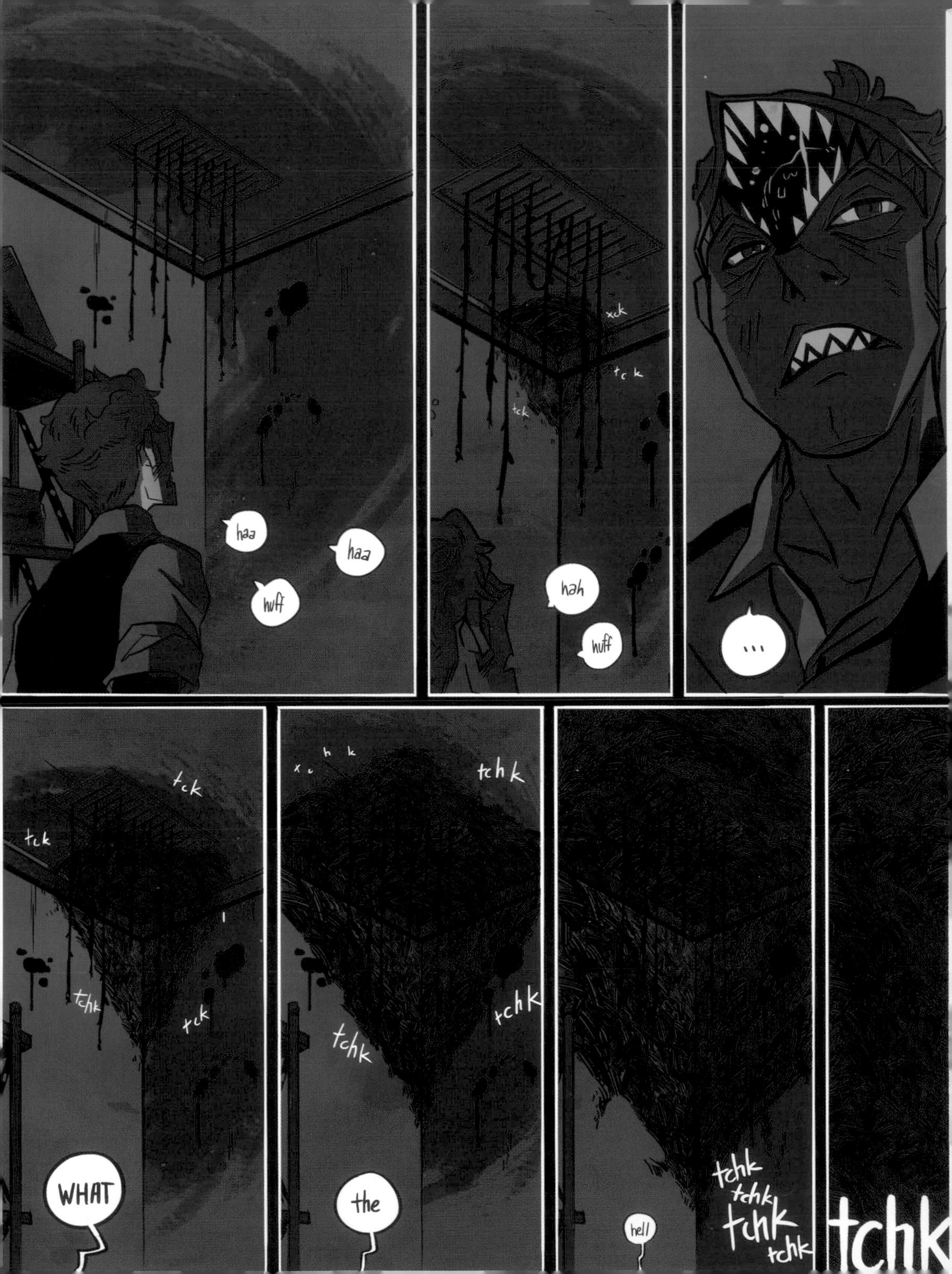
haa
huff
haa
xck
tck
tck
hah
huff
...
tck
tck
tchk
tck
WHAT
tchk
tchk
tchk
the
hell
tchk
tchk
tchk
tchk
tchk

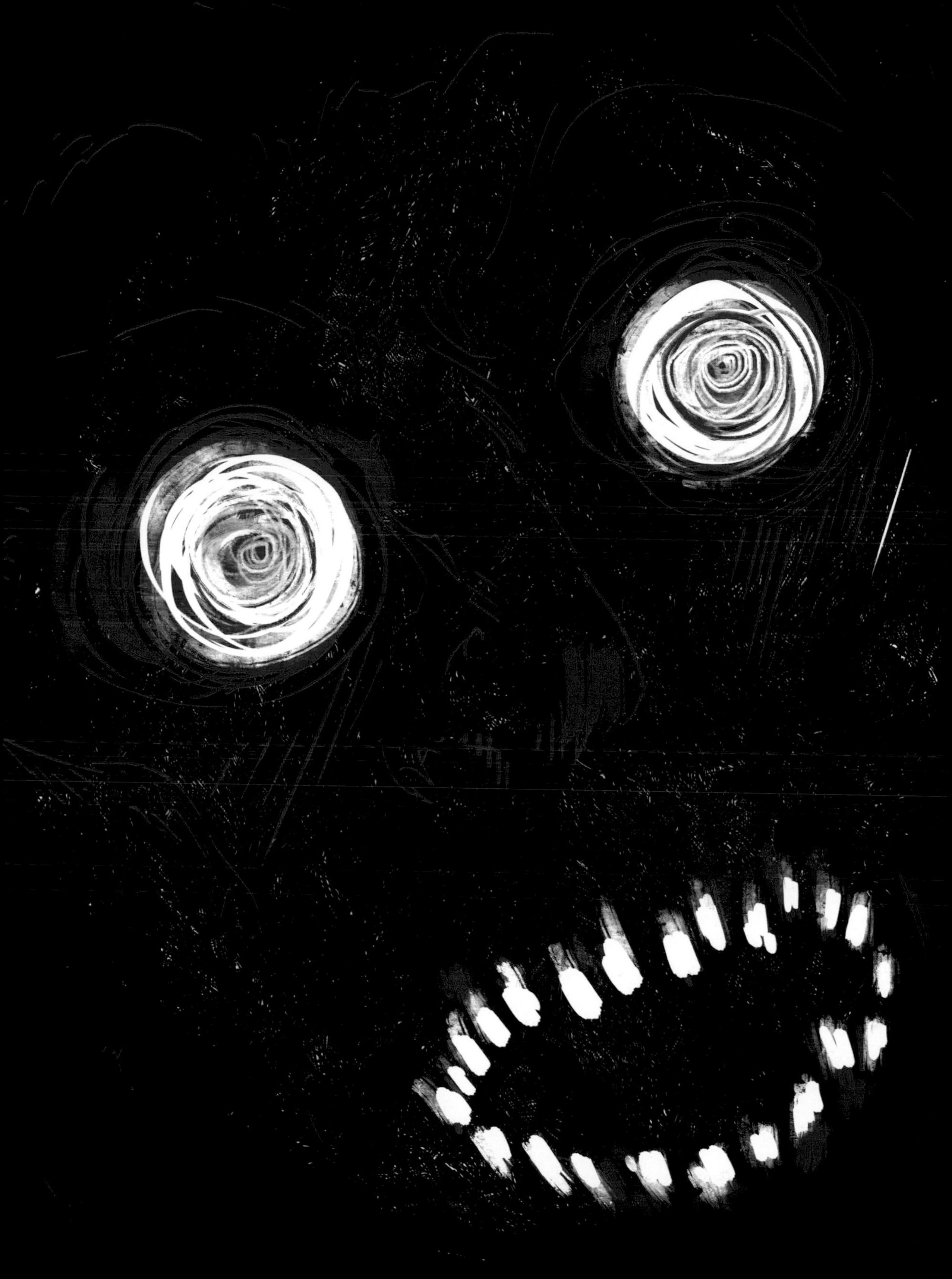

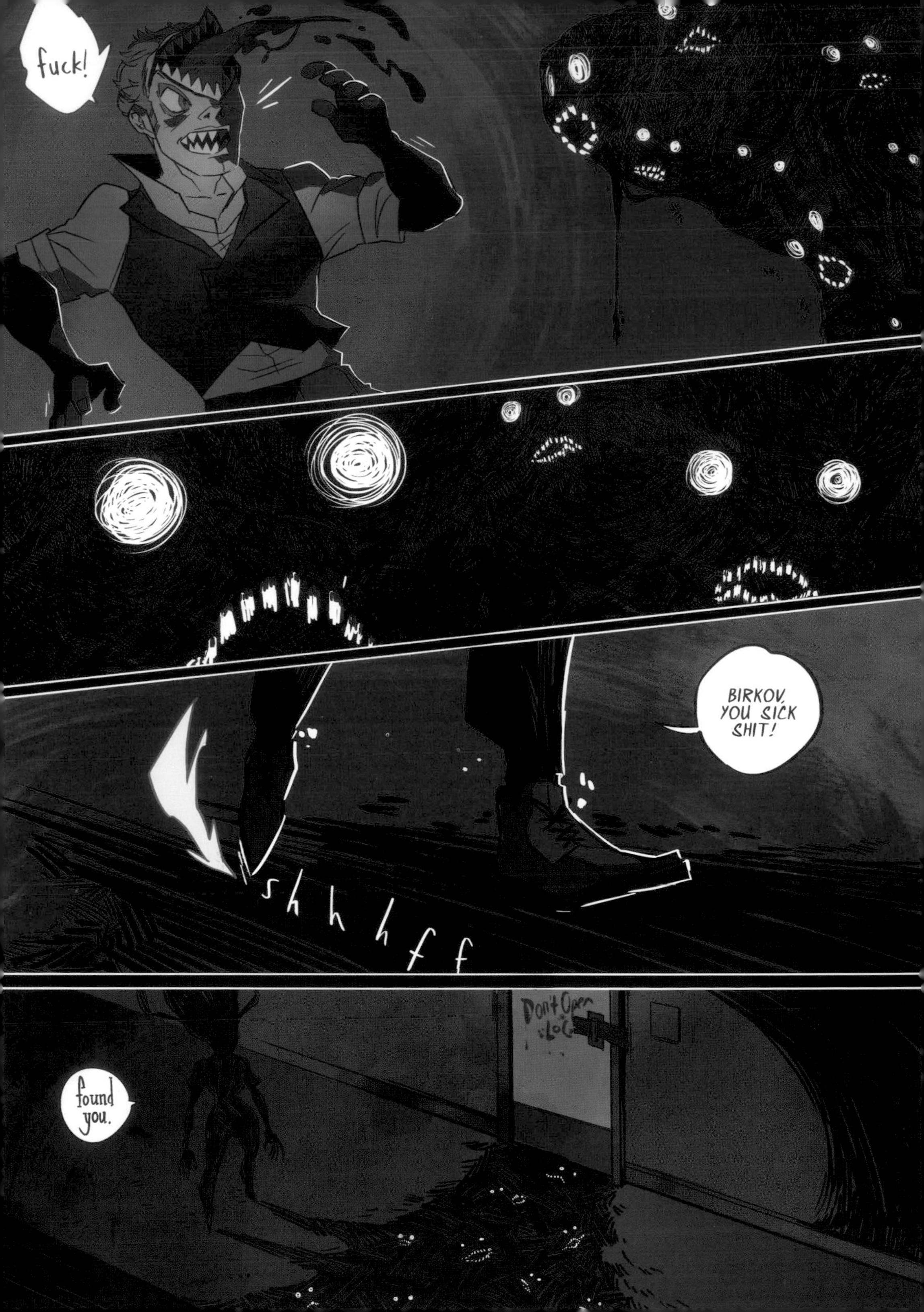
fuck!
BIRKOV, YOU SICK SHIT!
shhhff
Don't Open
found you.

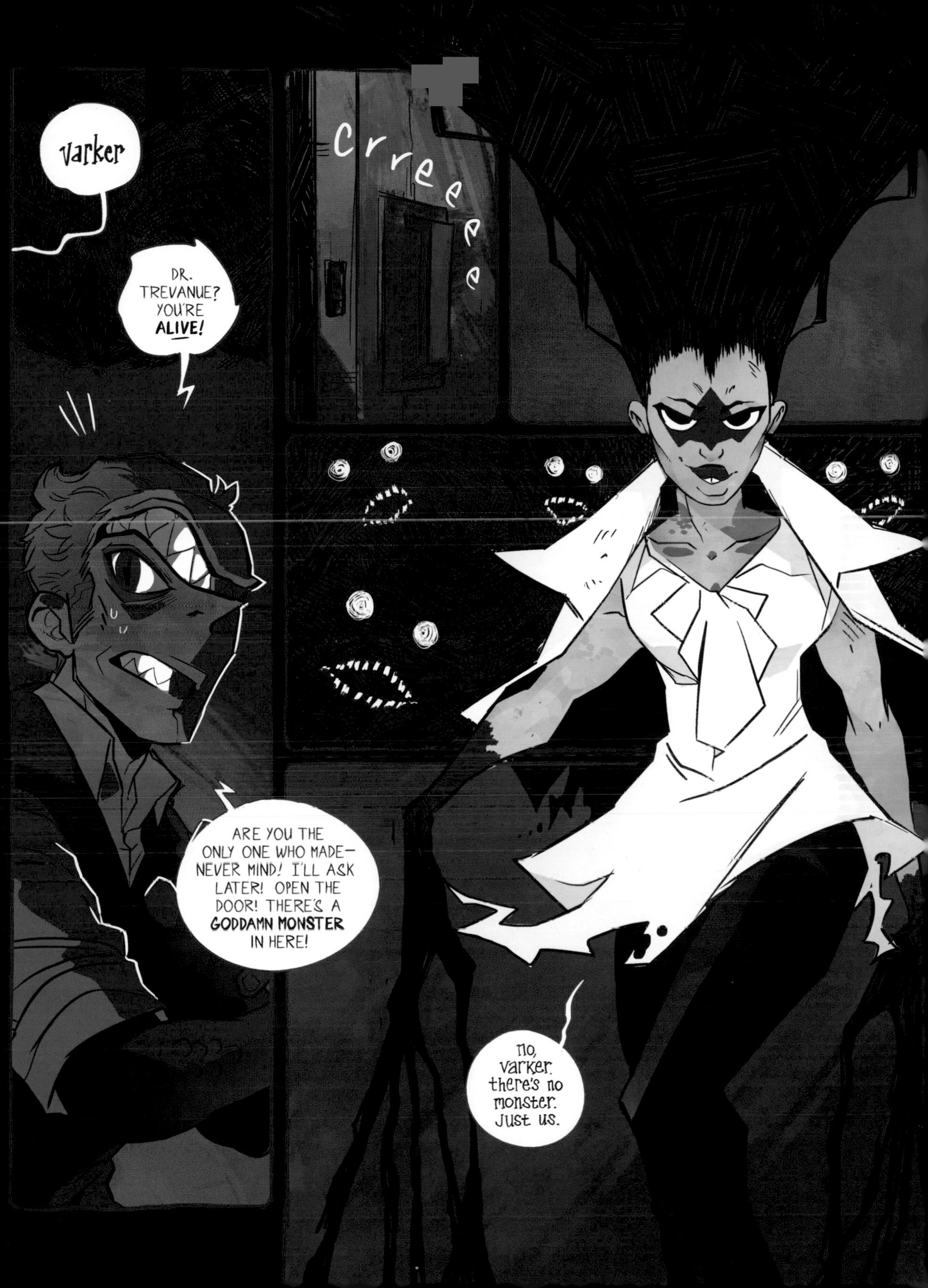

Varker
DR. TREVANUE? YOU'RE ALIVE!
Crreeeee
ARE YOU THE ONLY ONE WHO MADE— NEVER MIND! I'LL ASK LATER! OPEN THE DOOR! THERE'S A GODDAMN MONSTER IN HERE!
No, Varker. there's no monster. Just us.

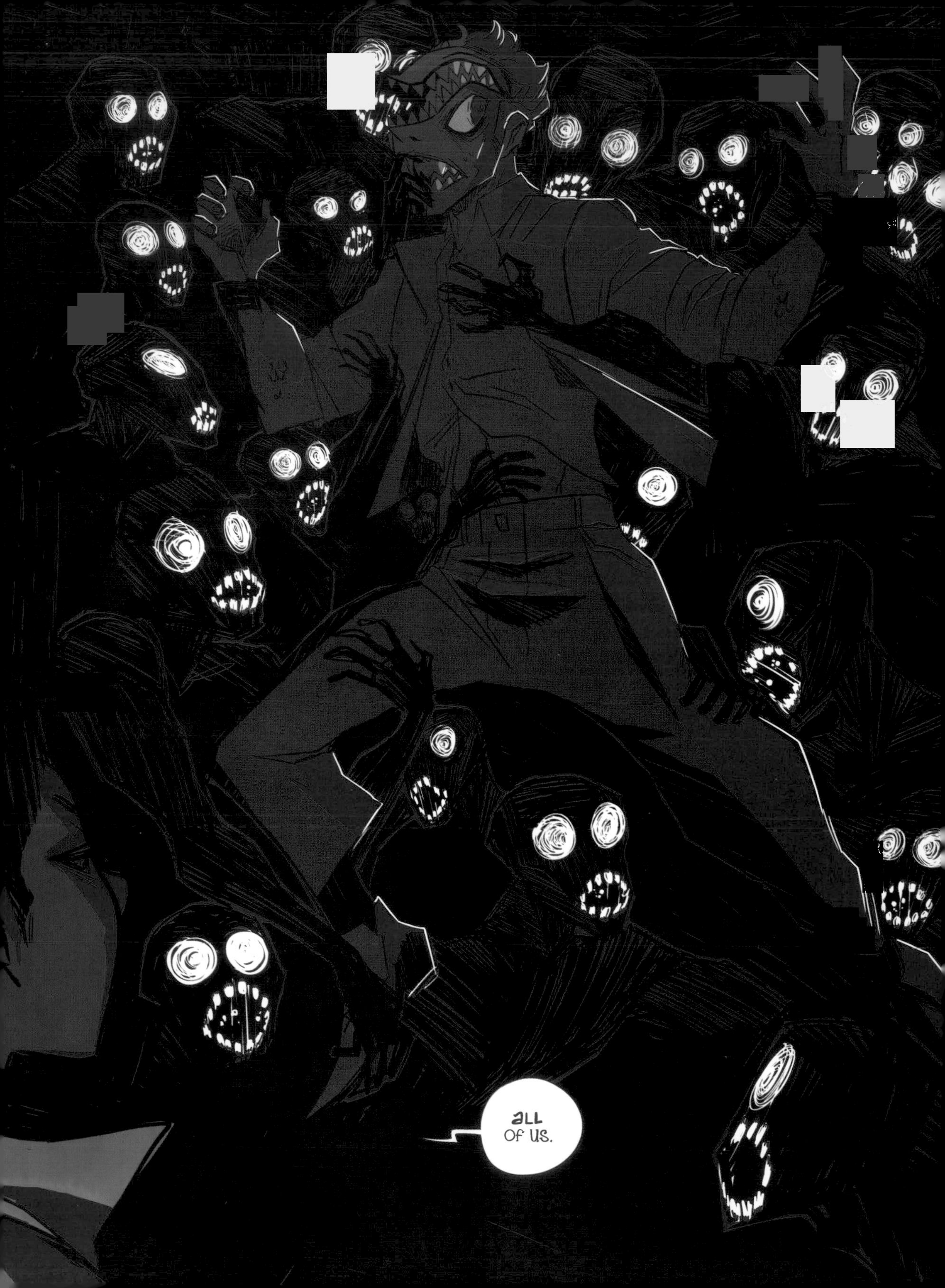
ALL OF US.

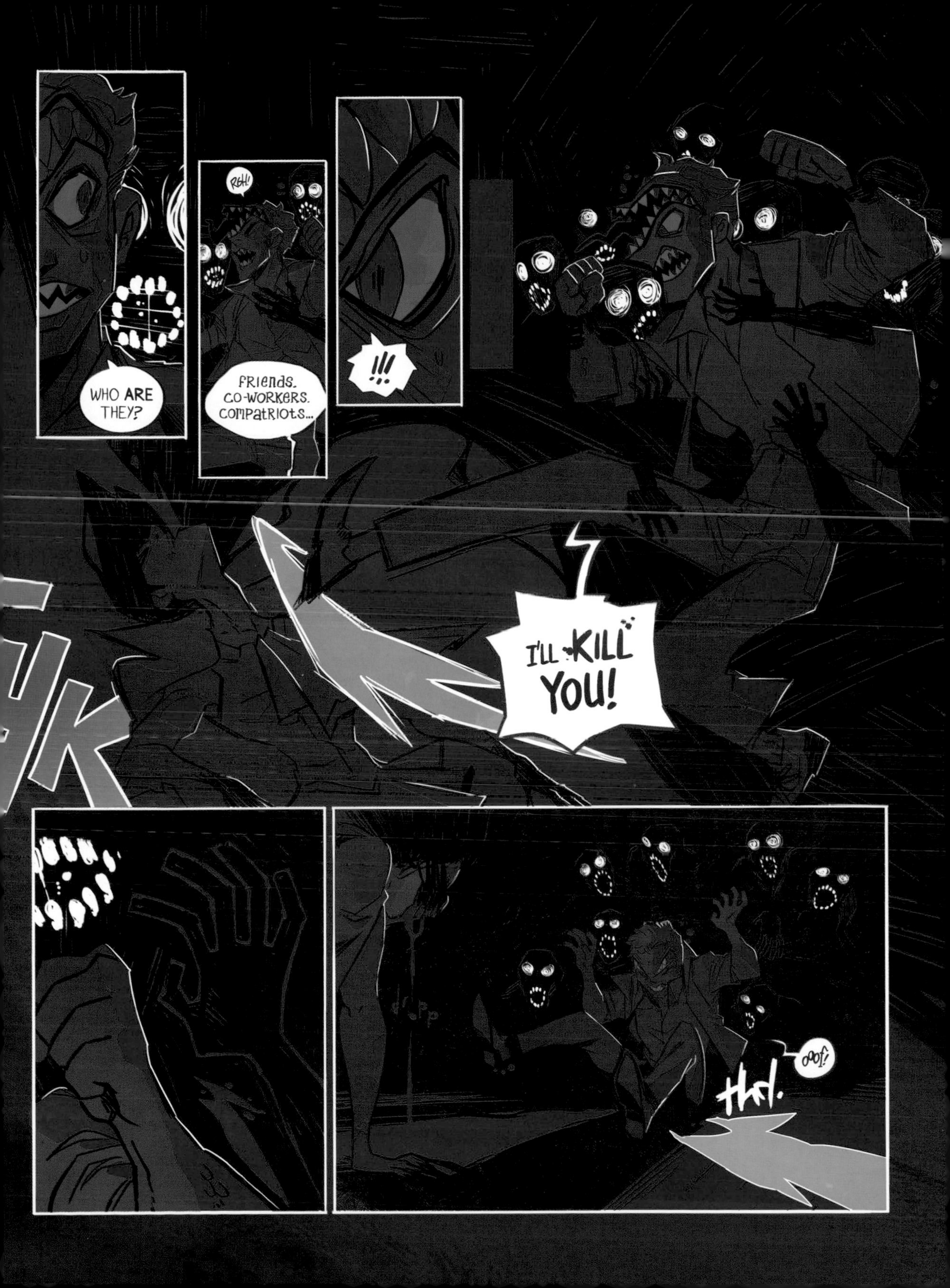
WHO ARE THEY?
RGH!
Friends. Co-workers. Compatriots...
!!!
I'LL KILL YOU!
thd.
ooof!

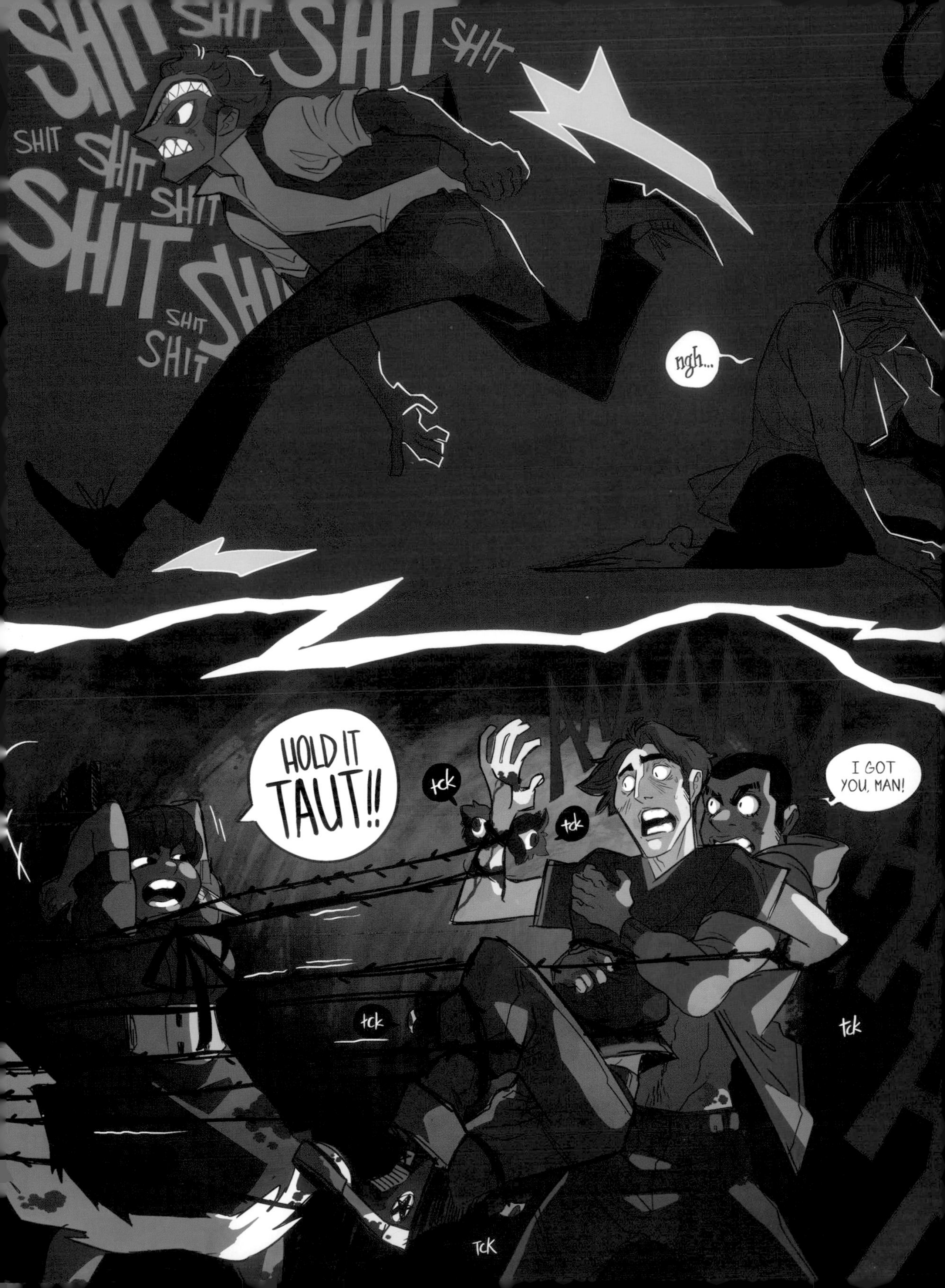
SHIT SHIT SHIT SHIT
SHIT SHIT SHIT
SHIT SHIT SHIT
SHIT SHIT SHIT
ngh...
HOLD IT TAUT!!
tck
tck
I GOT YOU, MAN!
tck
tck
TCK

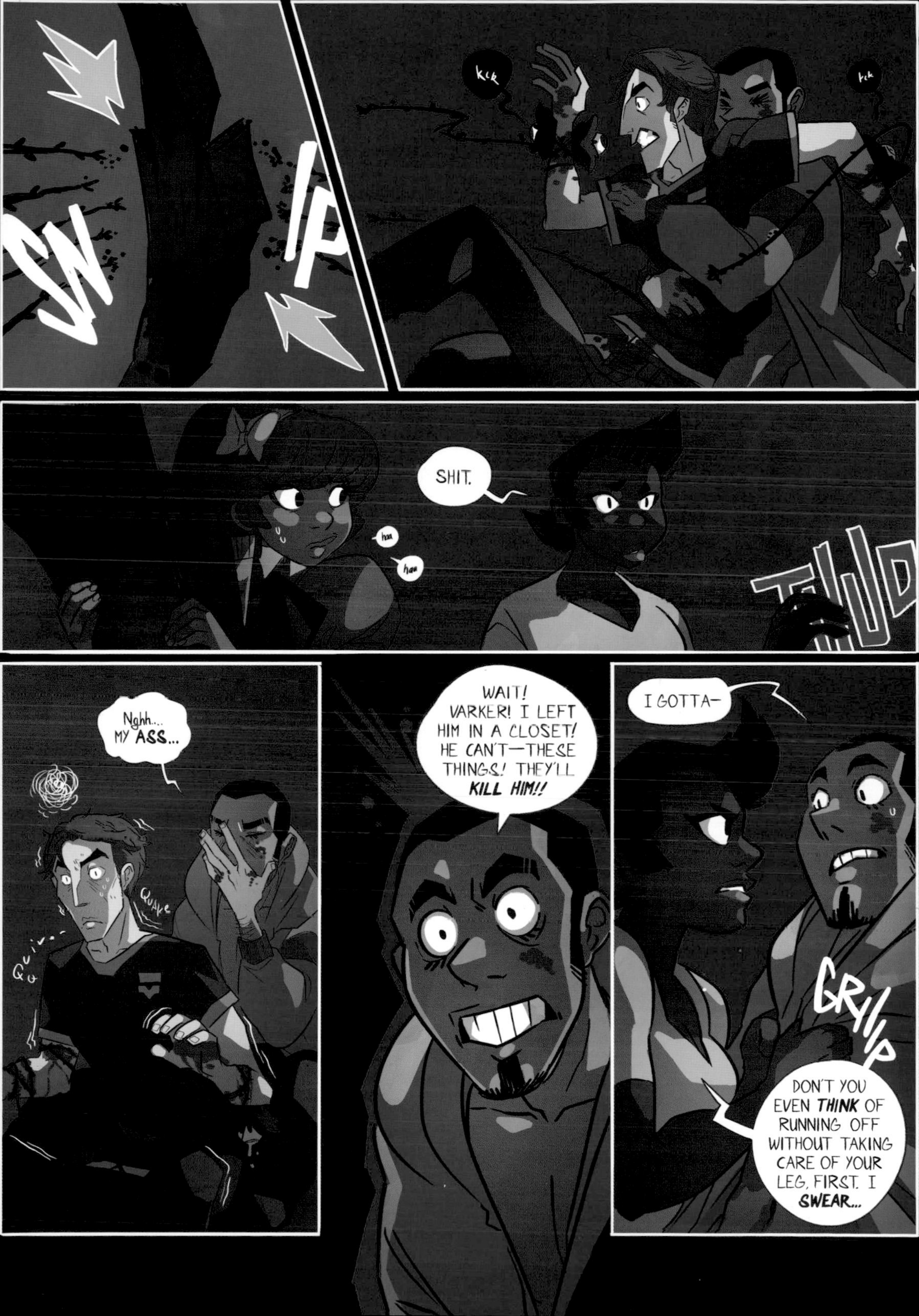
SWIP
kck
kck
SHIT.
haa
haa
THUD
Nghh... MY ASS...
Quake
Quiver
WAIT! VARKER! I LEFT HIM IN A CLOSET! HE CAN'T—THESE THINGS! THEY'LL KILL HIM!!
I GOTTA-
GRIP
DON'T YOU EVEN THINK OF RUNNING OFF WITHOUT TAKING CARE OF YOUR LEG, FIRST. I SWEAR...

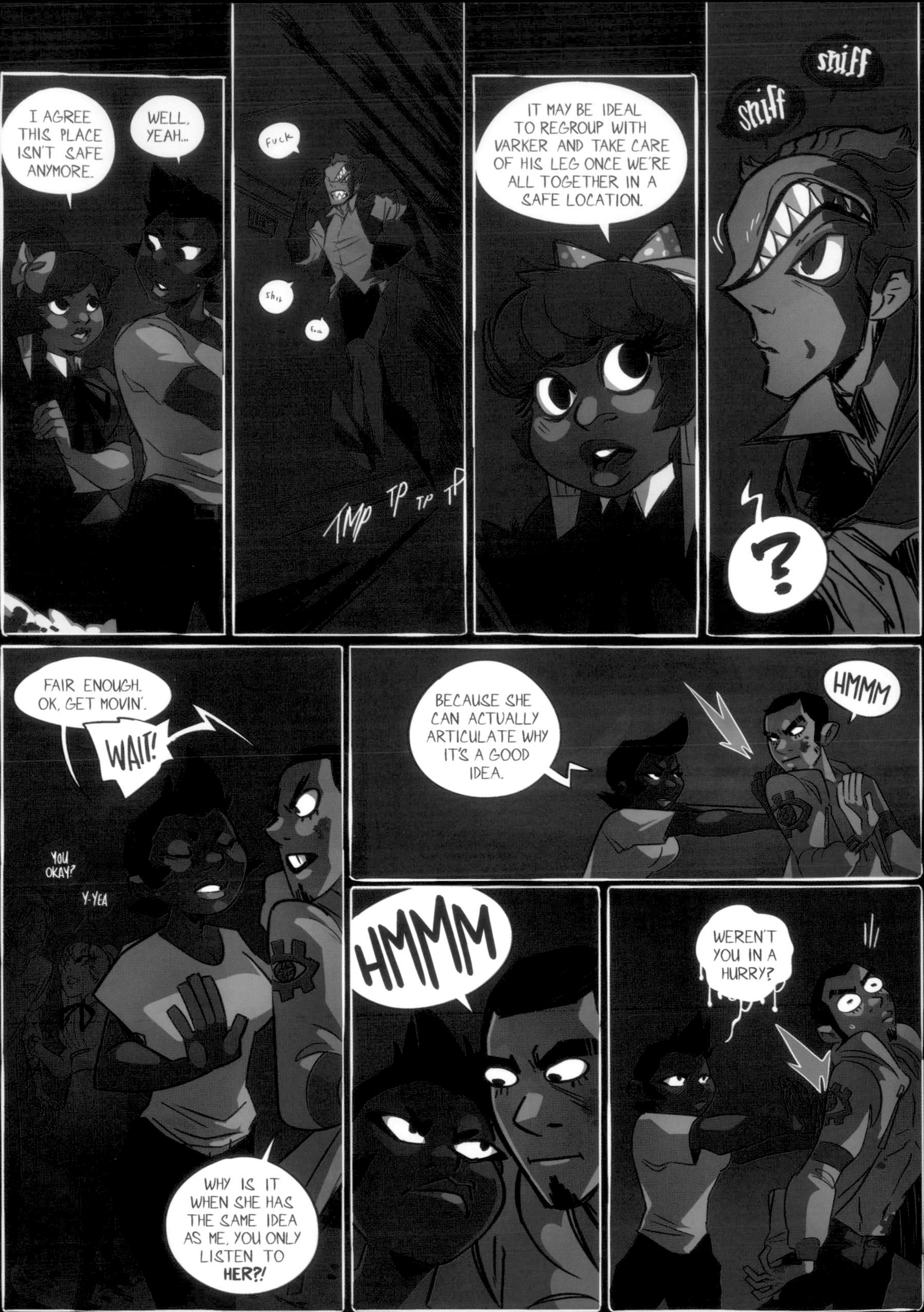

I AGREE THIS PLACE ISN'T SAFE ANYMORE.
WELL, YEAH...
Fuck
shit
fuck
TMP TP TP TP
IT MAY BE IDEAL TO REGROUP WITH VARKER AND TAKE CARE OF HIS LEG ONCE WE'RE ALL TOGETHER IN A SAFE LOCATION.
sniff
sniff
?
FAIR ENOUGH. OK, GET MOVIN'.
WAIT!
YOU OKAY?
Y-YEA
WHY IS IT WHEN SHE HAS THE SAME IDEA AS ME, YOU ONLY LISTEN TO **HER?!**
BECAUSE SHE CAN ACTUALLY ARTICULATE WHY IT'S A GOOD IDEA.
HMMM
HMMM
WEREN'T YOU IN A HURRY?

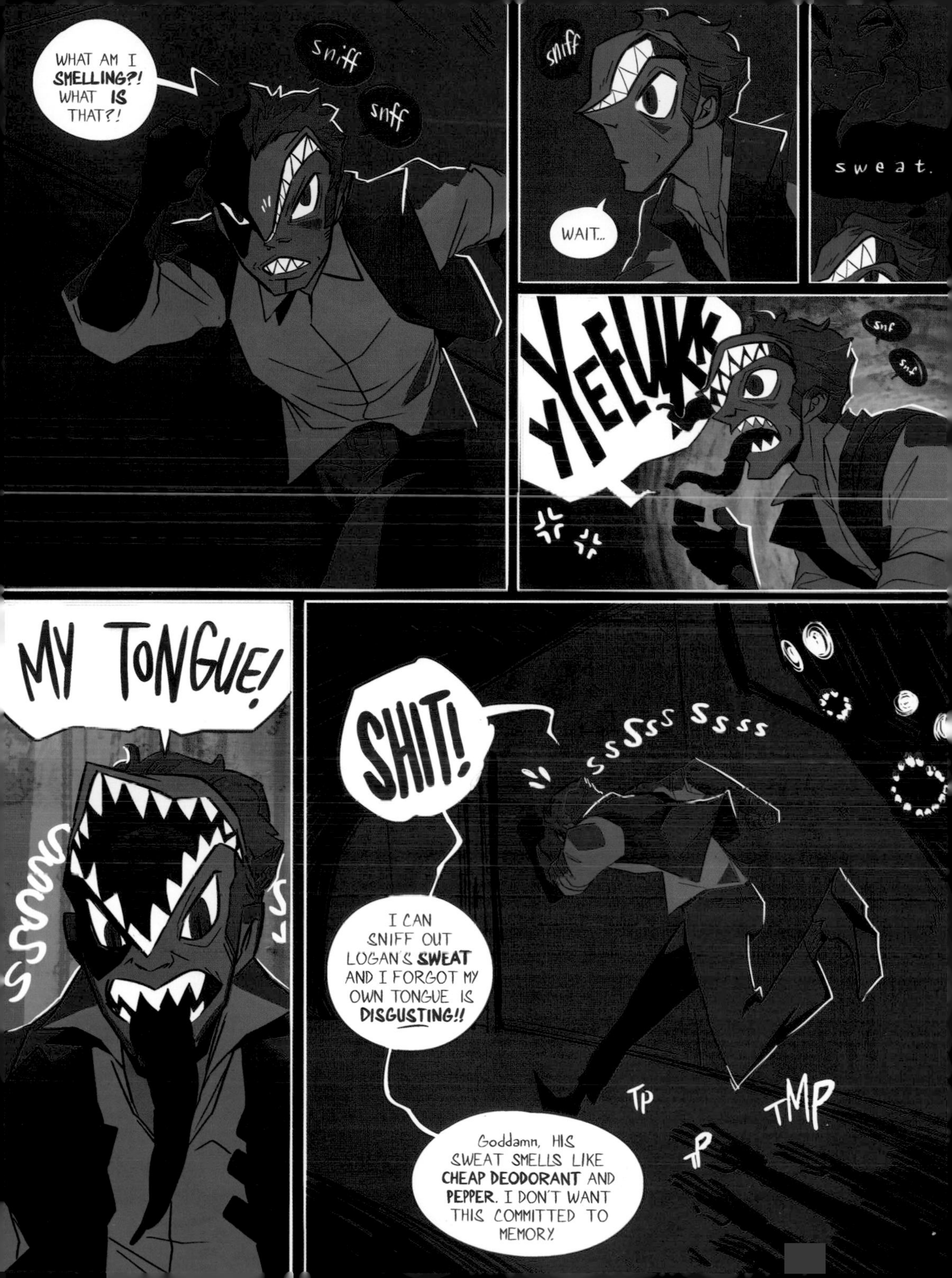
WHAT AM I SMELLING?! WHAT IS THAT?!
sniff
sniff
sniff
WAIT...
sweat.
YEEUKK
snf
snf
MY TONGUE!
SHIT!
SSSSS SSSS
I CAN SNIFF OUT LOGAN'S SWEAT AND I FORGOT MY OWN TONGUE IS DISGUSTING!!
Goddamn, HIS SWEAT SMELLS LIKE CHEAP DEODORANT AND PEPPER. I DON'T WANT THIS COMMITTED TO MEMORY.
TP
TP
TMP

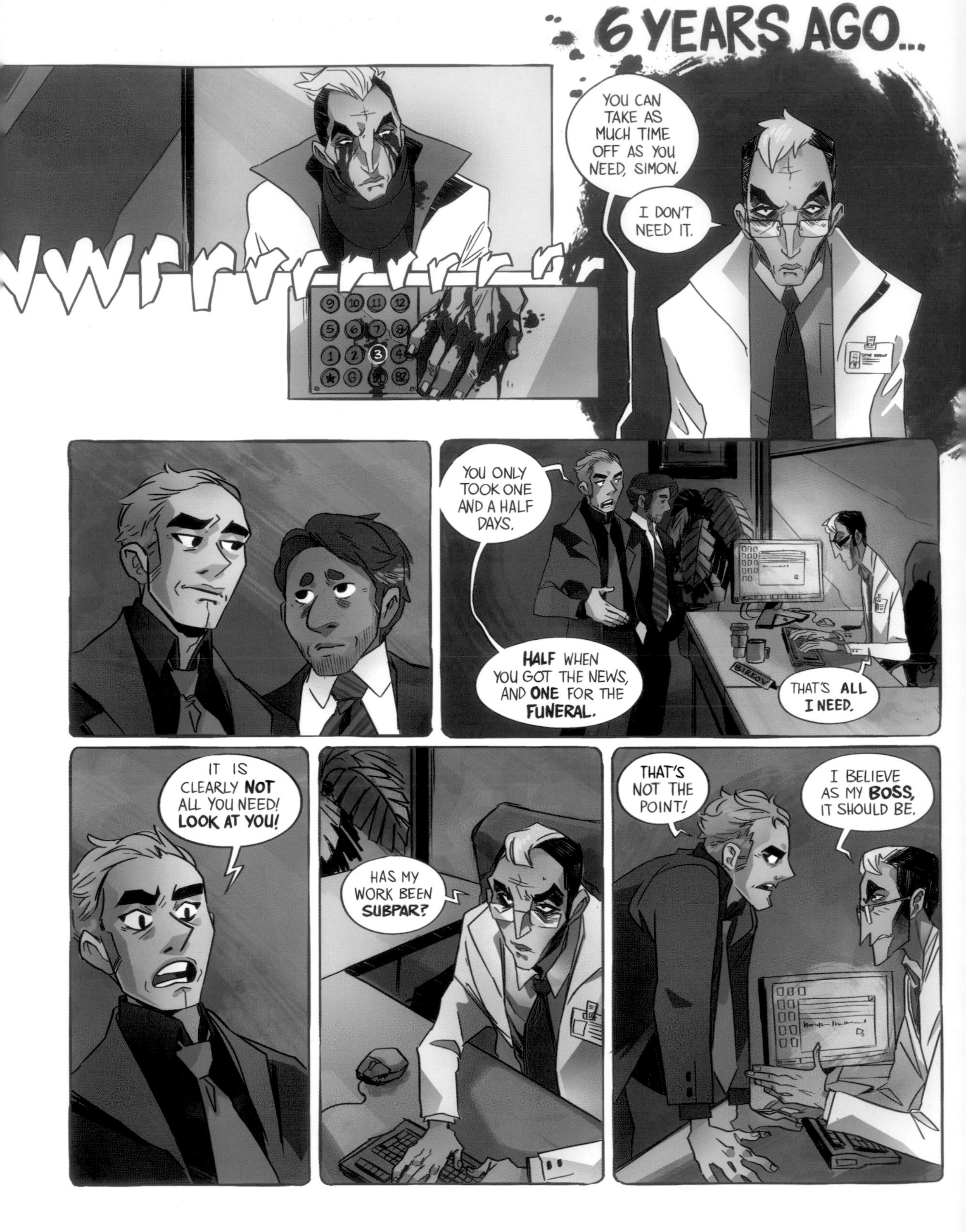
6 YEARS AGO...
VWRRRRRRRRR
YOU CAN TAKE AS MUCH TIME OFF AS YOU NEED, SIMON.
I DON'T NEED IT.
YOU ONLY TOOK ONE AND A HALF DAYS.
HALF WHEN YOU GOT THE NEWS, AND ONE FOR THE FUNERAL.
BIRKOV
THAT'S ALL I NEED.
IT IS CLEARLY NOT ALL YOU NEED! LOOK AT YOU!
HAS MY WORK BEEN SUBPAR?
THAT'S NOT THE POINT!
I BELIEVE AS MY BOSS, IT SHOULD BE.

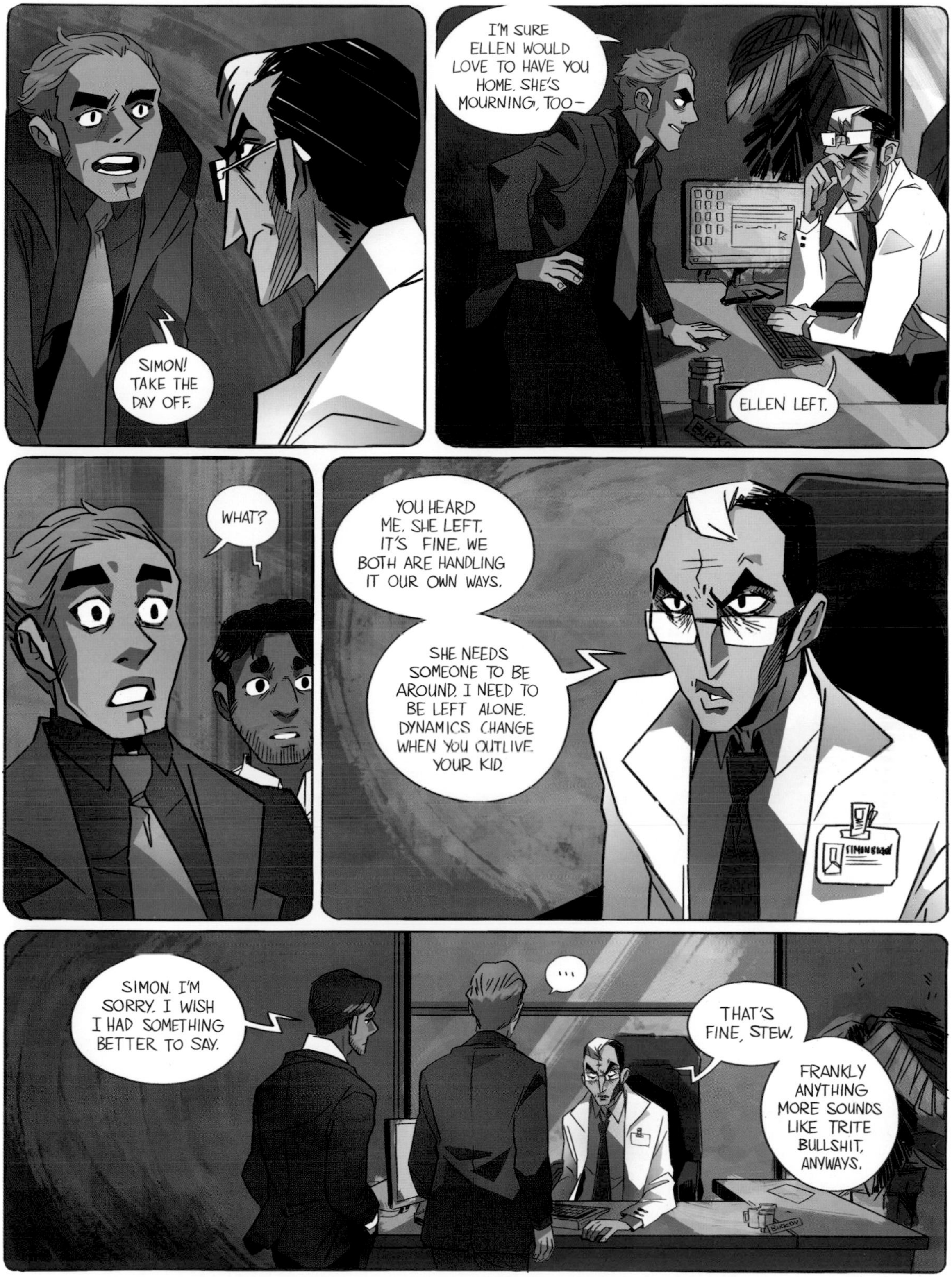
SIMON! TAKE THE DAY OFF.
I'M SURE ELLEN WOULD LOVE TO HAVE YOU HOME. SHE'S MOURNING, TOO—
ELLEN LEFT.
WHAT?
YOU HEARD ME. SHE LEFT. IT'S FINE. WE BOTH ARE HANDLING IT OUR OWN WAYS.
SHE NEEDS SOMEONE TO BE AROUND. I NEED TO BE LEFT ALONE. DYNAMICS CHANGE WHEN YOU OUTLIVE YOUR KID.
SIMON. I'M SORRY. I WISH I HAD SOMETHING BETTER TO SAY.
...
THAT'S FINE, STEW.
FRANKLY ANYTHING MORE SOUNDS LIKE TRITE BULLSHIT, ANYWAYS.

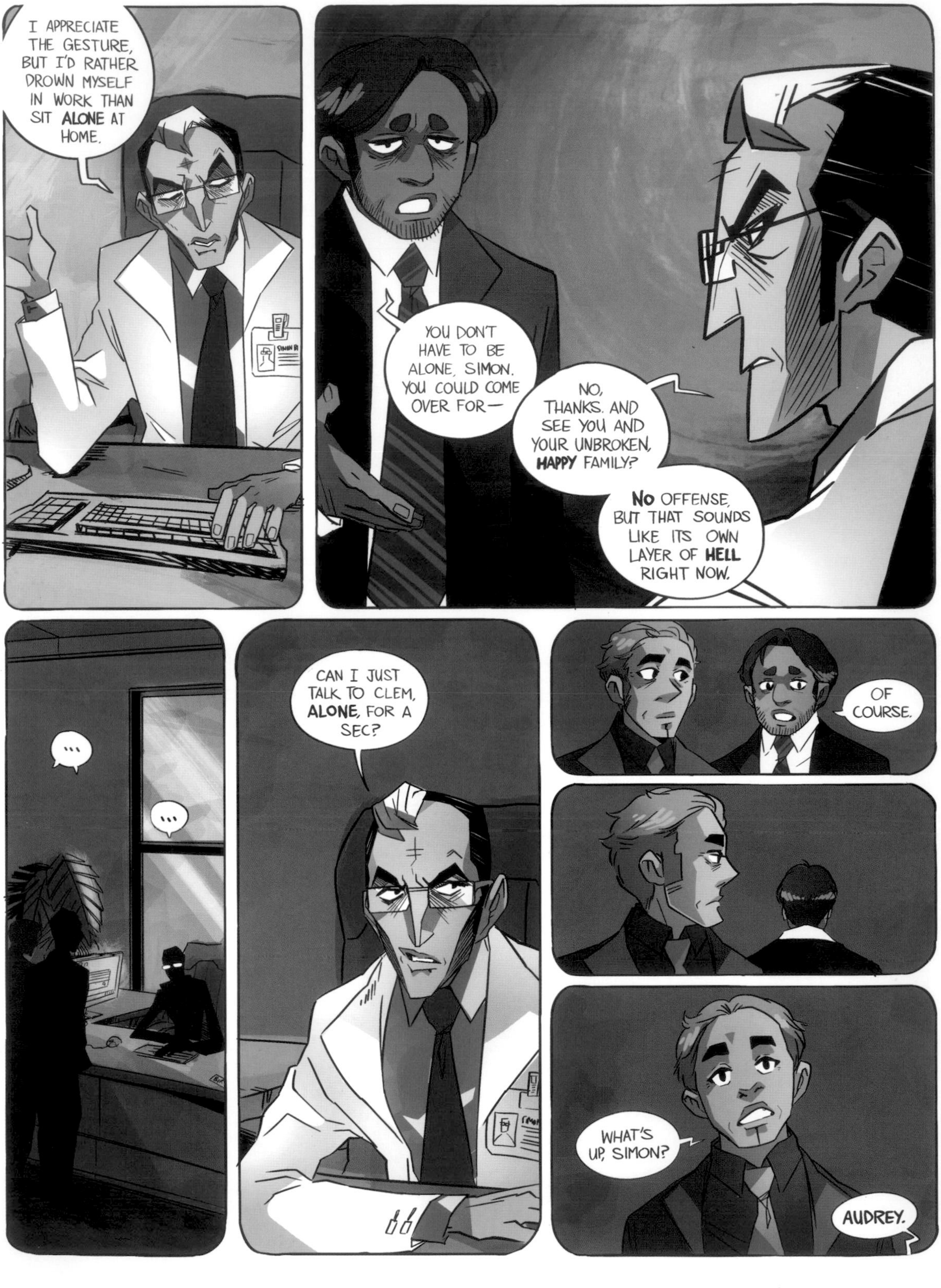
I APPRECIATE THE GESTURE, BUT I'D RATHER DROWN MYSELF IN WORK THAN SIT ALONE AT HOME.
YOU DON'T HAVE TO BE ALONE, SIMON. YOU COULD COME OVER FOR—
NO, THANKS. AND SEE YOU AND YOUR UNBROKEN, HAPPY FAMILY?
NO OFFENSE, BUT THAT SOUNDS LIKE ITS OWN LAYER OF HELL RIGHT NOW.
...
...
CAN I JUST TALK TO CLEM, ALONE, FOR A SEC?
OF COURSE.
WHAT'S UP, SIMON?
AUDREY.

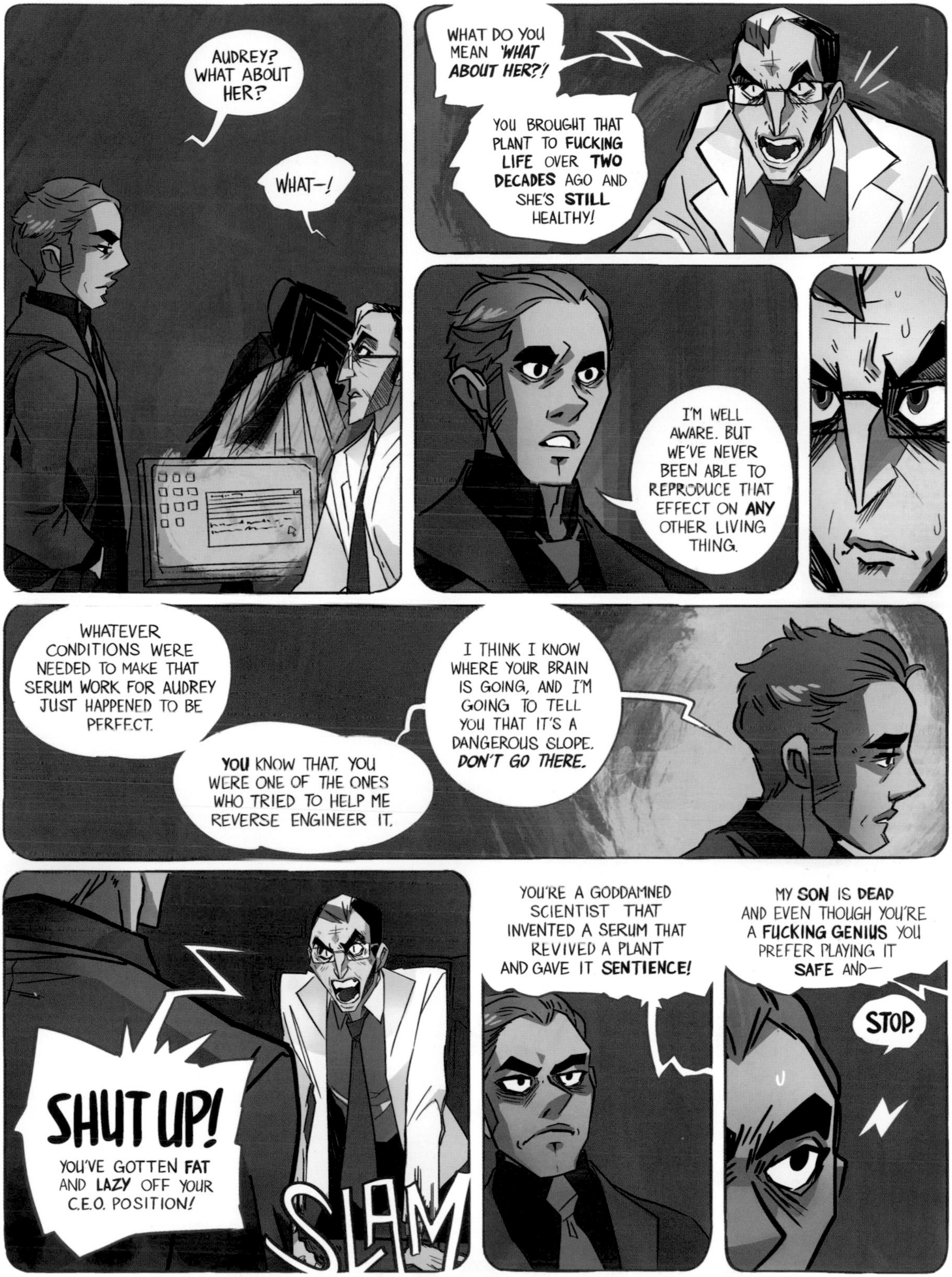
AUDREY? WHAT ABOUT HER?
WHAT—!
WHAT DO YOU MEAN 'WHAT ABOUT HER?'!
YOU BROUGHT THAT PLANT TO FUCKING LIFE OVER TWO DECADES AGO AND SHE'S STILL HEALTHY!
I'M WELL AWARE. BUT WE'VE NEVER BEEN ABLE TO REPRODUCE THAT EFFECT ON ANY OTHER LIVING THING.
WHATEVER CONDITIONS WERE NEEDED TO MAKE THAT SERUM WORK FOR AUDREY JUST HAPPENED TO BE PERFECT.
YOU KNOW THAT. YOU WERE ONE OF THE ONES WHO TRIED TO HELP ME REVERSE ENGINEER IT.
I THINK I KNOW WHERE YOUR BRAIN IS GOING, AND I'M GOING TO TELL YOU THAT IT'S A DANGEROUS SLOPE. DON'T GO THERE.
SHUT UP!
YOU'VE GOTTEN FAT AND LAZY OFF YOUR C.E.O. POSITION!
SLAM
YOU'RE A GODDAMNED SCIENTIST THAT INVENTED A SERUM THAT REVIVED A PLANT AND GAVE IT SENTIENCE!
MY SON IS DEAD AND EVEN THOUGH YOU'RE A FUCKING GENIUS YOU PREFER PLAYING IT SAFE AND—
STOP.

JUST **STOP.** ONLY AN IDIOT WOULD THINK THAT A SINGLE SUCCESS **TWENTY** YEARS AGO WITH PLANT LIFE COULD GARNER RESULTS WITH A **HUMAN BEING.**

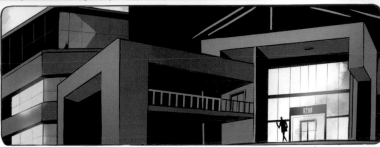

YOU'RE NOT IN YOUR **RIGHT MIND,** SIMON. WHAT YOU'RE PROPOSING WOULD REQUIRE **HUMAN** TEST SUBJECTS, WHICH IS NOT ONLY **ILLEGAL,** BUT **UNETHICAL.**

GO HOME. GET SOME REST. **PLEASE.**

I UNDERSTAND YOUR LOSS, SIMON, BUT OBSESSING OVER HIS REVIVAL WON'T **CHANGE** ANYTHING.

HEY, ABRAHM.

I FINALLY THOUGHT OF A FAVOR.

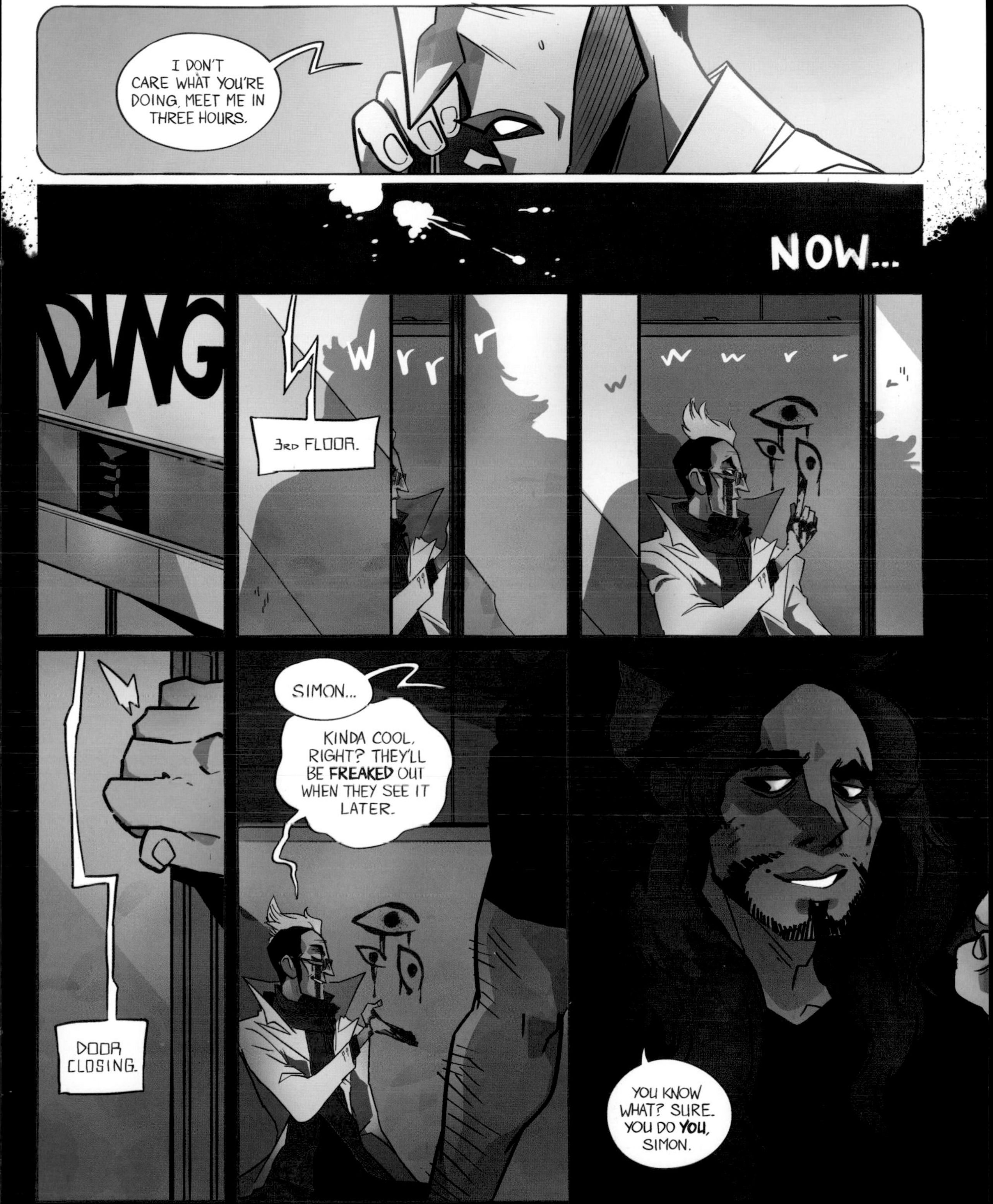

I DON'T CARE WHAT YOU'RE DOING, MEET ME IN THREE HOURS.
NOW...
DING
Wrrr
3RD FLOOR.
wwwrr
DOOR CLOSING.
SIMON...
KINDA COOL, RIGHT? THEY'LL BE FREAKED OUT WHEN THEY SEE IT LATER.
YOU KNOW WHAT? SURE. YOU DO YOU, SIMON.

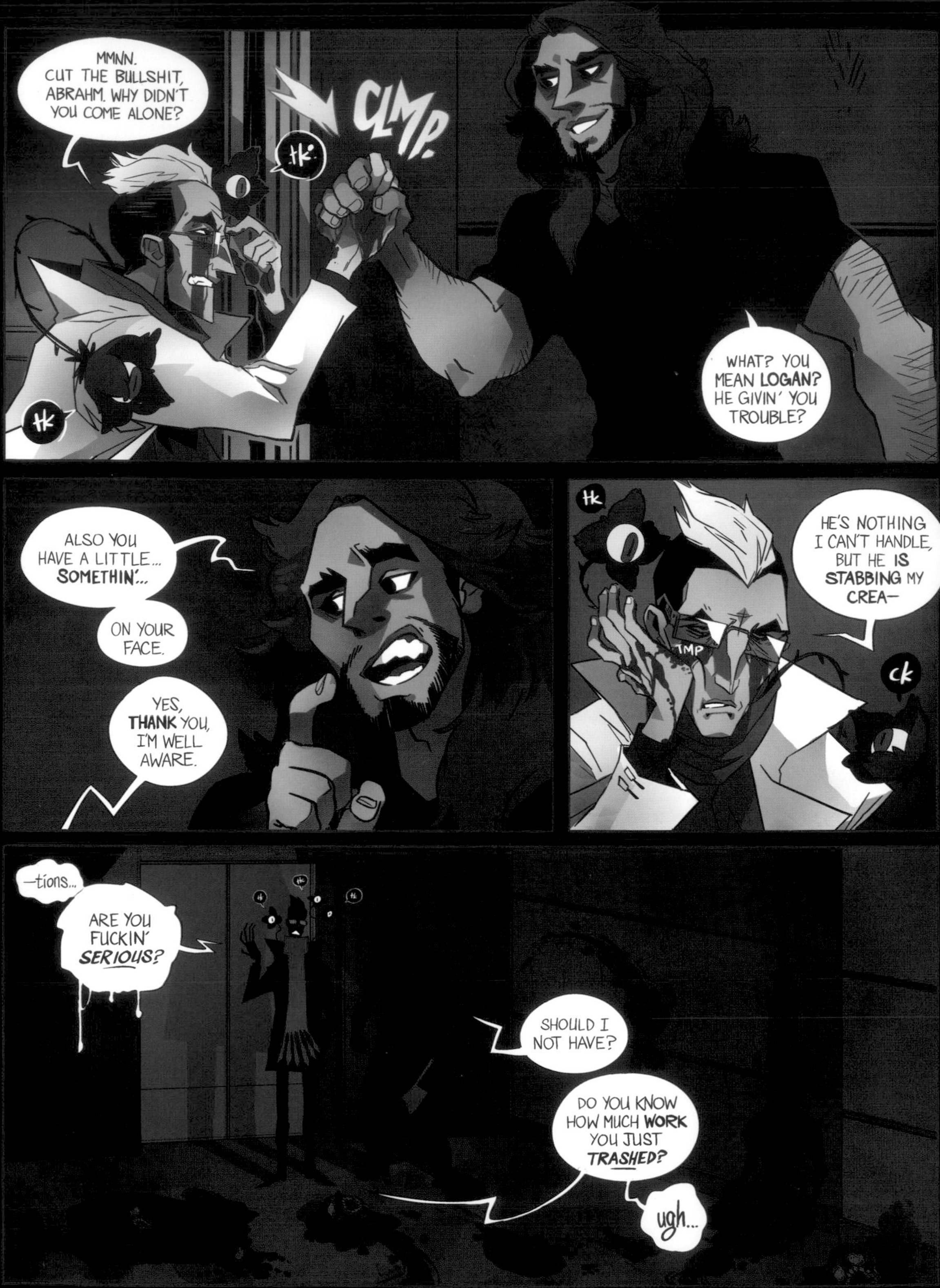
MMNN. CUT THE BULLSHIT, ABRAHM. WHY DIDN'T YOU COME ALONE?
tk
CLMP.
tk
WHAT? YOU MEAN LOGAN? HE GIVIN' YOU TROUBLE?
ALSO YOU HAVE A LITTLE... SOMETHIN'...
ON YOUR FACE.
YES, THANK YOU, I'M WELL AWARE.
tk
HE'S NOTHING I CAN'T HANDLE, BUT HE IS STABBING MY CREA—
TMP
ck
—tions...
ARE YOU FUCKIN' SERIOUS?
SHOULD I NOT HAVE?
DO YOU KNOW HOW MUCH WORK YOU JUST TRASHED?
ugh...

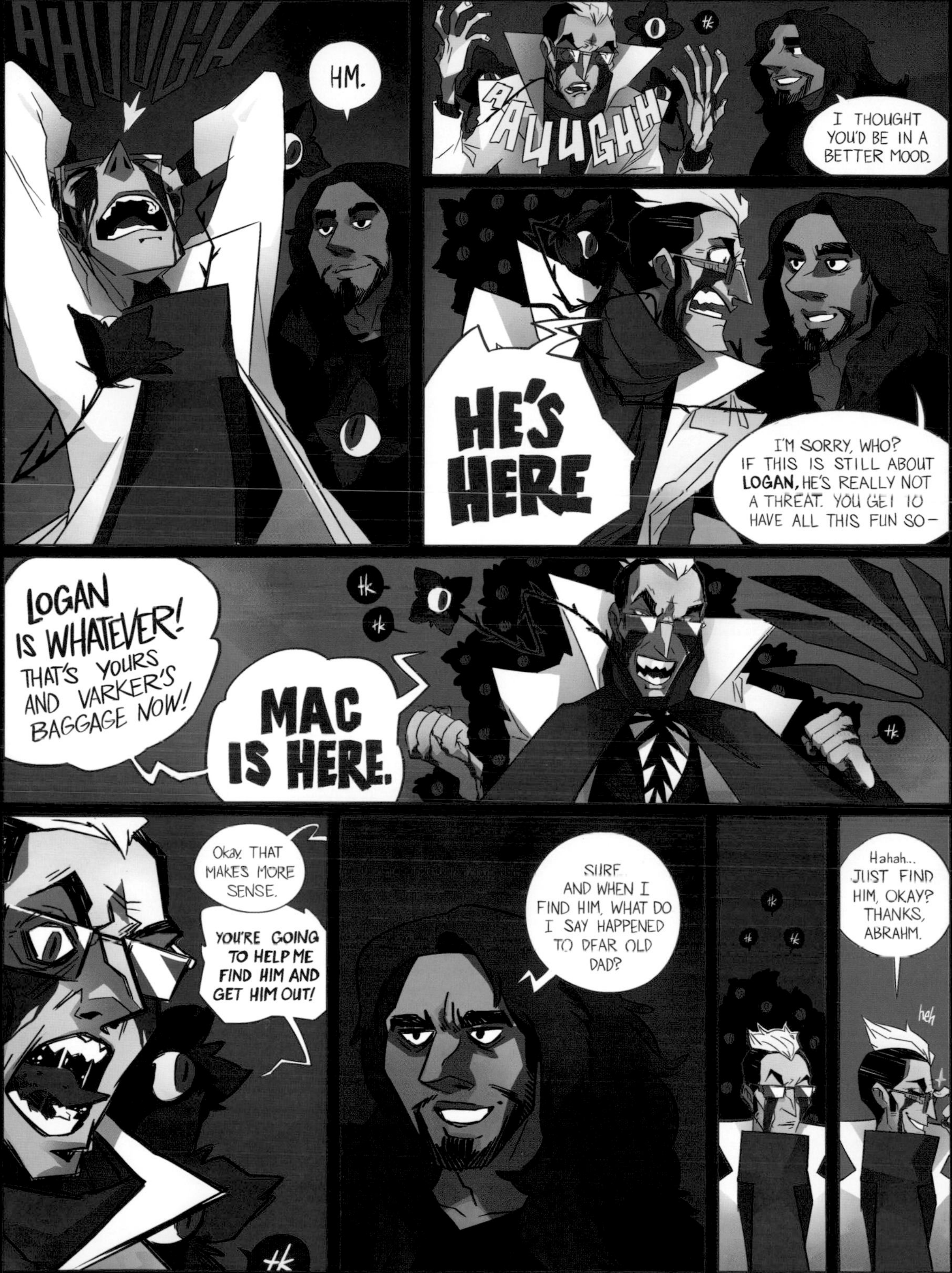
AHHUGH!
HM.
AAUUGHH
I THOUGHT YOU'D BE IN A BETTER MOOD.
HE'S HERE
I'M SORRY, WHO? IF THIS IS STILL ABOUT LOGAN, HE'S REALLY NOT A THREAT. YOU GET TO HAVE ALL THIS FUN SO—
LOGAN IS WHATEVER! THAT'S YOURS AND VARKER'S BAGGAGE NOW!
MAC IS HERE.
Okay. THAT MAKES MORE SENSE.
YOU'RE GOING TO HELP ME FIND HIM AND GET HIM OUT!
SURE. AND WHEN I FIND HIM, WHAT DO I SAY HAPPENED TO DEAR OLD DAD?
Hahah... JUST FIND HIM, OKAY? THANKS, ABRAHM.
heh

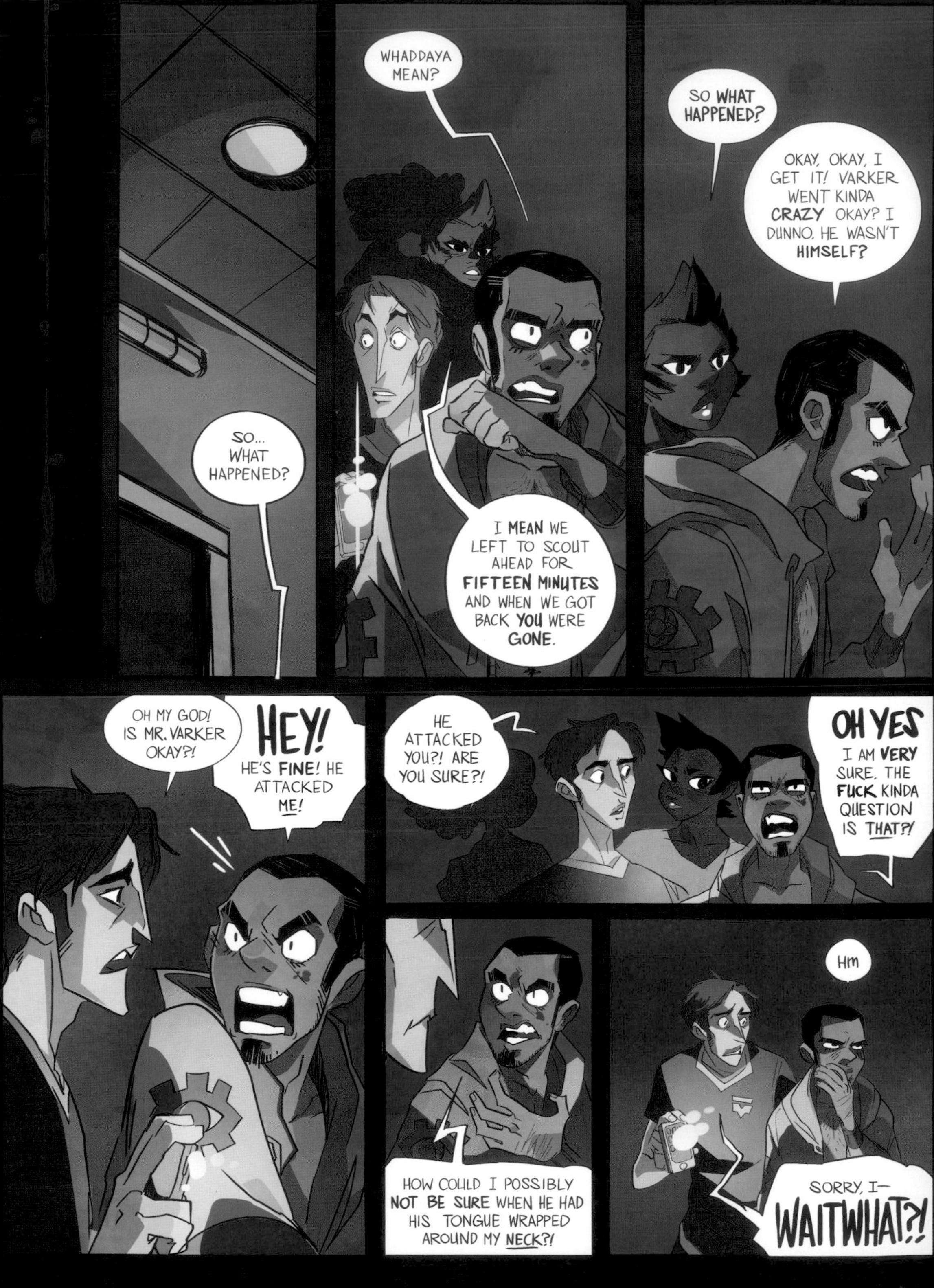
SO... WHAT HAPPENED?
WHADDAYA MEAN?
I MEAN WE LEFT TO SCOUT AHEAD FOR FIFTEEN MINUTES AND WHEN WE GOT BACK YOU WERE GONE.
SO WHAT HAPPENED?
OKAY, OKAY, I GET IT! VARKER WENT KINDA CRAZY OKAY? I DUNNO. HE WASN'T HIMSELF?
OH MY GOD! IS MR. VARKER OKAY?!
HEY!
HE'S FINE! HE ATTACKED ME!
HE ATTACKED YOU?! ARE YOU SURE?!
OH YES
I AM VERY SURE. THE FUCK KINDA QUESTION IS THAT?!
HOW COULD I POSSIBLY NOT BE SURE WHEN HE HAD HIS TONGUE WRAPPED AROUND MY NECK?!
Hm
SORRY, I—
WAITWHAT?!

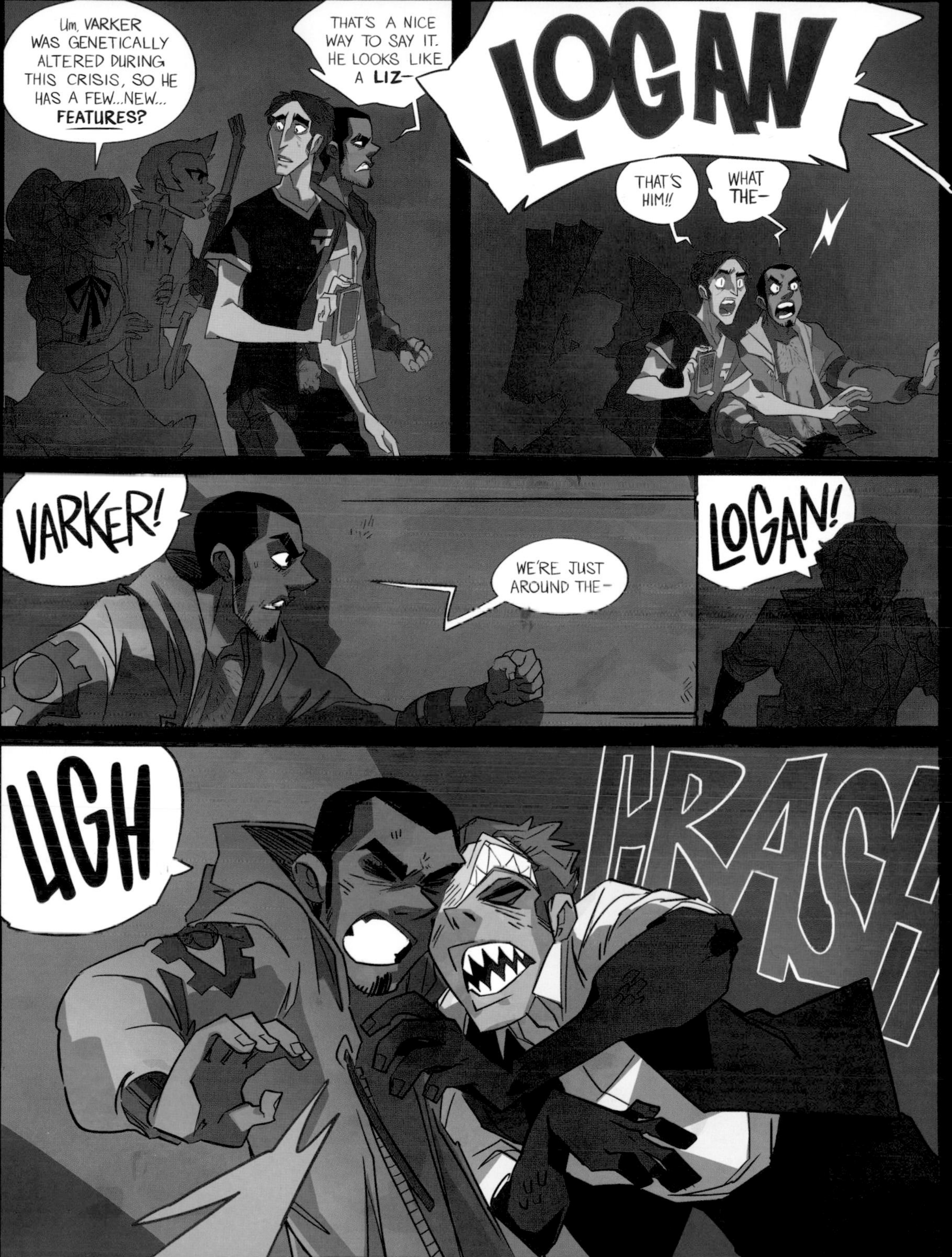

Um, VARKER WAS GENETICALLY ALTERED DURING THIS CRISIS, SO HE HAS A FEW...NEW... FEATURES?
THAT'S A NICE WAY TO SAY IT. HE LOOKS LIKE A LIZ-
LOGAN
THAT'S HIM!!
WHAT THE-
VARKER!
WE'RE JUST AROUND THE-
LOGAN!
UGH
KRASH

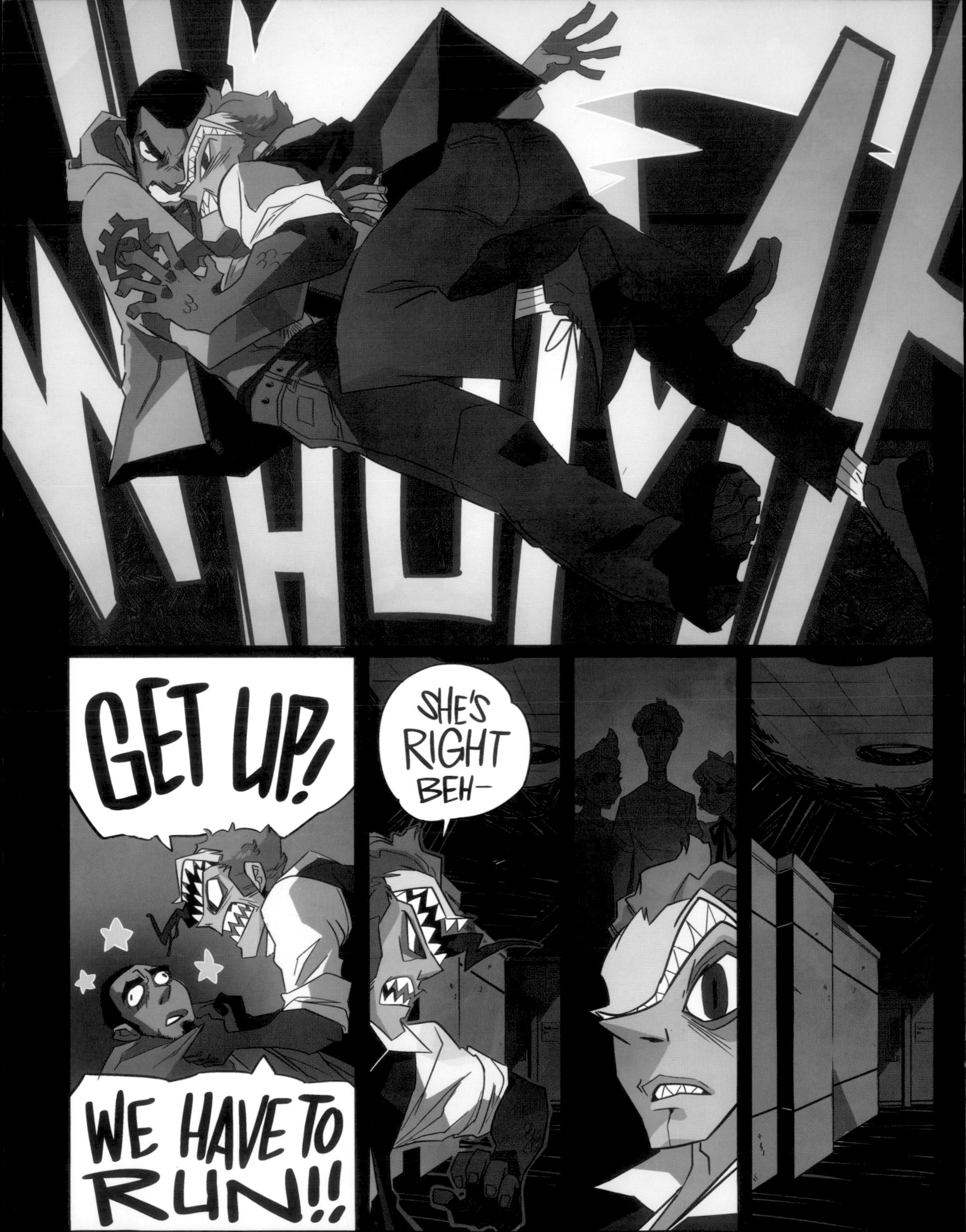
GET UP!
WE HAVE TO RUN!!
SHE'S RIGHT BEH-

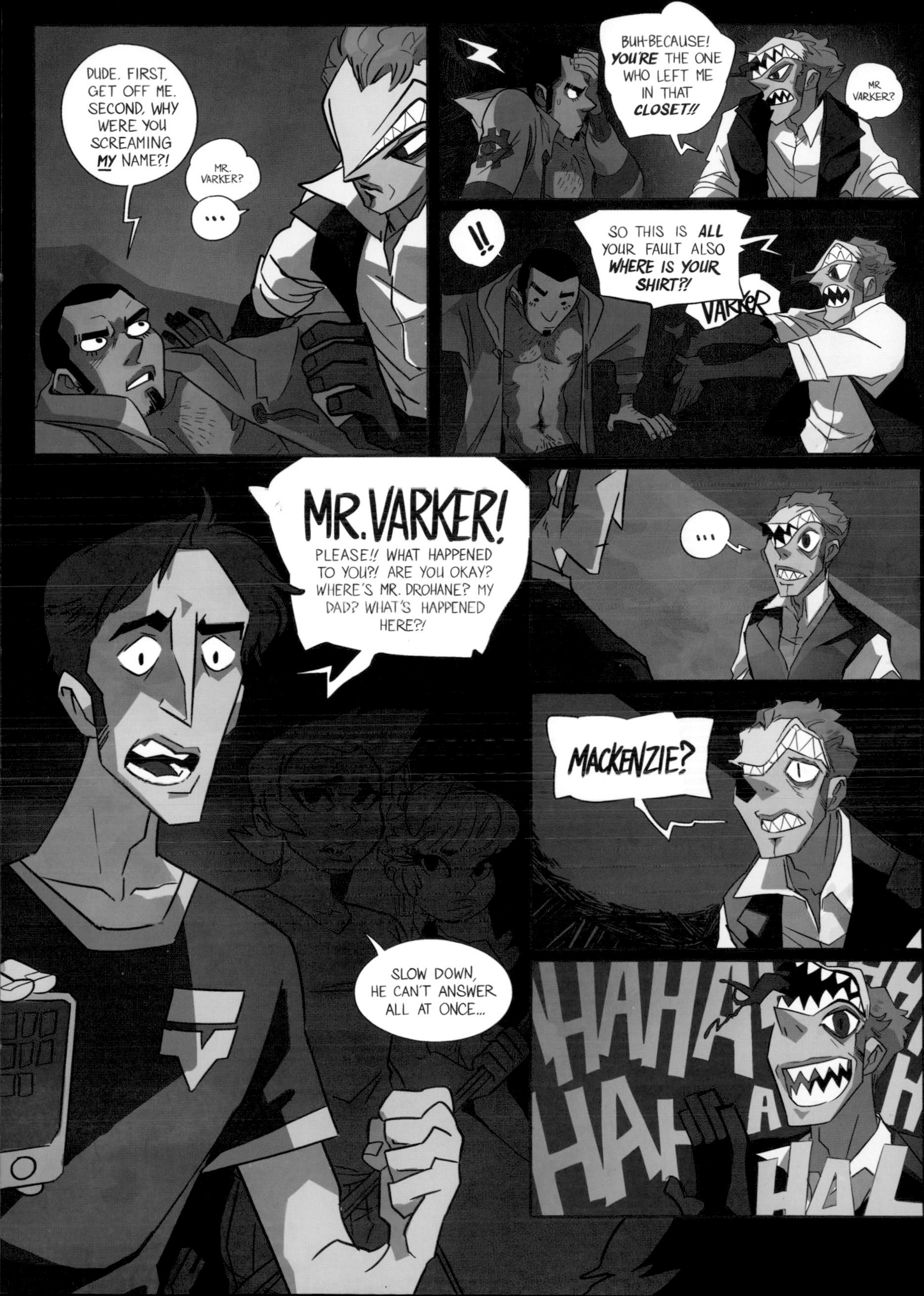
DUDE. FIRST, GET OFF ME. SECOND, WHY WERE YOU SCREAMING MY NAME?!
MR. VARKER?
...
BUH-BECAUSE! YOU'RE THE ONE WHO LEFT ME IN THAT CLOSET!!
MR VARKER?
!!
SO THIS IS ALL YOUR FAULT ALSO WHERE IS YOUR SHIRT?!
VARKER
MR. VARKER!
PLEASE!! WHAT HAPPENED TO YOU?! ARE YOU OKAY? WHERE'S MR. DROHANE? MY DAD? WHAT'S HAPPENED HERE?!
...
MACKENZIE?
SLOW DOWN, HE CAN'T ANSWER ALL AT ONCE...

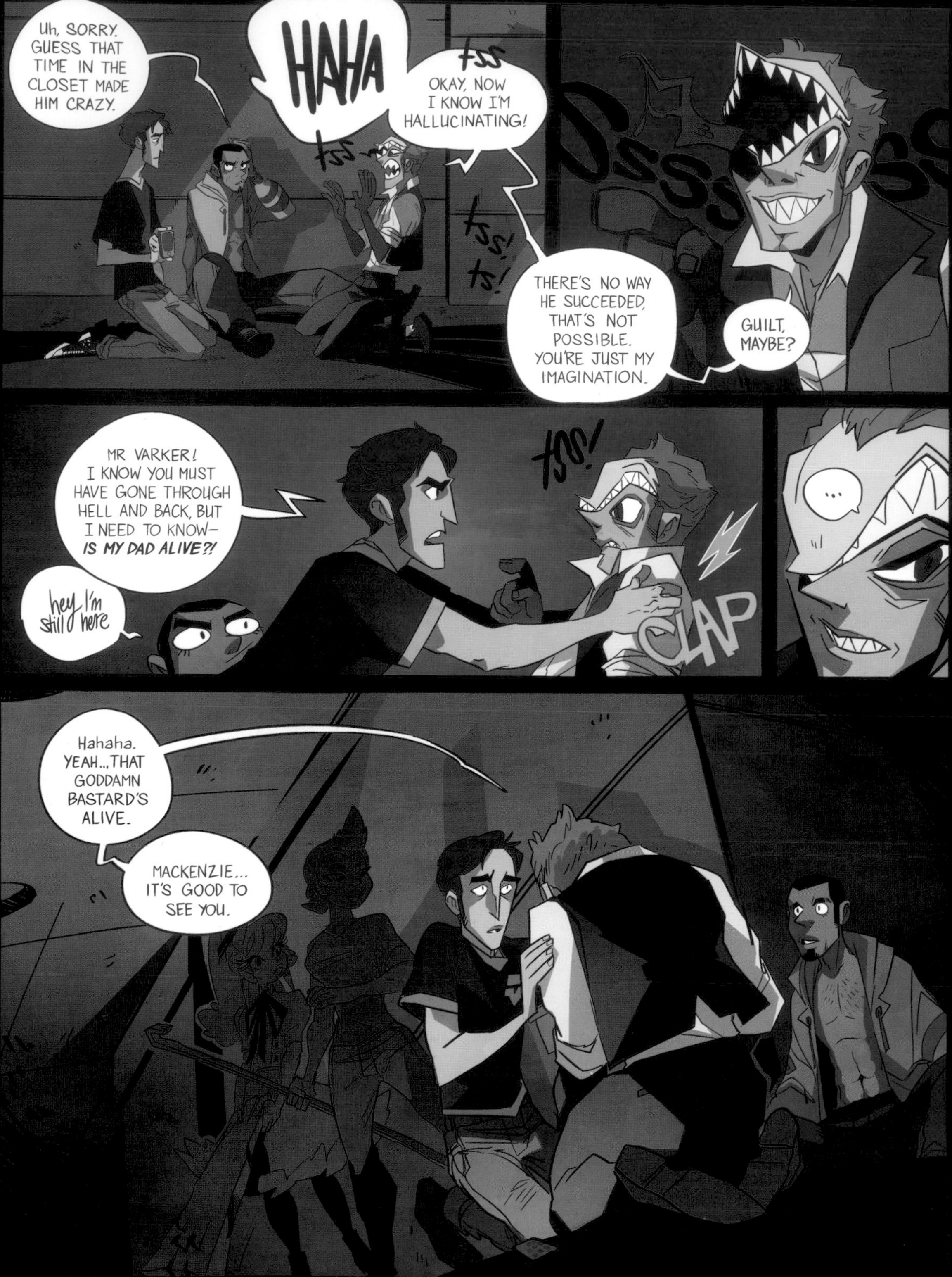
Uh, SORRY. GUESS THAT TIME IN THE CLOSET MADE HIM CRAZY.
HAHA
tss
OKAY, NOW I KNOW I'M HALLUCINATING!
tss
tss!
ts!
THERE'S NO WAY HE SUCCEEDED, THAT'S NOT POSSIBLE. YOU'RE JUST MY IMAGINATION.
GUILT, MAYBE?
MR VARKER! I KNOW YOU MUST HAVE GONE THROUGH HELL AND BACK, BUT I NEED TO KNOW— IS MY DAD ALIVE?!
tss!
hey I'm still here
CLAP
...
Hahaha. YEAH...THAT GODDAMN BASTARD'S ALIVE.
MACKENZIE... IT'S GOOD TO SEE YOU.

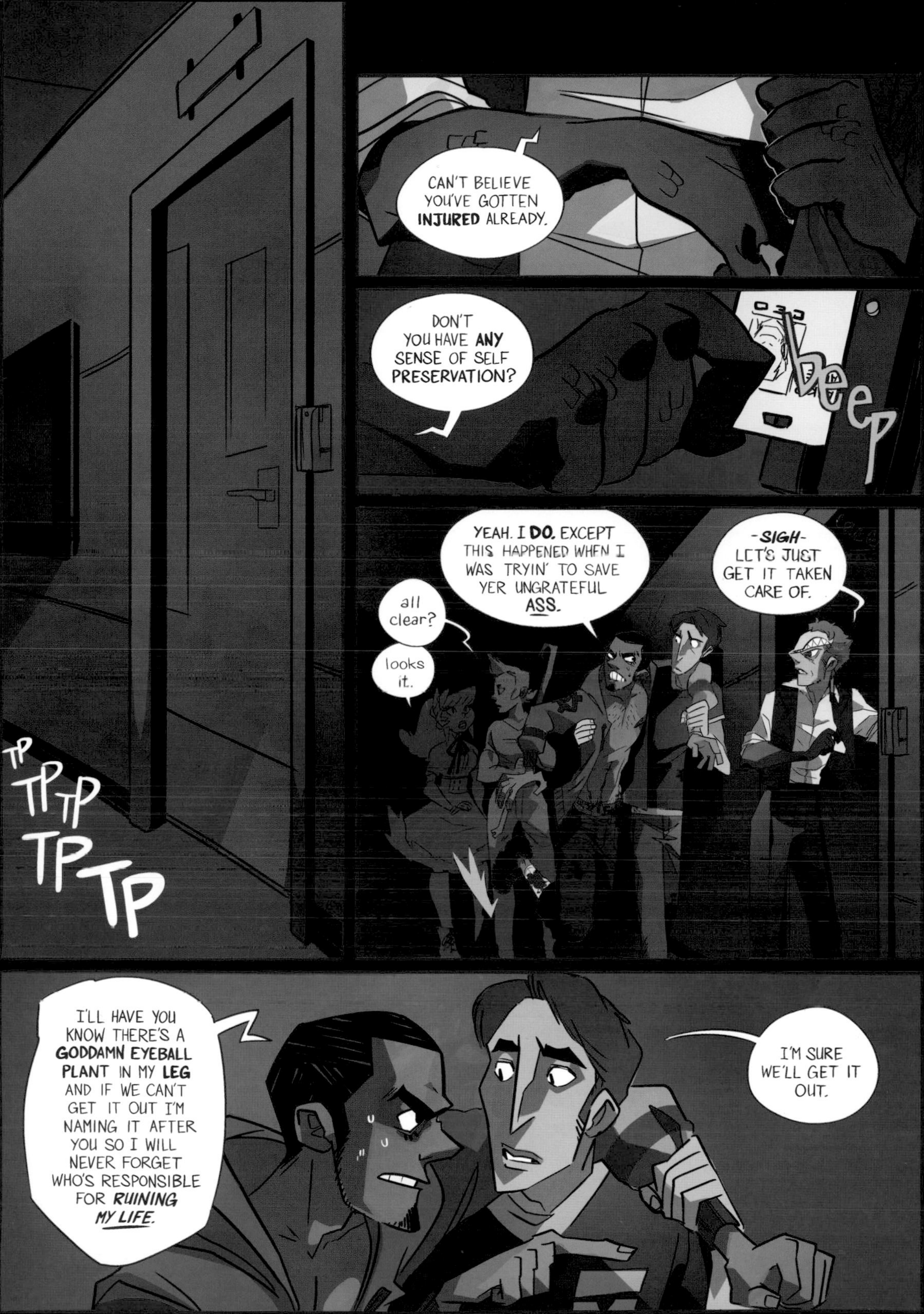
CAN'T BELIEVE YOU'VE GOTTEN **INJURED** ALREADY.
DON'T YOU HAVE **ANY** SENSE OF SELF **PRESERVATION**?
beeep
TP TP TP TP TP TP
all clear?
looks it.
YEAH. I **DO.** EXCEPT THIS HAPPENED WHEN I WAS TRYIN' TO SAVE YER UNGRATEFUL **ASS.**
-**SIGH**- LET'S JUST GET IT TAKEN CARE OF.
I'LL HAVE YOU KNOW THERE'S A **GODDAMN EYEBALL PLANT** IN MY **LEG** AND IF WE CAN'T GET IT OUT I'M NAMING IT AFTER YOU SO I WILL NEVER FORGET WHO'S RESPONSIBLE FOR ***RUINING MY LIFE.***
I'M SURE WE'LL GET IT OUT.

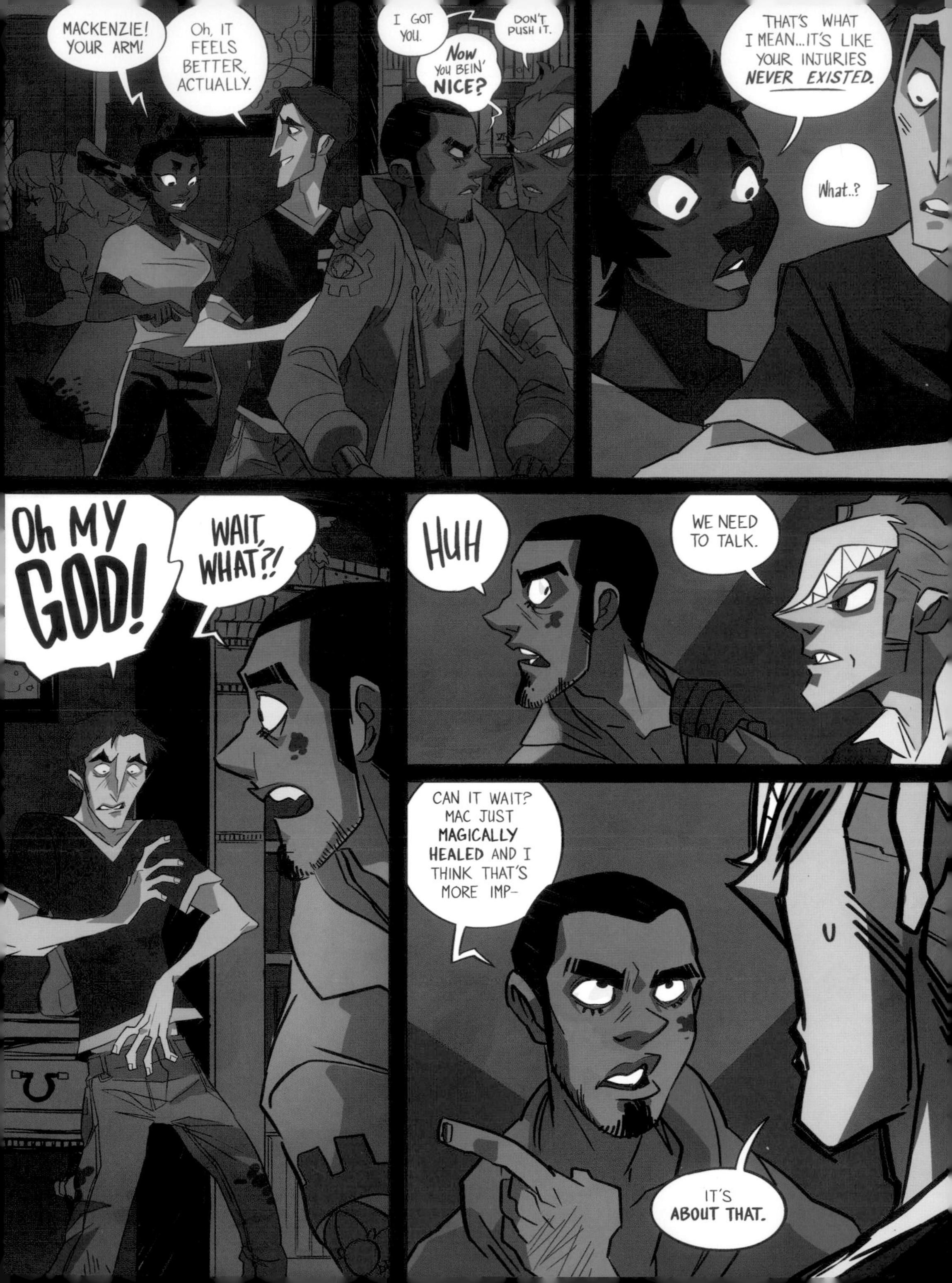
MACKENZIE! YOUR ARM!
Oh, IT FEELS BETTER, ACTUALLY.
I GOT YOU.
DON'T PUSH IT.
Now YOU BEIN' NICE?
THAT'S WHAT I MEAN...IT'S LIKE YOUR INJURIES NEVER EXISTED.
What..?
Oh MY GOD!
WAIT, WHAT?!
HUH
WE NEED TO TALK.
CAN IT WAIT? MAC JUST MAGICALLY HEALED AND I THINK THAT'S MORE IMP-
IT'S ABOUT THAT.

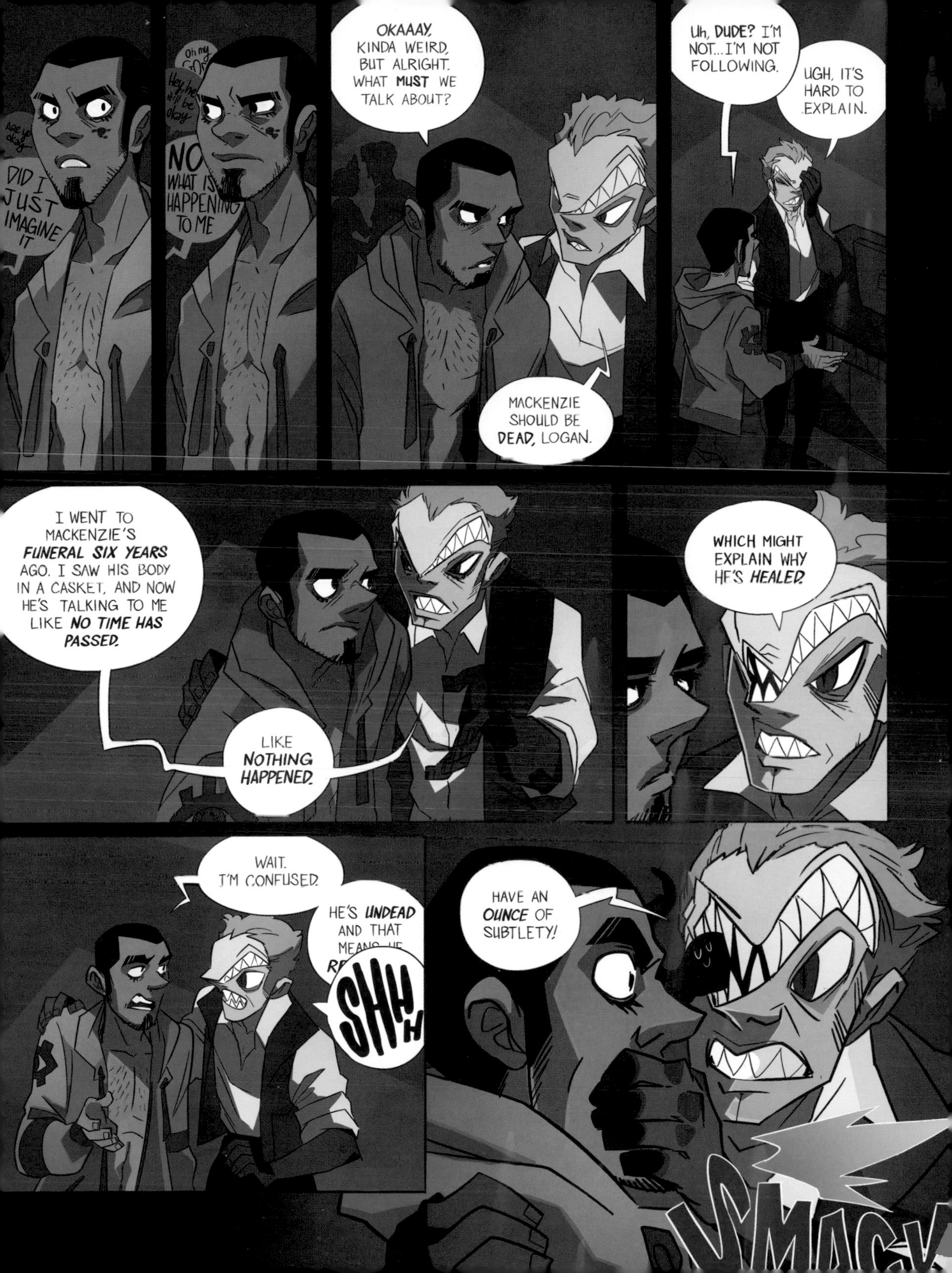

Are yo okay
DID I JUST IMAGINE IT
Oh my
Hey, he'll be okay
NO WHAT IS HAPPENING TO ME
OKAAAY, KINDA WEIRD, BUT ALRIGHT. WHAT **MUST** WE TALK ABOUT?
MACKENZIE SHOULD BE **DEAD**, LOGAN.
Uh, **DUDE?** I'M NOT...I'M NOT FOLLOWING.
UGH, IT'S HARD TO EXPLAIN.
I WENT TO MACKENZIE'S ***FUNERAL SIX YEARS*** AGO. I SAW HIS BODY IN A CASKET, AND NOW HE'S TALKING TO ME LIKE **NO TIME HAS PASSED.**
LIKE **NOTHING HAPPENED.**
WHICH MIGHT EXPLAIN WHY HE'S ***HEALED.***
WAIT. I'M CONFUSED.
HE'S ***UNDEAD*** AND THAT
SHHH
HAVE AN ***OUNCE*** OF SUBTLETY!
SMACK

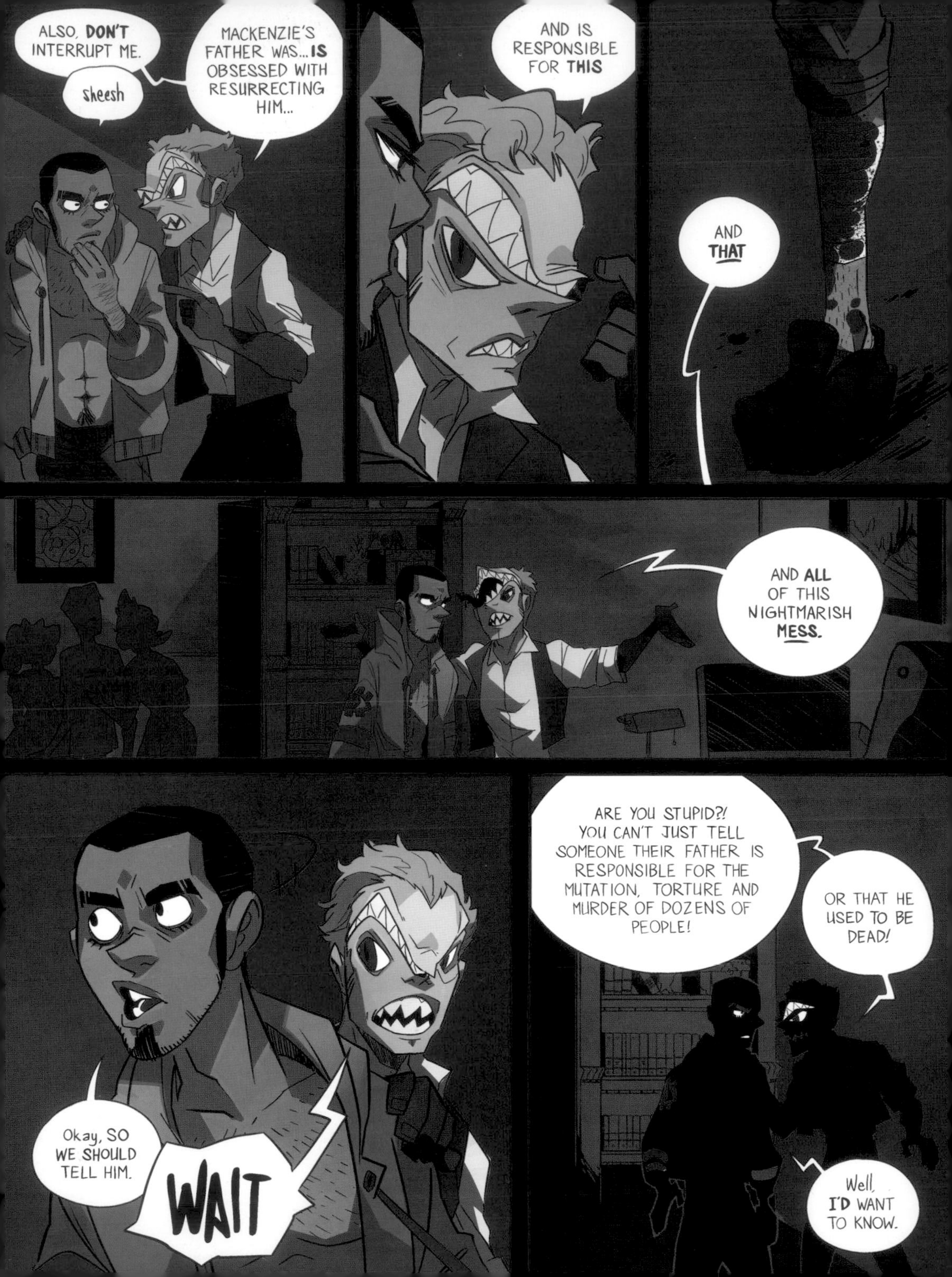
ALSO, DON'T INTERRUPT ME.
sheesh
MACKENZIE'S FATHER WAS... IS OBSESSED WITH RESURRECTING HIM...
AND IS RESPONSIBLE FOR THIS
AND THAT
AND ALL OF THIS NIGHTMARISH MESS.
Okay, SO WE SHOULD TELL HIM.
WAIT
ARE YOU STUPID?! YOU CAN'T JUST TELL SOMEONE THEIR FATHER IS RESPONSIBLE FOR THE MUTATION, TORTURE AND MURDER OF DOZENS OF PEOPLE!
OR THAT HE USED TO BE DEAD!
Well, I'D WANT TO KNOW.

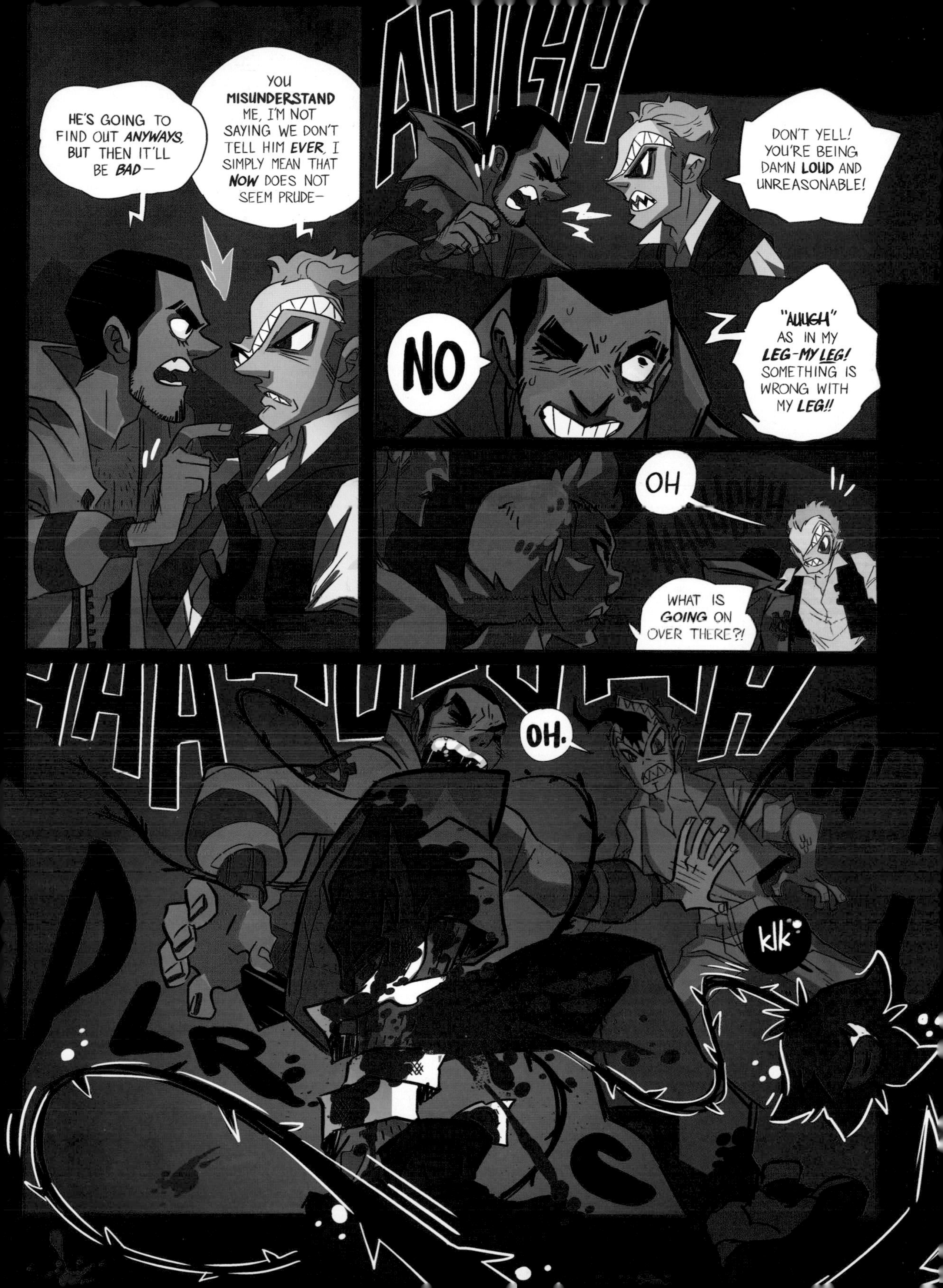
HE'S GOING TO FIND OUT ANYWAYS, BUT THEN IT'LL BE BAD—
YOU MISUNDERSTAND ME, I'M NOT SAYING WE DON'T TELL HIM EVER, I SIMPLY MEAN THAT NOW DOES NOT SEEM PRUDE—
AUGH
DON'T YELL! YOU'RE BEING DAMN LOUD AND UNREASONABLE!
NO
"AUUGH" AS IN MY LEG-MY LEG! SOMETHING IS WRONG WITH MY LEG!!
OH
WHAT IS GOING ON OVER THERE?!
OH.
klk

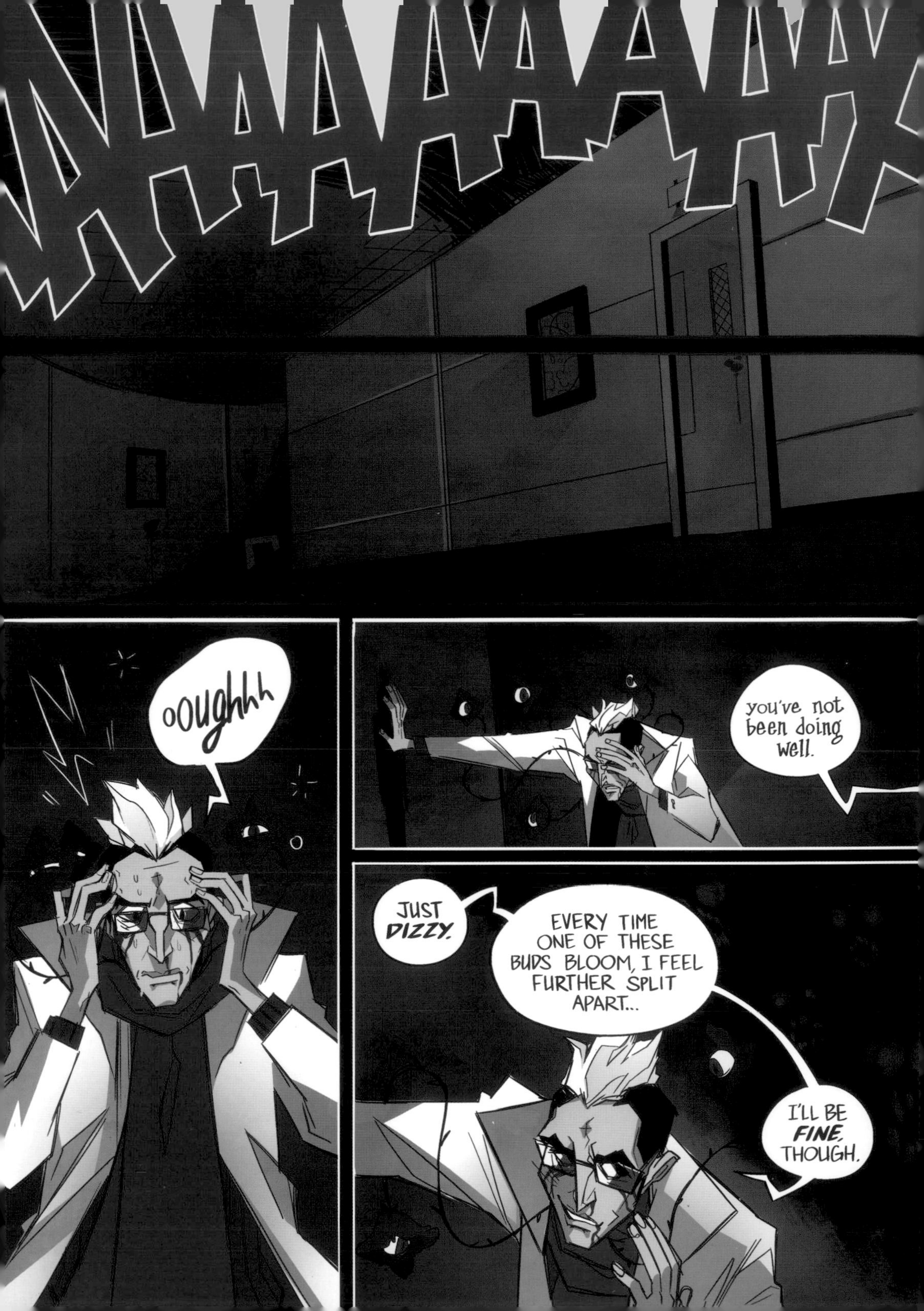
WAAAAAAAAAAAH
oOughhh
you've not been doing well.
JUST DIZZY.
EVERY TIME ONE OF THESE BUDS BLOOM, I FEEL FURTHER SPLIT APART...
I'LL BE FINE, THOUGH.

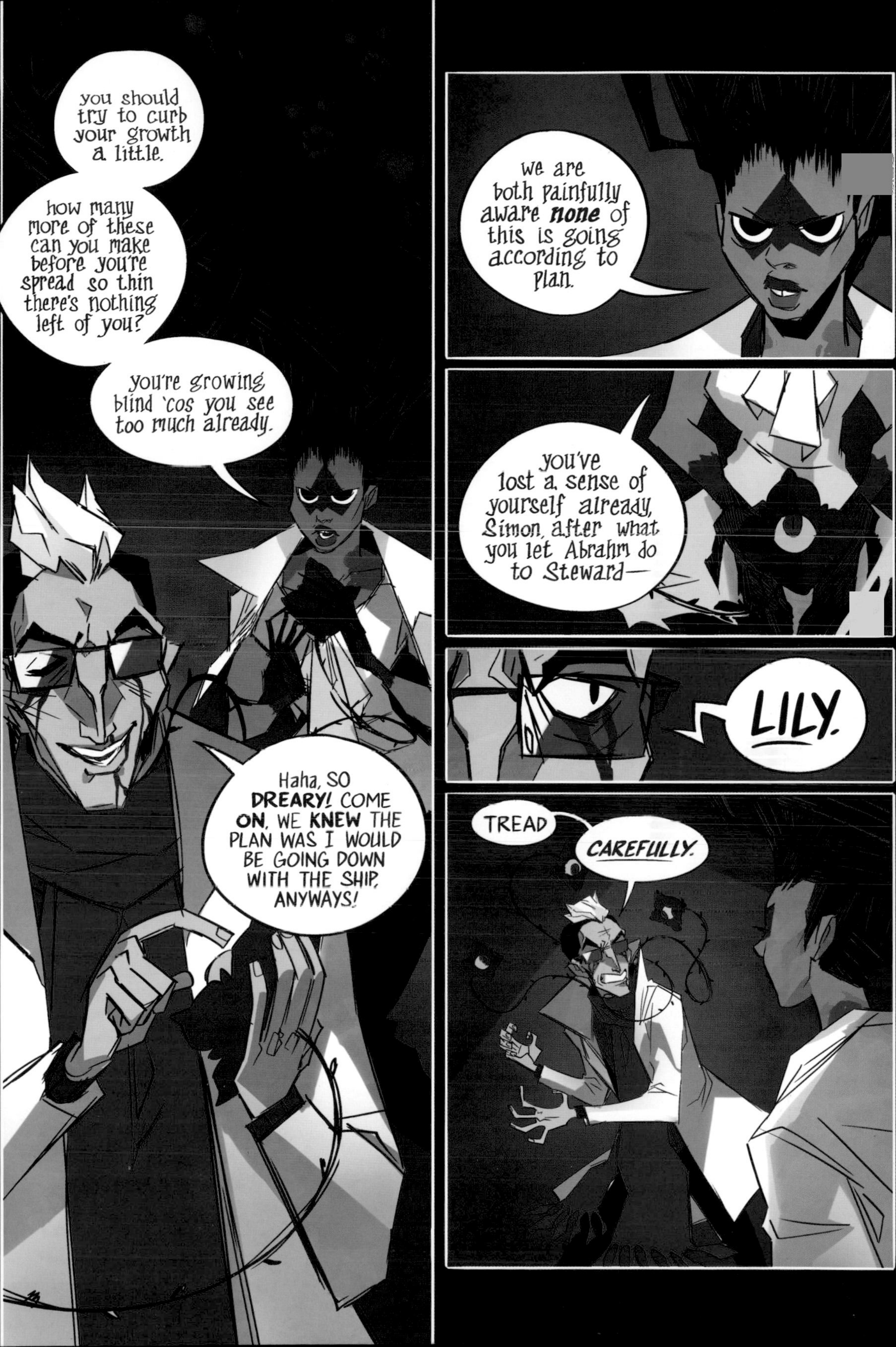
you should try to curb your growth a little.
how many more of these can you make before you're spread so thin there's nothing left of you?
you're growing blind 'cos you see too much already.
Haha, SO DREARY! COME ON, WE KNEW THE PLAN WAS I WOULD BE GOING DOWN WITH THE SHIP, ANYWAYS!
we are both painfully aware none of this is going according to plan.
you've lost a sense of yourself already, Simon, after what you let Abrahm do to Steward—
LILY.
TREAD
CAREFULLY.

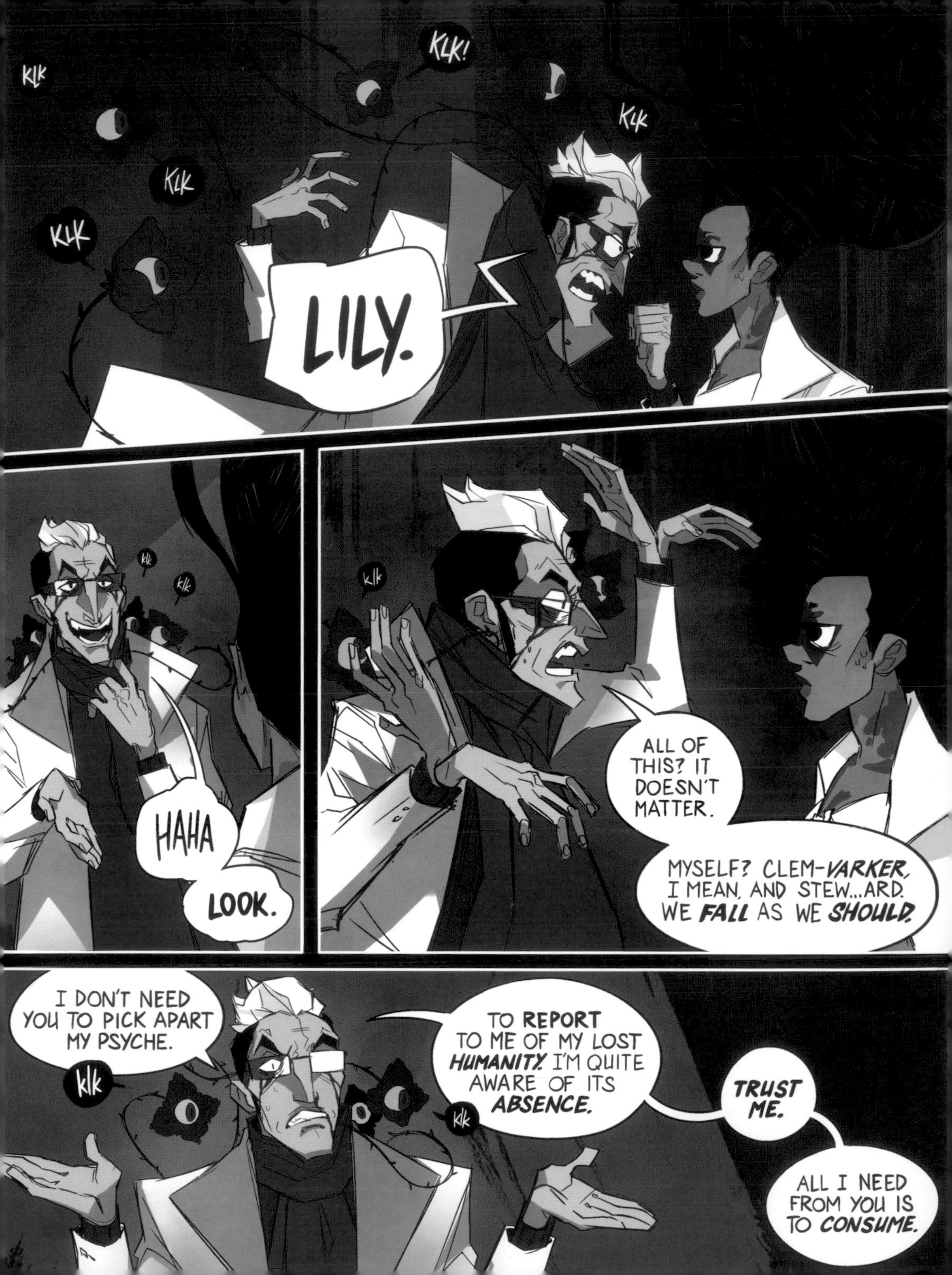
KLK
KLK!
KLK
KLK
KLK
LILY.
klk
klk
HAHA
LOOK.
klk
ALL OF THIS? IT DOESN'T MATTER.
MYSELF? CLEM-VARKER, I MEAN, AND STEW...ARD. WE FALL AS WE SHOULD.
I DON'T NEED YOU TO PICK APART MY PSYCHE.
klk
TO REPORT TO ME OF MY LOST HUMANITY. I'M QUITE AWARE OF ITS ABSENCE.
klk
TRUST ME.
ALL I NEED FROM YOU IS TO CONSUME.

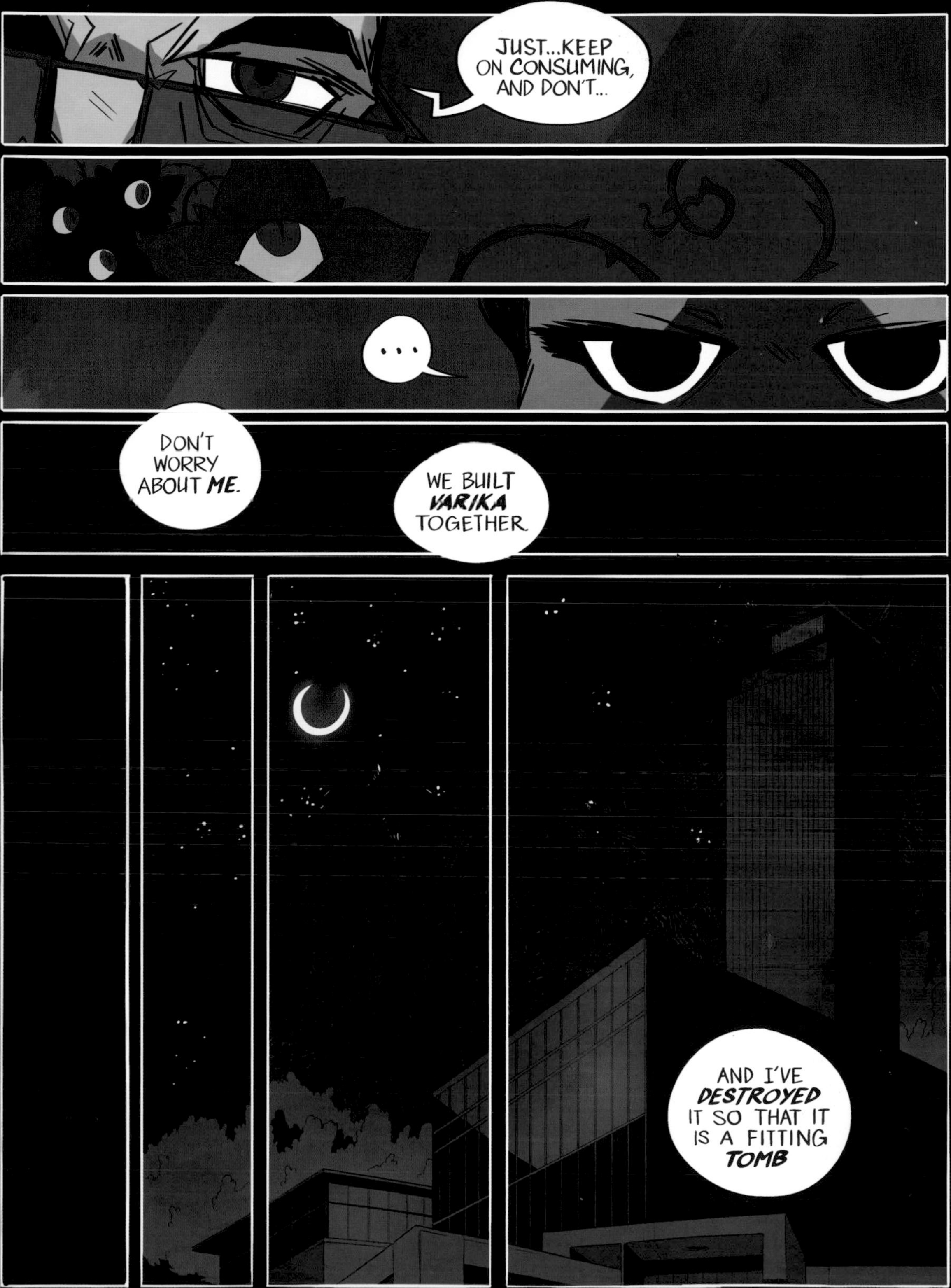
JUST...KEEP ON CONSUMING, AND DON'T...
...
DON'T WORRY ABOUT ME.
WE BUILT VARIKA TOGETHER.
AND I'VE DESTROYED IT SO THAT IT IS A FITTING TOMB

FOR US

THREE

MONSTERS.

END of BOOK 1

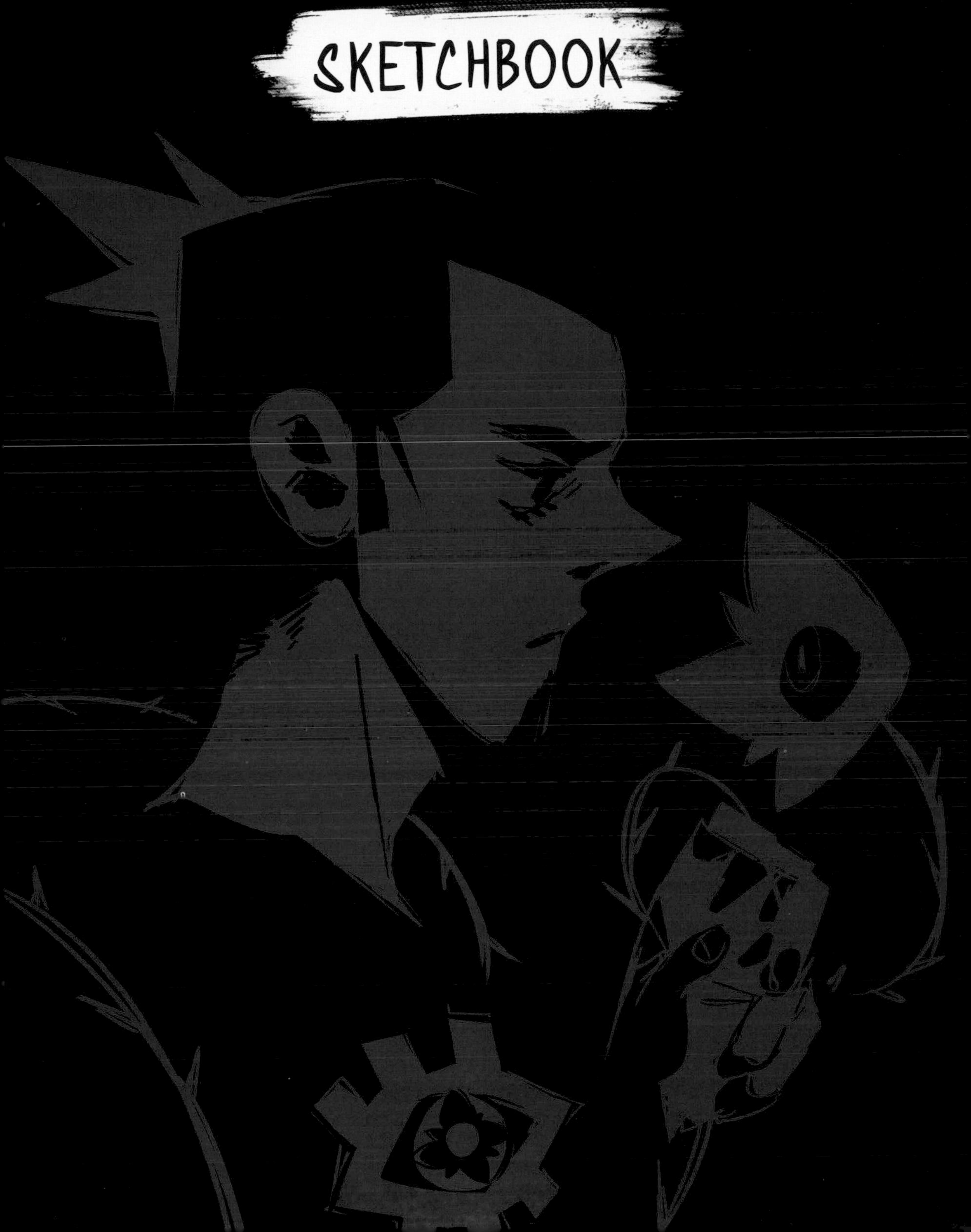
SKETCHBOOK

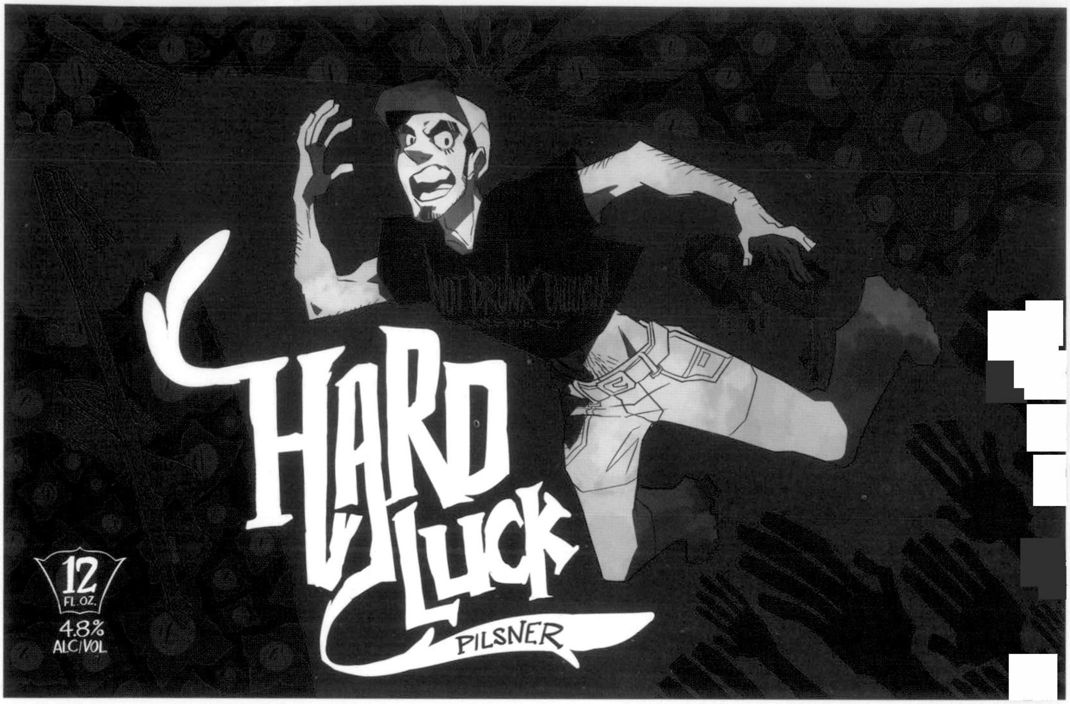
HARD LUCK
PILSNER
12
FL. OZ.
4.8%
ALC/VOL

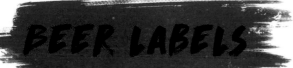

BEER LABELS

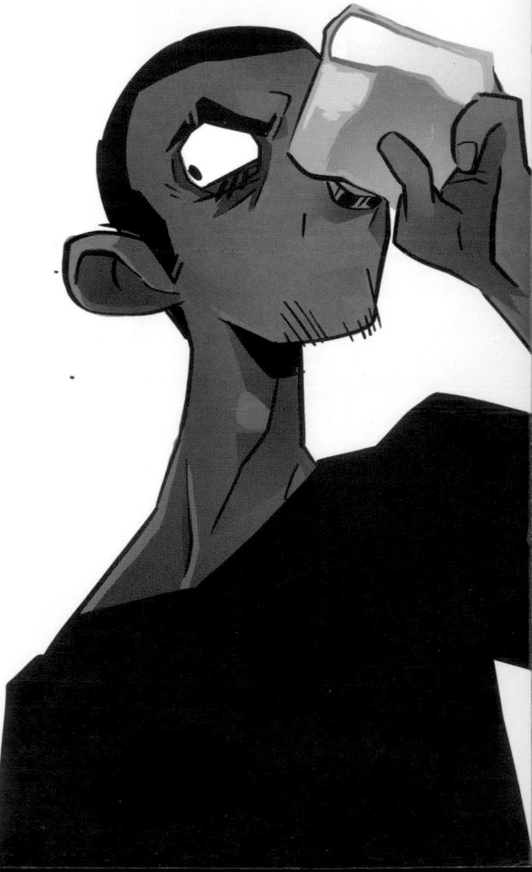

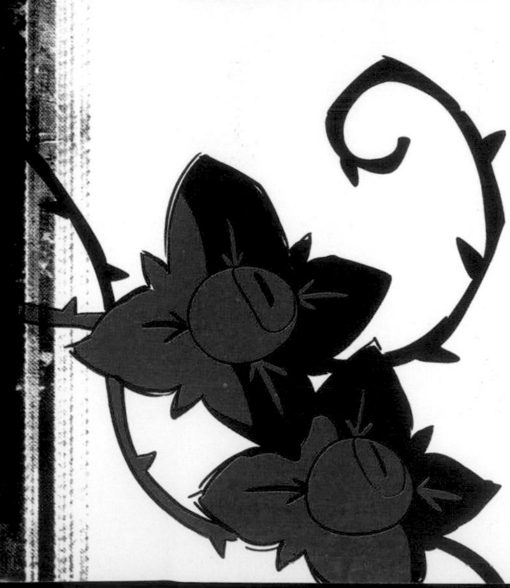

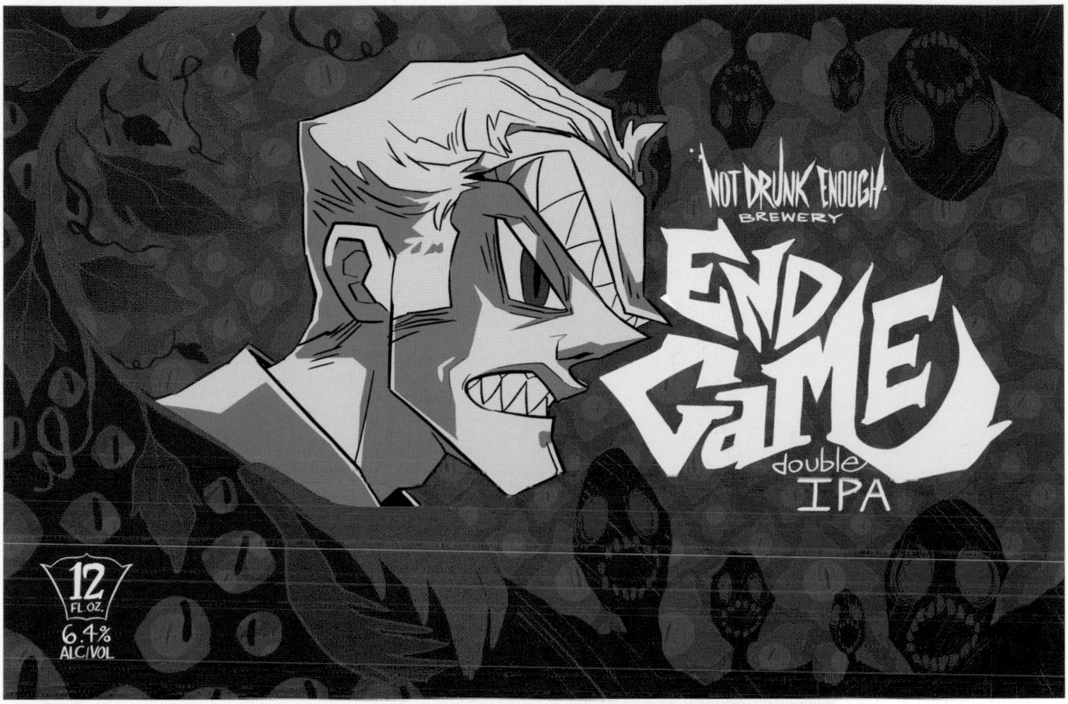
NOT DRUNK ENOUGH
BREWERY
END GAME
double
IPA
12
FL.OZ.
6.4%
ALC/VOL

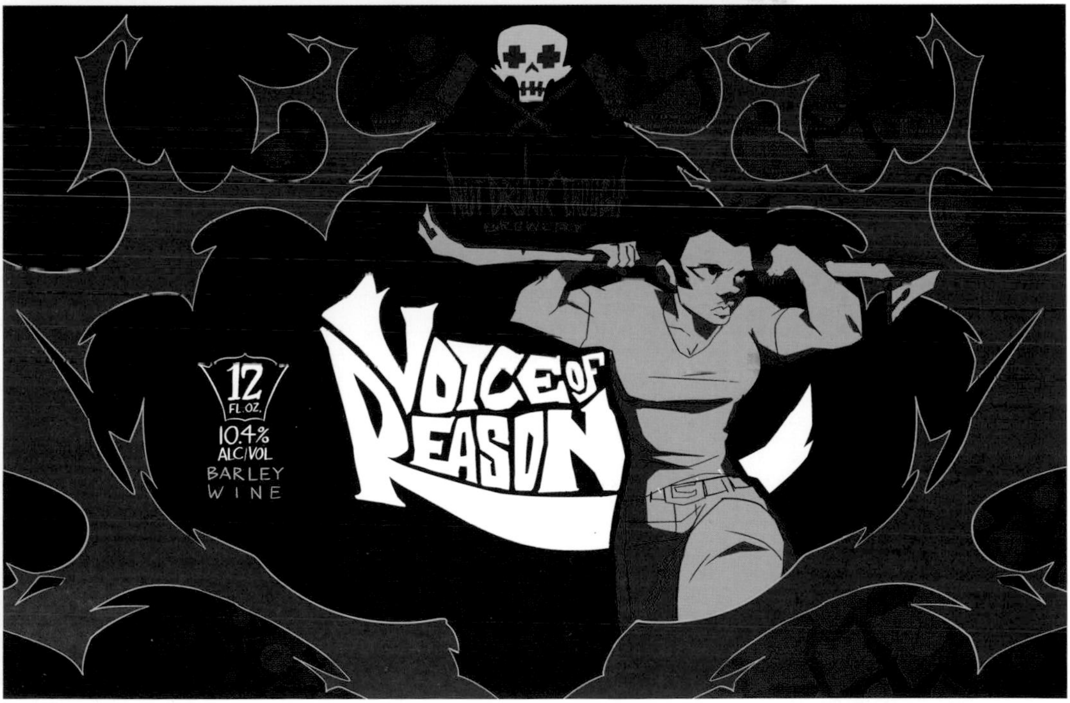
12
FL.OZ.
10.4%
ALC/VOL
BARLEY
WINE
VOICE OF
REASON

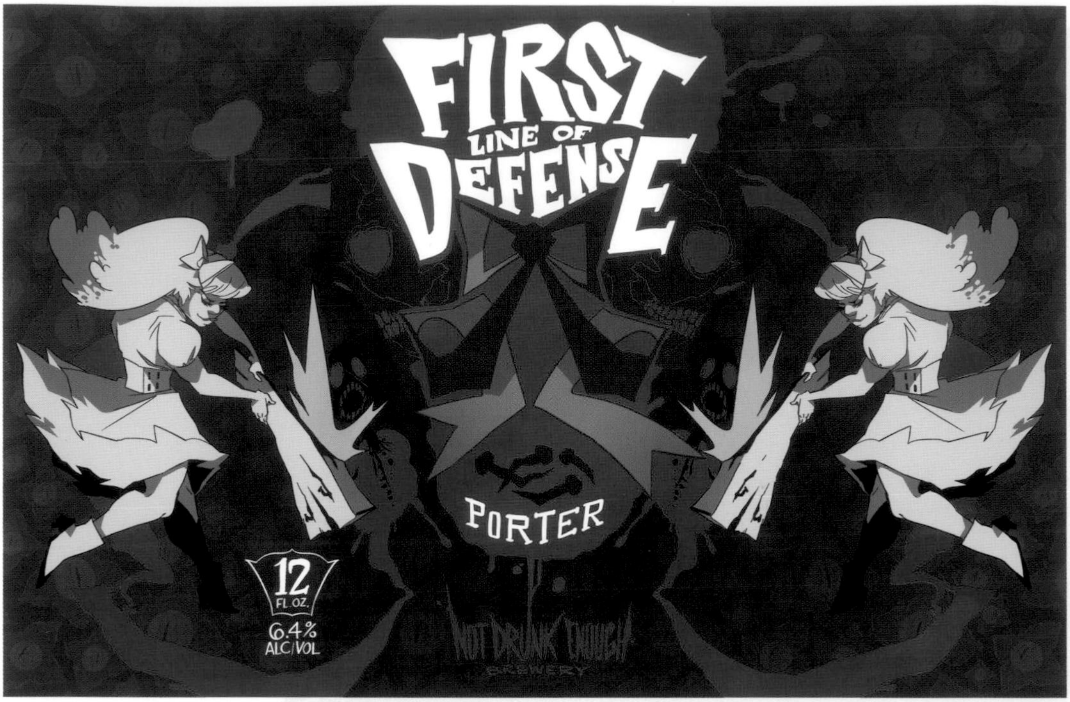
FIRST LINE OF DEFENSE
PORTER
12 FL OZ.
6.4% ALC/VOL
NOT DRUNK ENOUGH
BREWERY

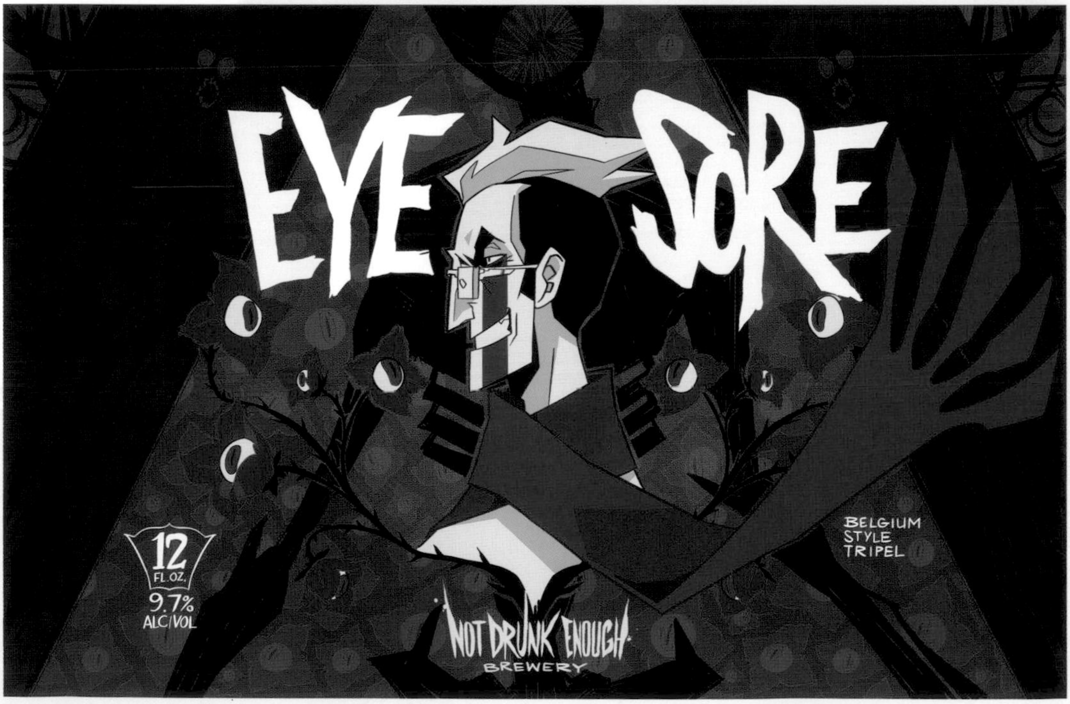
EYE SORE
BELGIUM STYLE TRIPEL
12 FL OZ.
9.7% ALC/VOL
NOT DRUNK ENOUGH
BREWERY

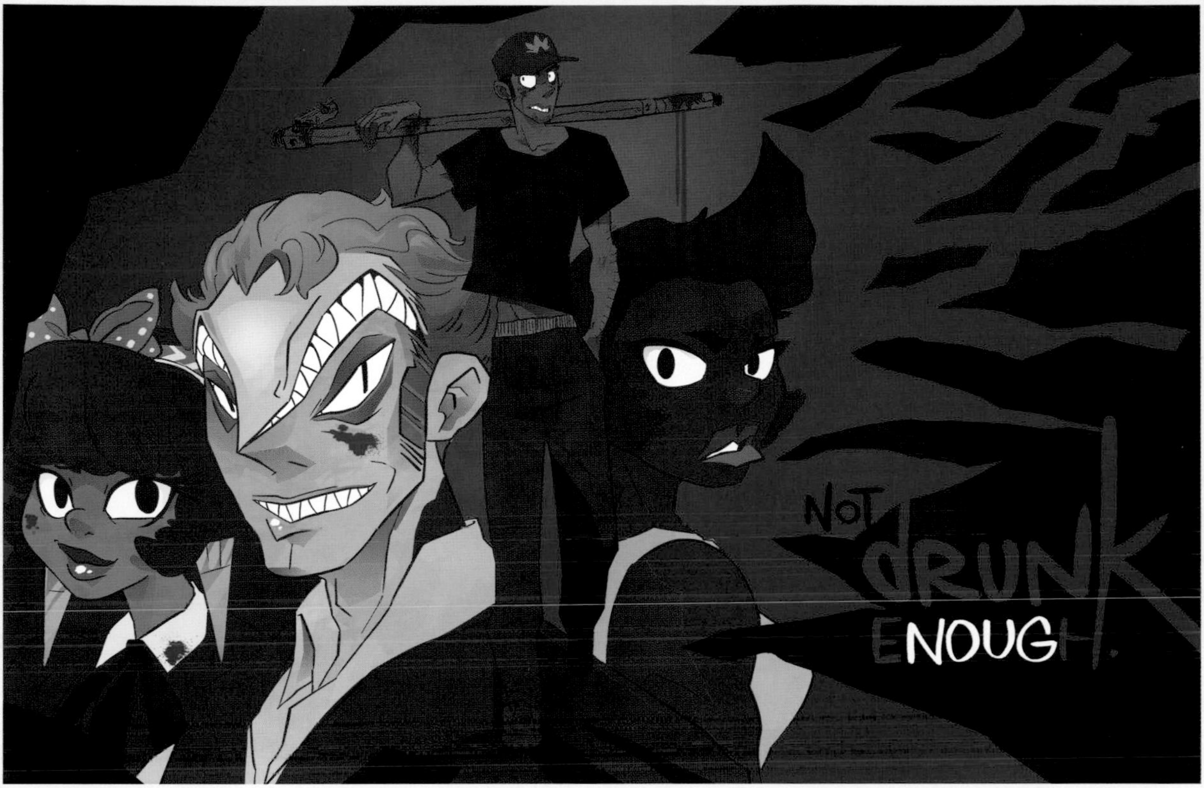
NOT DRUNK ENOUGH.

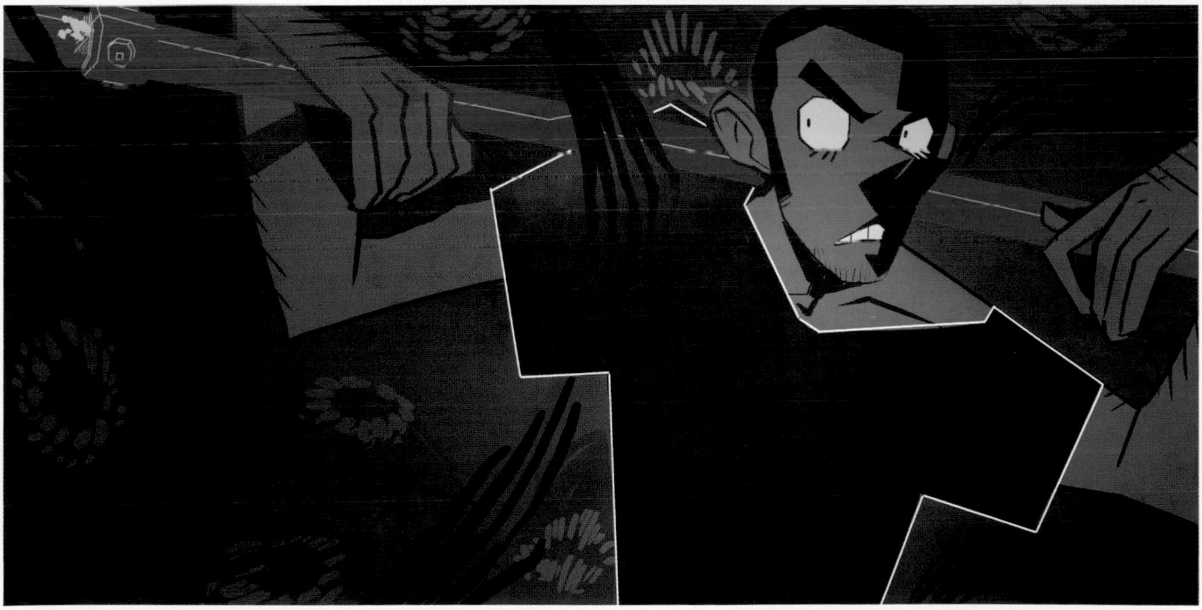

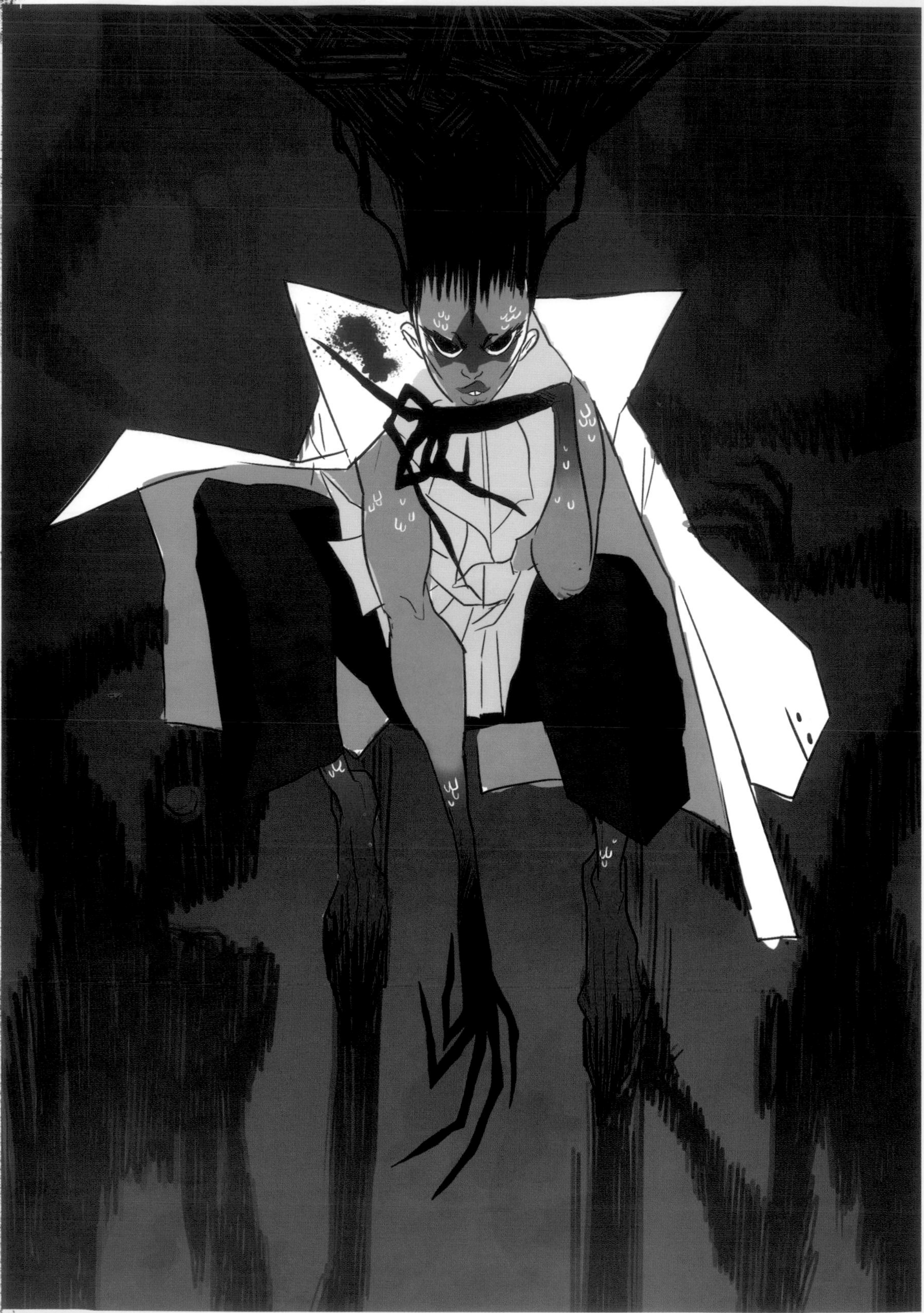

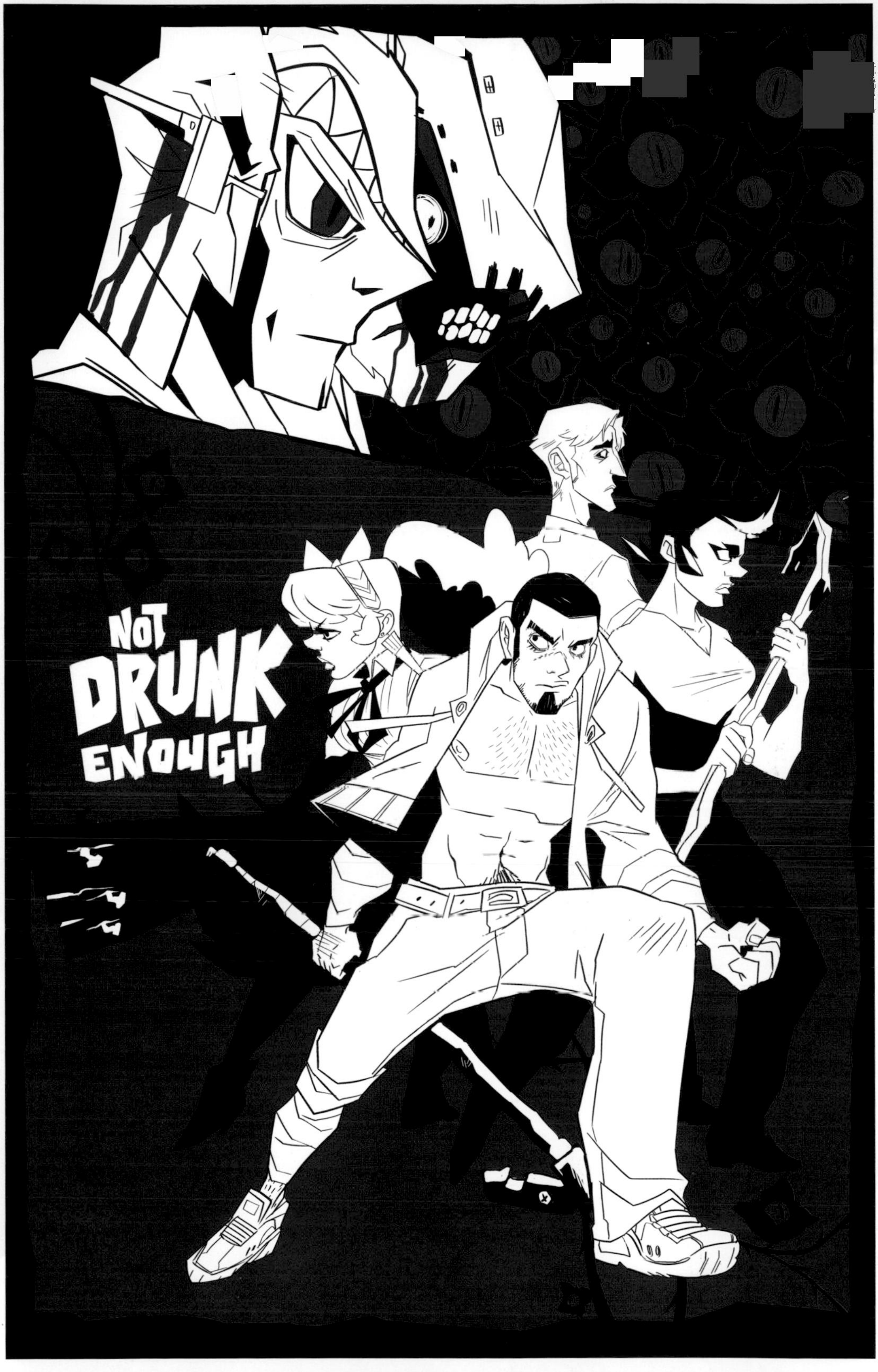
NOT DRUNK ENOUGH

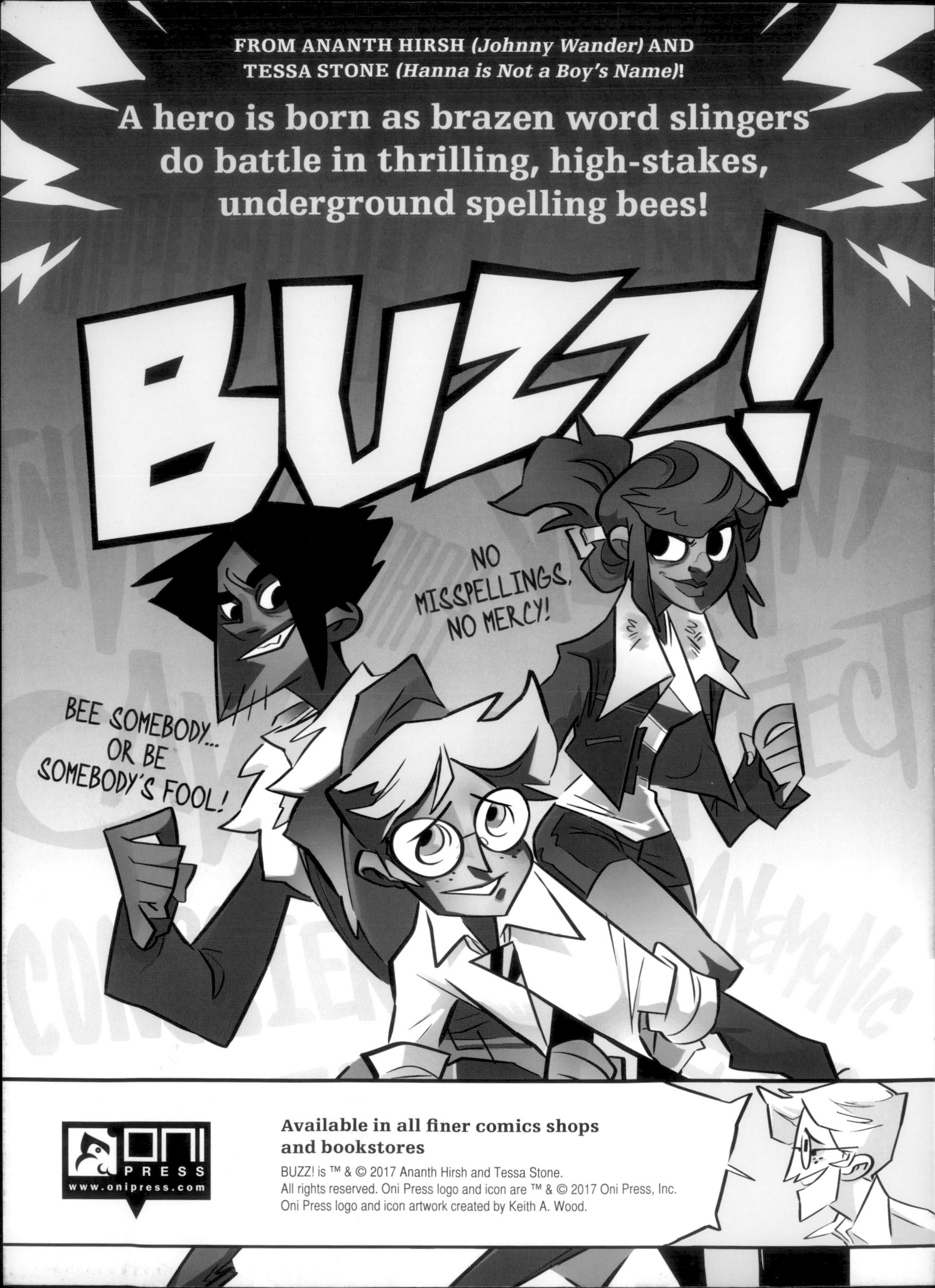
BUZZ!
NO MISSPELLINGS, NO MERCY!
BEE SOMEBODY... OR BE SOMEBODY'S FOOL!

IS THIS WHAT YOU W★ANTED

Ananth Hirsh · Tessa Stone · Sarah Stone

isthiswhatyouwanted.com

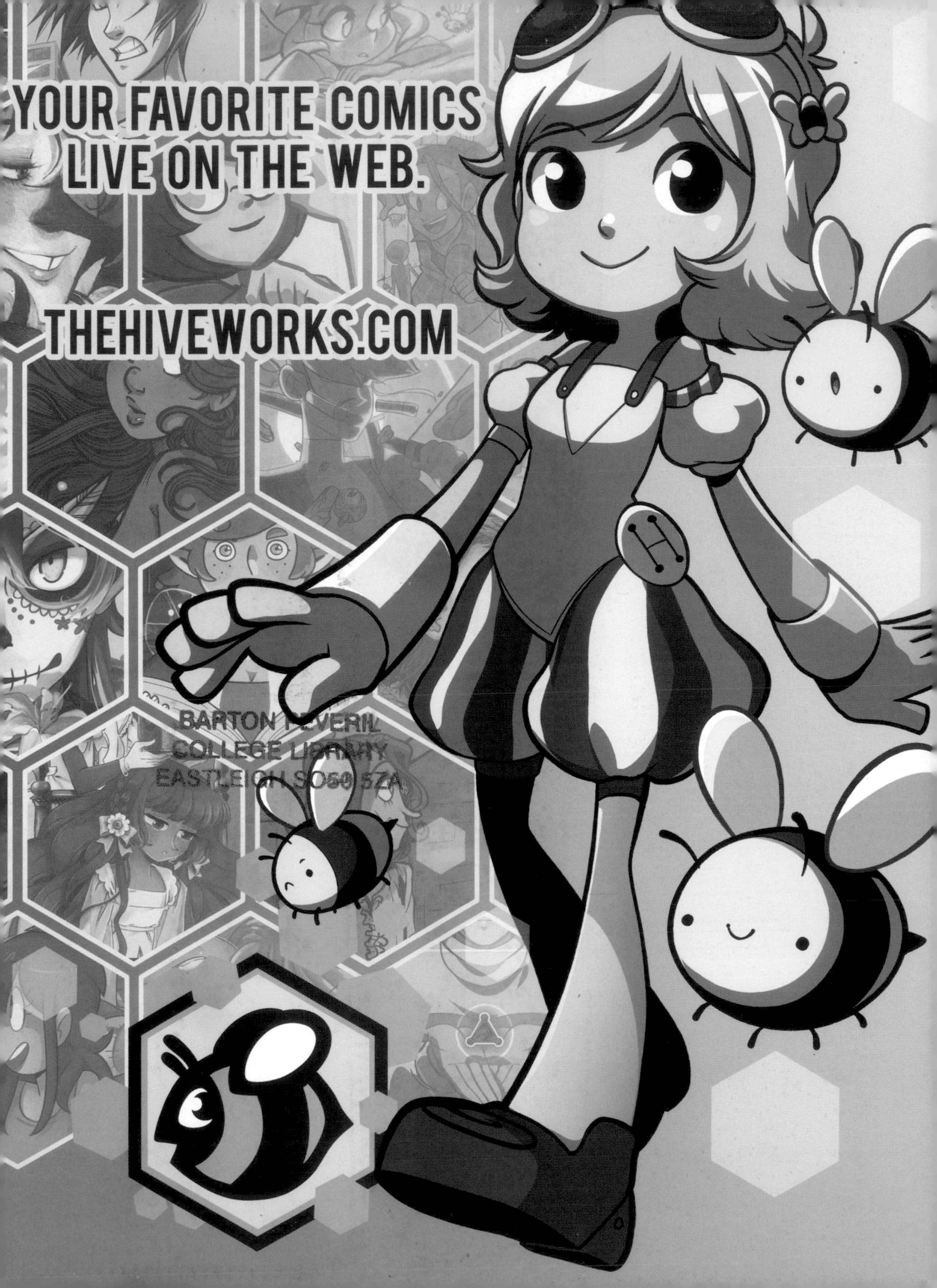
YOUR FAVORITE COMICS
LIVE ON THE WEB.
THEHIVEWORKS.COM